Essentials of
International Relations

Fourth Edition

Essentials of International Relations

Fourth Edition

KAREN A. MINGST
University of Kentucky

W. W. NORTON & COMPANY
NEW YORK · LONDON

Copyright © 2008, 2004, 2002, 1999 by W. W. Norton & Company, Inc.

All rights reserved.
Printed in the United States of America.

Manufacturing by Courier Companies
Book design by Chris Welch
Production manager: Diane O'Connor

Library of Congress Cataloging-in-Publication Data
Mingst, Karen A., 1947–
    Essentials of international relations / Karen A. Mingst. — 4th ed. p. cm.
    Includes bibliographical references and index.
ISBN 978-0-393-92897-6 (pbk.)
1. International realtions.   I. Title.
    JZ1305.M56 2008
    327—dc22

W. W. Norton & Company, Inc., 500 Fifth Avenue, New York, N.Y. 10110
www.wwnorton.com

W. W. Norton & Company Ltd., Castle House, 75/76 Wells Street,
London W1T 3QT

1 2 3 4 5 6 7 8 9 0

Contents

5   The State

Maps

Preface

More than twelve years have passed since Roby Harrington of W. W. Norton and Company appeared at my door to talk about an idea for a series of textbooks on international relations and world politics. He believed that faculty were "clamoring for smart, short textbooks with a clear sense of what's essential and what's not." He was right.

In this fourth edition of *Essentials of International Relations*, the guiding principles behind the book's structure remain the same. Students need a brief history of international relations to understand why we study the subject and how current scholarship is informed by what has proceeded it; this background is provided in Chapters 1 and 2. Theories provide interpretative frameworks for understanding what is happening in the world, and levels of analysis—the international system, the state, and the individual—help us further organize and conceptualize the material. In Chapters 3–6, competing theories are presented and used to illustrate how each level of analysis can be applied. The major issues of the twenty-first century—security, economics, and globalization—are also presented and analyzed.

The rich pedagogical program of previous editions has been preserved in the fourth edition. As in earlier editions, "Theory in Brief" boxes, "In Focus" boxes, "Essential Debates," and numerous maps and conceptual diagrams appear throughout the text. "Global Perspectives" boxes are new to this edition, giving students the opportunity to view a specific topic or issue from the vantage point of a particular state. This enables students to consider how people and leaders in various states see the world. Along with substantial updating throughout, this edition presents constructivist perspectives more consistently, introduces additional material on the European Union and NGOs, expands Chapter 8 on security, and presents a completely reorganized Chapter 9 on international political economy, with special attention to the issue of resources.

Many of these changes have been made at the suggestion of numerous reviewers, primarily faculty who have taught the book in the classroom.

While it is impossible to act on every suggestion (not all the critics themselves agree), I have carefully studied the various recommendations and thank the reviewers for taking time to offer critiques.

Over the course of the previous three editions, I have heard from students around the world who asked questions and offered their opinions on the book. I am indebted to these students for their comments.

In this edition, I owe special thanks to Angela Van Berkel, a M.A. graduate of the Patterson School of Diplomacy and International Commerce, who was instrumental in collating the various critiques, doing research, and offering suggestions to improve the writing. Other former students—Lt. Col. Tom Ruby and Angela Thomas—provided research assistance for earlier editions.

Three editors have piloted this book through the publishing process. Sarah Caldwell for the first edition, Rob Whiteside for the second, and Ann Shin for the last two editions. Ann has been a constant fountain of ideas and enthusiasm.

My husband, Robert E. Stauffer, and our kids—Ginger, now an attorney, and Brett, a wildlife biologist—have given support, encouragement, and love, despite going through their own traumas, big and small. I dedicate this book to my father, who died in 2004 in his eighty-ninth year—a loving family man and solid citizen who was lucky enough to enjoy a sharp and inquiring mind until the end.

Essentials of
International Relations

Fourth Edition

Africa, 2007

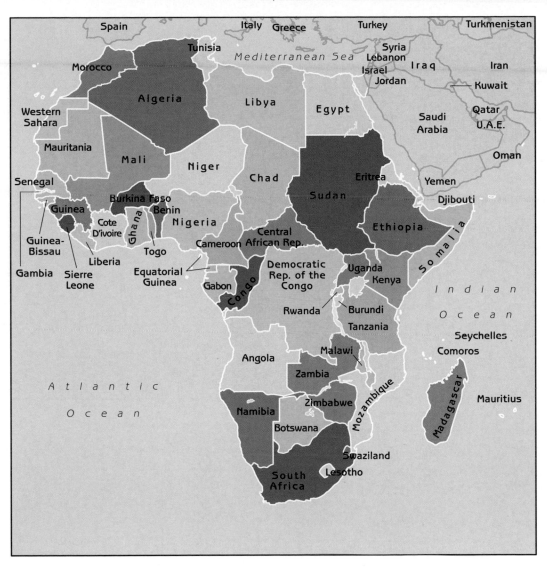

Asia, 2007

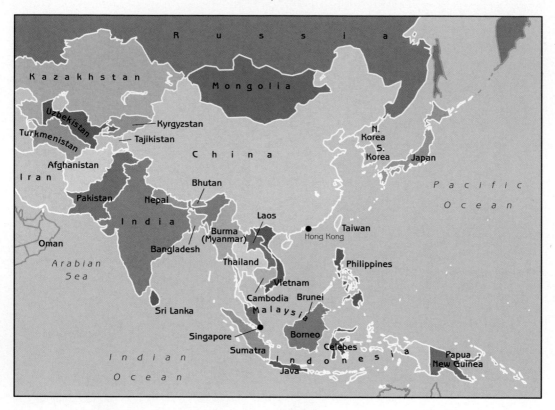

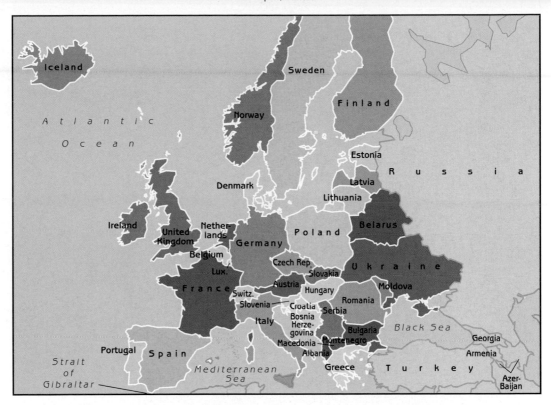

North America, 2007

Latin America, 2007

Asia

Middle
East

Africa

*Indian
Ocean*

Oceania

The Middle East, 2007

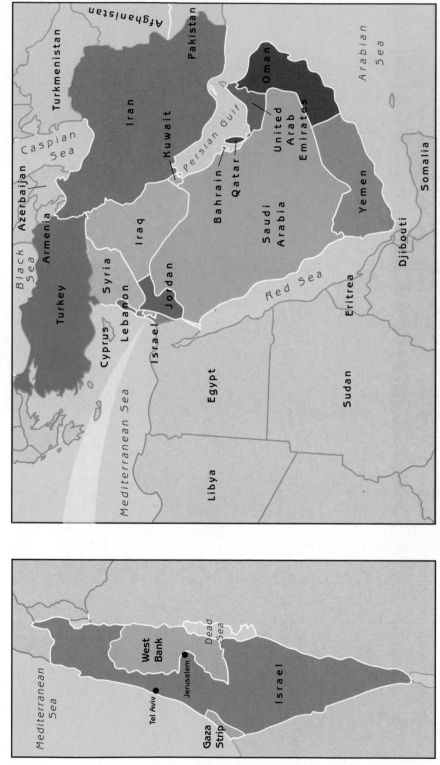

Approaches to International Relations

- *How does international relations affect you in your daily life?*
- *Why do we study international relations theory?*
- *How have history and philosophy been used to study international relations?*
- *What is the contribution of behavioralism?*
- *What alternative approaches have challenged traditional approaches? Why?*

International Relations in Daily Life

Reading a daily newspaper and listening to the evening news make us aware of international events far away from our everyday lives. But these events—terrorist bombings in Saudi Arabia, Israel, and Spain; starvation in North Korea and Sudan; the G-8 meeting in St. Petersburg; the dramatic growth of China's economy; and the intense efforts to stop Iran's nuclear program—may seem to most of us to be distant and unrelated to our own lives.

Yet these seemingly remote events quickly can become both highly related and personally salient to any or all of us. Those bombings killed visiting students from your university; your sibling or your uncle in the military responded to natural disasters such as the 2004 tsunami and devastating earthquakes in 2005 and 2006; groups from your area protested G-8 environmental policies; China, once a symbol of anticapitalism, is now a hotly contested terrain for your employer's investment dollars; nuclear weapons threaten us, even if located thousands of miles away. A slight change of the story line immediately transforms events "out there" to matters of immediate concern.

Historically, international activities such as these were overwhelmingly the results of decisions taken by central governments and heads of state, not by ordinary citizens. Increasingly, however, these activities involve different actors, some of whom *you* directly influence. In all likelihood, you, too, will be participating in international relations as you travel to foreign lands, purchase products made abroad, or work for a multinational corporation headquartered in another country. You may be a member of a nongovernmental organization—Amnesty International, the Red Cross, or Greenpeace—with a local chapter in your community or at your college. With your fellow members around the globe, you may try to influence the local, as well as the national and international, agenda. Your city or state may be actively courting foreign private investment, competing against both neighboring municipalities and other countries. These activities can directly affect the job situation in your community, creating new employment possibilities or taking away jobs to areas with cheaper wages. As a businessperson, you may be liberated or constrained by business regulations—internationally mandated standards established by the World Trade Organization to facilitate the movement of goods and commerce across national borders.

Thus the variety of actors in international relations includes not just the 192 states recognized in the world today, and their leaders and government bureaucracies, but also municipalities, for-profit and not-for-profit private organizations, international organizations, and you. **International relations** is the study of the interactions among the various actors that participate in international politics, including states, international organizations, nongovernmental organizations, subnational entities like bureaucracies and local governments, and individuals. It is the study of the behaviors of these actors as they participate individually and together in international political processes.

How, then, can we begin to study this multifaceted phenomenon called international relations? How can we understand why bombings occur in Saudi Arabia, Israel, and Spain; why the North Korean people have experienced food shortages; what the agenda was during the last G-8 meeting that elicited the antiglobalization protests; and why China is the investment bonanza of the twenty-first century? How can we begin to think theoretically about events and trends in international relations? How can we make sense of the seemingly disconnected events that we read about or hear about on the news? How can we begin to answer the foundational questions of international relations?

In Focus

FOUNDATIONAL QUESTIONS OF INTERNATIONAL RELATIONS

◆ How can human nature be characterized?

◆ What is the relationship between the individual and society?

◆ What is the relationship between societies?

◆ What are the characteristics of the state?

◆ What should be the role of the state?

◆ What ought to be the norms in international society?

◆ How might international society be structured to achieve order?

Thinking Theoretically

Political scientists develop theories or frameworks both to understand the causes of events that occur in international relations every day and to answer the foundational questions in the field. Although there are many contending theories, three of the more prominent theories are developed in depth in this book: liberalism and neoinstitutional liberalism, realism and neorealism, and radical perspectives whose origin lie in Marxism. Also introduced is the newer theory of constructivism.

In brief, liberalism is historically rooted in several philosophical traditions that posit that human nature is basically good. Individuals form into groups and later states. States generally cooperate and follow international norms and procedures that have been mutually agreed on. In contrast, realism posits that states exist in an anarchic international system. Each state bases its policies on an interpretation of national interest defined in terms of power. The structure of the international system is determined by the distribution of power among states. A third approach, radical theory, is rooted in economics. Actions of individuals are largely determined by economic class; the state is an agent of international capitalism; and the international system is highly stratified, dominated by an international capitalist system.

Theory development, however, is a dynamic process. Beginning in the late twentieth century, alternative critical approaches to international relations have challenged the traditional theories of liberalism and realism and substantially modified radicalism. Believing that a generalized theory based on historical, philosophical, or behavioral methods is impossible to achieve, critical theorists contend that theory is situated in a particular time and place, conditioned by ideological, cultural, and sociological influences. There is no single objective reality, only multiple realities based on individual experiences and perspectives.

Among the best-developed alternative theories are postmodernism and constructivism, both generalized approaches to examining all social interactions. As applied to international relations, postmodernism questions the whole notion of states, which postmodernists view as a fiction constructed by scholars and citizens alike. They contend that states do not act in regularized ways but are known only through the stories told about them, filtered through the perspectives of the storyteller. The task of postmodernist analysis is thus to deconstruct the basic concepts of the field and to replace them with multiple realities.

International relations constructivists, following in the radical tradition in their attention to the sources of change, argue that the key structures in the state system are not material but instead are intersubjective and social. The interest of states is not fixed but is malleable and ever changing. While constructivists, like the other theorists, differ among themselves, they share the common belief that discourse shapes how political actors define interests and thus modify their behavior. Constructivism has assumed increasing importance in twenty-first-century thinking about international relations.

Different theoretical approaches help us see international relations from different viewpoints. As political scientist Stephen Walt explains, "No single approach can capture all the complexity of contemporary world politics. Therefore we are better off with a diverse array of competing ideas rather than a single theoretical orthodoxy. Competition between theories helps reveal their strengths and weaknesses and spurs subsequent refinements, while revealing flaws in conventional wisdom."[1] We will explore these competing ideas, and their strengths and weaknesses, in the remainder of the book.

Developing the Answers

How do political scientists find the answers to the questions posed? How do they find information to assess the accuracy, relevancy, and potency of their theories?

History

Answers have often been discovered in history. Without any historical background, many of today's key issues are incomprehensible. History tells us that the bombings in Israel are part of a dispute over territory between Arabs and Jews, a dispute with its origins in biblical times and with its modern roots in the establishment of the state of Israel in 1948. Widespread famine in North Korea can be attributed to long-standing government neglect of the agricultural sector, while Sudan's difficulties stem from a two-decade-old civil war that disrupted the countryside, compounded by several natural disasters. The agenda discussed at G-8 summits includes economic, political, and social issues that are historically rooted in different views of the state's role in economic and social life. Finally, investors see China as ripe for economic opportunity. Like other countries that have developed over time, China has cheap labor markets for export industries and an enormous consumer market eager to buy consumer products, both of which make China an attractive target for investors.

Thus, history provides a crucial background for the study of international relations. History has been so fundamental to the study of international relations that there was no separate international relations subdiscipline until the early twentieth century. Before that time, especially in both Europe and the United States, international relations was simply considered diplomatic history in most academic institutions.

History invites its students to acquire detailed knowledge of specific events, but it also can be used to test generalizations. Having deciphered patterns from the past, students of history can begin to explain the relationship among various events. For example, having historically documented the cases when wars occur and described the patterns leading up to war, the diplomatic historian can search for explanations for, or causes of, war. The ancient Greek historian Thucydides (c. 460–401 B.C.), in *History of the Peloponnesian War*, used this approach. Distinguishing between the underlying and the immediate causes of wars, Thucydides found that what made that war inevitable was the growth of Athenian power. As that city-state's power increased, Sparta, Athens's greatest rival, feared its own loss of power. Thus, the changing distribution of power was the underlying cause of the Peloponnesian War.[2]

Many scholars following in Thucydides' footsteps use history in similar ways. But those using history must be wary. History may be a bad guide; the "lessons" of Munich and Allied appeasement of Germany before World War II or the "lessons" of the war in Vietnam or of the 1991 Gulf War are neither clear-cut nor agreed on. And periodically, fundamental changes in actors and in technology can make history obsolete as a guide to the present or the future. For example, Stephen Biddle argues that comparing Vietnam to the current war in Iraq is an oversimplification that is misapplied in a historical context. In Vietnam, the struggle was a "Maoist people's war"; one of national liberation led by an insurgency trying to overthrow an illegitimate, elite ruling regime supported by the United States. Vietnam was an ideological war based on ideas and nationalism. The Iraq war, however, is a communal civil war, where several subnational ethnic groups are vying for power. The conflict is not about ideology, class interests, or nationalism, but about "group survival." The insurgents do not oppose U.S. occupation, but act in defense of their own sect. Therefore, unlike in Vietnam, where insurgents were competing for the hearts and minds of the Vietnamese, Iraqi insurgents are fighting for their own self-interest. Thus, employing the strategies used in Vietnam to fight the Iraq war is counterproductive. Using "Vietnamization," Richard Nixon's policy to transfer the fighting over to the Vietnamese, does not translate into a similarly successful "Iraqization." This approach worked in Vietnam because it undermined the nationalist aspect of the insurgency, but turning the fighting over to Iraqi forces will only exacerbate the communal conflict and further increase tensions and mistrust among the Sunnis, Shiites, and Kurds. Such inaccurate application of the "lessons" of historical comparisons occasionally leads to poor policy prescriptions, yet history cannot be ignored.[3]

Philosophy

Answers to international relations questions also incorporate classical and modern philosophy. Much classical philosophizing focuses on the state and its leaders—the basic building blocks of international relations—as well as on methods of analysis. For example, the ancient Greek philosopher Plato (c. 427–347 B.C.), in *The Republic*, concluded that in the "perfect state" the people who should govern are those who are superior in the ways of philosophy and war. Plato called these ideal rulers "philosopher-kings."[4] While not directly discussing international relations, Plato introduced two ideas seminal to the discipline: class analysis and dialectical reasoning, both of which were bases for later Marxist analysts. Radicals, like Marxists, see economic class as the major divider in domestic and international politics; this viewpoint will be explored in depth in Chapters 3 and 9. Marxists also acknowledge the importance of dialectical reasoning—that is, reasoning from a dialogue or conversation that leads to the discovery of contradictions in the original assertions and in political reality. In contemporary Marxist terms, such an analysis reveals the contradiction between global and local policies, whereby, for example, local-level textile workers lose their jobs to foreign competition and are replaced by high-technology industries.

Just as Plato's contributions to contemporary thinking were both substantive and methodological, the contributions of his student, the philosopher Aristotle (384–322 B.C.), lay both in substance (the search for an ideal domestic political system) and in method (the comparative method). Analyzing 168 constitutions, Aristotle looked at the similarities and differences among states, becoming the first writer to use the comparative method of analysis. He came to the conclusion that states rise and fall largely because of internal factors—a conclusion still debated in the twenty-first century.[5]

After the classical era, many of the philosophers of relevance to international relations focused on the notion of the basic characteristics of man and how those characteristics might influence the character of international society. The English philosopher Thomas Hobbes (1588–1679), in *Leviathan*, imagined a state of nature, a world without governmental authority or civil order, where men rule by passions, living with the constant uncertainty of their own security. To Hobbes, the life of man is solitary, selfish, and even brutish. Extrapolating to the international level, in the absence of international authority, society is in a "state of nature," or **anarchy**. States left in this anarchic condition act as man does in the state of nature. For Hobbes the solution to the dilemma is a unitary state—a Leviathan—where power is centrally and absolutely controlled.[6]

The French philosopher Jean-Jacques Rousseau (1712–78) addressed the same set of questions but, having been influenced by the Enlightenment, saw a different solution. In "Discourse on the Origin and Foundations of Inequality among Men," Rousseau described the state of nature as an egocentric world, with man's primary concern being self-preservation—not unlike Hobbes's description of the state of nature. Rousseau posed the dilemma in terms of the story of the stag and the hare. In a hunting society, each individual must keep to his assigned task in order to find and trap the stag for food for the whole group. However, if a hare happens to pass nearby, an individual might well follow the hare, hoping to get his next meal quickly and caring little for how his actions will affect the group. Rousseau drew an analogy between these hunters and states. Do states follow short-term self-interest, like the hunter who follows the hare? Or do they recognize the benefits of a common interest?[7]

Rousseau's solution to the dilemma posed by the stag and the hare was different from Hobbes's Leviathan. Rousseau's preference was for the creation of smaller communities in which the "general will" could be attained. Indeed, according to Rousseau, it is "only the general will," not a Leviathan, that can "direct the forces of the state according to the purpose for which it was instituted, which is the common good."[8] In Rousseau's vision, "each of us places his person and all his power in common under the supreme direction of the general will; and as one we receive each member as an indivisible part of the whole."[9]

Still another philosophical view of the characteristics of international society was set forth by the German philosopher Immanuel Kant (1724–1804), in both *Idea for a Universal History* and *Perpetual Peace*. Kant envisioned a federation of states as a means to achieve peace, a world order in which man is able to live without fear of war. Sovereignties would remain intact, but the new federal order would be both preferable to a "super-Leviathan" and more effective and realistic than Rousseau's small communities. Kant's analysis was based on a vision of human beings that was different from that of either Rousseau or Hobbes. In his view, while admittedly selfish, man can learn new ways of cosmopolitanism and universalism.[10]

The tradition laid by these philosophers has contributed to the development of international relations by calling attention to fundamental relationships: those between the individual and society, between individuals *in* society, and between societies. These philosophers had varied, often competing visions of what these relationships are and what they ought to be. Some of their more important contributions are summarized in Table 1.1. The early philosophers have led contemporary international relations scholars to the examination of the characteristics of leaders, to the recognition of the importance of the internal dimensions of the state, to the analogy of the state and nature, and to descriptions of an international community.

History and philosophy permit us to delve into the foundational questions—the nature of man and the broad characteristics of the state and of international society. They allow us to speculate on the **normative** (or moral) element in political life: What *should be* the role of the state? What *ought to be* the norms in international society? How *might* international society be

TABLE 1.1

Contributions of Philosophers to International Relations Theory	
Plato (427–347 B.C.)	Greek political philosopher who argued that the life force in man is intelligent. Only a few people can have the insight into what is good; society should submit to the authority of these philosopher-kings. Many of these ideas are developed in *The Republic*.
Aristotle (384–322 B.C.)	Greek political philosopher who addressed the problem of order in the individual Greek city-state. The first to use the comparative method of research, observing multiple points in time and suggesting explanations for the patterns found.
St. Thomas Aquinas (1225–74)	Italian theorist who wrote during the height of feudal Europe. In *Treatise of the Laws*, developed the framework of natural law—a fusion of classical philosophy, Christian theology, and Roman law. Natural law is followed by man instinctively and releases man's good tendencies.
Thomas Hobbes (1588–1679)	English political philosopher who in *Leviathan* described life in a state of nature as solitary, selfish, and brutish. Individuals and society can escape from the state of nature through a unitary state, a Leviathan.
Jean-Jacques Rousseau (1712–78)	French political philosopher whose seminal ideas were tested by the French Revolution. In "Discourse on the Origin and Foundations of Inequality among Men," described the state of nature in both national and international society. Argued that the solution to the state of nature is the social contract, whereby individuals gather in small communities where the "general will" is realized.
Immanuel Kant (1724–1804)	German political philosopher key to the idealist or utopian school of thought. In *Idea for a Universal History* and *Perpetual Peace*, advocated a world federation of republics bound by the rule of law.

structured to achieve order? When is war just? Should economic resources be redistributed?

With its emphasis on normative questions, the philosophical tradition encourages examination of the role of law at both the societal and international levels. Indeed, St. Thomas Aquinas (1225–74), the Italian philosopher and theologian, was one of the first to make the connection. In *Treatise of the Laws*, he found the universe to be governed by "divine reason" and argued that human law needs to be made compatible with this natural law. Aquinas posited the existence of a law of nations, derived from the natural law: "To the law of nations belongs those things, which are derived from the law of nature as conclusions from premises, just buying and selling, and the like, without which men cannot live together, which is a point of the law of nature, since man is by nature a social animal, as is proved in the *Politics* of *Aristotle*."[11]

The study of law presumes a degree of order based on written and unwritten norms of behavior. The task of those employing the legal approach is not only to describe the "laws" and norms that govern behavior but to prescribe those laws that are most useful, fair, and just for states and societies seeking to achieve the normative goals elucidated by various philosophers. Whether international law has achieved these goals is discussed in Chapter 7.

Thus, from the beginning of time scholars interested in international relations became grounded in diplomatic history as a substantive focus and also became thoroughly versed in philosophy, posing the foundational questions and seeking normative answers.

Behavioralism

In the 1950s, some scholars became dissatisfied with examining historic events as idiosyncratic cases. They became disillusioned with philosophical discourse. They pondered new questions: Are there subtle and perhaps more intriguing patterns to diplomatic history than those found in the descriptive historical record? Is individual behavior more predictable than the largely contextual descriptions of the historian? Is it possible to test whether the trends found through historical inquiry or the "oughts" proposed by the philosophers are empirically valid? How do people—the foundation of the municipality, the state, and international society—actually behave? Is man as selfish as Hobbes and Rousseau posited? Are states as power hungry as those who compare the anarchic international system to the state of nature would have us believe?

Scholars seeking answers to these new questions were poised to contribute to the behavioral revolution in U.S. social sciences during the 1950s and 1960s. **Behavioralism** proposes that individuals, both alone and in groups, act in patterned ways. The task of the behavioral scientist is to suggest plausible hypotheses regarding those patterned actions and to systematically and empirically test those hypotheses. Using the tools of the scientific method to describe and explain human behavior, these scholars hope ultimately to predict future behavior. Many will be satisfied, however, with being able to explain patterns, as prediction in the social sciences remains an uncertain enterprise.

The Correlates of War project, research based at the University of Michigan, permits us to see the application of behavioralism. Beginning in 1963, political scientist J. David Singer and his historian colleague Melvin Small attacked one of the fundamental questions in international relations: Why is there war?[12] As Singer himself later acknowledged, he was motivated by the normative philosophical concern—how can there be peace? The two scholars chose a different methodological approach than their historian colleagues. Rather than focusing on one war, one of the "big ones" that change the tide of history, as Thucydides did in his study of the Peloponnesian War, they sought to find patterns among a number of different wars. Believing that there are generalizable patterns to be found across all wars, Singer and Small turned to statistical data to discover the patterns.

The initial task of the Correlates of War project was to collect data on international wars (not civil wars) between 1865 and 1965 in which 1,000 or more deaths had been reported. For each of the 93 wars that fit these criteria, the researchers found data on the magnitude, severity, and intensity of wars, as well as the frequency of war over time. This data collection process proved a much larger task than Singer and Small had anticipated, employing a bevy of researchers and graduate students.

Once the wars were codified, the second task was to generate specific, testable hypotheses that might explain the outbreak of war. Is there a relationship between the number of alliance commitments in the international system and the number of wars experienced? Is there a relationship between the number of great powers in the international system and the number of wars? Is there a relationship between the number of wars over time and the severity of the conflicts? In the Correlates of War studies and in subsequent studies using the same data, hundreds of such relationships have been verified, although the relative importance of some of these findings is questionable.

The ultimate goal of the project is to connect all the relationships that are found into a coherent theory of why wars occur. Which groups of factors are *most* correlated with the outbreak of war over time? And how are these factors related to one another? Although answering these questions will never *prove* that a particular group of factors is the cause of war, it could suggest some high-level correlations that merit theoretical explanation. Are characteristics within specific warring states most correlated with the outbreak of war? What is the correlation between international system–level factors—such as the existence of international organizations—and the outbreak of war? If the Correlates of War project finds consistently high correlations between alliances and war or between international organizations and war, then it can explain why wars break out, and perhaps policymakers may be able to predict the characteristics of the actors and the location for future wars. That is the goal of that research project. Yet methodological problems abound. The Correlates of War database looks at all international wars, irrespective of the different political, military, social, and technological contexts. So while the generalizations gleaned may be provocative, richer description is needed to really explain the different patterns between wars of the late 1800s and wars of the early 2000s.

Although the methods of behavioralism, as illustrated in the Correlates of War project, have never been an end in themselves, only a means to improve explanation, during the 1980s and 1990s scholars have seriously questioned the behavioral approach. Their disillusionment has taken several forms. To some, many of the foundational questions—the nature of man and society—are neglected by behavioralists because they are not easily testable by empirical methods. These critics suggest returning to the philosophical roots of international relations. To others, the questions behavioralists pose are the salient ones, but their attention to methods has overwhelmed the substance of their research. Few would doubt the importance of J. David Singer and Melvin Small's initial excursion into the causes of war, but even the researchers themselves admitted losing sight of the important questions in their quest to compile data and hone research methods. Some scholars, still within the behavioralist orientation, suggest simplifying esoteric methods in order to refocus on the substantive questions. Others remain firmly committed to the behavioral approach, pointing to the lack of funding and time as an explanation for their meager results.

Approaches of Alternative Theories

Alternative theorists are dissatisfied with using history, philosophy, or behavioral approaches. The postmodernists, for example, seek to deconstruct the basic concepts of the field, like the state, the nation, rationality, and realism, by searching the texts (or sources) for hidden meanings underneath the surface, in the subtext. Once those hidden meanings are revealed, the postmodernist seeks to replace the once-orderly picture with disorder, to replace the dichotomies with multiple portraits.

Researchers have begun to deconstruct core concepts and replace them with multiple meanings. Political scientist Cynthia Weber, for example, argues that sovereignty (the independence of a state) is neither well defined nor consistently grounded. Digging below the surface of sovereignty, going beyond evaluations of the traditional philosophers, she has discovered that conceptualizations of sovereignty are constantly shifting, based on the exigencies of the moment and sanctioned by different communities. The multiple meanings of sovereignty are conditioned by time, place, and historical circumstances.[13] This analysis has profound implications for the theory and practice of international relations, which are rooted in state sovereignty and accepted practices that reinforce sovereignty. It challenges conventional understandings.

Postmodernists also seek to find the voices of "the others," those individuals who have been disenfranchised and marginalized in international relations. Feminist Christine Sylvester illustrates her approach with a discussion of the Greenham Common Peace Camp, a group of mostly women who in the early 1980s left their homes and neighborhoods in Wales and walked more than a hundred miles to a British air force base to protest against plans to deploy missiles at the base. Although the marchers were ignored by the media—and thus were "voiceless"—they maintained a politics of resistance, recruiting other political action groups near the camp and engaging members of the military stationed at the base. The women learned how to maintain a peace camp, forcing down the barriers between the militarized and demilitarized and between women and men. In 1988, when the Intermediate Range Nuclear Force Treaty was signed, dismantling the missiles, the women moved on to another protest site, drawing public attention to the role of Britain in the nuclear era.[14]

Others, such as the constructivists, have turned to discourse analysis to answer the questions posed. To trace the impact of ideas on shaping identities, they analyze culture, norms, procedures, and social practices. They probe how identities are shaped and change over time. They use texts, interviews, and archival material, as well as research local practices by riding public transportation and standing in lines. By using multiple sets of data, they create thick description. The case studies found in Peter Katzenstein's edited volume *The Culture of National Security* utilize this approach. Drawing on analyses of Soviet foreign policy at the end of the Cold War, German and Japanese security policy from militarism to antimilitarism, and Arab national identity, the authors search for security interests defined by actors who are responding to changing cultural factors. These studies show how social and cultural factors shape national security policy in ways that contradict realist or liberal expectations.[15]

No important question of international relations today can be answered with exclusive reliance on any one approach. History, whether in the form of an extended case study (Peloponnesian War) or a study of multiple wars (Correlates of War), provides useful answers. Philosophical traditions offer the framework for the major discussions of the day. And the newer methods of deconstructionism and thick description and discourse analysis provide an even richer base from which the international relations scholar can draw.

In Sum: Making Sense of International Relations

How can we, as students, begin to make sense of international political events in our daily lives? How have scholars of international relations helped us make sense of the world around us? In this chapter, major theories of international relations have been introduced, including the liberal, realist,

TABLE 1.2

Approaches to Studying International Relations	
Type of Approach	**Method**
History	Examines individual or multiple cases.
Philosophy	Develops rationales from core texts and analytical thinking.
Behavioralism	Finds patterns in human behavior and state behavior using empirical methods.
Alternative	Deconstructs major concepts and uses discourse analysis to build thick description. Finds voices of "others."

radical, and constructivist frameworks. These theories provide frameworks for asking and answering core foundational questions. To answer these questions, international relations scholars turn to many other disciplines, including history, philosophy, behavioral psychology, and critical studies (see Table 1.2). International relations is a pluralistic and eclectic discipline.

Where Do We Go from Here?

To understand the development of international relations theory, we need to examine general historical trends to show developments in the state and the international system, particularly events in Europe during the nineteenth and twentieth centuries. This "stuff" of diplomatic history is the subject of Chapter 2. Chapter 3 is designed to help us think about the development of international relations theoretically through several frameworks—liberalism, realism, radicalism, and constructivism. Chapters 4, 5, and 6, examine the levels of analysis in international relations. Each of these chapters is organized around the theoretical frameworks. Thus, in Chapter 4 the international system is examined; in Chapter 5, the state; and in Chapter 6, the individual. In each of these chapters the focus is on comparing liberal, realist, and radical descriptions and explanations, augmented, when appropriate, with constructivism. Chapter 7 explores and analyzes the roles of international organizations, nongovernmental actors, and international law. In the last three chapters, the major issues of international relations are studied: in Chapter 8, war and strife; in Chapter 9, international political economy; and in Chapter 10, the globalizing issues of the twenty-first century.

Notes

1. Stephen M. Walt, "International Relations: One World, Many Theories," *Foreign Policy*, no. 110 (Spring 1998), 30.
2. Thucydides, *History of the Peloponnesian War*, trans. Rex Warner (Rev. ed.; Harmondsworth, Eng.: Penguin, 1972).
3. Stephen Biddle, "Seeing Bagdad, Thinking Saigon," *Foreign Affairs* 85.2 (March/April 2006), 2–14. For more on the use of historical analogies, see Yuen Foong Khong, *Analogies at War: Korea, Munich, Dien Bien Phu, and the Vietnam Decision of 1965* (Princeton, N.J.: Princeton Univ. Press, 1992).
4. Plato, *The Republic* (Harmondsworth, Eng.: Penguin, 1955).
5. Aristotle, *The Politics*, ed. Trevor J. Saunders, trans. T. A. Sinclair (Harmondsworth, Eng.: Penguin, 1981).
6. Thomas Hobbes, *Leviathan*, ed. C. B. Macpherson (Harmondsworth, Eng.: Penguin, 1968).
7. Jean-Jacques Rousseau, "Discourse on the Origin and Foundations of Inequality among Men," in *Basic Political Writings of Jean-Jacques Rousseau*, ed. and trans. Donald A. Cress (Indianapolis, Ind.: Hackett Publishing, 1987).
8. Jean-Jacques Rousseau, "On the Social Contract," Book 2, Ch. 1, in *Basic Political Writings of Jean-Jacques Rousseau*, Cress, 153.
9. Ibid., Book 1, Ch. 6, 148.
10. See Immanuel Kant, *Idea for a Universal History from a Cosmopolitan Point of View* (1784) and *Perpetual Peace: A Philosophical Sketch* (1795), both reprinted in *Kant Selections*, ed. Lewis White Beck (New York: Macmillan Co., 1988).
11. St. Thomas Aquinas, "Treatise of the Laws" (XCV:4), reprinted in *Great Books of the Western World*, vols. 19, 20, ed. Robert Maynard Hutchins (Chicago: Encyclopedia Britannica, 1952, 1986).
12. J. David Singer and Melvin Small, *The Wages of War, 1816–1965: A Statistical Handbook* (New York: Wiley, 1972).
13. Cynthia Weber, *Simulating Sovereignty: Intervention, the State, and Symbolic Interchange* (Cambridge, Eng.: Cambridge University Press, 1994).
14. Christine Sylvester, "Emphatic Cooperation: A Feminist Method for IR," *Millennium: Journal of International Studies* 23:2 (1994), 315–34.
15. Peter J. Katzenstein, ed., *The Culture of National Security: Norms and Identity in World Politics* (New York: Columbia University Press, 1996).

The Historical Context of Contemporary International Relations

- *Which historical periods have most influenced the development of international relations?*
- *What are the historical origins of the state?*
- *Why is the Treaty of Westphalia used as a benchmark for international relations scholars?*
- *What are the historical origins of the European balance-of-power system?*
- *How could the Cold War be both a series of confrontations between the United States and the Soviet Union and a "long peace"?*
- *What key events have shaped the post–Cold War world?*

Students of international relations need to understand the events and trends of the past. Theorists recognize that core concepts in the field—the state, the nation, sovereignty, power, balance of power—were developed and shaped by historical circumstances. Policymakers search the past for patterns and precedents to guide contemporary decisions. In large part, the major antecedents to the contemporary international system are found in European-centered Western civilization.

Great civilizations thrived in other parts of the world too, of course: India and China, among others, had extensive, vibrant civilizations long before the historical events covered below. But the European emphasis is justified on the basis that contemporary international relations, in both theory and practice, is rooted in the European experience, for better or worse. In this chapter, we will first look at the period before 1648 (a seminal year for students of international relations), then the post-Westphalian world after 1648, then Europe of the nineteenth century, and finally the major transitions in the twentieth century.

The purpose of this historical overview is to trace important trends over time—the emergence of the state and the notion of sovereignty, the development of the international state system, and the changes in the distribution of power among key states. These trends have a direct impact on international relations theory and practice today.

The Pre-Westphalian World

Many international relations theorists date the contemporary system from 1648, the year of the Treaty of Westphalia ending the Thirty Years War. This treaty marks the end of rule by religious authority in Europe and the emergence of secular authorities. With secular authority came the principle that has provided the foundation for international relations ever since: the notion of the territorial integrity of states—legally equal and sovereign participants in an international system. The Greek city-state system, the Roman Empire, and changing centralization and decentralization of the Middle Ages are each key developments leading to the new Westphalian order.

Greece and the City-State System of Interactions

The Greeks, organized in independent city-states, were at the height of their power in 400 B.C. and engaged in classic power politics, as cataloged by Thucydides in *History of the Peloponnesian War*. As the militaries of the great city-states struggled, states carried on economic relations and trade with each other to an unprecedented degree. This environment clearly fostered the flowering of the strong philosophical tradition of Plato and Aristotle that we studied in Chapter 1. In this setting, city-states—each an independent unit—conducted peaceful relations with each other as they vied for power—a precursor of the modern state system.

Rome: The Governing of an Empire

Many of the Greek city-states were eventually incorporated into the Roman Empire (50 B.C.–400 A.D.). The Roman Empire served as the precursor for larger political systems. Its leaders imposed order and unity by force on a large geographic expanse—covering much of Europe, the Mediterranean portions of Asia, the Middle East, and northern Africa. Having conquered far-flung and diverse peoples, the Roman leaders were preoccupied with keeping the various units—tribes, kingdoms, and states—within their sphere of influence and ensuring that the fluid borders of the empire remained secure from the roving hordes to the north and east. Indeed, from the Roman experience comes the word *empire* itself, from the Latin *imperium*. The leaders imposed various forms of government, from Roman proconsuls to local bureaucrats and administrators, disseminating the Latin language to the far reaches of the empire. They followed the practice of granting Roman citizenship to free peoples in the far-flung empire, while at the same time giving local rulers considerable autonomy to organize their own domain.

Greece, c. 450 B.C.

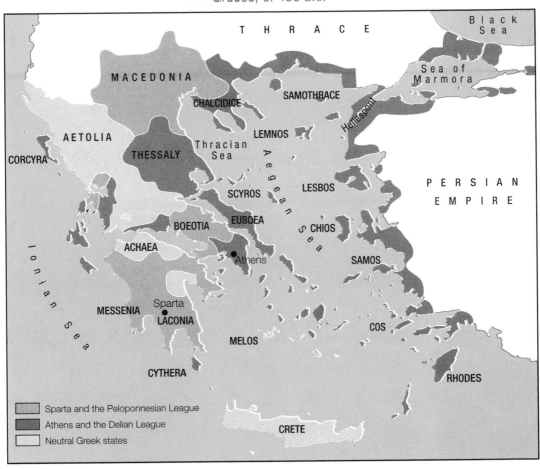

Roman philosophers provided an essential theoretical underpinning to the empire, as well as to future international relations theory. In particular, Marcus Tullius Cicero (106–43 B.C.) offered a mechanism for the uniting of the various parts of the empire. He proposed that men ought to be united by a law among nations applicable to humanity as a whole. But such a law among nations did not preclude Cicero's offering more practical advice to Rome's leaders: he emphasized the necessity of maintaining state security by expanding resources and boundaries, while at the same time ensuring domestic stability.[1] Above all, the Roman Empire itself and the writers it spawned provided the foundation for a larger geographic entity whose members, while retaining local identities, were united through the centralization of power.

The Roman Empire, c. 117 A.D.

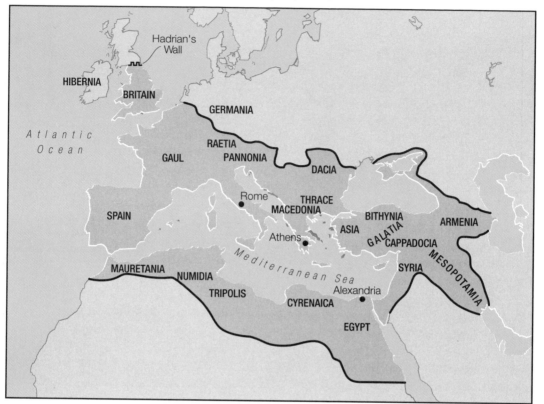

The Middle Ages: Centralization and Decentralization

When the Roman Empire disintegrated in the fifth century A.D., power and authority became decentralized in Europe, but other forms of interaction flourished—travel, commerce, and communication, not just among the elites but also among merchant groups and ordinary citizens. By 1000 A.D. three civilizations had emerged from the rubble of Rome. First among them was the Arabic civilization, which had the largest geographic expanse, stretching from the Middle East and Persia through North Africa to the Iberian Peninsula. United under the religious and political domination of the Islamic caliphate, the Arabic language, and advanced mathematical and technical accomplishments, the Arabic civilization was a potent force. Second was the Byzantine Empire, located nearer the core of the old Roman Empire in Constantinople and united by Christianity. Third was the rest of Europe, where with the demise of the Roman Empire central authority was absent, languages and cultures proliferated, and the networks of com-

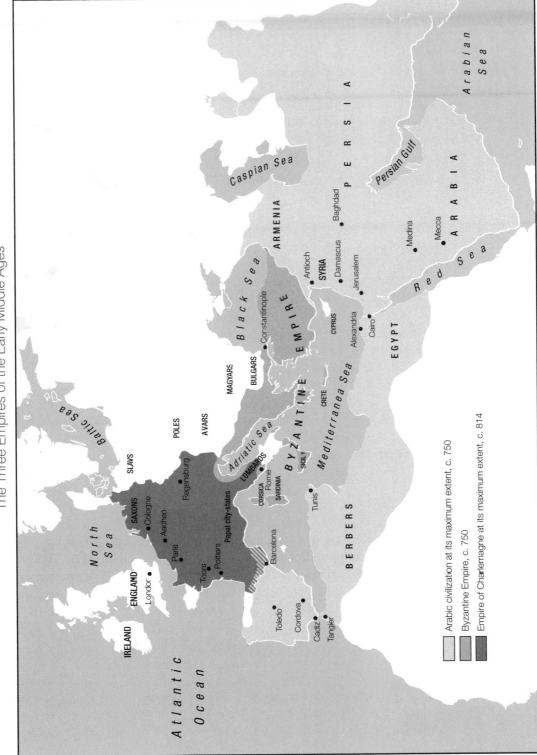

The Three Empires of the Early Middle Ages

Atlantic Ocean

IRELAND

ENGLAND
London

North Sea

Baltic Sea

SLAVS

SAXONS
Cologne
Aachen

Paris

Tours
Poitiers

Regensburg

POLES

AVARS

MAGYARS

BULGARS

Papal city-states

Rome
LOMBARDS
CORSICA
SARDINIA

Barcelona

Toledo
Cordova
Cadiz
Tangier

Tunis

BERBERS

SICILY

Adriatic Sea

Mediterranean Sea

CRETE

Black Sea

Corstantinople

BYZANTINE EMPIRE

ARMENIA

Caspian Sea

PERSIA

Baghdad

Antioch
SYRIA
Damascus
Jerusalem
CYPRUS
Alexandria
Cairo

EGYPT

Red Sea

Medina
Mecca

ARABIA

Persian Gulf

Arabian Sea

Arabic civilization at its maximum extent, c. 750

Byzantine Empire, c. 750

Empire of Charlemagne at its maximum extent, c. 814

munication and transportation developed by the Romans were beginning to disintegrate.

Much of Western Europe reverted to feudal principalities, controlled by lords and tied to fiefdoms that had the authority to raise taxes and exert legal authority. Lords exercised control over vassals, who worked for the lords in return for the right to work the land and acquire protection. Feudalism, which placed authority in private hands, was the response to the prevailing disorder. Power and authority were located at different overlapping levels.

The preeminent institution in the medieval period in Europe was the church; virtually all other institutions were local in origin and practice. Thus, authority was centered either in Rome (and in its agents, the bishops, dispersed throughout medieval Europe) or in the local fiefdom. Yet even the bishops seized considerable independent authority despite their overarching allegiance to the church. Economic life was also intensely local.

In the late eighth century, the church's monopoly on power was challenged by Carolus Magnus, or Charlemagne (742–814), the leader of the Franks in what is today France. Charlemagne was granted authority to unite western Europe in the name of Christianity against the Byzantine Empire in the east; the pope made him emperor of the Holy Roman Empire. In return, Charlemagne offered the pope protection. The struggle between religious and secular authority and the debate over which should rule would continue for hundreds of years, with writers periodically offering their views on the subject. One such writer was Dante Alighieri (1265–1321), who argued in "De Monarchia" that there should be a strict separation of the church from political life.[2] This question was not resolved until three hundred years later at the Treaty of Westphalia.

The Holy Roman Empire itself was a weak secular institution; as one famous saying goes, it was not very holy, very Roman, nor much of an empire. Yet successors to Charlemagne did provide a limited secular alternative to the church. The contradictions remained, however: the desire on the part of the church for universalism versus the medieval reality of small, fragmented, diverse authorities. These small units, largely unconnected to each other, with dispersed populations, all served to prevent the establishment of centralized governmental authority.

Similar trends of centralization and decentralization, political integration and disintegration, were also occurring in other geographic areas. In Africa, for example, the Ancient Kingdom of Ghana (not to be confused with the contemporary state) centralized power between the fifth and thirteenth centuries, and in the thirteenth and fourteenth centuries, the Kingdom of Mali prevailed. Each were powerful political and economic territories; each had a sophisticated system of tax collection and served as important centers of commerce with Muslims in North Africa, trading gold and salt with their Arab neighbors. Each was an empire with standing armies but with traditional rulers left in place in the outlying districts. And on the opposite side of the globe, in Latin America, independent civilizations flourished—the Mayans from 100 to 900 A.D. and the Aztecs and Incas from 1200.

Japan represented another country where centralization followed a period of warfare and decentralized authority. Whereas the fifteenth and sixteenth centuries can be largely characterized by turmoil, a period of two hundred years of more centralized control followed. During the Tokugawa period from 1603 to 1868, Japan was ruled by a shogun. This was a period of strict class hierarchy, led by the warrior-caste of samurai, followed by farmers, artisans, and traders. While unrest and violent confrontations occurred over the disparate economic conditions, none of these events posed a direct threat to the established feudal system. Yet in each region, it was intervention by Europeans in later centuries that challenged this order.

The Late Middle Ages: Developing Transnational Networks in Europe and Beyond

Although the intellectual debate was not yet resolved, after 1000 A.D. secular trends began to undermine both the decentralization of feudalism and the universalization of Christianity in Europe. Commercial activity expanded into larger geographic areas, as merchants traded along increasingly safer transportation routes. All forms of communication improved. New technology, such as water mills and windmills, not only made daily life easier but also provided the first elementary infrastructure to support agrarian economies. Municipalities, like the reinvigorated city-states of the northern Italian peninsula—Genoa, Venice, Milan, Florence—established trading relationships, setting up meeting places at key locations, arranging for the shipment of commercial materials, and even agreeing to follow certain diplomatic practices to facilitate commercial activities. These diplomatic practices—establishing embassies with permanent staff, sending special consuls to handle commercial disputes, and sending diplomatic messages through specially protected channels—were the immediate precursors of contemporary diplomatic practice.

These economic and technological changes led to fundamental changes in social relations. First, a new group of individuals emerged—a transnational business community—whose interests and livelihoods extended beyond its immediate locale. This group acquired more cosmopolitan experiences outside the realm of the church and its teachings, which had so thoroughly dominated education up to this point. The individual members developed new interests in art, philosophy, and history, acquiring considerable economic

Europe, c. 1360

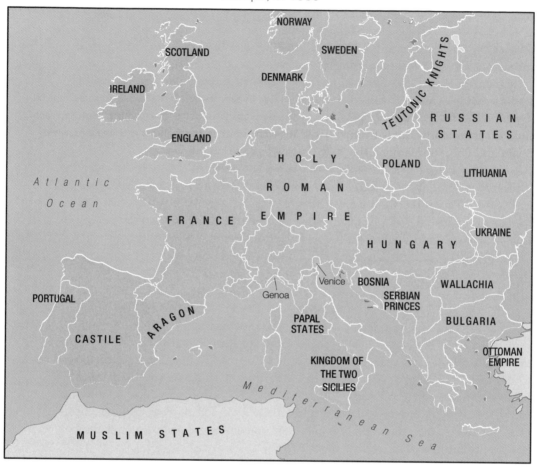

wealth along the way. They believed in themselves, becoming the individual-ists and humanists of the Renaissance. Second, writers and other individuals rediscovered classical literature and history, finding intellectual sustenance and revelation in Greek and Roman thought.

The Italian philosopher Niccolò Machiavelli (1469–1527), more than any other writer, illustrates the changes taking place and the ensuing gulf between the medieval world of the church and secular institutions. In *The Prince* Machi-avelli elucidated the qualities that a leader needs to maintain the strength and security of the state. Realizing that the dream of unity in Christianity was unat-tainable (and probably undesirable), Machiavelli called on leaders to articulate their own political interests. He argued that having no universal morality to guide them, leaders must act in the state's interest, answerable to no moral rules. The cleavage between the religiousness of medieval times and the humanism of the later Renaissance was thus starkly drawn.[3]

The desire to expand economic intercourse even further, coupled with the technological inventions that made ocean exploration safer, fueled a period of European territorial expansion. Individuals from Spain and Italy were among the earliest of these adventurers— Christopher Columbus sailing to the New World in 1492, Hernán Cortés to Mexico in 1519, Francisco Pizarro to the Andes in 1533, all disrupting the indigenous orders. During this age of exploration European civilization spread to distant shores. For some theorists, it is these events—the gradual incorporation of the underdeveloped peripheral areas into the world capitalist economy and the international capitalist system—that mark the beginning of history relevant for contemporary international relations.

In the 1500s and 1600s, as explorers and even settlers moved into the New World, the old Europe remained in flux. In some key locales such as France, England, and Aragon and Castile in Spain, feudalism was being replaced by an increasingly centralized monarchy. The move toward centralization did not go uncontested; the masses, angered by taxes imposed by newly emerging states, rebelled and rioted. New monarchs needed the tax funds to build armies; they used their armies to consolidate their power internally and conquer more territory. Other parts of Europe were mired in the secular-versus-religious controversy, and Christianity itself was torn by the Catholic and Protestant split. In 1648, that controversy inched its way toward resolution.

> **In Focus**
>
> ### KEY DEVELOPMENTS BEFORE 1648
>
> ◆ The sovereign Greek city-states reach the height of their power in 400 B.C.; they carry out cooperative functions through diplomacy and classic power politics.
>
> ◆ The Roman Empire (50 B.C.–A.D. 400) originates imperialism, develops the practice of expanding territorial reach. The empire is united through law and language, while allowing some local identity.
>
> ◆ The Middle Ages (400–1000) witness the centralization of religious authority in the church, with decentralization in political and economic life.
>
> ◆ The Late Middle Ages (1000–1500) foster the development of transnational networks during the age of exploration.

The Emergence of the Westphalian System

The formulation of **sovereignty**—a core concept in contemporary international relations—was one of the most important intellectual developments leading to the Westphalian revolution. Much of the development of the notion is found in the writings of the French philosopher Jean Bodin (1530–96). To Bodin, sovereignty was the "absolute and perpetual power vested in a commonwealth."[4] It resides not in an individual but in a state; thus it is perpetual. Sovereignty is "the distinguishing mark of the sovereign that he cannot in any way be subject to the commands of another, for it is he who makes law for the subject, abrogates law already made, and amends obsolete law."[5]

Although absolute, sovereignty, according to Bodin, is not without limits. Leaders are limited by divine law or natural law: " . . . all the princes on earth are subject to the laws of God and of nature." They are also limited by the type of regime—"the constitutional laws of the realm"—be it a monarchy, an aristocracy, or a democracy. And last, leaders are limited by covenants, contracts with promises to the people within the commonwealth, and treaties with other states, though there is no supreme arbiter in relations among states.[6] Thus, Bodin provided the conceptual glue of sovereignty that would emerge with the Westphalian agreement.

The Thirty Years War (1618–48) devastated Europe; the armies plundered the central European landscape, fought battles, and survived by ravaging the civilian population. But the treaty that ended the conflict had a profound impact on the practice of international relations. First, the **Treaty of Westphalia** embraced the notion of sovereignty. With one stroke, virtually all the small states in central Europe attained sovereignty. The Holy Roman Empire was dead. Monarchs in the west realized that religious conflicts had to be stopped, so they agreed not to fight on behalf of either Catholicism or Protestantism. Instead, each monarch gained the authority to choose the version of Christianity for his or her people. This meant that monarchs, and not the church, had religious authority over their populations. This development implied the general acceptance of sovereignty—that the sovereign enjoyed exclusive rights within a given territory. With the pope and the emperor stripped of power, the notion of the territorial state was accepted. The treaty not only legitimized territoriality and the right of states to choose their own religion, but it also established that states could determine their own domestic policies, free from external pressure and with full jurisdiction in their own geographic space. It also introduced the right of noninterference in the affairs of other states.

Second, the leaders had seen the devastating effects of mercenaries fighting wars. Thus, after the Treaty of Westphalia, the leaders sought to establish their own permanent national militaries. The growth of such forces led to increasingly centralized control, since the state had to collect taxes to pay for

In Focus

KEY DEVELOPMENTS AFTER WESTPHALIA

- ◆ Notion and practice of sovereignty develops.
- ◆ Centralized control of institutions under military grows.
- ◆ Capitalist economic system emerges.

Europe, c. 1648

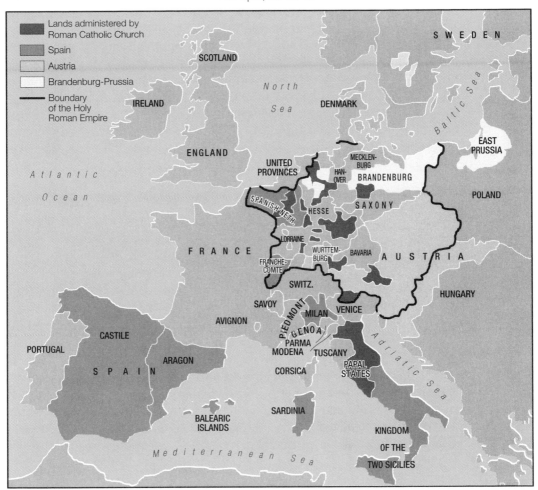

these militaries and the leaders assumed absolute control over the troops. The state with a national army emerged, its sovereignty acknowledged, and its secular base firmly established. And that state became increasingly more powerful. Larger territorial units gained an advantage as armaments became more sophisticated.

Third, the Treaty of Westphalia established a core group of states that dominated the world until the beginning of the nineteenth century: Austria, Russia, Prussia, England, France, and the United Provinces (the area now comprising the Netherlands and Belgium). Those in the west—England, France, and the United Provinces—underwent an economic revival under the aegis of capitalism, while those in the east—Prussia and Russia—reverted to feudal practices. In the west, private enterprise was encouraged. States improved their infrastructure to facilitate commerce, and great trading companies and banks emerged. In contrast, in the east, serfs remained on the land and economic change was stifled. Yet in both regions, absolutist states dominated: with Louis XIV (1638–1715) ruling in France, Peter the Great (1672–1725) in Russia, and Frederick II (1712–86) in Prussia. Until the end of the eighteenth century, European politics was dominated by multiple rivalries and shifting alliances. These rivalries were also played out in regions beyond Europe, where contending European states vied for power, most notably Great Britain and France in North America.

The most important theorist of the time was the Scottish economist Adam Smith (1723–90). In *An Inquiry into the Nature and Causes of the Wealth of Nations,* Smith argued that the notion of a market should apply to all social orders. Individuals—laborers, owners, investors, consumers—should be permitted to pursue their own interests, unfettered by state regulation. According to Smith, each individual acts rationally to maximize his or her own interests. With groups of individuals pursuing self-interests, economic efficiency is enhanced and more goods and services are produced and consumed. At the aggregate level, the wealth of the state and that of the international system are similarly enhanced. What makes the system work is the so-called invisible hand of the market; when individuals pursue their rational self-interests, the system (the market) operates effortlessly.[7] Smith's explication of how competing units enable capitalism to work to ensure economic vitality has had a profound effect on states' economic policies and political choices, which we shall explore in Chapter 9. But other ideas of the period would also dramatically alter governance in the nineteenth, twentieth, and twenty-first centuries.

Europe in the Nineteenth Century

Two revolutions ushered in the nineteenth century—the American Revolution (1776) against British rule and the French Revolution (1789) against absolutist rule. Each revolution was the product of Enlightenment thinking as well as social contract theorists. During the Enlightenment, thinkers began to see individuals as rational, capable of understanding the laws governing them and of working to improve their condition in society.

The Aftermath of Revolution: Core Principles

Two core principles emerged in the aftermath of the American and French Revolutions. The first was that absolutist rule is subject to limits imposed by man. In *Two Treatises on Government*, the English philosopher John Locke (1632–1704) attacked absolute power and the notion of the divine right of kings. Locke argued that the state is a beneficial institution created by rational men in order to protect both their natural rights (life, liberty, and property) and their self-interests. Men freely enter into this political arrangement. They agree to establish government to ensure natural rights for all. The crux of Locke's argument is that political power ultimately rests with the people, rather than with the leader or the monarch. The monarch derives his **legitimacy** from the consent of the governed.[8]

The second core principle that emerged at this time was **nationalism,** wherein the masses identify with their common past, their language, customs, and practices. Individuals who share such characteristics are motivated to participate actively in the political process as a group. For example, during the French Revolution, a patriotic appeal was made to the masses to defend the nation and its new ideals. This appeal forged an emotional link between the masses and the state. These two principles—legitimacy and nationalism—arose out of the American and French Revolutions to provide the foundation for politics in the nineteenth and twentieth centuries.

Peace at the Core of the European System

Following the defeat of Napoleon in 1815 and the establishment of peace by the Congress of Vienna, the five powers of Europe—Austria, Britain, France, Prussia, and Russia—ushered in a period of relative peace in the international political system, the so-called Concert of Europe. No major wars among these great powers were fought after the demise of Napoleon until the Crimean War in 1854, and in that war both Austria and Prussia remained neutral. Other local wars of brief duration were fought in which some of the five major powers remained neutral. Held together by agreements reached at a series of ad hoc conferences, all five powers were never involved in conflict with one another. Meeting over thirty times before World War I, the group became a club of like-minded leaders, and through these meetings they legitimized both the independence of new European states and the division of Africa by colonial powers.

The fact that general peace prevailed during this time is surprising, since major economic, technological, and political changes were radically altering the landscape. The population growth rate soared and commerce surged as transportation corridors were strengthened. Political changes were dramatic: Italy was unified in 1870; Germany was formed out of thirty-nine different fragments in 1871; Holland was divided into the Netherlands and Belgium in the 1830s; and the Ottoman Empire gradually disintegrated, leading to independence for Greece in 1829 and for Moldavia and Wallachia (Romania) in

Europe, c. 1815

1856. With such dramatic changes under way, what factors explain the peace? At least three factors explain this phenomenon.

First, the European states enjoyed a solidarity among themselves, based on their being European, Christian, "civilized," and white. These traits differentiated "them"—white Christian Europeans—from the "other"—the rest of the world. With their increasing contact with the colonial world, Europeans saw more than ever their commonalities, the uniqueness of being European. This was, in part, a return to the unity found in the Roman Empire and in Roman law, a secular form of medieval Christendom, and a larger Europe as envisioned in the writings of Kant and Rousseau. The Congress of Vienna and the Concert of Europe gave form to these beliefs.

Second, European elites were united in their fear of revolution from the masses. In fact, at the Congress of Vienna, the Austrian diplomat Klemens von Metternich (1773–1859), the architect of the Concert of Europe, believed that Europe could best be managed by returning it to the age of absolutism. Elites envisioned grand alliances that would bring European leaders together to fight revolution from below. In the first half of the century, these alliances were not altogether successful. In the 1830s, Britain and France sided together against the three eastern powers (Prussia, Russia, and Austria), and in 1848, all five powers were confronted by the masses with demands for reform. But in the second half of the century, European leaders acted in concert, ensuring that mass revolutions did not move from state to state. In 1870, Napoleon III was isolated quickly for fear of a revolution that never occurred. Fear of revolt from below thus united European leaders, making interstate war less likely.

Third, two of the major issues confronting the core European states were internal ones: the unifications of Germany and Italy. Both German and Italian unification had powerful proponents and opponents among the European powers. For example, Britain supported Italian unification, making possible Italy's annexation of Naples and Sicily; Austria, on the other hand, was preoccupied with the increasing strength of Prussia and thus did not actively oppose what may well have been against its national interest—the creation of two sizable neighbors out of myriad independent units. German unification was acceptable to Russia as long as its interest in Poland was respected, and German unification got support from the dominant middle class in Britain, as they viewed a stronger Germany as a potential counterbalance to France. Thus, although the unification of both were finally solidified through small local wars, a general war was averted since Germany and Italy were preoccupied with territorial unification.

Industrialization, a critical development at the time, was a double-edged sword. In the second half of the nineteenth century, all attention was focused on the processes of industrialization. Great Britain was the leader, outstripping all rivals in the output of coal, iron, and steel, and the export of manufactured goods. In addition, Britain became the source of finance capital, the banker for the Continent and, in the twentieth century, for the world. Industrialization spread through virtually all areas of Western Europe as the masses flocked to the cities and entrepreneurs and middlemen scrambled for economic advantage.

The industrial revolution provided the European states with the military and economic capacity to engage in territorial expansion. Some imperial states were motivated by economic gains, as they sought new external markets for manufactured goods and obtained, in turn, raw materials to fuel their industrial growth. For others, the motivation was cultural and religious—to spread the Christian faith and the ways of white "civilization" to the "dark" continents and beyond. To still others, the motivation was political.

Since the European balance of power prevented direct confrontation in Europe, European state rivalries were played out in Africa and Asia.

To satisfy Germany's ambitions, the major powers during the Congress of Berlin in 1885 divvied up Africa, giving Germany a sphere of influence in East Africa (Tanganyika), West Africa (Cameroon and Togo), and southern Africa (southwest Africa). European imperialism provided a convenient outlet for Germany's aspirations as a unified power without endangering the delicate balance of power within Europe itself. By the end of the nineteenth century, eighty-five percent of Africa was under the control of European states.

In Asia, only Japan and Siam (Thailand) were not under direct European or U.S. influence. China is an excellent example of external domination. Under the Qing dynasty, which began in the seventeenth century, the Chinese territory had slowly been losing political, economic, and military power for several hundred years. In the nineteenth century, British merchants began to trade with China in exchange for tea, silk, and porcelain, paying for them with smuggled opium. In 1842, the British defeated China in the Opium War, forcing China to cede various political and territorial rights to foreigners through a series of unequal treaties. Both European states and Japan were able to occupy large portions of Chinese territory where each claimed to have exclusive trading rights in a particular region. Foreign powers, then, exercised separate "spheres of influence" in China. By 1914, Europeans controlled four-fifths of the world.

The United States was an imperial power as well. Having won the 1898 Spanish-American War, pushing the Spanish out of the Philippines, Puerto Rico, Cuba, and other small islands, the United States acquired its own colonies.

The struggle for economic prowess led to heedless exploitation of the colonial areas, particularly in Africa and Asia. But the five European powers did not fight major wars directly against each other. By the end of the century, however, this economic competition became destabilizing, as European states coalesced into two competing alliance systems.

Balance of Power

How was this period of relative peace in Europe managed and preserved for so long? The answer lies in a concept called the **balance of power.** In the nineteenth century a *balance of power* emerged because the independent European states, each with relatively equal power, feared the emergence of any predominant state (**hegemon**) among them. Thus, they formed alliances to counteract any potentially more powerful faction—creating a balance of power. The treaties signed after 1815 were designed not only to quell revolution from

Europe, c. 1878

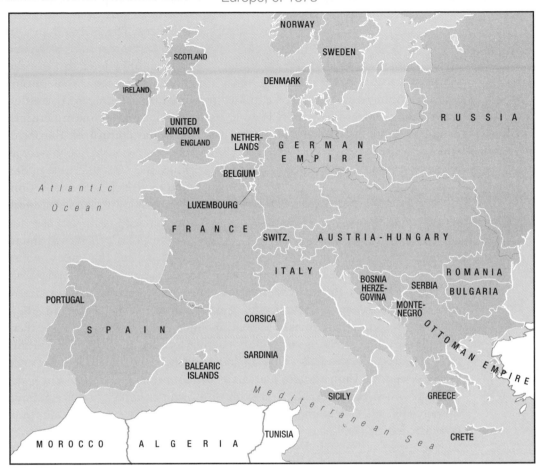

below but to prevent the emergence of a hegemon, such as France under Napoleon had become. Britain and Russia, at least later in the century, could have assumed a dominant leadership position—Britain because of its economic prowess and naval capability, and Russia because of its relative geographic isolation and extraordinary manpower—but neither sought to exert hegemonic power because the status quo was acceptable to each state.

Britain and Russia did play different roles in the balance of power. Britain most often played the role of balancer. For example, by intervening on behalf of the Greeks in their struggle for independence from the Turks in the late 1820s, on behalf of the Belgians during their war of independence against Holland in 1830, on behalf of Turkey against Russia in the Crimean War in 1854–56 and again in the Russo-Turkish War in 1877–78, Britain ensured that other states did not interfere in these conflicts and that Europe

In Focus

KEY DEVELOPMENTS IN
NINETEENTH-CENTURY EUROPE

◆ From revolutions emerge two concepts: absolutist rule subject to limitations, and nationalism.

◆ A system managed by the balance of power brings relative peace to Europe. Elites are united in fear of the masses, and domestic concerns are more important than foreign policy.

◆ European imperialism in Asia and Africa helps to maintain the European balance of power.

◆ The balance of power breaks down due to solidification of alliances, resulting in World War I.

thus remained balanced. Russia's role was as a builder of alliances. The Holy Alliance of 1815 kept Austria, Prussia, and Russia united against revolutionary France, and Russia used its claim on Poland to build a bond with Prussia. Russian interests in the Dardanelles, the strategic waterway linking the Mediterranean Sea and the Black Sea, and in Constantinople (today's Istanbul) overlapped with those of Britain. Thus, these two states, located at the margins of Europe, played key roles in making the balance-of-power system work.

During the last three decades of the nineteenth century, the Concert of Europe frayed, beginning with the Russian invasion of Turkey in 1877. Alliances began to solidify as the balance-of-power system began to weaken. Outside of the core European region, conflict escalated. All the Central and South American states had won their independence from Spain and Portugal by 1830, and the United States and Great Britain prevented further European competition in South America. But the European colonial powers—Britain, France, Holland, Belgium, and Italy—fought wars to conquer and retain their colonies in Africa and Asia.

The Breakdown: Solidification of Alliances

By the waning years of the nineteenth century, that balance-of-power system had weakened. Whereas previously alliances had been fluid and flexible, with allies changeable, now alliances had solidified. Two camps emerged: the Triple Alliance (Germany, Austria, and Italy) in 1882 and the Dual Alliance (France and Russia) in 1893. In 1902, Britain broke from the "balancer" role, joining in a naval alliance with Japan to prevent a Russo-Japanese rapprochement in China. This alliance marked a significant turn: for the first time, a European state (Great Britain) turned to an Asian one (Japan) in order to thwart a European ally (Russia). And in 1904, Britain joined with France in the Entente Cordiale.

The end of the balance-of-power system, as well as the historic end of the nineteenth century, came with World War I. The two sides were enmeshed in a struggle between competitive alliances, made all the more dangerous by the

Europe, 1914

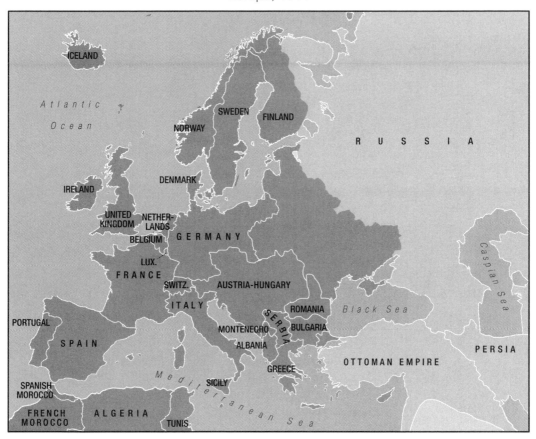

German position. Germany had not been satisfied with the solutions meted out at the Congress of Berlin. Germany still sought additional territory; if that meant European territory, then the map of Europe would have to be redrawn. Being a "latecomer" to the core of European power, Germany did not receive the diplomatic recognition and status its leaders desired. Thus, with the assassination of Archduke Franz Ferdinand, the heir to the throne of the Austro-Hungarian Empire, in 1914 in Sarajevo, Germany encouraged Austria to crush Serbia. After all, Germany did not want to see the disintegration of the Austro-Hungarian Empire, its major ally.

Under the system of alliances, once the fateful shot was fired, states honored their commitments to their allies, sinking the whole continent in warfare. Through their support of Serbia, the unlikely allies of Russia, France, and Great Britain became involved; through its support of Austria-Hungary, Germany entered the fray. It was anticipated that the war would be short and decisive, but it was neither. Between 1914 and 1918, soldiers from more than a dozen countries endured the persistent degradation of trench warfare and the horrors of gas warfare. More than 8.5 million soldiers and 1.5 million civilians lost their lives. Symbolically, the nineteenth century had come to a close: the century of relative peacefulness ended in a systemwide confrontation.

The Interwar Years and World War II

The end of World War I saw critical changes in international relations. First, three European empires were strained and finally broke up during or near the end of World War I. With those empires went the conservative social order of Europe; in its place emerged a proliferation of nationalisms. Russia exited the war in 1917, as revolution raged within its territory. The czar was overthrown and eventually replaced by not only a new leader (Vladimir I. Lenin) but a new ideology that would have profound implications for the rest of the twentieth century. The Austro-Hungarian Empire also broke apart, replaced by Austria, Hungary, Czechoslovakia, part of Yugoslavia, and part of Romania. Also reconfigured was the Ottoman Empire. Having gradually lost power throughout the nineteenth century, the Ottomans were allied with the Triple Alliance powers. Their defeat resulted in the final demise of the Ottomans. Arabia rose against Turkish rule, and British forces occupied Jerusalem and Baghdad. A diminished Turkey was the successor state.

The end of the empires produced proliferating nationalisms. In fact, one of President Woodrow Wilson's Fourteen Points in the treaty ending World War I called for self-determination, the right of national groups to self-rule. The nationalism of these various groups (Austrians, Hungarians) had been stimulated by technological innovations in the printing industry, which made it easy and cheap to publish material in the multitude of different European languages and so offer differing interpretations of history and national life. Yet in reality, many of these newly created entities had neither shared histories nor compatible political histories, nor were they economically viable.

Second, Germany emerged out of World War I an even more dissatisfied power. Not only had Germany been defeated on the military battlefield and its territorial ambitions been thwarted, the Treaty of Versailles, which formally ended the war, made the subsequent generation of Germans pay the economic cost of the war through reparations—$32 billion for wartime damages. This dissatisfaction provided the climate for the emergence of Adolf Hitler, who was dedicated to righting the "wrongs" that had been imposed on the German people.

Third, enforcement of the Versailles Treaty was given to the ultimately unsuccessful **League of Nations,** the intergovernmental organization designed to prevent all future wars. But the organization itself did not have the political weight, the legal instruments, or the legitimacy to carry out the task. The political weight of the League was weakened by the fact that the United States, whose president had been the principal architect of the League, itself refused to join, retreating instead to an isolationist foreign policy. Nor did Russia join, nor were any of the vanquished of the war permitted to participate. The League's legal authority was weak, and the instruments it had for enforcing the peace were ineffective.

Fourth, a vision of the post–World War I order had clearly been expounded, but it was a vision stillborn from the start. That vision was spelled out in Wilson's Fourteen Points. He called for open diplomacy—"open covenants of peace, openly arrived at, after which there shall be no private international understandings of any kind but diplomacy shall proceed always frankly and in public view."[9] Point three was a reaffirmation of economic liberalism, the removal of economic barriers among all the nations consenting to the peace. And, of course, the League, as a "general association of nations," was designed to ensure that war would never occur again. But that vision was not to be: In the words of the historian E. H. Carr, "The characteristic feature of the twenty years between 1919 and 1939 was the abrupt descent from the visionary hopes of the first decade to the grim despair of the second, from a utopia which took little account of reality to a reality from which every element of utopia was rigorously excluded."[10] Liberalism and its utopian and idealist elements were to be replaced by realism as the dominant international relations theory—a fundamentally divergent theoretical perspective; both liberalism and realism are developed in Chapter 3.

And the world from which the realists emerged was a turbulent one: a world economy in collapse; a German economy imploding; the U.S. stock market plummeting; Japan marching into Manchuria in 1931 and into the rest of China in 1937; Italy overrunning Ethiopia in 1935; fascism, liberalism, and communism clashing. These were the symptoms of the interwar period.

Germany proved to be the real challenge. Having been rearmed under Hitler in the 1930s, buoyed by helping the Spanish fascists during the Spanish Civil War, and successful in reuniting ethnic Germans from far-flung territories, Germany was ready to right the "wrongs" imposed by the Treaty of Versailles. For various reasons, Britain and France acquiesced to Germany's resurgence. Britain agreed in 1938 to let Germany

In Focus

KEY DEVELOPMENTS IN THE INTERWAR YEARS

- ◆ Three empires collapse: Russia by revolution, the Austro-Hungarian Empire by dismemberment, and the Ottoman Empire by external wars and internal turmoil. This leads to a resurgence of nationalisms.
- ◆ German dissatisfaction with the World War I settlement leads to facism. Germany finds allies in Italy and Japan.
- ◆ A weak League of Nations is unable to respond to Japanese, Italian, and German aggression, nor does it respond to widespread economic unrest.

Europe, 1939

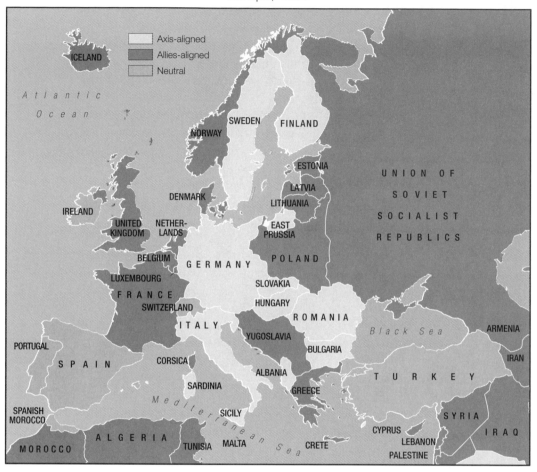

occupy Czechoslovakia, in the hope of averting more general war. But this was an idle hope. German fascism uniquely mobilized the masses in support of the state. It drew on the belief that war and conflict were noble activities, from which ultimately superior civilizations would be formed. It drew strength from the belief that certain racial groups were superior, others inferior, and mobilized the disenchanted and the economically weak on behalf of its cause.

The power of fascism—German, Italian, and Japanese versions—led to the uneasy (unholy) alliance between the communist Soviet Union and the liberal United States, Great Britain, and France, among others. That alliance was intended to check the Axis powers, by force if necessary. Thus, when World War II broke out, those fighting against the Axis acted in unison, regardless of their ideological divergence.

The Allies at the end of the war were successful. Both the German Reich and imperial Japan lay in ruins at the end of the war, the former as a result of traditional firepower and the latter as a result of the new instrument of atomic warfare. The end of World War II resulted in a major redistribution of power (the victorious United States would now be pitted against the equally victorious Soviet Union) and changed political borders (the Soviet Union absorbed the Baltic states and portions of Finland, Czechoslovakia, Poland, and Romania; Germany and Korea were divided; and Japan was ousted from much of Asia). Each of these changes contributed to the new international conflict: the Cold War.

The Cold War

The leaders of the "hot" World War II, Britain's prime minister Winston Churchill, the United States' president Franklin Roosevelt, and the Soviet Union's premier Joseph Stalin planned during the war for the postwar order. Indeed, the Atlantic Charter of August 14, 1941, called for collaboration on economic issues and prepared for a permanent system of security. These plans were consolidated in 1943 and 1944 and came to fruition in the United Nations in 1945. Yet several other outcomes of World War II provided the foundation for the **Cold War** that followed.

Origins of the Cold War

The most important outcome of World War II was the emergence of two **superpowers**—the United States and the Soviet Union—as the primary actors in the international system and the attendant decline of Europe as the epicenter of international politics. Both the United States and the Soviet Union were reluctant powers. Neither had been anxious to fight; each entered the war only after a direct attack on its territory. But by the end of the war, each had become a military superpower.

The second outcome of the war was the recognition of fundamental incompatibilities between these two superpowers in both national interests and ideology. Differences surfaced immediately over geopolitical national interests. Russia, having been invaded from the west on several occasions, including during World War II, used its newfound power to solidify its sphere of influence in the buffer states of Eastern Europe—Poland, Czechoslovakia, Hungary, Bulgaria, and Romania. The Soviet leadership believed that ensuring friendly neighbors on its western borders was vital to Soviet national interests. As for the United States, as early as 1947, U.S. policymakers argued that U.S. interests lay in containing the Soviet Union. The diplomat and historian George Kennan published in *Foreign Affairs* the famous "X" article, in which he argued that because the Soviet Union would always feel military insecurity, it would conduct an aggressive foreign policy. Containing the Soviets, Kennan therefore wrote, should become the cornerstone of the United State's postwar foreign policy.[11]

The United States put the notion of **containment** into action in the Truman Doctrine of 1947. Justifying material support in Greece against the communists, President Truman asserted, "I believe that it must be the policy of the United States to support free peoples who are resisting attempted subjugation by armed minorities or by outside pressures. I believe that we must assist free peoples to work out their own destinies in their own way."[12] But almost immediately, the United States retreated from containment, drastically reducing the size of its armed forces in hopes of returning to a more peaceful world. Then in 1948, when the Soviets blocked western transportation corridors to Berlin, the German capital, which had been divided into sectors by the Potsdam Conference, in 1945, the United States realized that its interests were broader. Thus, containment, based on U.S. geostrategic interests, became the fundamental doctrine of U.S. foreign policy during the Cold War.

The United States and the Soviet Union also had major ideological differences. These differences pitted two contrasting visions of society and of the international order. The United States' democratic liberalism was based on a social system that accepted the worth and value of the individual, a political system that depended on the participation of individuals in the electoral process, and an economic system, **capitalism,** that provided opportunities to individuals to pursue what was economically rational with little or no government interference. At the international level, this logically translated into support for other democratic liberal regimes and support of capitalist institutions and processes, including, most critically, free trade.

Soviet communist ideology also affected that country's conception of the international system and state practices. The Soviet state embraced Marxist ideology, which holds that under capitalism one class (the bourgeoisie) controls the ownership of the means of production and uses its institutions and authority to maintain that control. The solution to the problem of class rule, according to Marxism, is revolution, wherein the exploited proletariat takes control from the bourgeoisie by using the state to seize the means of production. Thus, capitalism is replaced by **socialism.** The leaders of the Soviet Union saw themselves in an interim period—after the demise of the capitalist state and before the victory of socialism. This ideology had critical international elements, as well: capitalism will try to extend itself through imperialism in order to generate more capital, larger markets, and greater control over raw materials. Soviet leaders thus felt themselves surrounded by a

Europe during the Cold War

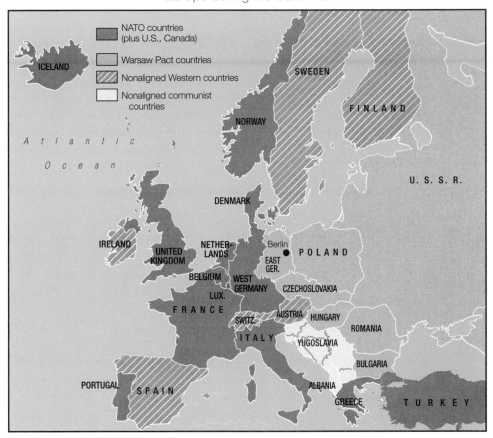

hostile capitalist camp and argued that the Soviet Union "must not weaken but must in every way strengthen its state, the state organs, the organs of the intelligence service, the army, if that country does not want to be smashed by the capitalist environment."[13] Internationally, they believed, it must support movements whose goals are both to undermine the capitalists and to promote a new social order.

Differences between the two superpowers were exacerbated by mutual misperceptions. Kennan cites powerful examples of misperceptions on the part of each superpower:

> The Marshall Plan, the preparations for the setting up of a West German government, and the first moves toward the establishment of NATO [the North Atlantic Treaty Organization] were taken in Moscow as the beginnings of a campaign to deprive the Soviet Union of the fruits of its

victory over Germany. The Soviet crackdown on Czechoslovakia [1948] and the mounting of the Berlin blockade, both essentially defensive . . . reactions to these Western moves, were then similarly misread on the Western side. Shortly thereafter there came the crisis of the Korean War, where the Soviet attempt to employ a satellite military force in civil combat to its own advantage, by way of reaction to the American decision to establish a permanent military presence in Japan, was read in Washington as the beginning of the final Soviet push for world conquest; whereas the active American military response, provoked by this move, appeared in Moscow . . . as a threat to the Soviet position in both Manchuria and in eastern Siberia.[14]

While such misperceptions did not cause the Cold War, they certainly added fuel to the confrontation.

The third outcome of the end of World War II was the beginning of the end of the colonial system, a development few predicted. The defeat of Japan and Germany led to the immediate end of their respective imperial empires. The other colonialists—spurred by the U.N. Charter's endorsement of the principle of national self-determination, faced with the reality of their economically and politically weakened position, and confronted with indigenous movements for independence—granted independence to their former colonies, beginning with Britain's granting India independence in 1947. It took the military defeat of France in Indochina in the early 1950s to bring decolonization to that part of the world. African states, too, became independent between 1957 and 1963. While the process of decolonization occurred over an extended time period, it was a relatively peaceful transition. The Europeans, together with their U.S. ally, were more interested in fighting communism than in retaining control of their colonial territories.

The fourth outcome was the realization that the differences between the two emergent superpowers would be played out indirectly, on third-party stages, rather than through direct confrontation between the two protagonists. As the number of newly independent states proliferated in the postwar world as the result of decolonialization, the superpowers vied for influence in these new states as the way to project power to areas outside of their traditional spheres of influence. Thus, the Cold War resulted in the globalization of conflict to all continents. International relations became truly global.

Other parts of the world did not just react to Cold War imperatives. They developed new ideologies or recast the dominant discourse of Europe in ways that addressed their own experience. Nowhere was this more true than in Asia. Both Ho Chi Minh of Vietnam and Chou En-lai of China lived in Europe for a time, where they joined communist parties. Returning home, they imported communist ideology, reinterpreting it in ways compatible with their national circumstances. For example, in China, the beginning of the communist revolution predated World War II. Taking to the countryside to build a revolution of agrarian peasants, Chou En-lai and his colleague Mao Zedong insisted that China was a semifeudal society in which the proletariat was the rural peasantry. The Chinese Communist party became the vanguard of this

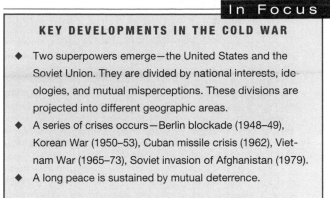

KEY DEVELOPMENTS IN THE COLD WAR

◆ Two superpowers emerge—the United States and the Soviet Union. They are divided by national interests, ideologies, and mutual misperceptions. These divisions are projected into different geographic areas.

◆ A series of crises occurs—Berlin blockade (1948–49), Korean War (1950–53), Cuban missile crisis (1962), Vietnam War (1965–73), Soviet invasion of Afghanistan (1979).

◆ A long peace is sustained by mutual deterrence.

group and the People's Army its instrument for guerrilla action. Mao's revolution was successful: the communists took control of mainland China in 1949 and established the People's Republic of China.

The globalization of post–World War II politics thus meant the rise of new contenders for power. Although the United States and the Soviet Union retained their dominant positions, new alternative ideologies acted as powerful magnets for populations in the independent and developing states of Africa, Asia, and Latin America. Later in the 1970s, these countries developed a new economic ideology, summarized in the program of the New International Economic Order.

The Cold War as a Series of Confrontations

The Cold War itself (1945–89) can be characterized as forty-five years of overall high-level tension and competition between the superpowers but with no direct military conflict. The advent of nuclear weapons created a bipolar stalemate, in which each side acted cautiously, only once coming close to the precipice of direct war. Each state backed down from particular confrontations, either because its national interest was not sufficiently strong to risk a nuclear confrontation or because its ideological resolve wavered in light of military realities.

The Cold War, then, was a series of events that directly or indirectly pitted the superpowers against each other. Some of those events were confrontations just short of war, while others were confrontations between proxies (North Korea vs. South Korea, North Vietnam vs. South Vietnam, Ethiopia vs. Somalia) that, in all likelihood, neither the United States nor the Soviet Union had intended to escalate as they did. Still other confrontations were fought over words; these usually ended in treaties and agreements. Some of these confrontations involved only the United States and the Soviet

Union, but more often than not, the allies of each became involved. Thus, the Cold War comprised not only superpower confrontations but confrontations between two blocs of states: the United States, with Canada, Australia, and much of Western Europe (allied in the **North Atlantic Treaty Organization, or NATO**); and the Soviet Union, with its **Warsaw Pact** allies in Eastern Europe. Over the life of the Cold War, these blocs loosened, and states sometimes took positions different from that of the dominant power. But for much of the time period, bloc politics was operative. Table 2.1 shows a time line of major events related to the Cold War.

One of those high-level, direct confrontations between the superpowers took place in Germany. Germany had been divided immediately after World War II into zones of occupation. The United States, France, and Great Britain administered the western portion; the Soviet Union, the eastern. Berlin, Germany's capital, was similarly divided but lay within Soviet-controlled East Germany. In the 1949 Berlin blockade, the Soviet Union blocked land access to Berlin, prompting the United States and Britain to airlift supplies for thirteen months. In 1949, the separate states of West and East Germany were declared. In 1961, East Germany erected the Berlin Wall around the West German portion of the city in order to stem the tide of East Germans trying to leave the troubled state; U.S. president John F. Kennedy responded with "Ich bin ein Berliner" ("I am a Berliner"), committing the United States to Berlin at any cost. Not surprisingly, it was the crumbling of that same wall in November 1989 that symbolized the end of the Cold War.

In Asia, Korea became the symbol of the Cold War. It, too, was divided geographically—between north and south—and ideologically—between a communist and a noncommunist state. The first Asian confrontation came in 1950 as communist North Korean troops, prodded by the Soviet military (hoping to improve its defensive position), marched into a weak South Korea. The Soviets never fought directly, but the United States (under the aegis of the United Nations) and the Chinese (acting on behalf of the Soviet Union) did. The North Korean offensive was eventually repelled, and the two sides became mired in a three-year stalemate. The war finally ended in 1953. But as with the Berlin crisis, that one event was to be followed over the years by numerous diplomatic skirmishes—over the basing of U.S. troops in South Korea, the use of the demilitarized zone between the north and the south, and North Korean attempts to become a nuclear power even after the end of the Cold War, the last a source of conflict still today.

The 1962 Cuban missile crisis was a high-profile direct confrontation between the superpowers in yet another area of the world. The Soviet Union's installation of missiles in Cuba was viewed by the United States as a direct threat to its territory: no weapons of a powerful enemy had ever been located so close to U.S. shores. The way in which the crisis was resolved suggests

TABLE 2.1

Important Events of the Cold War	
Year	**Event**
1945–48	Soviet Union establishes communist regimes in Eastern Europe.
1947	Announcement of Truman Doctrine; United States proposes Marshall Plan for the rebuilding of Europe.
1948	Marshal Tito separates Yugoslavia from the Soviet bloc.
1948–49	Soviets blockade Berlin; United States and allies carry out airlift.
1949	Soviets test atomic bomb, ending U.S. nuclear monopoly; Chinese communists under Mao win civil war, establish People's Republic of China; United States and Allies establish NATO.
1950–53	Korean War
1953	Death of Stalin leads to internal Soviet succession crisis.
1956	Soviets invade Hungary; Nasser of Egypt nationalizes the Suez Canal, leading to confrontation with Great Britain, France, and Israel.
1957	Soviets launch Sputnik, symbolizing superpower scientific competition.
1960–63	Congo crisis and U.N. action to fill power vacuum.
1960	United States' U-2 spy plane shot down over Soviet territory, leading to the breakup of the Paris summit meeting.
1961	Bay of Pigs invasion of Cuba, sponsored by the United States, fails; Berlin Wall constructed.
1962	United States and Soviet Union brought to the brink of nuclear war following the discovery of Soviet missiles in Cuba; eventually leads to thaw in superpower relations.
1965	United States begins large-scale intervention in Vietnam.
1967	Israel defeats Egypt, Syria, and Jordan in the Six-Day War; Glassboro summit signals detente, loosening of tensions between the superpowers.
1968	Czech government liberalization halted by Soviet invasion; Nuclear Nonproliferation Treaty (NPT) signed.
1972	Nixon visits China and Soviet Union; United States and Soviet Union sign SALT I arms limitation treaty.
1973	United States ends official military involvement in Vietnam; Arab-Israeli War leads to energy crisis.
1975	Proxy and anticolonial wars fought in Angola, Mozambique, Ethiopia, and Somalia.
1979	Shah of Iran, a U.S. ally, overthrown by Islamic revolution; United States and Soviet Union sign SALT II; Soviet Union invades Afghanistan; U.S. Senate does not ratify SALT II.
1981–89	Reagan Doctrine provides basis for U.S. support of "anticommunist" forces in Nicaragua and Afghanistan.
1983	United States invades Grenada.
1985	Gorbachev starts economic and political reforms in Soviet Union.
1989	Peaceful revolutions in Eastern Europe replace communist governments; Berlin Wall is dismantled.
1990	Germany reunified.
1991	Resignation of Gorbachev; Soviet Union collapses.
1992–93	Russia and other former Soviet republics become independent states.

GLOBAL PERSPECTIVES

The Cold War: A View from Cuba

Cuba, like Berlin, was one of the geopolitical flashpoints during the Cold War. American policymakers saw Cuba's revolutionary communist government as a threat, and when the Soviet Union installed missiles on Cuban territory, the U.S. government felt that national survival was at stake. However, from the Cuban perspective, the United States was a hostile neighbor and the Soviet Union was a needed ally.

In 1959 a band of guerrilla fighters led by Fidel Castro seized power in Cuba. The new regime immediately expropriated American property and nationalized American-owned oil refineries. In retaliation, the United States imposed a trade embargo, and rumors circulated that the CIA was training Cuban exiles for invasive action against Cuba. In 1961 the Bay of Pigs operation, launched by the Cuban exiles in an attempt to overthrow Castro, confirmed Castro's suspicions. The operation failed: 90 exiles were killed and 1,200 were captured. The complicity of the U.S. government was proven when it later ransomed those who had been captured.

In the midst of this confrontation with the United States, Castro found a friend in the Soviet Union. Formal diplomatic ties between the two countries were established in 1960. The Bay of Pigs incident helped cement that relationship as Soviet Premier Khrushchev voiced support for the Cuban position and warned that further U.S. interference would result in an international incident. Castro's announcement in 1961 that his revolution was a socialist one and that he had always been a Marxist deepened Cuba's ties with the Soviet Union.

When the Soviet Union proposed situating ballistic missiles on Cuban soil in 1962, Castro agreed, eager to please his ally in the struggle against the United States. Cuba viewed the missiles as a deterrent against an American invasion, while the Soviet Union considered this action a way to compensate for its lagging missile program. Moreover, Cuba "owed" the Soviet Union, since the Soviets were supplying Castro with other arms and economic assistance, and Soviet trade was helping keep the Cuban economy afloat. The ensuing confrontation between the Soviet Union and the United States over the Cuban missiles became a symbol of the Cold War.

After the Soviets were forced to dismantle the missiles, Cuba recognized that its best defense was to take the offensive, spreading its ideology and political support to developing countries. The regime turned its foreign policy focus to promoting revolution in other developing countries. Castro's long-time colleague Ernesto "Che" Guevara spent most of the 1960s trying to foment revolution in Latin America. In the 1970s Cuba sent 36,000 soldiers to Angola and 16,000 troops to Ethiopia. While Soviet interests were not as strong in the former case, Cuban support of Ethiopia shows a confluence of Soviet/Cuban intentions. Expansion of Cuban and Soviet power through an Ethiopian proxy meant a setback for their mutual enemy, the United States, partly because it would be more difficult for the West to control vital sea links.

For Critical Analysis

1. *In the Cold War, was Cuba a proxy between the United States and the Soviet Union?*
2. *What were Cuba's own national interests during the Cold War?*

unequivocally that neither party sought a direct confrontation. The United States chose to blockade Cuba to prevent further Soviet shipments of missiles; importantly, it rejected as first options more coercive military alternatives—land invasion or air strikes—although those options were never entirely foreclosed. Through behind-the-scenes unofficial contacts in Washington and direct communication between President Kennedy and Soviet premier Nikita Khrushchev, the crisis was defused and war was averted.

Vietnam provided a test of a different kind. The Cold War was played out there not in one dramatic crisis but in an extended civil war, in which communist North Vietnam and its Chinese and Soviet allies were pitted against the "free world"—South Vietnam, allied with France, the United States, and assorted supporters including South Korea, the Philippines, and Thailand. To most U.S. policymakers in the late 1950s and early 1960s, Vietnam represented yet another test of the containment doctrine: communist influence must be stopped, they argued, before it spread like a chain of falling dominos through the rest of Southeast Asia and beyond (hence the term **domino effect**). Thus, the United States supported the South Vietnamese dictators Ngo Dinh Diem and Nguyen Van Thieu against the rival communist regime of Ho Chi Minh in the north, which was underwritten by both the People's Republic of China and the Soviet Union. But as the South Vietnamese government and military faltered on its own, the United States stepped up its military support, increasing the number of U.S. troops on the ground and escalating the air war over the north.

In the early stages the United States was fairly confident of victory; after all, a superpower with all its military hardware and technically skilled labor force could surely beat a poorly trained guerrilla force. Policymakers in the United States were quickly disillusioned, however, as U.S. casualties mounted and the U.S. public grew disenchanted. Should the United States use all of its conventional military capability to prevent the "fall" of South Vietnam and stave off the domino effect? Should the United States fight until victory was guaranteed for liberalism and capitalism? Or should it extricate itself from the unpopular quagmire? Should the United States capitulate to the forces of ideological communism? These questions, posed in both geostrategic and ideological terms, defined the middle years of the Cold War, from the Vietnam War's slow beginning in the late 1950s until the dramatic departure of U.S. officials from the South Vietnamese capital, Saigon, in 1975, symbolized by U.S. helicopters leaving the U.S. embassy while hordes of Vietnamese tried to grab on and escape with them.

The U.S. effort to avert a communist takeover in South Vietnam failed, yet contrary to expectations, the domino effect did not occur. Cold War alliances were shaken on both sides: the friendship between the Soviet Union and China had long before degenerated into a geostrategic fight and a struggle over the proper form of communism, especially in Third World countries. But the Soviet bloc was left relatively unscathed by the Vietnam War. The U.S.-led Western alliance was seriously jeopardized, as several U.S. allies (including Canada) strongly opposed U.S. policy toward Vietnam. The bipolar structure of the Cold War international system was coming apart. Confidence in military alternatives was shaken in the United States, undermining for over a decade the United States' ability to commit itself militarily. The power of the United States was supposed to be righteous power, but in Vietnam there was neither victory nor righteousness.

It was not always the case that when one of the superpowers acted the other side responded. In some cases, the other side chose not to act, or at least not to respond in kind, even though it could have escalated the conflict. For example, the Soviet Union invaded Hungary in 1956 and Czechoslovakia in 1968, both sovereign states and allies in the Warsaw Pact. The United States verbally condemned these aggressive actions by the Soviets, which under other circumstances may have been met with counterforce, but the actions themselves went unchecked. In 1956, the United States, preoccupied with the Suez Canal crisis, kept quiet, aware that it was ill prepared to respond militarily. In 1968, the United States was mired in Vietnam and beset by domestic turmoil and a presidential election. So, too, was the United States relatively complacent, although angry, when the Soviets invaded Afghanistan in 1979. The Soviets likewise kept quiet when the United States took aggressive action within its sphere of influence, invading Grenada in 1983 and Panama in 1989. Thus, during the Cold War, even blatantly aggressive actions by one of the superpowers did not always lead to a response by the other.

Many of the events of the Cold War involved the United States and the Soviet Union only indirectly; proxies fought in their place. Nowhere has this been as true as in the Middle East. For both the United States and the Soviet Union, the Middle East was a region of vital importance, because of its natural resources (including approximately one-third of the world's oil and more than one-half of the world's oil reserves), its strategic position as a transportation hub between Asia and Europe, and its cultural significance as the cradle of three of the world's major religions. Not surprisingly, following the establishment of Israel in 1948, recognized diplomatically first by the United States, the region was the scene of superpower confrontation by proxy: between a U.S.-supported Israel and the Soviet-backed Arab states of Syria, Iraq, and Egypt. During the Six-Day War in 1967, Israel crushed the Soviet-equipped Arabs in six short days, seizing the strategic territories of the Golan Heights, Gaza, and the West Bank. In 1973 during the Yom Kippur War, the Israeli victory was not as overwhelming, because the United States and the Soviets negotiated a cease-fire before more damage could be done. But throughout the Cold War, these "hot" wars were followed by guerrilla actions committed by all parties. As long as the basic balance of power was maintained between Israel (and the United States) on one side and the Arabs (and the Soviets) on the other, the region was left alone; when that balance was threatened, the superpowers acted through proxies to maintain the balance. Other controversies plagued the region, as evidenced by events after the end of the Cold War.

In parts of the world that are of less strategic importance, confrontation through proxies was even more the modus operandi during the Cold War. Events in Africa present numerous examples of this. When the colonialist Belgians abruptly left the Congo in 1960, a power vacuum arose. Civil war broke out, as various contending factions sought to take power and bring order out of the chaos. One of the contenders, the Congolese premier Patrice Lumumba (1925–61), appealed to the Soviets for help in fighting the Western-backed insurgents and received both diplomatic support and military supplies. However, Lumumba was dismissed by the Congolese president, Joseph Kasavubu, an ally of the United States. Still others, such as Moise Tshombe, leader of the copper-rich Katanga province, who was also closely identified with Western interests, fought for control. The three-year civil war could have become another protracted proxy war between the United States and the Soviet Union for influence in this emerging continent. However, the United Nations averted the proxy confrontation by sending in supposedly neutral peacekeepers, whose primary purpose was to fill the vacuum and prevent the superpowers from making the Congo yet another terrain of the Cold War.

In both Angola and the Horn of Africa (Ethiopia and Somalia), however, participants in civil wars were able to transform their struggles into Cold War confrontations by proxy, thereby gaining military equipment and technical expertise from one of the two superpowers. Such proxy warfare served the interests of the superpowers, permitting them to project power and support geostrategic interests (oil in Angola, transportation routes around the Horn) and ideologies without directly confronting each other.

The Cold War was also fought and moderated in words, at **summits** (meetings between leaders) and in treaties. Some Cold War summits were relatively successful: the 1967 Glassboro summit (between U.S. and Soviet leaders) began the loosening of tensions known as detente, but the meeting between President Dwight Eisenhower and Premier Nikita Khrushchev in Vienna in 1960 ended abruptly when the Soviets shot down a U.S. U-2 spy plane over Soviet territory. Treaties between the two parties placed self-imposed limitations on nuclear arms. For example, the first Strategic Arms Limitations Treaty (SALT I), in 1972, placed an absolute ceiling on the numbers of intercontinental ballistic missiles (ICBMs), deployed nuclear warheads, and multiple independently targetable reentry vehicles (MIRVs) and limited the number of antiballistic missile sites maintained by each superpower. So the superpowers did enjoy periods of accommodation, when they could agree on principles and policies.

The Cold War as a Long Peace

If the Cold War is largely remembered as a series of crises and some direct and indirect confrontations, why then has the Cold War been referred to as the "long peace"? The term itself was coined by diplomatic historian John Lewis Gaddis to dramatize the absence of war between great powers during the Cold War. Just as general war was averted in nineteenth-century Europe, so too has general war been avoided since World War II. Why?

Gaddis attributes the long peace to five factors, no single explanation being sufficient. Probably the most widely accepted explanation revolves around the role of nuclear **deterrence**. Once both the United States and the Soviet Union had acquired nuclear weapons, neither was willing to use them, since their very deployment jeopardized both states' existence. This argument will be elaborated on further in Chapter 8. Another explanation attributes the long peace to the division of power between the United States and the Soviet Union. Such a parity of power led to stability in the international system, as will be explained in Chapter 4. However, since the advent of nuclear weapons occurred simultaneously with the emergence of the bipolar system, it is impossible to disentangle one explanation from the other.

A third explanation for the long peace is the stability imposed by the hegemonic economic power of the United States. Being in a superior economic position for much of the Cold War, the United States willingly paid the price of maintaining stability. It provided military security for Japan and much of northern Europe, and its currency was the foundation of the international monetary system. Yet while this argument explains why the United States acted to enhance postwar economic stability, it does not explain Soviet actions.

A fourth explanation gives credit for maintaining the peace not to either of the superpowers but to economic liberalism. During the Cold War, the liberal economic order solidified and became a dominant factor in international relations. Politics became **transnational** under liberalism—based on interests and coalitions across traditional state boundaries—and thus great powers became increasingly obsolete. Cold War peace is therefore attributed to the dominance of economic liberalism.

Finally, Gaddis explores the possibility that the long peace of the Cold War was predetermined, as just one phase in a long historical cycle of peace and war. He argues that every 100 to 150 years, war occurs on a global scale; these cycles are driven by uneven economic growth. This explanation suggests that the Cold War is but a blip in one long cycle, and specific events or conditions occurring during the Cold War offer no explanatory power.[15]

Whatever the "right" combination of explanations, international relations theorist Kenneth Waltz has noted the irony in the long peace: that both the United States and the Soviet Union, "two states, isolationist by tradition, untutored in the ways of international politics, and famed for impulsive behavior, soon showed themselves—not always and everywhere, but always in crucial cases—to be wary, alert, cautious, flexible, and forbearing."[16] The United States and the Soviet Union, wary and cautious of each other, also became predictable and familiar to each other. Common interests in economic growth and system stability overcame the long adversarial relationship.

The Post-Cold War Era

The fall of the Berlin Wall in 1989 symbolized the end of the Cold War, but actually its end was gradual. The Soviet premier then, Mikhail Gorbachev, and other Soviet reformers had set in motion two domestic processes—*glasnost* (political openness) and *perestroika* (economic restructuring)—as early as the mid-1980s. *Glasnost* opened the door to criticism of the political system, culminating in the emergence of a multiparty system and the massive reorientation of the once-monopolistic Communist party. *Perestroika* undermined the foundation of the planned economy, an essential part of the communist system. At the outset, Gorbachev and his reformers sought to save the system, but once initiated, these reforms led to the dissolution of the Warsaw Pact, Gorbachev's resignation in December 1991, and the disintegration of the Soviet Union itself in 1992–93.

Gorbachev's domestic reforms also led to changes in the orientation of Soviet foreign policy. Needing to extricate the country from the political quagmire and economic drain of the war in Afghanistan, yet seeking to "save face," Gorbachev suggested that the permanent members of the U.N. Security Council "could become guarantors of regional security."[17] Afghanistan was a test case, where a small group of U.N. observers monitored and verified the withdrawal of more than one hundred thousand Soviet troops in 1988 and 1989—an action that would have been impossible during the height of the Cold War. Similarly, the Soviets agreed to and supported the 1988 withdrawal of Cuban troops from Angola. The Soviet Union had retreated internationally from commitments near its borders, as well as in far-flung places. Most important, the Soviets agreed to cooperate in multilateral activities to preserve regional security.

These changes in Soviet policy and the eventual demise of the empire itself mark the beginning of the post–Cold War era and are the subject of much study in international relations today. What explains these remarkable changes? Did the West's preparations for war or its strong alliance system force the Soviet Union into submission? Was Western power and policy responsible for the Soviet demise and thus the end of the Cold War? Was it Western military strength that led the Soviets to become less bellicose and less threatening? Or did events within the Soviet Union itself lead to its demise? Was it the fault of communism, an impractical economic structure? Was it due to the resistance of those who opposed communism in Soviet domestic politics? Or was it the fact that communism not only failed to deliver on its promises but actually led to more poverty and more political repression? Or was it the failure of the Soviet bureaucratic system that led to the country's ultimate disintegration? Did the United States, too, exhaust its capacity to carry on global confrontation, as Russian realist theorists contend? No single answer suffices; elements of each played a role.

The first post–Cold War test of the so-called New World Order came in response to Iraq's invasion and annexation of Kuwait in August 1990. Despite the Soviets' long-standing relationship with Iraq, the Soviet Union (and later Russia), along with the four other permanent members of the U.N. Security Council, agreed first to take economic sanctions against Iraq. Then they agreed in a Security Council resolution to support the means to restore the status quo—to oust Iraq from Kuwait with a multinational military force. Finally, they supported sending the U.N. Iraq-Kuwait Observer Mission to monitor the zone and permitted the U.N. to undertake humanitarian intervention and create safe havens for the Kurdish and Shiite populations of Iraq. Although forging a consensus on each of these actions (or in the case of China, convincing it to abstain) was difficult, the coalition held, a unity unthinkable during the Cold War.

The end of the Cold War denotes a major change in international relations, the end of one historical era and the beginning of another, which a few have labeled the age of globalization. This era appears

---

In Focus

KEY DEVELOPMENTS IN THE POST–COLD WAR ERA

◆ Changes are made in Soviet/Russian foreign policy, with the withdrawals from Afghanistan and Angola in the late 1980s monitored by the United Nations.

◆ Iraqi invasion of Kuwait in 1990 and the multilateral response unite the former Cold War adversaries.

◆ *Glasnost* and *perestroika* continue in Russia, as reorganized in 1992–93.

◆ The former Yugoslavia disintegrates into independent states; civil war ensues in Bosnia and Kosovo, leading to U.N. and NATO action.

◆ Widespread ethnic conflict arises in central and western Africa, Central Asia, and the Indian subcontinent.

◆ Al Qaeda terrorist network commits terrorist acts against the homeland of the United States and U.S. interests abroad; U.S. and coalition forces respond militarily in Afghanistan and Iraq.

◆ Terrorist attacks occur in Saudi Arabia, Spain, and Great Britain.

to be marked by U.S. primacy in international affairs to a degree not even matched by the Romans or Alexander the Great. The United States is seemingly able to impose its will on other states even when it wishes to go in directions not favored by its allies. Yet this primacy is still not able to prevent ethnic conflict, civil wars, and human rights abuses from occurring.

The 1990s was a decade marked by dual realities, the first being U.S. primacy, and the second being civil and ethnic strife. Yugoslavia's violent disintegration played itself out over the entire decade despite Western attempts to resolve the conflict peacefully. At the same time, the world witnessed ethnic tension and violence in the Great Lakes region of central Africa. Genocide in Rwanda and Burundi went unchallenged by the international community, further emboldening rebels and elites who stand to gain from anarchy in the region to continue these activities in the future. And despite U.S. primacy, Russia maintains enough military power and political influence to prevent U.S. intervention in ethnic hostilities in the Transcaucasus region.

These dual realities converged and diverged throughout the 1990s and continue to do so today. The disintegration of Yugoslavia culminated in an American-led war against Serbia to halt ethnic attacks on the Albanian population in Kosovo. Despite European hesitancy to engage militarily and the inability to obtain a U.N. resolution supporting military action, the United States drove NATO to intervene. The seventy-eight-day air war ended with the capitulation of the Serbs and the turning over of the province of Kosovo to U.N. administration.

On September 11, 2001, the world witnessed deadly, psychologically devastating, and economically disruptive terrorist attacks against two important cities in the United States. These attacks set into motion a U.S.-led global war on terrorism. Buoyed by an outpouring of support from around the world and by the first-ever invocation of Article V of the NATO Charter, which declares an attack on one NATO member an attack on all, the United States undertook to lead an ad hoc coalition to combat terrorist organizations with global reach. This new war on terror combines many elements into multiple campaigns with different foci in different countries. Many countries are arresting known terrorists and their supporters and freezing their monetary assets. The United States fought a war in Afghanistan to oust the Taliban regime, which was providing safe haven to Osama bin Laden's Al Qaeda organization and a base from which it freely planned, organized, trained, and carried out a global terror campaign against the United States and its allies.

Following a successful campaign in Afghanistan that specifically targeted terrorists and their supporters and installed an elected leader in that country, the United States used its position of primacy to diverge from its allies. The United States, convinced that Iraq maintained a clandestine weapons of mass destruction program and posed a continued threat through support of terrorist organizations, attempted to build support in the United Nations for authorization to remove forcibly Saddam Hussein from power and find hidden weapons of mass destruction. When the United Nations refused to back the U.S. request, the United States built its own coalition along with the United Kingdom, destroyed the Iraqi military, and overthrew the Iraqi government. The fight in Iraq continues today, although Hussein himself was executed in 2006.

Even after the economic downturn following the September 11 terrorist attacks on New York and Washington, D.C., the U.S. military and economy are still the strongest in the world. Yet despite its primacy, the United States does not feel it is secure from attack. The global war against terrorism is far from over, and the issue of whether U.S. power will be balanced by an emerging power is also far from resolved. It may turn out that U.S. success or failure in Iraq and against global terror organizations will determine whether its position of primacy strengthens or wanes and hence set the international stage for the remainder of the first decade of the twenty-first century.

In Sum: Learning from History

Will the post–Cold War era be characterized by cooperation among the great powers, or will the era be one of conflict among states and over new ideas? Does the post–Cold War world signal a return to the **multipolar** system of the nineteenth century? Or is this era to see a **unipolar** system dominated by the United States, comparable to the British hegemony of the nineteenth century? How can we begin to predict how the current era will best be characterized or what the future will bring?

We have taken the first step toward answering these questions by looking to the past. Our examination of the development of contemporary international relations has focused on how core concepts of international relations have emerged and evolved over time, most notably the state, sovereignty, the nation, and the international system. These concepts, developed within a specific historical context, provide the building blocks for contemporary international relations. The state is well established, but its sovereignty may be eroding from without (Chapters 7, 9, 10) and from within (Chapter 5). The principal characteristics of the contemporary international system are in the process of change with the end of the **bipolarity** of the Cold War (Chapter 4).

To help us understand the trends of the past and how those trends influence contemporary thinking and to predict future developments, we turn to theory. Theory gives order to analysis; it takes specific events and provides generalized explanations. In Chapter 3 we will look at competing theories and perspectives about international relations. These theories view the past from quite different perspectives.

Notes

1. Cicero, *Res Publica: Roman Politics and Society according to Cicero,* trans. W. K. Lacey and B. W. J. G. Wilson (London: Oxford University Press, 1970).
2. Dante, "De Monarchia," in *The Portable Dante,* ed. Paolo Milano (New York: Penguin, 1977).
3. Niccolò Machiavelli, *The Prince and the Discourses* (New York: Random House, 1940).
4. Jean Bodin, *Six Books on the Commonwealth* (Oxford, Eng.: Basil Blackwell, 1967), 25.
5. Ibid., 28.
6. Ibid.
7. Adam Smith, *An Inquiry into the Nature and Causes of the Wealth of Nations* (New York: Modern Library, 1937).
8. John Locke, *Two Treatises on Government* (Cambridge, Eng.: Cambridge University Press, 1960).
9. Quoted in A. C. Walworth, *Woodrow Wilson* (Baltimore: Penguin, 1969), 148.
10. Edward Hallett Carr, *The Twenty Years' Crisis, 1919–1939: An Introduction to the Study of International Relations* (New York: Harper Torchbooks, 1939, rep. 1964), 224.
11. George F. Kennan ["X"], "The Sources of Soviet Conduct," *Foreign Affairs* 25 (July 1947), 566–82.
12. Quoted in Charles W. Kegley, Jr., and Eugene R. Wittkopf, *World Politics: Trend and Transformation* (5th ed.; New York: St. Martin's, 1995), 94.
13. Josef Stalin, "Reply to Comrades," *Pravda,* August 2, 1950.
14. George F. Kennan, "The United States and the Soviet Union, 1917–1976," *Foreign Affairs* 54 (July 1976), 683–84.
15. John Lewis Gaddis, "The Long Peace: Elements of Stability in the Postwar International System," *International Security* 10:4 (Spring 1986), 92–142.
16. Kenneth N. Waltz, *Theory of International Politics* (Reading, Mass: Addison-Wesley, 1979), 173.
17. Mikhail Gorbachev, "Secure World," as reported in Foreign Broadcast Information Service, *Daily Report, Soviet Union,* September 17, 1987, 25.

Contending Perspectives: How to Think about International Relations Theoretically

- *What is the value of studying international relations from a theoretical perspective?*

- *Why do scholars pay attention to the levels-of-analysis problem?*

- *What are the major theoretical underpinnings of liberalism and its newer variant, neoliberal institutionalism? Of realism and neorealism? Of radicalism? Of constructivism?*

- *Can you analyze a contemporary event by using theoretical perspectives?*

Thinking Theoretically

How can theory help us make sense of international relations? In this chapter we will use the example of the 2003 Iraq war to explore major international relations theories and their explanations for political events.

Why did the United States and its coalition partners invade Iraq? Why did Iraq continue to refuse to comply with the demands of the international community? We need to begin by examining the historical record. That provides the key context for understanding the actions of the United States.

The international community was concerned about Saddam Hussein's behavior, Iraq's weapons, and the possibility that Saddam was supporting international terrorist activities, especially after his ouster of U.N. weapons inspectors from Iraq in 1998. Following the September 11, 2001, attacks on U.S. territory, that concern became urgent. In his 2002 State of the Union address, President George W. Bush included Iraq in what he described as an "axis of evil." The administration subsequently lobbied for U.N. resolutions during the fall of 2002 to have Iraq declared in material breach of prior U.N. resolutions. Although successful in convincing U.N. Security Council members to declare a material breach, the United States was unable to muster support for a U.N.-authorized military action against Iraq. In March 2003, the United States went ahead without U.N. authorization and launched a military attack against Iraq. Three weeks later, the Iraqi regime fell, and the

TABLE 3.1

Major Events Leading Up to and of the 2003 Iraq War	
Date	**Event**
September 11, 2001	Terrorist attacks against the World Trade Center and the Pentagon are answered by an immediate commitment by the U.S. government to fight global terrorism and punish those responsible.
October 7, 2001	United States strikes targets in Afghanistan in order to oust the Taliban from power, whose government harbors Al Qaeda terrorists.
November 14, 2001	United States announces ouster of Taliban from power in Afghanistan.
January 29, 2002	President George W. Bush labels Iraq, Iran, and North Korea members of an "axis of evil" threatening world peace.
October 2, 2002	U.S. Congress authorizes the president to use U.S. armed forces against Iraq.
October 8, 2002	U.N. resolution holds Iraq in material breach of previous resolutions.
March 2003	United States stops trying to fashion a U.N. resolution authorizing use of military force, acknowledging failure to get approval of five permanent members of the Security Council.
March 17, 2003	United States issues a 48-hour ultimatum for the Baathist regime and its leader, Saddam Hussein, to leave Iraq.
March 19, 2003	Decapitation attack is launched against Saddam. U.S. Special Operations forces enter Iraq, followed by the movement of coalition ground forces into Iraq.
April 9, 2003	Iraqi regime falls.
April 2003– present	Efforts continue to establish security in midst of resistance to U.S. presence and rising sectarian violence

United States imposed temporary rule over Iraq. Table 3.1 lists the major events of the crisis and the war.

This examination of history shows that the United States was motivated by several factors: regret over not having ousted Saddam in the 1991 Gulf War; the possibility that the regime possessed weapons of mass destruction; concern that Saddam's regime was involved in both domestic and international terrorism; the need for stability in the oil-rich state; and the hope that a democratic Iraq could be the centerpiece of a new liberal democratic order in the Middle East. Similarly, to understand Iraq's refusal to comply with international demands, we must understand the roots of its strong nationalism, its history of being controlled by Western colonialists, and a Saddam Hussein whose power and legitimacy was augmented by standing up to the West. Theories will help explain more generally why these events occurred.

A **theory** is a set of propositions and concepts that seeks to explain phenomena by specifying the relationships among the concepts; theory's ultimate purpose is to predict phenomena. Good theory generates groups of testable **hypotheses:** specific statements positing a particular relationship between two or more variables. By testing groups of interrelated hypotheses, theory is verified and refined and new relationships are found that demand subsequent testing.

Moving from description to explanation to theory and from theory to testable hypotheses is not a unilinear process. Although theory depends on a logical deduction of hypotheses from assumptions, and a testing of the hypotheses, as more and more data are collected in the empirical world, theories have to be revised or adjusted. This is, in part, a creative exercise, in which one must be tolerant of ambiguity, concerned about probabilities, and distrustful of absolutes.

International relations theories come in a variety of forms. In this chapter, we introduce three general theories, or theoretical perspectives, in the study of international relations: liberalism (and its newest variant, neoliberal institutionalism), realism (and neorealism), and radical theories based in Marxism. In addition, we present an overview of constructivism as one of the newest theoretical perspectives in international relations. Before we examine these theories more closely, we must consider the various levels at which we can analyze events and trends.

Theory and the Levels of Analysis

Why did the United States and its coalition partners invade Iraq in 2003? The list of possible explanations can be organized according to three **levels of analysis** (see Figure 3.1). There are good reasons to pay attention to levels of analysis. They help orient our questions and suggest the appropriate type of evidence to explore. Paying attention to levels of analysis helps us make logical deductions and enables us to explore all categories of explanation.

In a categorization first used by Kenneth Waltz and amplified by J. David Singer, three different sources of explanations are offered. If the *individual level* is the focus, then the personality, perceptions, choices, and activities of individual decisionmakers (Saddam Hussein and George W. Bush) and individual participants (Defense Secretary Donald Rumsfeld, Saddam's sons) provide the explanation. If the *state level*, or domestic factors, are the focus, then the explanation is derived from characteristics of the state: the type of government (democracy or authoritarianism), the type of economic system (capitalist or socialist), interest groups within the country, or even the national interest. If the *international system level* is the focus, then the explanation rests with the anarchic characteristics of that system or with international and regional organizations and their strengths and weaknesses.[1]

Box 3.1 categorizes possible explanations of the conflict according to these three levels of analysis. Of course, explanations from all three levels

FIGURE 3.1

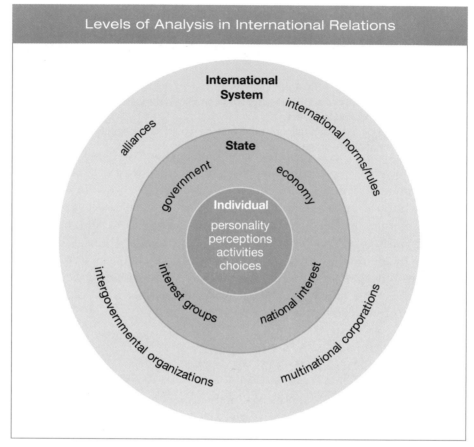

Levels of Analysis in International Relations

International System

international norms/rules

alliances

State

government

economy

Individual
personality
perceptions
activities
choices

interest groups

national interest

intergovernmental organizations

multinational corporations

probably contributed to the United States's decision to invade Iraq in 2003. The purpose of theory is to guide us toward an understanding of which of these various explanations are the necessary and sufficient explanations for the invasion.

Although all scholars acknowledge the utility of paying attention to levels of analysis, they differ on how many levels are useful in explaining events. Most political scientists use between three and six levels. Although adding more layers may provide more descriptive context, it makes explanation and prediction more problematic. The most important differentiation in theory must be made between the international level and the domestic level. In this book we will use the three levels explained above: individual, state, and international system.

Good theory, then, should be able to explain phenomena at a particular level of analysis; better theory should also offer explanations across different levels of analysis. The general theories outlined in the rest of this chapter are

BOX 3.1

Possible Explanations for the United States' Invasion of Iraq in 2003 by Level of Analysis

Individual Level

1. Saddam Hussein was an evil leader who committed atrocities against his own people and defied the West.
2. Saddam Hussein was irrational, otherwise he would have capitulated to the superior capability of the U.S. and British coalition.
3. George W. Bush and his advisers have targeted Saddam Hussein and Iraq since the late 1990s.

State Level

4. The United States must protect its national security, and Iraq's weapons of mass destruction threatened U.S. security.
5. Ousting the Taliban from Afghanistan was only the first step in the war on terrorism; Iraq, a known supporter of terrorism, was the second.
6. The United States must be assured of a stable oil supply, and Iraq has the world's second largest reserves.
7. The United States must not permit states who support terrorism or terrorist groups access to destructive weapons.
8. It is in the U.S. national interest to build a progressive Arab regime in the region.

International Level

9. U.N. resolutions condemning Iraq had to be enforced in order to maintain the legitimacy of the United Nations.
10. A unipolar international system is uniquely capable of responding to perceived threats to the stability of the system, and the U.S. invasion was one manifestation of this.
11. There is an international moral imperative for humanitarian intervention—to oust evil leaders and install democratic regimes.

all comprehensive, meaning they incorporate all three levels of analysis. Yet each of the theories is not as simple or as unified as presented. Many authors have introduced variations, modifications, and problematics, and even the same authors have changed positions over time. Thus, the theories are discussed only in terms of their essential characteristics.

Liberalism and Neoliberal Institutionalism

Liberalism (sometimes referred to as idealism) holds that human nature is basically good and that people can improve their moral and material conditions, making societal progress possible. Bad or evil human behavior, such as injustice and war, are the products of inadequate or corrupt social institutions and of misunderstandings among leaders. Thus, liberals believe that injustice, war, and aggression are not inevitable but can be moderated or even eliminated through institutional reform or collective action. According to liberal thinking, the expansion of human freedom is best achieved in democracies and through market capitalism.

The origins of liberal theory are found in Enlightenment optimism, nineteenth-century political and economic liberalism, and twentieth-century Wilsonian idealism. The contribution of the eighteenth-century Enlightenment to liberalism rests on the Greek idea that individuals are rational human beings, able to understand the universally applicable laws governing both nature and human society. Understanding such laws means that people have the capacity to improve their condition by creating a just society. If a just society is not attained, then the fault rests with inadequate institutions, the result of a corrupt environment.

The writings of the French philosopher Baron de La Brède et de Montesquieu (1689–1755) reflect Enlightenment thinking. He argued that it is not human nature that is defective, but problems arise as man enters civil society and forms separate nations. War is a product of society, not an attribute inherent in individuals. To overcome defects in society, education is imperative; it prepares one for civil life. Groups of states are united according to the law of nations, which regulates conduct even during war. Montesquieu optimistically stated that "different nations ought in time of peace to do one another all the good they can, and in time of war as little harm as possible, without prejudicing their real interests."[2]

Likewise, the writings of Immanuel Kant form the core of Enlightenment beliefs. According to Kant, international anarchy can be overcome through some kind of collective action—a federation of states in which sovereignties would be left intact. Kant offered hope that humans would learn ways to avoid war, though as he admitted, the task will not be easy.[3]

Nineteenth-century liberalism took the rationalism of the eighteenth-century Enlightenment and reformulated it by adding a preference for democracy over aristocracy and for free trade over national economic self-sufficiency. Sharing the Enlightenment's optimistic view of human nature, nineteenth-century liberalism saw man as capable of satisfying his natural needs and wants in rational ways. These needs and wants could be achieved most efficiently by each individual's pursuing his own freedom and autonomy, unfettered by excessive state structures. According to liberal thought, individual freedom and autonomy can best be realized in a democratic state unfettered by excessive governmental restrictions. Likewise, political freedoms are most easily achieved in capitalist states where rational and acquisitive human beings can improve their own conditions, maximizing both individual and collective economic growth and economic welfare. Free markets must be allowed to flourish and governments must permit the free flow of trade and commerce. Liberal theorists believe that free trade and commerce create interdependencies between states, thus raising the cost of war.

Twentieth-century idealism also contributed to liberalism, finding its greatest adherent in U.S. president Woodrow Wilson, who authored the covenant of the League of Nations—hence the term "Wilsonian idealism." The basic proposition of this idealism is that war is preventable; more than half of the League covenant's twenty-six provisions focused on preventing war. The covenant even included a provision legitimizing the notion of **collective security,** wherein aggression by one state would be countered by collective action, embodied in a "league of nations."

Thus, the League of Nations illustrated the importance that liberals place on international institutions to deal with war and the opportunity for collective problem solving in a multilateral forum. Liberals also place faith in international law and legal instruments—mediation, arbitration, and international courts. Still other liberals think that all war can be eliminated through disarmament. Whatever the specific prescriptive solution, the basis of liberalism remains firmly embedded in the belief of the rationality of humans and in the unbridled optimism that through learning and education, humans can develop institutions to bring out their best characteristics.

During the interwar period, when the League of Nations proved incapable of maintaining collective security, and during World War II, when human atrocities made many question the basic goodness of humanity, liberalism came under intense scrutiny. Was humankind inherently good? How could an institution fashioned under the best assumptions have failed so miserably? Liberalism as a theoretical perspective fell out of favor.

Since the 1970s, liberalism has been revived under the rubric of **neoliberal institutionalism.** Neoliberal institutionalists such as the political scientists Robert Axelrod and Robert O. Keohane ask *why* states choose to cooperate most of the time even in the anarchic condition of the international system. One answer is found in the simple but profound story of the prisoner's dilemma.[4]

The **prisoner's dilemma** is the story of two prisoners, each being interrogated separately for an alleged crime. The interrogator tells each prisoner that if one of them confesses and the other does not, the one who confessed will go free and the one who kept silent will get a long prison term. If both confess, both will get somewhat reduced prison terms. If neither confesses, both will receive short prison terms based on lack of evidence. Let's say that both prisoners confess, and thus each serves a longer sentence than if they had cooperated and kept silent. Why did cooperation fail to occur? Each prisoner is faced with a one-time choice. Neither prisoner knows how the other will respond; the cost of not confessing if the other confesses is extraordinarily high. So both will confess, leading to a less-than-optimal outcome for both. This dilemma is discussed further in Chapter 5.

But if the situation is repeated, the possibility of reciprocity makes it rational to cooperate. Had the two prisoners cooperated with each other by both remaining silent, then the outcome would have been much better for both. It was actually in the self-interest of each to cooperate! Similarly, states are not faced with a one-time situation; they confront each other over and over again on specific issues. Unlike classical liberals, neoliberal institutionalists do not believe that individuals naturally cooperate out of an innate characteristic of humanity. The prisoner's dilemma provides neoliberal institutionalists with a rationale for mutual cooperation in an environment where there is no international authority mandating such cooperation.

Neoliberal institutionalists arrive at the same prediction as liberals do—cooperation—but their explanation for why cooperation occurs is different. For classical liberals, cooperation emerges from man's establishing and reforming institutions that permit cooperative interactions and prohibit coercive actions. For neoliberal institutionalists, cooperation emerges because for actors having continuous interactions with each other, it is in the self-interest of each to cooperate. Institutions may be established, affecting the possibilities for cooperation, but they do not guarantee cooperation.

For neoliberal institutionalists, security is essential, and institutions help to make security possible. Institutions provide a guaranteed framework of interactions; they suggest that there will be an expectation of future interactions. These interactions will occur not just on security issues but on a whole suite of international issues including human rights (a classic liberal concern), the environment, immigration, and economics.[5]

With the end of the Cold War in the 1990s, liberalism as a general theoretical perspective has achieved new credibility. Two particular areas stand out. First, researchers of the so-called democratic peace (discussed in more detail in Chapter 5) are trying to determine *why* democracies do not fight each other. A variety of liberal explanations provide the answer. One argument is that shared democratic norms and culture inhibit aggression; leaders in democracies hear from a multiplicity of voices that tend to restrain decisionmakers and therefore lessen the chance of war. Another argument is that transnational and international institutions that bind democracies together through dense networks act to constrain behavior. These explanations are based on liberal theorizing.

Second, post–Cold War theorists such as the scholar and former policy analyst Francis Fukuyama see not just a revival but a victory for international liberalism, in the absence of any viable theoretical alternatives. He admits that some groups, such as Palestinians and Israelis, Sinhalese and Tamils, or

Armenians and Azeris, will continue to have grievances against each other. But large-scale conflict is less frequent than in earlier eras. For the first time, Fukuyama argues, the possibility exists for the "universalization of Western liberal democracy as the final form of human governance."[6] Indeed, political scientist John Mueller makes the liberal argument even more strongly. Just as dueling and slavery, once acceptable practices, have become morally unacceptable, war is increasingly seen in the developed world as

THEORY IN BRIEF	
Liberalism / Neoliberal Institutionalism	
Key actors	States, nongovernmental groups, international organizations
View of the individual	Basically good; capable of cooperating
View of the state	Not an autonomous actor; having many interests
View of the international system	Interdependence among actors; international society; anarchy
Beliefs about change	Probable; a desirable process
Major theorists	Montesquieu, Kant, Wilson, Keohane, Mueller

immoral and repugnant. The terrifying moments of World Wars I and II have led to the obsolescence of war, says Mueller (see Chapter 8).[7]

As liberalism as an accepted theoretical perspective has waxed and waned, so too has realism, the major theoretical counterpoint to liberalism. While these two theories differ in many respects, they are both rationally based.

Realism and Neorealism

Realism, like liberalism, is the product of a long historical and philosophical tradition, even though its direct application to international affairs is of more recent vintage. Realism is based on a view of the individual as primarily selfish and power seeking. Individuals are organized in states, each of which acts in a unitary way in pursuit of its own **national interest,** defined in terms of power. These states exist in an anarchic international system, characterized by the absence of an authoritative hierarchy. Under this condition of anarchy, states in the international system can rely only on themselves. Their most important concern, then, is to manage their insecurity, which arises out of the anarchic system. They rely primarily on balancing the power of other states and deterrence to keep the international system intact and as nonthreatening as possible.

At least four of the essential assumptions of realism are found in Thucydides' *History of the Peloponnesian War*.[8] First, for Thucydides, the state (Athens or Sparta) is the *principal actor* in war and in politics in general, just as latter-day realists posit. While other actors, such as international institutions, may participate, they are not important.

Second, the state is assumed to be a **unitary actor:** although Thucydides included fascinating debates among different officials from the same state, he argued that once a decision is made to go to war or capitulate, the state speaks and acts with one voice. There are no subnational actors trying to overturn the decision of the government or subvert the interests of the state.

Third, decisionmakers acting in the name of the state are assumed to be **rational actors.** Like most educated Greeks, Thucydides believed that individuals are essentially rational beings and that they make decisions by weighing the strengths and weaknesses of various options against the goal to be achieved. Thucydides admitted that there are potential impediments to rational decisionmaking, including wishful thinking on the part of leaders, confusing intentions and national interests, and misperceptions about the characteristics of the counterpart decisionmaker. But the core notion that rational decisionmaking leads to the pursuit of the national interest remains. Likewise for modern realists, rational decisions advance the national interest—the interests of the state—however ambiguously that national interest is formulated.

Fourth, Thucydides, like contemporary realists, was concerned with security issues—the state's need to protect itself from enemies both foreign and domestic. A state augments its security by increasing its domestic capacities, building up its economic prowess, and forming alliances with other states based on similar interests. In fact, Thucydides found that before and during the Peloponnesian War, it was fear of a rival that motivated states to join alliances, a rational decision on the part of the leader. In the Melian dialogue, a section of *History of the Peloponnesian War*, Thucydides posed the classic dilemma between realist and liberal thinking: "the strong do what they can and the weak suffer what they must." More generally, do states have rights based on the conception of an international ethical or moral order, as liberals suggest? Or is a state's power, in the absence of an international authority, the deciding factor?

Thucydides did not identify all the tenets of realism. Indeed, the tenets and rationale of realism have unfolded over centuries, and not all realists agree on what they are. For example, six centuries after Thucydides lived, the Christian bishop and philosopher St. Augustine (354–430) added a fundamental assumption of realism, arguing that humanity is flawed, egoistic, and selfish, although not predetermined to be so. St. Augustine blames war on this basic characteristic of humanity.[9] Although subsequent realists dispute Augustine's biblical explanation for humanity's flawed, selfish nature, few realists dispute the fact that humans are basically power seeking and self-absorbed.

The implications of humanity's flawed nature for the state are developed further in the writings of the Italian political philosopher Niccolò Machiavelli (1469–1527). He argued in *The Prince* that a leader needs to be ever mindful of threats to his personal security and the security of the state. Machiavelli promoted the use of alliances and various offensive and defensive strategies to protect the state.[10]

The central tenet accepted by virtually all realist theorists is that states exist in an anarchic international system. This tenet was originally articulated by Thomas Hobbes (see Chapter 1). Hobbes maintained that just as individuals in the state of nature have the responsibility and the right to preserve themselves, so too does each state in the international system. Hobbes depicted a state of international anarchy, where the norm for states is "having their weapons pointing, and their eyes fixed on one another."[11] In the absence of international authority, there are few rules or norms that restrain states.

In the aftermath of World War II, at the height of disillusionment with liberalism, international relations theorist Hans Morgenthau (1904–80) wrote the seminal synthesis of realism in international politics and offered a methodological approach for testing the theory. For Morgenthau, just as for Thucydides, Augustine, and Hobbes, international politics is a struggle for power. That struggle can be explained at the three levels of analysis: (1) the flawed individual in the state of nature struggles for self-preservation; (2) the autonomous and unitary state is constantly involved in power struggles, balancing power with power and reacting to preserve what is in the national interest; and (3) because the international system is anarchic—there is no higher power to put the competition to an end—the struggle is continuous. Because of the imperative to ensure a state's survival, leaders are driven by a morality quite different from that of ordinary individuals. Morality, for realists, is to be judged by the political consequences of a policy.[12]

Morgenthau's textbook, *Politics among Nations*, became the realist bible for the years following World War II. Policy implications flowed naturally from the theory: the most effective technique for managing power is balance of power. Both George Kennan (1904–2005), writer and chair of the State Department's Policy Planning Staff in the late 1940s and later the U.S. ambassador to the Soviet Union, and Henry Kissinger (b. 1923), scholar, foreign policy adviser, and secretary of state to Presidents Richard Nixon and Gerald Ford, are known to have based their policy recommendations on realist theory.

As we saw in Chapter 2, Kennan was one of the architects of the U.S. Cold War policy of containment, an interpretation of balance of power. The goal of containment was to prevent Soviet power from extending into regions beyond that country's immediate, existing sphere of influence (Eastern Europe). Containment was achieved by balancing U.S. power against Soviet power. Kissinger, during the 1970s, encouraged the classic realist balance of power by supporting weaker powers such as China and Pakistan to exert leverage over the Soviet Union and to offset India's growing power, respectively (India was an ally of the Soviets).

Whereas realists offer clear policy prescriptions, not all realists agree on what the correct policy is. Defensive realists argue, for example, that all states in the international system should pursue policies of restraint, whether through military, diplomatic, or economic channels. Such defensive moderate postures can be pursued without leading to dangerous levels of mistrust among states. Offensive realists, on the other hand, argue that under conditions of international anarchy, states cannot be certain of others' intentions with 100 percent confidence. They posit that all states should seek opportunities to improve their relative positions and that states should strive for power even if their goal is merely to preserve their own independence. States may thus pursue expansionist politics, building up their relative power positions. Yet even among both defensive and offensive realists, there are significant differences of view about the appropriate course of action.[13]

In fact, realism encompasses a family of related arguments, sharing common assumptions and premises. It is not a single unified theory. Among the various reinterpretations of realism, the most powerful is **neorealism** (or structural realism), as delineated in Kenneth Waltz's *Theory of International Politics*.[14] Waltz undertook this reinterpretation of classical realism in order to make political realism a more rigorous theory of international politics. Neorealists are so bold as to propose general laws to explain events: they therefore attempt to simplify explanations of behavior in anticipation of being better able to explain and predict general trends.

Neorealists give precedence in their analyses to the structure of the international system as an explanatory factor, over states, which are emphasized by traditional realists, and over the innate characteristics of human beings. According to Waltz, the most important unit to study is the structure of the international system. The structure of a particular system is determined by the ordering principle, namely the absence of overarching authority, and the distribution of capabilities among states. Those capabilities define a state's position in the system. The international structure is a force in itself; it constrains state behavior, and states may not be able to control it. According to neorealists, the international structure, rather than the characteristics of individual states, determines outcomes.[15]

As in classical realism, balance of power is a core principle of neorealism. But unlike earlier realists, neorealists believe that the balance of power among states is largely determined by the structure of the system. In such a system, the possibilities for international cooperation are logically slim:

> When faced with the possibility of cooperating for mutual gain, states that feel insecure must ask how the gain will be divided. They are compelled to ask not "Will both of us gain?" but "Who will gain more?" If an expected gain is to be divided, say, in the ratio of two to one, one state may use its disproportionate gain to implement a policy intended to damage or destroy the other. Even the prospect of large absolute gains for both parties does not elicit their cooperation so long as each fears how the other will use its increased capabilities.[16]

A problem arises with states' concerns about relative gains because states always act to maximize their power relative to other states in order to improve their chances of survival. The importance of relative power means that states hesitate to engage in cooperation if the benefits to be gained may be distributed unevenly among participating states. Even if cooperation could produce absolute gains for any one state, these gains will be discounted by that state should cooperation produce greater gains for other states. In a neorealist's balance-of-power world, a state's survival depends on having more power than other states, thus all power (and gains in power) are viewed in relative terms.[17]

Neorealists are also concerned with cheating. States may be tempted to cheat on agreements in order to gain a relative advantage over other states. Fear that other states will renege on existing cooperative agreements is especially potent in the military realm, in which changes in military weaponry can result in a major shift in the balance of power. Self-interest provides a powerful incentive for one state to take advantage of another. The awareness that such incentives exist, combined with states' rational desire to protect their own interests, tends to preclude cooperation among states.

Scholars have developed other interpretations of realism as well. While neorealism simplifies the classical realist theory and focuses on a few core concepts (system structure and balance of power), other reinterpretations add increased complexity to realism. Princeton University professor Robert Gilpin, in *War and Change in World Politics*, offers one such reinterpretation. Accepting the realist assumptions that states are the principal actors, decisionmakers are basically rational, and the international system structure plays a key role in determining power, Gilpin examines 2,400 years of history, finding that "the distribution of power among states constitutes the principal form of control in every international system."[18] What Gilpin adds is the notion of dynamism, of history as a series of cycles—cycles of birth, expansion, and demise of dominant powers. Whereas classical realism offers no satisfactory rationale for the decline of powers, Gilpin does, on the basis of the importance of economic power.

<table>
<tr><td colspan="2" style="text-align:center">**THEORY IN BRIEF**</td></tr>
<tr><td colspan="2" style="text-align:center">Realism / Neorealism</td></tr>
<tr><td>Key actors</td><td>International system, states</td></tr>
<tr><td>View of the individual</td><td>Power seeking; selfish; antagonistic</td></tr>
<tr><td>View of the state</td><td>Power seeking; unitary actor; following its national interest</td></tr>
<tr><td>View of the international system</td><td>Anarchic; reaches stability in a balance-of-power system</td></tr>
<tr><td>Beliefs about change</td><td>Low change potential; slow structural change</td></tr>
<tr><td>Major theorists</td><td>Thucydides, St. Augustine, Machiavelli, Hobbes, Morgenthau, Waltz, Gilpin, Mearsheimer</td></tr>
</table>

Hegemons decline because of three processes: the increasingly marginal returns of controlling an empire, a state-level phenomenon; the tendency for economic hegemons to consume more over time and invest less, also a state-level phenomenon; and the diffusion of technology, a system-level phenomenon through which new powers challenge the hegemon. As Gilpin explains, "disequilibrium replaces equilibrium, and the world moves toward a new round of hegemonic conflict."[19]

Whereas Gilpin adds dynamism to a largely static theory of realism, the feminist political scientist Ann Tickner and her colleagues add gender, and hence more complexity, to realism. Classical realism is based on a very limited notion of both human nature and power, according to Tickner. She argues that human nature is not fixed and inalterable; it is multidimensional and contextual. Power cannot be equated exclusively with control and domination. Tickner thinks that realism must be reoriented toward a more inclusive notion of power, where power is the ability to act in concert (not just conflict) or to be in a symbiotic relationship (instead of outright competition). In other words, power can also be a concept of connection rather than one only of autonomy.[20]

In short, there is no single tradition of political realism; there are "realisms." Although each is predicated on a key group of assumptions, each attaches different importance to the various core propositions. Yet what unites proponents of realist theory—their emphasis on the unitary autonomous state in an international anarchic system—distinguishes them clearly from both the liberals and the radicals.

The Radical Perspective

Radicalism offers the third overarching theoretical perspective on international relations. Whereas there is widespread agreement concerning the appropriate assignment of the liberal and realist labels, there is no such agreement about the label radicalism.

The writings of Karl Marx (1818 83) are fundamental to all radical thought, even though he did not directly address all the issues of today. Marx theorized on the evolution of capitalism on the basis of economic change and class conflict: the capitalism of nineteenth-century Europe emerged out of the earlier feudal system. According to Marx, in capitalism, private interests control labor and market exchanges, creating bondages from which certain classes try to free themselves. A clash inevitably arises between the controlling, capitalist bourgeois class and the controlled workers, called the proletariat. It is from this violent clash that a new socialist order is born.[21]

There is a group of core beliefs that unite those espousing a radical, largely Marxist, perspective. The first set of beliefs in radicalism is found in historical analysis. Whereas for most liberals and realists, history provides various data points from which generalizations can be gleaned when appropriate, radicals see historical analysis as fundamental. Of special relevance is the history of the production process. During the evolution of the production process from feudalism to capitalism, new patterns of social relations were developed. Radicals are concerned most with explaining the relationship between the means of production, social relations, and power.

Basing their analyses of history on the importance of the production process, most radical theorists also assume the primacy of economics for explaining virtually all other phenomena. This clearly differentiates radicalism from either liberalism or realism. For liberals, economic interdependence is one possible explanation for international cooperation, but only one among many factors. For realists and neorealists, economic factors are one of the ingredients of power, one component of the international structure. In neither theory, though, is economics the determining factor. In radicalism, on the other hand, economic factors assume primary importance. For example, radical feminists based in the Marxist tradition suggest that the roots of oppression against women are found in the exploitive capitalist system.

A third group of radical beliefs centers on the structure of the global system. That structure, in Marxist thinking, is hierarchical and is largely the by-product of **imperialism,** or the expansion of certain economic forms into other areas of the world. The British economist John A. Hobson (1858–1940) theorized that expansion occurs because of three conditions: overproduction of goods and services in the more developed countries, underconsumption by workers and the lower classes in developed nations because of low wages, and oversavings by the upper classes and the bourgeoisie in the dominant developed countries. In order to solve these three economic problems, developed states historically have expanded abroad, and radicals argue that developed countries still see expansion as a solution: goods find new markets in underdeveloped regions, workers' wages are kept low because of foreign competition, and savings are profitably invested in new markets rather than in improving the lot of the workers. Imperialism leads to rivalry among the

THEORY IN BRIEF	
Radicalism / Dependency Theory	
Key actors	Social classes, transnational elites, multinational corporations
View of the individual	Actions determined by economic class
View of the state	An agent of the structure of international capitalism and the executing agent of the bourgeoisie
View of the international system	Highly stratified; dominated by international capitalist system
Beliefs about change	Radical change desired
Major theorists	Marx, Wallerstein, Hobson, Lenin

developed countries, evoking, in the realist's interpretation, a "scramble" to balance power.[22]

To radicals, imperialism produces the hierarchical international system, in which there are opportunities for some states, organizations, and individuals and significant constraints on behavior for others. Developed countries can expand, enabling them to sell goods and export surplus wealth that they cannot use at home. Simultaneously, the developing countries are increasingly constrained and dependent on the actions of the developed world. Hobson, who condemned imperialism as irrational, risky, and potentially conflictual, did not see it as necessarily inevitable.

Radical theorists emphasize the techniques of domination and suppression that arise from the uneven economic development inherent in the capitalist system. Uneven development empowers and enables the dominant states to exploit the underdogs; the dynamics of capitalism and economic expansion make such exploitation necessary if the top dogs are to maintain their position and the capitalist structure is to survive. Whereas realists see balancing the power of other states and diplomacy as the mechanisms for gaining and maintaining power, Marxists and radicals view the economic techniques of domination and suppression as the means of power in the world; the choices for the underdog are few and ineffective.

The Russian revolutionary and communist leader V. I. Lenin (1870–1924), in *Imperialism: The Highest Stage of Capitalism,* argued that imperialism inevitably leads to war. Lenin believed that capitalist countries have to expand through imperialism; it is not a choice, but a necessity. Once the developed capitalist states have divided up control over the developing markets, then war among the developed capitalist states over control of those markets becomes inevitable. War, then, is an outcome of capitalist economic competition.[23]

While contemporary radical interpretations begin with the writings of Marx, they have developed in quite different directions. Sociologist Immanuel Wallerstein (b. 1930), for one, links history and the rise of capitalism in what is known as the world-capitalist-system perspective. In *The Modern World-System,* he carefully and systematically examines the emergence of capitalism in Europe since the sixteenth century in terms of classes of states. At each stage of the historical process, he identifies core geographic areas where development is most advanced and the agricultural sector is able to provide sustenance for the industrial workers. Wallerstein identifies peripheral areas as well, where raw materials are extracted for the developed core and unskilled labor is mired in less-productive activities. These areas are prevented from developing by the developed core, which maintains its position at the expense of the periphery. In between the core and periphery lies the semiperiphery, where a mix of different activities occurs.[24]

Wallerstein's rendering of history intrinsically recognizes change. States of the semiperiphery can at another historic period move into the core, and occasionally vice versa. For example, in the 1980s and 1990s, semiperipheral countries such as South Korea and Taiwan moved into the core, and a few members of the periphery such as Thailand and Malaysia entered the semiperiphery. Thus, for Wallerstein and his disciples, as for most other radical theorists, attention is riveted on the changes in the systemwide phenomenon of capitalism. No political configuration can be explained without reference to the underlying structure of capitalism: "If there is one thing which distinguishes a world-system perspective from any other, it is its insistence that the unit of analysis is a *world*-system defined in terms of *economic* processes and links, and not any units defined in terms of juridical, political, cultural, geographical, or other criteria."[25]

Other latter-day radicals recognize that capitalists can use additional, more sophisticated techniques of control over developing markets. Contemporary radicals, such as **dependency theorists,** attribute primary importance to the role of **multinational corporations (MNCs)** and international banks based in developed countries in exerting fundamental controls over the developing countries. These organizations are seen as key players in establishing and maintaining dependency relationships; they are agents of penetration, not benign actors, as liberals would characterize them, or marginal actors, as realists would. These organizations are able to forge transnational relationships with elites in the developing countries, so that domestic elites in both exploiter and exploited countries are tightly linked in a symbiotic relationship.

Dependency theorists, particularly those from Latin America (Raul Prebisch, Enzo Faletto, Fernando Henrique Cardoso), believe that options for states on the periphery are few. Since the basic terms of trade are unequal, these states have few external options. And they have few internal options either, since their internal constraints are just as real: land tenure and social and class structures.[26] Thus, like the realists, dependency theorists are rather pessimistic about the possibility of change.

Finally, virtually all radical theorists, regardless of their specific emphases, are uniformly normative in their orientation. They evaluate the hierarchical capitalist structure as "bad," its methods exploitative. They have clear normative and activist positions about what should be done to ameliorate inequalities among both individuals and states—ranging from forming radical organizations supported by Leninists to more incremental changes suggested by dependency theorists.

In some quarters, radicalism has been discredited as an international relations theory. Radicalism cannot explain why there was emerging cooperation even before the end of the Cold War between capitalist and socialist states. And it cannot explain why there was such divisiveness among noncapitalist states. Neither can radicalism explain why and how some of the developing countries have been able to adopt a capitalist approach and escape from economic and political dependency. Radicalism could not have predicted such developments. And radicalism, just like liberalism and realism, did not foresee or predict the demise of the Soviet Union, arguably one of the most significant changes in the twentieth century. Each theory, despite claims of comprehensiveness, has significant shortcomings.

In other circles, radicalism has survived as a theory of economic determinism and as a theory advocating major change in the structure of the international system. Radicalism helps us understand the role of economic forces both within and between states and to explain the dynamics of late-twentieth-century economic globalization, as discussed in Chapter 9.

Constructivism

Although a relatively new approach to international relations, **constructivism** has returned international scholars to the foundational questions, including the nature of the state and the concepts of sovereignty and citizenship. In addition, constructivism has opened new substantive areas to inquiry, such as the roles of gender and ethnicity, which have been largely absent from international relations approaches.

Like liberalism, realism, and radicalism before it, constructivism is not a uniform theory. Some question whether it is a substantive theory at all. Indeed, many of the variables in the theory are loosely defined. But constructivists do share the position that since the world is so complicated, no overarching theory in international relations is possible.

The major theoretical proposition that all constructivists subscribe to is that state behavior is shaped by elite beliefs, identities, and social norms. Individuals in collectivities forge, shape, and change culture through ideas and practices. State and national interests are the result of the social identities of these actors. Thus, the object of study is the norms and practices of individuals and the collectivity, with no distinction made between domestic politics and international politics.[27] Ted Hopf offers a simple analogy:

The scenario is a fire in a theater where all run for the exits. But absent knowledge of social practices of constitutive norms, structure, even in this seemingly overdetermined circumstance, is still indeterminate. Even in a theater with just one door, while all run for that exit, who goes first? Are they the strongest or the disabled, the women or the children, the aged or the infirm, or is it just a mad dash? Determining the outcome will require knowing more about the situation than about the distribution of material power or the structure of authority. One will need to know about the culture, norms, institutions, procedures, rules, and social practices that constitute the actors and the structure alike.[28]

Constructivists eschew the concept of material structures. One of the most well-known constructivist theorists, Alexander Wendt, argues that political structure, whether one of anarchy or a particular distribution of material capabilities, explains nothing. It tells us little about state behavior: "It does not predict whether two states will be friends or foes, will recognize each other's sovereignty, will have dynastic ties, will have revisionist or status quo powers, and so on."[29] Many constructivists emphasize normative structures. What we need to know is identity, and identities change as a result of cooperative behavior and learning. Whether the system is anarchic depends on the distribution of identities, not the distribution of military capabilities, as the realist would have us believe. If a state identifies only with itself, then the system may be anarchic. If a state identifies with other states, then there is no anarchy.

Like the realists and neoliberal institutionalists, constructivists see power as important. But whereas the former just see power in material terms (military, economic, political), constructivists also see power in discursive terms—the power of ideas, culture, and language. Power exists in every exchange among actors, and the goal of constructivists is to find the sources of power. Their unique contribution may well be in elucidating the sources of power in ideas and in showing how ideas shape and change identity. An example of constructivist contributions can be seen in the discussion of sovereignty. Constructivists see sovereignty not as an absolute, but as a contested concept. They point out that states have never had exclusive control over territory but that state sovereignty has always been challenged and is being challenged continuously by new institutional forms and new national needs.

For all the renewed intellectual vigor that constructivism has fostered, this approach has been criticized. If, as constructivists claim, there is no objective reality, if "the world is in the eye of the beholder," then there can be no right or wrong answers, only individual perspectives. With no authoritative texts, all texts are equally valid—both the musings of the elites and the practices of everyday men and women. In this book, selective examples from

Contending Theoretical Perspectives

	Liberalism / Neoliberal Institutionalism	Realism / Neorealism	Radicalism / Dependency Theory	Constructivism
Key actors	States, nongovernmental groups, international organizations	International system, states	Social classes, transnational elites, multinational corporations	Individuals, collective identities
View of the individual	Basically good; capable of cooperating	Power seeking; selfish; antagonistic	Actions determined by economic class	Major unit, especially elites
View of the state	Not an autonomous actor; having many interests	Power seeking; unitary actor; following its national interest	Agent of the structure of international capitalism; executing agent of the bourgeoisie	State behavior shaped by elite beliefs, collective norms, and social identity
View of the international system	Interdependence among actors; international society; anarchic	Anarchic; reaches stability in balance-of-power system	Highly stratified; dominated by international capitalist system	Nothing explained by international material structures alone
Beliefs about change	Probable; a desirable process	Low change potential; slow structural change	Radical change desired	Belief in evolutionary change

constructivist scholarship will allow you to see the approach in use and to begin to develop a feel for this theoretical alternative.

Theory in Action: Analyzing the 2003 Iraq War

The contending theoretical perspectives discussed in the preceding sections see the world and even specific events quite differently. What theorists and policymakers choose to see, what they each seek to explain, and what implications they draw—all these elements of analysis can vary, even though the facts of the event may be the same. Analyzing the 2003 Iraq war by using these different theories allows us to compare and contrast the theories in action.

A liberal view of the 2003 Iraq war would utilize all three levels of analysis. With respect to the individual level, Saddam was clearly an abusive leader whose atrocities against his own population were made evident in the aftermath of the war, with the discovery of mass graves. He was aggressive not only against domestic opponents of his regime but also against other people within the region, and even supported terrorist activities against enemies in the West. With respect to the state level, liberals would emphasize the characteristics of the Iraqi state—mainly its authoritarian nature—and the notion that replacement by a democracy would lessen the coercive threat of the state, provide enhanced stability in the Middle East region, and be a beacon for other nascent democracies nearby. The fact that many liberals believed that the regime had or was very close to acquiring weapons of mass destruction only added to the urgency of regime change. With respect to the international level, liberals would emphasize that Iraq was not conforming to its obligations under various U.N. Security Council resolutions. Thus, there was an obligation by the international community to support sanctions and continue inspections, and failing that, for the international community to undertake collective action, fighting a war to punish Saddam's regime and allow an alternative government to take root.

Why did the international community not respond as some liberals would have predicted? The inability of the United States to win the endorsement of the U.N. Security Council for collective action can be attributed to the fact that some members of the council, including France and Russia, and some other powerful states including Germany, believed that containment of the Iraqi regime was effective, that there was insufficient evidence for the presence of the weapons of mass destruction, and that there was no need to take immediate action in light of the higher priority given to fighting Al Qaeda in Afghanistan.

In contrast, realist interpretations of the 2003 Iraq war would focus on state-level and international-level factors. Realists see the international system as anarchic, with no international authority and few states other than the United States able and willing to act to rid the world of the Iraq threat. Iraq posed a security threat to the United States with its supposed holdings of weapons of mass destruction, and the United States therefore saw a need to eliminate those weapons and at the same time to assure a stable oil supply to the West. The only way to achieve these objectives was to oust the Baathist regime from power in Iraq. Having escalated its threats and amassed its troops on Iraq's borders to coerce the regime to give up power, the United States had no choice but to act militarily when that coercion failed.

Yet not all realists agree that the policy the United States pursued was the correct one. There is an interesting discussion among realists about whether or not the U.S. operation was necessary. John Mearsheimer, an offensive realist, and Stephen Walt, a defensive realist, have jointly argued that the war was not necessary. They write that any threat posed by Saddam, even his possible attainment of nuclear weapons, could have been effectively deterred by U.S. military power. They further argue that even if the war went well and had positive long-term consequences, it would be unnecessary and could engender long-term animosity toward the United States within the Middle East region and around the world. The policy of deterrence employed by the United States had worked previously and could have continued to work.[30] Yet George W. Bush, and many realist theorists, believed that Saddam was not being effectively deterred. Bush argued that Saddam's use of chemical weapons against the Kurds in the past meant that it was probable he would use these weapons to threaten the United States. This perceived threat influenced the Bush administration's decision to invade. Realists, like liberals, clearly can draw different policy prescriptions from theory.

A radical interpretation would tend to focus mainly on the international system structure. That system structure, for radicals, is embedded in the historical colonial system and its contemporary legacies. Political colonialism spawned an imperialist system in which the economic needs of the capitalist states were paramount. In the Middle East, that meant imperialism by the West to secure oil resources. In colonial times, imperialism was state organized; today imperialism is practiced by multinational corporations.

The instability of the oil supply coming from Iraq explains the U.S. invasion of Iraq in 2003 in this view. In the belief of many radicals (and many in the Arab world), the United States wants to control Iraq's oil. They point to the fact that one of the United States's first military objectives was the seizure of the Rumaila oil field in southern Iraq. Oil fields all over the country were protected by U.S. troops even when civil disorder and looting of

International Relations Theories: A French View of the U.S. Iraq Policy

Explanations for policy decisions made by states may differ depending on the state's theoretical perspective. France opposed a United Nations resolution authorizing use of military action against Iraq in 2003, as supported by the United States. Here we examine the contending explanations for the French position.

Immediately after 9/11, France voiced solidarity with the United States and contributed troops to Operation Enduring Freedom in Afghanistan. However, after President George W. Bush's "axis of evil" speech in 2002, which emphasized preemptive action, the policies of France and the United States diverged. When the United States pressured the United Nations Security Council for a resolution authorizing the use of force against Iraq, France believed that weapons inspectors should be given time to investigate. Subsequently, France denounced any such military action without U.N. approval and threatened to use its Security Council veto against any premature military campaign. What explains France's position?

A liberal theorist would suggest that the French position reflects a firm belief in the legitimacy of international institutions, multilateral solutions, and international law. International law and institutions posit that states should not intervene in the affairs of others without a just and well-documented cause. That position was reinforced by the French government's domestic constituency: public opinion in France was overwhelmingly opposed to using military force against Iraq. France does not find sufficient cause for intervention.

A radical theorist might say that the United States is merely acting as it has in the past—as an imperialist power. But as the United States becomes more dependent on others, particularly for oil, it has, one French author asserts, "resorted to making a show of empire by choosing to pursue military and diplomatic actions among a series of puny powers dubbed for dramatic effect 'the axis of evil'. . . ."[a] France opposes that policy.

A realist would point to two factors that may explain the French position. First, France is acting out of its own self-interest. French leaders believed that an invasion of Iraq would make France less secure, rather than more secure. From this perspective, taking action against Iraq would lead to more terrorists being recruited to the radical cause, making Al Qaeda stronger and fueling anti-Western sentiment in the Middle East. Exercising force in Iraq would be unlikely to deter terrorism since most terrorists have no geographic home. Additionally, France has a sizeable Muslim population and home-grown terrorist groups might be more prone to focus on French targets, making the country less secure.

A second, albeit less satisfactory, explanation from the realist perspective is that France's position is part of a long-standing attempt to balance American power and make the international system a multipolar one. This would reestablish France as a great power in international relations, restoring "la gloire et la grandeur de la France."

For Critical Analysis

1. *Which explanation of France's position do you find convincing? Why?*
2. *Which explanation of the United States's actions discussed in this chapter do you find convincing?*

a. Immanuel Todd, *After the Empire: The Breakdown of the American Order* (New York: Columbia University Press, 2002), x.

precious monuments went unchecked. Restarting the oil pipelines was given priority over providing for the basic needs of the Iraqi people.

Radicals, especially world-system and dependency theorists, would not be surprised at all that the core states of the capitalist system—the United States and its allies—responded with force when Iraq threatened their critical interests in oil. Nor would they expect the end of the Cold War to make any difference in the structure of the system. The major changes in international power relationships that radicals seek—and predict—have not yet come.

In Sum: Seeing the World through Theoretical Lenses

How each of us sees international relations depends on his or her own theoretical lens. Do you see things through a realist framework, are you inclined toward a liberal interpretation, or do you adhere to a radical or constructivist view of the world? These theoretical perspectives differ not only in who they identify as key actors, but in their views about the individual, the state, and the international system—the three levels of analysis. Equally important, these perspectives hold different views about the possibility and desirability of change in the international system.

In the next four chapters, we examine in more detail how each of these three dominant perspectives sees the international system, the state, the individual, and international organizations. Where applicable, constructivist interpretations will also be included. First we will examine the most general level of analysis—the international system.

Notes

1. Kenneth N. Waltz, *Man, the State, and War* (New York: Columbia University Press, 1954); and J. David Singer, "The Levels of Analysis Problem," *International Politics and Foreign Policy*, ed. James N. Rosenau (Rev. ed.; New York: Free Press, 1961), 20–29.
2. Baron de La Brède et de Montesquieu, *The Spirit of the Laws*, vol. 36, ed. David Wallace Carrithers (Berkeley: University of California Press, 1971), 23.
3. Immanuel Kant, *Perpetual Peace*, ed. Lewis White Beck (New York: Macmillan Co., 1957).
4. Robert Axelrod and Robert O. Keohane, "Achieving Cooperation under Anarchy: Strategies and Institutions," *Cooperation under Anarchy*, ed. Kenneth Oye (Princeton, N.J.: Princeton University Press, 1986), 226–54.

5. Robert O. Keohane and Joseph Nye, *Power and Interdependence* (3d ed.; New York: Longman, 2001); and Robert O. Keohane and Joseph Nye, "Transnational Relations and World Politics," *International Organization* 25:3 (Summer 1971), 329–50, 721–48.

6. Francis Fukuyama, "The End of History?" *National Interest* 16 (Summer 1989), 4.

7. John Mueller, *Retreat from Doomsday: The Obsolescence of Major War* (New York: Basic Books, 1989).

8. Thucydides, *History of the Peloponnesian War*, trans. Rex Warner (Rev. ed.; Harmondsworth, Eng.: Penguin, 1972).

9. St. Augustine, "Confessions" and "City of God," in *Great Books of the Western World*, vol. 18, ed. Robert Maynard Hutchins (Chicago: Encyclopedia Britannica, 1952, 1986).

10. Niccolò Machiavelli, *The Prince and the Discourses* (New York: Random House, 1940).

11. Thomas Hobbes, *Leviathan*, ed. C. B. Macpherson (Harmondsworth, Eng.: Penguin, 1968), 13.

12. Hans J. Morgenthau, *Politics among Nations* (5th ed. rev.; New York: Knopf, 1978).

13. John J. Mearsheimer, *The Tragedy of Great Power Politics* (New York: Norton, 2001), 19–22.

14. Kenneth N. Waltz, *Theory of International Politics* (Reading, Mass: Addison-Wesley, 1979).

15. Kenneth N. Waltz, "Realist Thought and Neorealist Theory," in *Controversies in International Relations Theory: Realism and the Neoliberal Challenge,* ed. Charles W. Kegley, Jr. (New York: St. Martin's, 1995), 67–82.

16. Waltz, *Theory of International Politics*, 105.

17. John J. Mearsheimer, "The False Promise of International Institutions," *International Security* 19:3 (Winter 1994–95), 5–49.

18. Robert Gilpin, *War and Change in World Politics* (Cambridge, Eng.: Cambridge University Press, 1981), 29.

19. Ibid., 210.

20. Ann Tickner, "Hans Morgenthau's Principles of Political Realism: A Feminist Reformulation," *Millennium: Journal of International Studies* 17:3 (1988), 429–40.

21. Karl Marx, *Capital: A Critique of Political Economy* (New York: Random House, n.d.).

22. John A. Hobson, *Imperialism: A Study*, ed. Philip Siegelman (Ann Arbor: University of Michigan Press, 1965).

23. V. I. Lenin, *Imperialism: The Highest Stage of Capitalism* (New York: International Publishers, 1939)

24. Immanuel Wallerstein, *The Modern World-System*, vol. 2, *Mercantilism and the Consolidation of the European World-Economy, 1600–1750* (New York: Academic Press, 1980).

25. Terence K. Hopkins et al., "Patterns of Development in the Modern World-System," in *World-Systems Analysis: Theory and Methodology,* ed. Terence K. Hopkins et al. (Beverly Hills, Calif.: Sage, 1982), 72. Emphasis in the original.

26. Tony Smith, "The Underdevelopment of the Development Literature: The Case of Dependency Theory," *World Politics* 31:2 (January 1979), 247–88.

27. Stephen M. Walt, "International Relations: One World, Many Theories," *Foreign Policy*, no. 110 (Spring 1998), 29–46.

28. Ted Hopf, "The Promise of Constructivism in International Relations Theory," *International Security* 23:1 (Summer 1989), 172.

29. Alexander Wendt, "Anarchy Is What States Make of It: The Social Construction of Power Politics," *International Organization* 46:2 (Spring 1992), 396. For a more complete analysis, see Alexander Wendt, *Social Theory of International Politics* (Cambridge, Eng.: Cambridge University Press, 1999).

30. John J. Mearsheimer and Stephen M. Walt, "An Unnecessary War," *Foreign Policy*, no. 134 (January–February 2003), 50–59.

The International System

- *Why is the concept of a system a powerful descriptive and explanatory device?*
- *How would a liberal theorist view the international system?*
- *What concepts do realists employ to analyze the international system?*
- *How do radicals view the international system?*
- *How do each of the contending theoretical perspectives explain change in the international system?*

The Notion of a System

Each of the contending theoretical perspectives examined in Chapter 3 described an international system. For realists and radicals, the concept of an international system is vital to their analyses, whereas for liberals, the international system is less precise as an explanatory mechanism and less consequential, and for constructivists, the concept of an international system is tied to notions of change.

To understand the international system, the notion of a system itself must be clarified. Broadly defined, a **system** is an assemblage of units, objects, or parts united by some form of regular interaction. The concept of systems is essential to the physical and biological sciences; systems are composed of different interacting units, whether at the micro (cell, plant, animal) or the macro (natural ecosystem or global climate) level. Because these units interact, a change in one unit causes changes in all the others. Systems, with their interacting parts, tend to respond in regularized ways; there are patterns to their actions. Boundaries separate one system from another, but there can be exchanges across these boundaries. A system can break down, meaning that changes within the system become so significant that in effect a new system emerges.

In the 1950s, the behavioral revolution in the social sciences and growing acceptance of political realism in international relations led scholars to conceptualize international politics as a system, using the language of systems theory. Beginning with the supposition that people act in regularized ways and that their patterns of interaction with each other are largely habitual, both realists and behavioralists made the conceptual leap that international politics is a system whose major actors are individual states.[1] This notion of a system is embedded in the thoughts of the three dominant theoretical schools of international relations. Of particular interest is how change occurs.

The International System according to Liberals

The international system is not central to the view of liberals. It is therefore not surprising to find at least three different conceptions of the international system in liberal thinking.

The first conception sees the international system not as a structure but as a process, in which multiple interactions occur among different parties and where various actors learn from the interaction. Actors in this process include not only states but also international governmental organizations (such as the United Nations), nongovernmental organizations (such as Human Rights Watch) and multinational corporations, and substate actors (such as parliaments and bureaucracies). Each different type of actor has interactions with all of the other ones. With so many different kinds of actors, a plethora of national interests defines the liberal international system. While security interests, so dominant for realists, are still important to liberals, other interests such as economic and social issues are also considered, depending on the time and circumstance. In their book *Power and Interdependence,* political scientists Robert Keohane and Joseph Nye describe the international system as an interdependent system in which the different actors are both sensitive to (affected by) and vulnerable to (suffering costly effects from) the actions of others. In interdependent systems, there are multiple channels connecting states; these channels exist between governmental elites and among nongovernmental elites and transnational organizations, as well. Multiple issues and agendas arise in the interdependent system. Military force may be useful in some situations, but is not useful for all issues.[2]

A second liberal conception of the international system comes from the English tradition of international society. According to two of the principal architects of this tradition, scholars Hedley Bull and Adam Watson, while the international system comprises a group of independent political communities, an **international society** is more than that. In an international society, the various actors communicate; they consent to common rules and institutions and recognize common interests. Actors in international society share a common identity, a sense of "we-ness"; without such an identity, a society cannot exist. This conception of the international system has normative

implications: liberals view
the international system as
an arena and process for
positive interactions.[3]

A third liberal view of
the international system is
that of neoliberal institutionalism, a view that comes
closer to realist thinking.
Neoliberal institutionalists
see the international system
as an anarchic one in which
each individual state acts in
its own self-interest. But unlike many realists, they see
the product of the interaction among actors as a potentially positive one, where
institutions created out of
self-interest serve to moderate state behavior, as states realize they will have
future interactions with the other actors involved.

THEORY IN BRIEF	
The Liberal Perspective on the International System	
Characterization	Three liberal interpretations: interdependence among actors, international society, and anarchy
Actors	States, international governmental institutions, nongovernmental organizations, multinational corporations, substate actors
Constraints	From anarchy and interdependence
Possibility of change	Low likelihood of radical change, but may occur; constant incremental change as actors are involved in new relationships

All liberals acknowledge and welcome change in the international system.
Liberals see changes coming from several sources. First, changes in the international system occur as the result of exogenous technological developments—
that is, progress occurring independently, or outside the control of actors in
the system. For example, changes in communication and transportation are
responsible for the increasing level of interdependence among states within
the international system.

Second, change may occur because of changes in the relative importance
of different issue areas. While realists give primacy to issues of national security, liberals identify the relative importance of other issue areas. Specifically,
in the last decades of the twentieth century, economic issues replaced
national security issues as the topic of the international agenda, while in the
twenty-first century, globalizing issues such as human rights and the environment may assume primacy. These represent fundamental changes in the
international system, according to liberal thinking.

Third, change may occur as new actors, including multinational corporations, nongovernmental organizations, or other participants in global civil society, may augment or replace state actors. The various new actors may enter into
new kinds of relationships and are apt to alter both the international system and
state behaviors. These types of changes are compatible with liberal thinking and
are discussed by liberal writers. Yet, like their realist counterparts, liberal

thinkers also acknowledge that change may occur in the overall power structure among the states. This is the view of change most in line with realist thinking.

The International System according to Realists

Political realists have clear notions of the international system and its essential characteristics. All realists characterize the international system as anarchic. No authority exists above the state; the state is sovereign. This anarchic structure constrains the actions of decisionmakers and affects the distribution of capabilities among the various actors. Realists differ among themselves, however, about the degree of a state's autonomy in the international system. Traditional realists acknowledge that states act and shape the system, whereas neorealists believe that states are constrained by the structure of the system. Yet for both, anarchy is the basic ordering principle and each state in the system must, therefore, look out for its own interests above all.

Realists differentiate the international system largely along the dimension of polarity.

Polarity

System polarity simply refers to the number of blocs of states that exert power in the international system. Realists are particularly interested in polarity because of its focus on power. There are three types of system polarity: multipolarity, bipolarity, and unipolarity (see Figure 4.1).

If there are a number of influential actors in the international system, a balance-of-power or a multipolar system is formed. In classical balance of power, the actors are exclusively states, and there should be at least five of them. The nineteenth-century balance of power—between Great Britain, Russia, Prussia, France, and Austria—is the real-world antecedent discussed in Chapter 2. In multipolar systems, several states—at least three or more—enjoy relative power parity.

In a balance-of-power system, the essential norms of the system are clear to each of the state actors. The In Focus box below lists those basic norms of behavior. If an essential actor does not follow these norms, the balance-of-power system may become unstable. If the number of states declines to three, stability is threatened, because coalitions between any two are possible, which would leave the third alone and weak. When alliances are formed in balance-of-power systems, they are formed for a specific purpose, have a short duration, and shift according to advantage rather than ideology. Any wars that do break out are probably limited in nature, designed to preserve the balance of power.

FIGURE 4.1

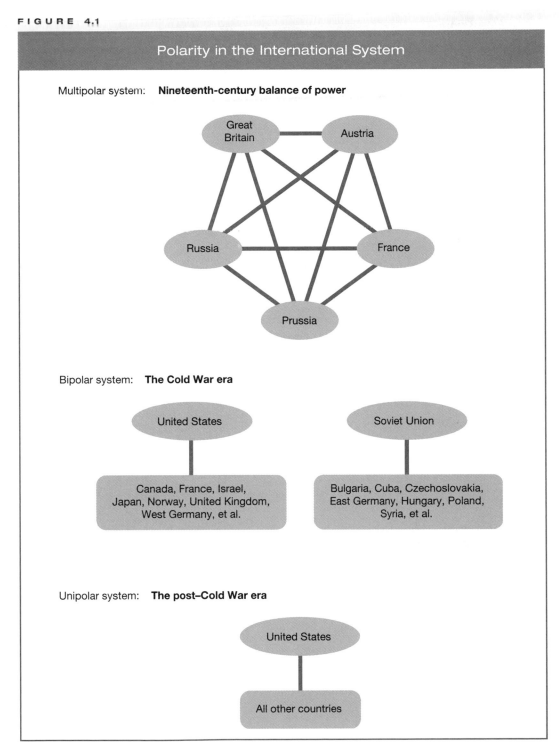

Polarity in the International System

Multipolar system: **Nineteenth-century balance of power**

Bipolar system: **The Cold War era**

Unipolar system: **The post–Cold War era**

BASIC NORMS OF A BALANCE-OF-POWER SYSTEM

◆ Any actor or coalition that tries to assume dominance must be constrained.

◆ States want to increase their capabilities by acquiring territory, increasing their population, or developing economically.

◆ Negotiating is better than fighting.

◆ Fighting is better than failing to increase capabilities, because no one else will protect a weak state.

◆ Other states are viewed as potential allies.

◆ States seek their own national interests defined in terms of power.

In bipolar systems, the essential norms are different. In the bipolar system of the Cold War, each of the blocs (the North Atlantic Treaty Organization (NATO) and the Warsaw Pact) sought to negotiate rather than fight, to fight minor wars rather than major ones, and to fight major wars rather than fail to eliminate the rival bloc, although the Cold War never erupted into a "hot" war. In the bipolar system, alliances tend to be long term, based on relatively permanent, not shifting, interests.

In a tight bipolar system, international organizations either do not develop or are completely ineffective, as the United Nations was during the height of the Cold War. In a looser bipolar system, international organizations may develop primarily to mediate between the two blocs, and individual states within the looser coalitions may try to use the international organizations for their own advantage.

Is the system a unipolar one; that is, is there just one group or even one state that commands influence in the international system? Immediately at the end of the Gulf War in 1991, many states, including the United States's closest allies and virtually all developing states, grew concerned that the international system had become unipolar, with no effective counterweight to the power of the United States. During much of the Cold War era, particularly in the 1950s and 1960s, the international system was bipolar—the United States, its allies in NATO and Japan versus the Soviet Union and its Warsaw Pact allies. But over the course of the Cold War, the relative tightness or looseness of the bipolar system varied, as powerful states such as the People's Republic of China and France pursued independent paths.

System Management and Stability

Polarity is also an important characteristic of the realist international system because of its relationship to system management and stability. Are certain polarities more manageable and hence more stable than others? Are wars more likely to occur in bipolar systems, multipolar systems, or unipolar systems? These questions have dominated much of the discussion among realists, but the studies of these relationships are inconclusive.

Bipolar systems are very difficult to regulate formally, since neither uncommitted states nor international organizations are able to direct the behavior of either of the two blocs. Informal regulation may be easier. If either of the blocs is engaged in disruptive behavior, its consequences are immediately seen, especially if, as a result, one of the blocs gains in strength or position. Kenneth Waltz, for one, argues that because of this the bipolar international system is the most stable structure in the long run: the two sides are "able both to moderate the other's use of violence and to absorb possibly destabilizing changes that emanate from uses of violence that they do not or cannot control."[4] In such a system, there is a clear difference in the amount of power held by the two poles as compared to that held by the rest of the state actors. Because of the power disparity, each of the two sides is able to focus its activity almost exclusively on the other, and can anticipate the other's actions and accurately predict its responses because of their history of repeated interactions. Each tries to preserve this balance of power in order to preserve itself and the bipolar system.

Pointing to the stability attained in the bipolar Cold War system, John Mearsheimer provoked controversy by suggesting that the world will miss the stability and predictability that the Cold War forged. With the end of the Cold War bipolar system, Mearsheimer argued, more conflict pairs would develop and hence more possibilities for war. He felt that deterrence would be more difficult and miscalculations more probable. He drew a clear policy implication: "The West has an interest in maintaining peace in Europe. It therefore has an interest in maintaining the Cold War order, and hence has an interest in the continuation of the Cold War confrontation; developments that threaten to end it are dangerous. The Cold War antagonism could be continued at lower levels of East-West tension than have prevailed in the past; hence the West is not insured by relaxing East-West tension, but a complete end to the Cold War would create more problems than it would solve."[5] Most analysts do not share this provocative conclusion, in part because factors other than polarity can affect system stability.

Theoretically, in multipolar and balance-of-power systems, the regulation of system stability ought to be easier than in bipolar systems. The whole purpose of the balancer role, such as that played by Great Britain in the nineteenth century, is to act as a regulator for the system, stepping in to correct a perceived imbalance—as when Great Britain intervened in the Crimean War of 1854–55, opposing Russia on behalf of Turkey. Under multipolarity, numerous interactions take place among all the various parties, and thus there is less opportunity to dwell on a specific relationship. Interaction by any one state actor with a variety of states leads to crosscutting loyalties and alliances and therefore moderates hostility or friendship with any one other state actor. States are less likely to respond to the arms buildup of just one party in the system, and so war becomes less likely.

Advocates of unipolarity claim that it is the most stable system. Hegemonic stability theorists claim that unipolarity, or dominance by a hegemon, leads to the most stable international system. Historian Paul Kennedy, in *The Rise and Fall of the Great Powers,* argues that it was the hegemony (though not unipolarity) of Britain in the nineteenth century and that of the United States in the immediate post–World War II era that led to the greatest stability.[6] Other proponents of this theory, such as Keohane, contend that hegemonic states are willing to pay the price to enforce norms unilaterally if necessary in order to ensure the continuation of the system that benefits them. When the hegemon loses power and declines, then system stability is jeopardized.[7]

It is clear, then, that realists do not agree among themselves on how polarity matters. Individual and group efforts to test the relationship between polarity and stability have been inconclusive. The Correlates of War project (discussed in Chapter 1) did test two hypotheses flowing from the polarity-stability debate. Singer and Small hypothesized that the greater the number of alliance commitments in the system, the more war the system will experience. They also hypothesized that the closer the system is to bipolarity, the more war it will experience. On the basis of the data between 1815 and 1945, however, neither argument was proven valid across the whole time span. During the nineteenth century, alliance commitments prevented war, whereas in the twentieth century, proliferating alliances seemed to predict war.[8]

Behavioral evidence for hegemonic stability theory is explored by the political scientists Michael Webb and Stephen Krasner.[9] During the 1970s, the United States began to decline as a hegemon, according to most aggregate economic measures, although that decline was relative and has been stabilized. Yet through the period of the United States's decline, the international economic system remained relatively stable. These findings suggest that system stability may persist even when the hegemon is in relative decline. Thus system stability is not solely dependent on hegemonic power. The behavioral evidence drawn from the analysis of realists themselves regarding the relationship between polarity and system stability is, therefore, inconclusive.

From a policy perspective, the international system of the twenty-first century is confronted by a unique problem. Currently, one state dominates: the defense expenditures of the United States are greater than those of the next fifteen states combined; its economy is three times stronger than those of the next three rivals combined. These statistics suggest a unipolar international system. What are the normative and practical implications of such a world? Will a unipolar world with the United States as the global hegemon lead to international peace?

**POLICY
DEBATE**

Will the United States' pursuit of global hegemony lead to international peace?

YES:

◆ U.S. hegemony is necessary to prevent a power vacuum in international relations.

◆ Other countries have abrogated their international responsibilities, so that the United States must take the lead.

◆ The United States has had a long and exceptional commitment to democracy, human rights, and liberal values and should marshal those values in the pursuit of international peace.

NO:

◆ U.S. primacy engenders strong animosity toward the United States among both friends and foes.

◆ To maintain its hegemony, the United States will be forced to employ ruthless methods that are antithetical to American values.

◆ The United States is not the only force for peace and a liberal international order; other states can and should be mobilized.

◆ Like all hegemons, the United States will eventually decline as a power and hence must be prepared to cooperate with others as an "ordinary state."

How the International System Changes

Although realists value the continuity of systems, they recognize that international systems do change. For example, at the end of the nineteenth century the multipolar balance of power broke down and was replaced by a tight alliance system pitting the Triple Alliance against the Triple Entente. Why do systems change? Realists attribute system change to either changes in the actors and hence the distribution of power or changes emanating from outside of the system.

Changes in either the number of major actors or the relative power relationship among the actors may result in a fundamental change in the international system. Wars are usually responsible for such fundamental changes in power relationships. For example, the end of World War II brought the relative demise of Great Britain and France, even though they were the victors.

The war also signaled the end not only of Germany's and Japan's imperial aspirations but of their basic national capabilities as well. Their respective militaries were soundly defeated; civil society was destroyed and infrastructure demolished. Two other powers emerged into dominant positions—the United States, now willing to assume the international role that it had shunned after World War I, and the Soviet Union, buoyed by its victory although economically weak. The international system had fundamentally changed; the multipolar world had been replaced by a bipolar one.

Robert Gilpin, in *War and Change in World Politics*, sees another form of system change, where states act to preserve their own interests and thereby change the international system. Such changes can occur because states respond at different rates to political, economic, and technological developments. For example, the rapidly industrializing states in Asia—South Korea, Taiwan, and Hong Kong (though now part of China)—have responded to technological change the fastest. By responding rapidly and with single-mindedness, these states have been able to improve their relative positions in terms of system stratification. Thus, characteristics of the international system can be changed by the actions of a few.[10]

Exogenous changes may also lead to a shift in the international political system. Advances in technology—the instruments for oceanic navigation, the airplane for transatlantic crossings, and satellites and rockets for exploration of outer space, for example—not only have expanded the boundaries of accessible geographic space, but also brought about changes in the boundaries of the international political system. With these changes came an explosion of new state actors, reflecting different political interests and different cultural traditions.

No technological change has had more of an impact on the international system than the development of nuclear weapons and their use in warfare. The destructiveness of these weapons, their inability to discriminate between combatants and civilians, and their evident harm to future generations are all characteristics that have led policymakers to change the rules of the game. During the Cold War this meant that the superpowers did not directly fight but preferred to spar through nonnuclear proxies using conventional military technology. Since these weapons have not been used since 1945, they are no longer seen as credible weapons in some circles. Nevertheless, the weapons remain much feared, and efforts by nonnuclear states to develop such weapons, or even the threat to do so, has met sharp resistance, as occurred when North Korea and Iran announced their respective intentions to become nuclear. The nuclear states do not want a change in the status quo; in their view, nuclear proliferation, particularly in the hands of rogue states, leads to international system instability.

Thus, in the view of realists, international systems can change, yet the inherent bias among realist interpretations is for continuity. All realists agree that there are patterns of change in the system, although they may disagree about what time frame to look at in order to study the changes. Efforts by realists to test many of the ideas coming from their notions about the international system have proven inconclusive.

The International System according to Radicals

Whereas realists define the international system in terms of its polarity and stability, radicals seek to describe and explain the structure in terms of stratification. The system that they see is totally different from the system described by liberals and realists, and hence the radicals advocate for a different future.

Stratification

The structure of the international system is described by stratification. **Stratification** refers to the uneven division of resources among different groups of states; the international system is stratified according to which states have vital resources, such as oil or military strength or economic power. Stratification is the key to understanding the radical notion of the international system.

Different international systems have had varying degrees of stratification. Indeed, system stratification is strong. According to one set of measures, several of the world's powers (the United States, Japan, Germany, France, Britain, Russia, and China) accounted for about one-half of the world's total gross domestic product (GDP), while the other 180-plus states shared the other half (see Figure 4.2). From the stratification of power and resources comes the division between the haves, loosely characterized as the **North,** and the have-nots, states largely positioned in the **South.** This distinction is vital to the discussion of international political economy found in Chapter 9.

Stratification of influence and resources has implications for the ability of a system to regulate itself, as well as for system stability. When the dominant

FIGURE 4.2

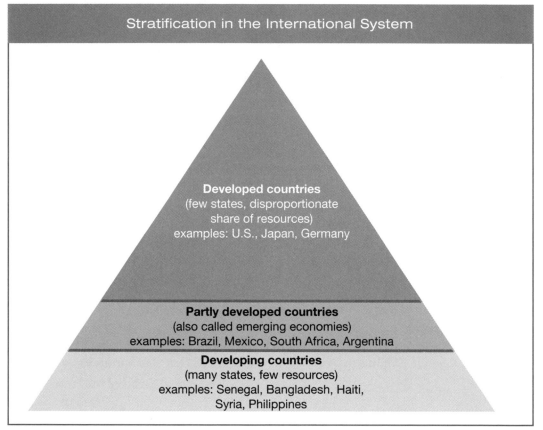

Stratification in the International System

Developed countries
(few states, disproportionate
share of resources)
examples: U.S., Japan, Germany

Partly developed countries
(also called emerging economies)
examples: Brazil, Mexico, South Africa, Argentina

Developing countries
(many states, few resources)
examples: Senegal, Bangladesh, Haiti,
Syria, Philippines

powers are challenged by those states just beneath them in terms of access to resources, the system may become highly unstable. For example, Germany's and Japan's attempts to obtain and reclaim resources during the 1930s led to World War II. Such a group of second-tier powers has the potential to win a confrontation, whereas the real underdogs in a severely stratified system do not (although they can cause major disruptions). The rising powers, especially those who are acquiring resources, seek first-tier status and are willing to fight wars to get it. If the challengers do not begin a war, the top powers may do so to quell the threat of a power displacement.

The Implications of Stratification

For Marxists, as well as most other radicals, crippling stratification in the international system is caused by capitalism. Capitalism structures the relationship between the advantaged and the disadvantaged, empowering the rich and disenfranchising the weak. Marxists assert that capitalism breeds its own instruments of domination, including international institutions whose rules are structured by capitalist states to facilitate capitalist processes, multi-national corporations whose headquarters are in capitalist states but whose loci of activity are in dependent areas, and even individuals (often leaders) or classes (the national bourgeoisie) residing in weak states who are co-opted to participate in and perpetuate an economic system that places the masses in a permanently dependent position.

Radicals believe that the greatest amount of resentment will be felt in systems where the stratification is most extreme. There, the poor are likely to be not only resentful but aggressive. They want change, but the rich have very little incentive to change their behavior. The call for the **New International Economic Order (NIEO)** in the 1970s was voiced by radicals and liberal reformers alike in most developing countries. The poorer, developing states of the South, the underdogs with a dearth of resources, sought fundamental changes, including debt forgiveness, international controls on multinational corporations, and major changes in how primary commodities were priced. They sought a greater share of the world's resources and an ability to exercise greater power. Other states of the South, including those which were further along in developing (emerging economies) and their northern allies, sought a more reformist agenda, including debt refinancing (not forgiveness), more concessionary aid, and voluntary controls on multinational corporations.

In short, radicals believe that great economic disparities are built into the structure of the international system and that all actions and interactions are constrained by this structure. World-system theorists like Immanuel Wallerstein and others, do see the possibility of change within the capitalist system. Change is evident in the shuffling of the states at the core of the system: the Dutch were replaced by the British and the British by the Americans. Change may occur in the semiperiphery and periphery, as states change their relative positions vis-à-vis one another. And capitalism goes through cycles of growth and expansion, as occurred during the age of colonialism and imperialism, followed by periods of contraction and decline. So capitalism itself is a dynamic force.

But can the capitalist system itself be changed? In other words, is system transformation—like the change from the feudal to the capitalist system—possible? Here, the radicals differ among themselves. Wallerstein, for example, is quite pessimistic,

THEORY IN BRIEF

The Radical Perspective on the International System

Characterization	Highly stratified
Actors	Capitalist states vs. developing states
Constraints	Capitalism; stratification
Possibility of change	Radical change desired but limited by the capitalist structure

claiming that any change that does occur is painfully slow. Others are more optimistic. Just as realists disagree among themselves about policy implications, radicals disagree about the likelihood that the system stratification that they all abhor will be altered.

Constructivism and International System Change

Constructivists, perhaps more than other theorists, have developed ideas on how the international system changes. Changes in the social norms of a system can lead to a fundamental shift in that system, although not all norm changes will be transforming. Social purposes of the international system have altered over time; there have been different international orders with changing purposes, different views of threat, and reliance on different ways to maintain order. Martha Finnemore traces at least four European international orders: an eighteenth-century balance order, a nineteenth-century concert one, a sphere-of-influence system for much of the twentieth century, and after the end of the Cold War an evolving new order whose purposes are the promotion of liberal democracy, capitalism, and human rights. What is unique about the constructivist approach is the specification of the mechanisms through which that change occurs. At the collective level, while coercion may still lead to change, more critical are international institutions and law, the legal profession, and social movements. At the individual level, change occurs through persuasion and through internationalization of the new norms. So while material capabilities do matter in explaining change, just as the realists and many liberals argue, and those conditions set the constraints of what order is possible, "why one order emerges rather than another," can only be seen, Finnemore argues, "by examining the ideas, culture, and social purpose of the actors involved."[11]

Advantages and Disadvantages of the International System as a Level of Analysis

For adherents of all theoretical perspectives, there are clear advantages to using the international system as a level of analysis. The language of systems theory allows comparison and contrasts between systems: the international system at one point in time may be compared with one at another point in time; international systems may be compared with internal state systems; political systems may be contrasted with social or even biological systems. How these various systems interact is the focus of both the social and natural sciences.

For all the sciences, the most significant advantage to this level of analysis lies in the comprehensiveness of systems theory. It enables scholars to organize the seemingly disjointed parts into a whole; it allows them to hypothesize about and then to test how the various parts, actors, and rules of the system are related and show how change in one part of the system results in changes in other parts. In this sense, the notion of a system is a significant research tool.

In short, systems theory is a holistic, or top-down, approach. Although it cannot provide descriptions of events at the micro level (such as why a particular individual acted a certain way), it does allow plausible explanations at the more general level. For the realists, generalizations derived from systems theory provide the fodder for prediction, the ultimate goal of all behavioral science. For liberals and radicals, these generalizations have definite normative implications; in the former case they affirm movement toward a positive system, and in the latter case they confirm pessimistic assessments about the place of states in the economically determined international system.

But systems theory also has some glaring weaknesses and inadequacies. The emphasis at the international system level means that the "stuff" of politics is often neglected, while the generalizations are broad and sometimes obvious. Who disputes that most states seek to maintain their relative capability or that most states prefer to negotiate rather than fight under all but a few circumstances? Who doubts that some states occupy a preeminent economic position that determines the status of all others?

Just as systems theory has a number of weaknesses, so is the testing of such theories very difficult. In most cases, theorists are constrained by a lack of historical information. After all, few systems theorists, besides some radical and cyclical theorists, discuss systems predating 1648. In fact, most begin with the nineteenth century. Those using earlier time frames are constrained both by a poor grounding in history and by glaring lapses in the historical record. Although these weaknesses are not fatal ones, they restrict the scholar's ability to test specific hypotheses over a long time period.

International system theorists have always been hampered by the problem of boundaries. If they use the notion of the international system, do they mean the international *political* system? What factors lie outside of the system? In fact, much realist theorizing systematically ignores this critical question by differentiating several different levels within the system, but only one international-system-level construct. Liberals do better, differentiating factors external to the system and even incorporating those factors into their expanded notion of an interdependent international system. Yet if you cannot clearly distinguish between what is inside and what is outside of the system,

The International System: A View from China

Realists posit that the international system changes as great powers gain or lose power vis à vis other states. As China's economic and political power has grown, many have speculated whether China will catch up to the United States, leading to a new bipolarity, or surpass the United States in a new unipolar system. Chinese government officials have stated their intentions.

China's view of the international system and its new role in the system have gradually emerged. Following almost a century of seeing itself as a victim of the great powers and after decades of internal revolution when it was closed to the world, China is becoming a confident great power. The country wields a great deal of economic and political influence, and is creating a place for itself and seeking to influence others. Chinese foreign policy objectives and interests have become more sophisticated and more closely aligned to those of a major power, and the country now works within the international system.

The economic revolution in China, its embrace of capitalism and unleashing of the productive capacity of its people, and the opening of foreign investment and enterprise, have led to two decades of impressive economic growth. China's annual GDP averages 9.4 percent and accounts for 4 percent of the world economy. The country's export-led growth has made it highly dependent on world markets to sell its products and provide rising incomes for Chinese consumers who are eager for the benefits of industrialization. This growth has made China highly dependent on natural resources, including oil and natural gas which are increasingly imported from abroad. To meet these economic needs, China engages in diplomatic activity, trying to cement relationships with resource-rich developing countries. In 2006 and 2007, Africa has been a special target of Chinese economic initiatives, with offers of foreign aid in exchange for access to resources.

The political evolution in China has been directed outward rather than inward. China is now an active participant in international institutions, exerting its power through membership in the Security Council and serving as a mediator between North Korea and other states. Since the mid-1990s, China has been actively involved in regional bodies like ASEAN, engaged Japan and South Korea economically and diplomatically, and sought an increased role in Central Asia, serving as a counterpoint to U.S. and Russian influence.

Symbolic of China's rise to great power status is its hosting of the 2008 Olympic games. The event has served as a motivator for improving infrastructure and sprucing up cities in China which will showcase its arrival on the world scene.

China's growing prominence reflects a "peaceful rise," according to Chinese officials. President Hu Jintao's 2006 visit to the United States noted that China can emerge as a great power in the international system without resorting to violence as other great powers have. Other Chinese leaders have made similar arguments. China will never go for territorial expansion, nor will it seek hegemony, and the current international order has operated to benefit China's so it has no intention of upsetting the status quo. The country's priorities are domestic ones—a growing urban-rural split, environmental problems, water deficits— problems within China that will demand significant attention from Chinese authorities for the next several decades. As President Hu assured U.S. authorities, China has neither the will nor the means to challenge America's dominance in the world.

For Critical Analysis

1. Why does China have an interest in sustaining the current international system even if it does not dominate it?
2. Is China's peaceful rise argument best explained by a realist, liberal, or radical perspective?

	THEORY IN BRIEF		
	Contending Perspectives on the International System		
	Liberalism / Neoliberal Institutionalism	**Realism / Neorealism**	**Radicalism / Dependency Theory**
Characterization	Three liberal interpretations: interdependence among actors, international society, and anarchy	Anarchic	Highly stratified
Actors	States, international governmental institutions, nongovernmental organizations, substate actors	State is primary actor	Capitalist states vs. developing states
Constraints	None; ongoing interactions	Polarity; distribution of power	Capitalism; stratiflcation
Possibility of change	No possibility of radical change; constant incremental change as actors are involved in new relationships	Slow change when the balance of power shifts	Radical change desired but limited by the capitalist structure

do you in fact have a system? And even more important, what shapes the system? What is the reciprocal relationship between international system constraints and unit (state) behavior? By way of contrast, constructivists do not acknowledge such boundaries. They argue that there is no relevant distinction between the international system and the state or between international politics and domestic politics and no distinction between endogenous and exogenous sources of change.

In Sum: From the International System to the State

Of all the theoretical approaches, realists and radicals pay the most attention to the international system level of analysis. For realists, the defining characteristic of the international system is polarity; for radicals, it is stratification. In both perspectives, the international system constrains state behavior. Realists generally view such constraints as positive, depending on the distribution of power, whereas for radicals the constraint is negative—preventing economically depressed states from achieving equality and justice. For liberals, the international system is viewed from a more neutral perspective, as an arena and process for interaction. Constructivists take an evolutionary approach, emphasizing how changes in norms and ideas shape the system, seeing little differentiation between the international and domestic system and eschewing the importance attached to international system structure.

States and foreign-policy decisionmakers operate within the confines of the international system. In the next chapter we examine the state, models of state decisionmaking, as well as challenges to the state.

Notes

1. See especially Morton Kaplan, *System and Process in International Politics* (New York: Krieger, 1976).
2. Robert O. Keohane and Joseph S. Nye, *Power and Interdependence* (3rd ed.; New York: Longman, 2001).
3. Hedley Bull and Adam Watson, eds., *The Expansion of International Society* (Oxford, Eng.: Oxford University Press, 1984).
4. Kenneth N. Waltz, "International Structure, National Force, and the Balance of World Power," *Journal of International Affairs* 21:2 (1967), 229.
5. John J. Mearsheimer, "Back to the Future: Instability after the Cold War," *International Security* 15:1 (Summer 1990), 52.
6. Paul M. Kennedy, *The Rise and Fall of the Great Powers: Economic Change and Military Conflict from 1500 to 2000* (New York: Random House, 1987).
7. Robert O. Keohane, *After Hegemony: Cooperation and Discord in the World Political Economy* (Princeton, N.J.: Princeton University Press, 1984).
8. J. David Singer and Melvin Small, "Alliance Aggregation and the Onset of War," in *Quantitative International Politics*, ed. J. David Singer (New York: Free Press, 1968), 246–86.
9. Michael C. Webb and Stephen D. Krasner, "Hegemonic Stability Theory: An Empirical Assessment," *Review of International Studies* 15 (1989), 183–98.
10. Robert Gilpin, *War and Change in World Politics* (Cambridge, Eng.: Cambridge University Press, 1981).
11. Martha Finnemore, *The Purpose of Intervention: Changing Beliefs about the Use of Force* (Ithaca, N.Y.: Cornell University Press, 2003), 95.

The State

- *How is the state, the major actor in international relations, defined?*
- *What are the different views of the state held by the various theoretical perspectives?*
- *How is state power measured?*
- *What methods do states use to exercise their power?*
- *Do democracies behave differently from nondemocracies?*
- *What models help us explain how states make foreign-policy decisions?*
- *What are the major contemporary challenges to the state?*

In thinking about international relations, the state is central. We see the United States versus Russia, France and Germany as allies, and North and South Korea as enemies. Much of the history traced in Chapter 2 was the history of how the state developed, emerging from the post-Westphalian framework, and how the state, sovereignty, and the nation developed in tandem. Two of the theoretical perspectives—realism and liberalism—acknowledge the primacy of the state. Yet despite this emphasis on the state, it is inadequately conceptualized. As the scholar James Rosenau laments, "All too many studies posit the state as a symbol without content, as an actor whose nature, motives, and conduct are so self-evident as to obviate any need for precise conceptualizing. Often, in fact, the concept seems to be used as a residual category to explain that which is otherwise inexplicable in macro politics."[1] We need to do better.

The State and the Nation

For an entity to be considered a **state,** four fundamental conditions must be met. First, a state must have a territorial base, a geographically defined boundary. Second, within its borders, a stable population must reside. Third, there should be a government to which this population owes allegiance. Finally, a state has to be recognized diplomatically by other states.

These legal criteria are not absolute. Most states do have a territorial base, though the precise borders are often the subject of dispute. Until the Palestinian Authority was given a measure of control over the West Bank and Gaza, for instance, Palestine was not territorially based. It was, however, given special observer status in international bodies and was viewed as a quasi state. Most states have a stable population, but migrant communities and nomadic peoples cross borders, as the Masai peoples of Kenya and Tanzania do, undetected by state authorities. Most states have some type of institutional structure for governance, but whether the people are obedient to it can be unknown, because of lack of information, or it can be problematic, because the institutional legitimacy of the government is constantly questioned. A state need not have a particular form of government, but most of its people must acknowledge the legitimacy of the government. In 1997, the people of Zaire (now the Democratic Republic of the Congo) told the rest of the international community that they no longer recognized the legitimacy of the government led by Mobutu Sese Seko, thus plunging the country into a civil war. Finally, other states must recognize the state diplomatically; but how many states' recognition does it take for this criterion to be fulfilled? The Republic of Transkei—a tiny piece of real estate carved out of South Africa—was recognized by just one state, South Africa. This action, designed to quell international outrage over South Africa's racist apartheid policy, proved insufficient to give Transkei status as a state, and the territory was soon reincorporated into South Africa. So while the legal conditions for statehood provide a yardstick, that measuring stick is not absolute. Some entities that do not fulfill all the legal criteria are still states.

The definition of a state differs from that of a **nation.** A nation is a group of people who share a set of characteristics. Do a people share a common history and heritage, a common language and customs, or similar lifestyles? If so, then the people make up a nation. It was this feeling of commonality, of people uniting together for a cause, that provided the foundation for the French Revolution and spread to the Americas and to central Europe. It was nationalism—the belief that nations should form their own states—that propelled the formation of a unified Italy and Germany in the nineteenth century. At the core of the concept of a nation is the notion that people having commonalities owe their allegiance to the nation and to its legal representative, the state. The recognition of commonalities among people (and hence of differences from other groups) spread with new technologies and education. When the printing press became widely used, the masses could read in their national languages; with improved methods of transportation, people could travel, witnessing firsthand similarities and differences among peoples. With better communications, elites could use the media to promote unity or sometimes to exploit differences.

Some nations, like Denmark and Italy, formed their own states. This coincidence between state and nation, the **nation-state,** is the foundation for national self-determination, the idea that peoples sharing nationhood have a right to determine how and under what conditions they should live. Other nations are spread among several states. For example, Germans resided and still live not only in a united Germany but in the far-off corners of eastern Europe; Kurds live in Iraq, Iran, and Turkey; Somalis live in Kenya, Ethiopia, and Djibouti as well as in Somalia. Still other states have within their borders several different nations—India, Russia, and South Africa are prominent examples. In these cases, the state and the nation do not coincide. Some nations want to have their own states, as the Kurds have for decades. Other nations, such as the Basques in Spain and France, desire adequate and fair representation within the existing state—special seats in representative bodies, concessions for language diversity, or even territory demarcated for special nationalities. Thus, the post-Westphalian state can take various forms. It may be a nation-state, where there is a congruence between state and nation, such as Denmark and Italy. It may be a state with several nations, like South Africa and India. The United States and Canada present yet another form. In each, a number of different Native American nations are a part of the state, as are multiple immigrant communities. The state and the nation do not coincide. Yet over time, a common identity and nationality is forged, even in the absence of religious, ethnic, or cultural similarity. In the case of the United States, national values reflecting commonly held ideas are expressed in public rituals including reciting the Pledge of Allegiance, singing the national anthem, and civic volunteerism.[2] States are both complex and constantly evolving.

Disputes over state territories and the desires of nations to form their own states have been major sources of instability and even conflict. Of these conflicts none has been as intractable as the conflict between Israeli Jews and Palestinian Arabs, who each claim the same territory. Complicated by several factors—that Jews, Christians, Muslims, and Bahais each claim land or some monuments as sacred, the intense opposition from Arab states to the existence of the state of Israel, and Israel's gradual expansion of its territory through war and settlements—five interstate wars have been fought and two uprisings by the Palestinian people within the territory occupied by Israel have occurred since the formation of the state of Israel in 1948. This leads to a major debate: Should Israel and the Palestinian territories be divided into two separate independent states, Israel and Palestine?

Should Israel and the Palestinian territories be divided into two separate, independent states?

YES:

◆ A Palestinian state would reinforce the democratic commitment to the principle of self-determination.

◆ A Palestinian state would provide stability in the region, resulting in formalized relations between Israel and other Arab states in the region.

◆ A Palestinian state would encourage the return of refugees who fled the territory during the wars between Arabs and Israel.

◆ The establishment of a Palestinian state would frustrate the rise to leadership of more extreme factions such as Hamas or Hezbollah.

◆ The creation of a Palestinian state would end Israeli occupation of the West Bank and shift the burden from Israel to the Palestinians for governing the people there, ensuring their security, and providing for their welfare.

◆ Palestinians living in Israel may choose to move to the newly created Palestine.

NO:

◆ Israel's security would be jeopardized by the neighboring Palestinian state's military capability.

◆ Israel's internal security would be compromised as right-wing Jewish settlers are forced to move from the settlements back to a space-poor Israel.

◆ Separate states would result in a massive population transfer, making war more likely when ethnic tensions are reinforced.

◆ Separate states can only be maintained with a third-party buffer between Israel and Palestine.

◆ Too many issues need to be resolved: determination of borders; the status of Jerusalem and other religious and holy sites; the status of Israeli settlements; water rights.

Contending Conceptualizations of the State

Just as the nation is more than a historic entity, the state is more than a legal entity. There are numerous competing conceptualizations of the state, many of which emphasize concepts absent from the legalistic approach.

Central Middle Eastern Region, 2006

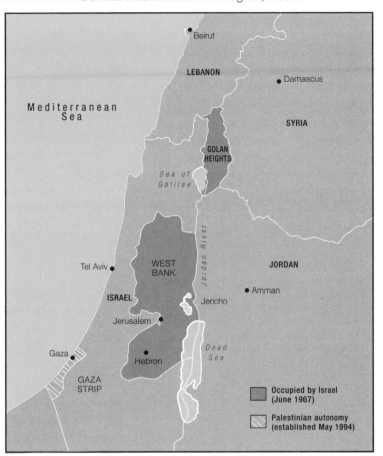

Other concepts of the state include: The state is a normative order, a symbol for a particular society and the beliefs that bind the people living within its borders. It is also the entity that has a monopoly on the legitimate use of violence within a society. The state is a functional unit that takes on a number of important responsibilities, centralizing and unifying them. The perspectives of the state parallel the general theories discussed in Chapters 3 and 4. For two of these theoretical perspectives, the state is paramount.

The Liberal View of the State

In the liberal view, the state enjoys sovereignty but is not an autonomous actor. Just as liberals believe the international system represents a process occurring among many actors, they see the state as a pluralist arena whose

In Focus

THE LIBERAL VIEW OF THE STATE

The state is:

♦ a process, involving contending interests.

♦ a reflection of both governmental and societal interests.

♦ the repository of multiple and changing national interests.

♦ the possessor of fungible sources of power.

function is to maintain the basic rules of the game. These rules ensure that various interests (both governmental and societal) compete fairly and effectively in the game of politics. There is no explicit or consistent national interest; there are many. These interests often compete against each other within a pluralistic framework. A state's national interests change, reflecting the interests and relative power positions of competing groups inside and sometimes also outside of the state.

The Realist View of the State

Realists generally hold a statist, or state-centric, view. They believe that the state is an autonomous actor constrained only by the structural anarchy of the international system. The state enjoys sovereignty, that is, the authority to govern matters that are within its own borders and affect its people, economy, security, and form of government. As a sovereign entity, the state has a consistent set of goals—that is, a national interest—defined in terms of power. Different kinds of power can be translated into military power. While power is of primary importance to realists, as we will see later in this chapter, ideas also matter in their estimation; ideology, for example, can determine the nature of the state, as with the North Korean state under communism. But in international relations, once the state (with power and ideas) acts, according to the realists, it does so as an autonomous, unitary actor.

In Focus

THE REALIST VIEW OF THE STATE

The state is:

♦ an autonomous actor.

♦ constrained only by the anarchy of the international system.

♦ sovereign.

♦ guided by a national interest that is defined in terms of power.

The Radical View of the State

Radicals offer two alternative views of the state, each emphasizing the role of capitalism and the capitalist class in the formation and functioning of the state. The *instrumental* Marxist view sees the state as the executing agent of the bourgeoisie. The bourgeoisie reacts to direct societal pressures, especially to pressures from the capitalist class. The *structural* Marxist view sees the state as operating within the structure of the capitalist system. Within that system, the state is driven to expand, not

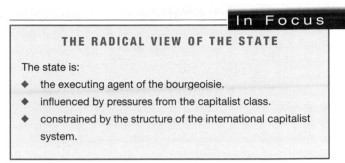

In Focus

THE RADICAL VIEW OF THE STATE

The state is:

◆ the executing agent of the bourgeoisie.

◆ influenced by pressures from the capitalist class.

◆ constrained by the structure of the international capitalist system.

because of the direct pressure of the capitalists but because of the imperatives of the capitalist system. In neither view is there a national interest: state behavior reflects economic goals. In neither case is real sovereignty possible, as the state is continually reacting to external (and internal) capitalist pressures.

The Constructivist View of the State

Since constructivists see both national interests and national identities as social constructs, the state is conceptualized very differently from any of the other theoretical perspectives. To constructivists, national interests are neither material nor given. They are ideational and ever-changing and evolving, both in response to domestic factors and in response to international norms and ideas. States share a variety of goals and values, which they are socialized into by international and nongovernmental organizations. Those norms can change state preferences, which in turn can influence state behavior. So, too, do states have multiple identities, including a shared understanding of national identity, which also changes, altering state preferences and hence state behavior. In short, the state "makes" the system and the system "makes" the state.[3]

Contrasting the Various Views of the State

Conceptualizations of the state can be easily contrasted using the example of an important primary commodity—oil.[4]

In Focus

THE CONSTRUCTIVIST VIEW OF THE STATE

The state is:

◆ a socially constructed entity.

◆ the repository of national interests that change over time.

◆ shaped by international norms that change preferences.

◆ influenced by changing national interests that shape and reshape identities.

◆ socialized by IGOs and NGOs.

Liberals believe that multiple national interests influence state actions: consumer groups desire the oil at the lowest price possible; manufacturers, who depend on bulk supplies to run their factories, prefer stability of the supply of oil, otherwise they risk losing their jobs; producers of oil, including domestic producers, want high prices, so that they will make profits and have incentives to reinvest in drilling. The state itself reflects no consistent viewpoint about the oil; its task is to ensure that the "playing field is level" and the procedural rules are the same for the various players in the market. The substantive outcome of the game—which group's interests predominate—changes depending on circumstances and is of little import to the state. When negotiations occur, the state assures that the various interests have a voice and provides a forum for the interactions. There is no single or consistent national interest: at times, it is low consumer prices; at other times, stability of prices; and at still other times, high prices in order to stimulate domestic production.

A realist interpretation, on the other hand, posits a uniform national interest that is articulated by the state. Oil is a key strategic commodity that is vital for national security. Thus, the state desires stability in the availability and prices of primary commodities. For example, the United States needs to be assured that there will be a safe and secure supply of oil and seeks to obtain it at relatively uniform prices. When the United States negotiates in international forums, with individual supplier states, or with multinational companies, the national interest of the state defined in strategic terms is the bottom line of the negotiations.

In the radical perspective, primary commodity policy reflects the interests of the owner capitalist class aligned with the bourgeoisie (in the instrumental Marxist view) and reflects the structure of the international capitalist system (in structural Marxist thinking). Both views would more than likely see the negotiating process as exploitative, where the weak (poor and dependent groups or states) are exploited for the advancement of strong capitalists or capitalist states. According to radical thinking, the international petroleum companies are the capitalists, aligned with hegemonic states. They are able to negotiate favorable prices to the detriment of developing, oil-producing states such as Mexico or Nigeria.

Thus, liberals, realists, and radicals hold different views about the state. These differences can be seen in four topic areas: the nature of state power (what is power? what are important sources of power?), the exercise of state power (the relative importance of different techniques of statecraft), how foreign policy is made (the statist vs. the bureaucratic or the pluralist view of decisionmaking), and the determinants of foreign policy (the relative importance of domestic vs. international factors).

The Nature of State Power

States are critical actors because they have **power,** which is the ability not only to influence others but to control outcomes so as to produce results that would not have occurred naturally. States have power vis-à-vis each other and with respect to those actors within the state. Yet power itself is multidimensional; there are different kinds of power. The outcome of the power relationship—whether and to what extent power is used or abused—is determined, in part, by the power potential of each of the parties involved.

All theoretical perspectives acknowledge the importance of power. But to realists, power is the currency of international relations. It is the means by which international actors deal with each other. For this reason, we will pay particular attention to the realist view of power, then show how liberals, radicals, and constructivists see power differently.

Natural Sources of Power

Through the exercise of power, states have influence over others and can control the direction of policies and events. Whether power is effective at influencing outcomes depends, in part, on the **power potential** of each party. A state's power potential depends in part on its natural sources of power, each of which is critical to both realist and radical perspectives. The three most important natural sources of power are geographic size and position, natural resources, and population.

Geographic size and position are the natural sources of power recognized first by international relations theorists. A large geographic expanse gives a state automatic power (when one thinks of power, one thinks of large states—Russia, China, the United States, Australia, India, Canada, or Brazil, for instance). Long borders, however, may be a weakness: they must be defended, an expensive and often problematic task.

Two different views about the importance of geography in international relations emerged at the turn of the century within the realist tradition. In the late 1890s, the naval officer and historian Alfred Mahan (1840–1914) wrote of the importance of controlling the sea. He argued that the state that controls the ocean routes controls the world. To Mahan, sovereignty over land was not as critical as having access to and control over sea routes.[5] In 1904, the British geographer Sir Halford Mackinder (1861–1947) countered this view. To Mackinder, the state that had the most power was the one that controlled the Eurasian geographic "heartland": "He who rules Eastern Europe commands the Heartland of Eurasia; who rules the Heartland commands the World Island of Europe, Asia, and Africa, and who rules the World Island commands the world."[6]

Both views have empirical validity. British power in the eighteenth and nineteenth centuries was determined largely by its dominance on the seas, a power that allowed Britain to colonialize distant places, including India, much of Africa, and North and Central America. Russia's lack of easy access to the sea and its resultant inability to wield naval power has been viewed as a persistent weakness in that country's power potential. Control of key oceanic choke points—the Straits of Malacca, Gibraltar, and Hormuz; the Dardanelles; the Persian Gulf; and the Suez and Panama Canals—is viewed as a positive indicator of power potential.

Yet geographic position in Mackinder's heartland of Eurasia has also proven to be a significant source of power potential. More than any other country Germany has acted to secure its power through its control of the heartland of Eurasia, acting very clearly according to Mackinder's dictum, as interpreted by the German geographer Karl Haushofer (1869–1946). Haushofer, who had served in both the Bavarian and the German armies, was disappointed by Germany's loss in World War I. Arguing that Germany could become a powerful state if it could capture the Eurasian heartland, he set out to make geopolitics a legitimate area for academic inquiry. He founded an institute and a journal, thrusting himself into a position as the leading supporter and proponent of Nazi expansion.

But geographic power potential is magnified or constrained by natural resources, a second source of natural power. Controlling a large geographic expanse is not a positive ingredient of power unless that expanse contains natural resources. Petroleum-exporting states like Kuwait, Qatar, and the United Arab Emirates, which are geographically small but have a crucial natural resource, have greater power potential than their sizes would suggest. States need oil and are ready to pay dearly for it, and will even go to war when access to it is denied. States that have such valuable natural resources, regardless of their geographic size, wield power over states that do not. The United States, Russia, and South Africa exert vast power potential because of their diverse natural resources—oil, copper, bauxite, vanadium, gold, and silver. Of course, having a sought-after resource may prove a liability, making states targets for aggressive actions, as Kuwait soberly learned in 1990. The absence of natural resources does not mean that a state has no power potential, however; Japan is not rich in natural resources, but it has parlayed other elements of power so as to make itself an economic powerhouse.

Population is a third natural source of power. Sizable populations, like those found in China (1.3 billion people), India (1.1 billion), the United States (300 million), and Russia (143 million), automatically give power potential, and often great power status, to a state. Although a large population pro-

FIGURE 5.1

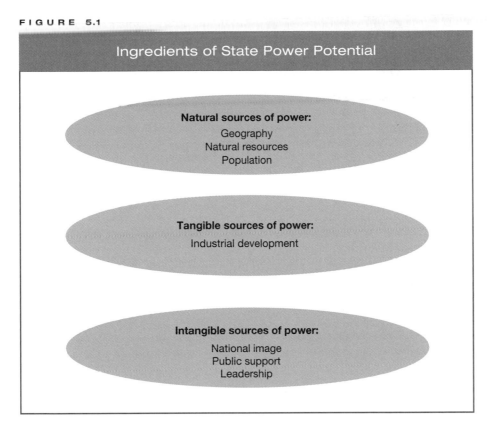

Ingredients of State Power Potential

Natural sources of power:
Geography
Natural resources
Population

Tangible sources of power:
Industrial development

Intangible sources of power:
National image
Public support
Leadership

duces a variety of goods and services, characteristics of that population (poor educational levels, low levels of social services) may serve as a constraint on state power. States with small, highly educated, skilled populations, such as Switzerland, Norway, Austria, and Singapore, can nevertheless fill disproportionately large economic and political niches.

These natural sources of power are modified by the use and organization of power into tangible and intangible sources. These sources are used to enhance, modify, or constrain power potential, as shown in Figure 5.1.

Tangible Sources of Power

Among the tangible sources of power, industrial development is among the most critical. With an advanced industrial capacity, the advantages and disadvantages of geography diminish. Air travel, for example, makes geographic expanse less of a barrier to commerce, yet at the same time makes even large states militarily vulnerable. With industrialization, the importance of population is modified, too. Large but poorly equipped armies are no match for small armies with advanced equipment. Industrialized states generally have higher educational levels, more-advanced technology, and more-efficient use of capital, all of which add to their tangible power potential.

Like realists, radicals acknowledge the importance of power sources and power potential. But where realists organize power around the state, radicals see power in class terms. According to radicals, differences in who has access to the sources of power lead to the creation of different classes, some more powerful (the capitalist class that owns the means of production) than others (the workers). These classes transcend state and national borders.

Intangible Sources of Power

Intangible power sources—national image, public support, leadership—may be as important as the tangible ones, although not to radicals who emphasize material sources of power. People within states have images of their own state's power potential—images that translate into an intangible power ingredient. Canadians have typically viewed themselves as internationally responsible and eager to participate in multilateral peacekeeping missions, to provide generous foreign aid packages, and to respond unselfishly to international emergencies. The state has acted on and, indeed, helped to shape that image, making Canada a more powerful actor than its small population (32 million) would otherwise dictate.

The perception by other states of public support and cohesion is another intangible source of power. China's power was magnified during the leadership of Mao Zedong (1893–1976), when there appeared to be unprecedented public support for the communist leadership and a high degree of societal cohesion. And Israel's successful campaigns in the Middle East in the 1967 and 1973 wars can be attributed in large part to strong public support, including the willingness of Israeli citizens to pay the cost and die for their country when necessary. When that public support is absent, particularly in democracies, the power potential of the state is diminished. Witness the U.S. loss in the Vietnam War, when challenges to and disagreement with the war effort undermined military effectiveness. Loss of public support may also inhibit authoritarian systems. In both the 1991 Gulf War and the 2003 Iraq war, Saddam Hussein's support from his own troops was woefully inadequate: many were not ready to die for the Iraqi regime.

Leadership is another source of intangible power. Visionaries and charismatic leaders such as India's Mohandas Gandhi, France's Charles de Gaulle, the United States's Franklin Roosevelt, Germany's Otto von Bismarck, and Britain's Winston Churchill were able to augment the power potential of their states by taking bold initiatives. Poor leaders, those who squander public resources and abuse the public trust, such as Libya's Muammar Qaddafi, Zaire's Mobutu Sese Seko, and Iraq's Saddam Hussein, diminish the state's power capability and its capacity to exert power over the long term. Liberals, in particular, pay attention to leadership: good leaders can avoid resorting to war; bad leaders may not be able to prevent it.

Clearly, when coupled with the tangible, intangible power sources either augment a state's capacity or diminish its power. Liberals, who have a more expansive notion of power, would more than likely place greater importance on these intangible ingredients, since several are characteristics of domestic processes. Yet different combinations of the sources of power may lead to varying outcomes. The victory by the NATO alliance over Milošević's Yugoslavian forces in 1999 can be explained by the alliance's overwhelming natural sources of power coupled with its strong tangible sources of power. But how can Afghanistan's victory over the Soviet Union in the early 1980s be explained, or the North Vietnamese victory over the United States in the 1970s, or the Algerian victory over France in the early 1950s? In those cases, countries with limited natural and tangible sources of power were able to prevail over those with strong natural and tangible power resources. In these cases, the intangible sources of power, including the willingness of the populations to continue to fight against overwhelming odds, explains victory by the objectively weaker side.[7] Success in using various forms of state power clearly depends on the specific context.

Constructivists, by way of contrast, offer a unique perspective on power. They argue that power includes not only the tangible and intangible sources. In addition, power includes the power of ideas and language—as distinguished from ideology, which fueled the unlikely victory of the objectively weaker side in the cases described above. It is through the power of ideas, and norms, that state identities and nationalism are forged and changed.

The Exercise of State Power

In all theoretical perspectives, power is not just to be possessed, it is to be used. Using state power is a difficult task.

States use a variety of techniques to translate power potential into effective power, namely, diplomacy, economic statecraft, and force. In a particular situation, a state may begin with one approach and then try a number of others to influence the intended target. In other cases, several different techniques may be utilized simultaneously. Which techniques political scientists think states emphasize varies across the theoretical perspectives. And different types of states may make different choices.

The Art of Diplomacy

Traditional **diplomacy** entails states trying to influence the behavior of other actors by negotiating, by taking a specific action or refraining from such an action, or by conducting public diplomacy. In using diplomacy to project power, a state might:

- Express to the target state, either publicly or privately, unhappiness with its policy choice.
- Suggest that a better relationship would follow if the target state's actions changed in a specific way.
- Threaten that negative consequences will follow if the target state continues to move in a specific direction.
- Turn to an international body to seek multilateral legitimization for its position, thus enlisting the support of other states on its behalf.
- Give the target state what it wants (diplomatic recognition, foreign aid) in return for desired actions.
- Remove what the target state wants (reduce foreign aid, withdraw diplomats, sever diplomatic ties) when it takes undesirable actions.

Diplomacy usually begins with bargaining, through direct or indirect communication, in an attempt to reach agreement on an issue. This bargaining may be conducted tacitly among the parties, each of which recognizes that a move in one direction leads to a response by the other that is strategic. The bargaining may be conducted openly in formal negotiations, where one side offers a formal proposal and the other responds in kind; this is generally repeated many times until a compromise is reached. In either case, reciprocity usually occurs, wherein each side responds to the other's moves in kind.

Yet for bargaining to be successful, each party needs to be credible, that is, each party needs to make believable statements, assume likely positions, and be able to back up its position by taking action. Well-intentioned and credible parties will have a higher probability of engaging in successful negotiations.

States seldom enter diplomatic bargaining or negotiations as power equals. Each has information of its own and its opponent's power potential, as well as knowledge of its own goals, even though that information may be imperfect, incomplete, or even just wrong. Thus, although the outcome of the bargaining is almost always mutually beneficial (if not, why bother?), that outcome is not likely to please each of the parties equally. And the satisfaction of each party may change as new information is revealed or as conditions change over time.

Bargaining and negotiations are complex processes, complicated by at least two critical factors. First, most states carry out two levels of bargaining simultaneously: international bargaining between and among states and the bargaining that must occur between the state's negotiators and its various domestic constituencies, both to arrive at a negotiating position and to ratify the agreement reached by the two states. Political scientist Robert Putnam refers to this as the "two-level game."[8] International trade negotiations within the World Trade Organization are such a two-level game. For example, Japan and South Korea bargain with the United States over the liberalization of rice markets. The United States supports liberalization in order to improve the balance of trade between it and the respective Asian powers; by advocating this position, the United States supports its own domestic rice producers, located in the key electoral states of California and Texas. Japan and South Korea have powerful domestic interests opposing liberalization, including rice farmers strategically located in virtually all voting constituencies. Thus, in each case, the United States and Japan or South Korea are each conducting two sets of negotiations: one with the foreign state and the other within the domestic political arena. What makes the game unusually complex is that "moves that are rational for one player at one board . . . may be impolitic for that same player at the other board."[9] The negotiator is the formal link between the two levels of negotiation. Realists see the two-level game as constrained primarily by the structure of the international system, whereas liberals more readily acknowledge domestic pressures and incentives.

Second, bargaining and negotiating are, in part, a culture-bound activity. Approaches to bargaining vary across cultures—a view accepted among liberals, who place importance on state differences. At least two styles of negotiations have been identified.[10] These two different styles may lead to contrasting outcomes.

In the negotiations during the 1970s for the New International Economic Order (NIEO), for example, culture influenced the negotiating style adopted by the South. Specifically, during bargaining on specific issues, the South argued in a deductive style—from general principles to particular applications. The task that the South saw for itself, then, was for its states to agree among themselves on basic principles of the NIEO and leave the particular details to be worked out at a later date. This approach conveniently masked conflict over details until a later stage. The South's approach contrasted sharply with that preferred by many countries in the North, who favored discussion of concrete detail, eschewing grand philosophical debate. The United States and Great Britain, key actors in the North, both favored pragmatically addressing concrete problems and resolving specific issues before broader principles were crystallized. These differences in negotiating approaches led, in part, to a stalemate in negotiations and eventually the failure to achieve any meaningful concessions.[11]

The use of **public diplomacy** is an increasingly popular diplomatic technique in a communication-linked world. Public diplomacy involves targeting both foreign publics and elites, attempting to create an overall image that enhances a country's ability to achieve its diplomatic objectives. For instance, former First Lady Hillary Rodham Clinton's international travels highlighting the role of women were designed to project a humanitarian image of the United States, built around caring about people, including women and children, and promoting values, democracy, and human rights.

Before and during the 2003 Iraq war, public diplomacy became a particularly useful diplomatic instrument. American administration officials, notably Secretary of State Colin Powell, National Security Advisor Condoleezza Rice, and Secretary of Defense Donald Rumsfeld, not only made the case for war to the American people in news interviews and newspaper editorials, but lobbied friendly and opposing states both directly in negotiations and indirectly through various media outlets, including independent Arab media such as the Al Jazeera television station. The Department of State ran media campaigns aimed at the Arab world and has since allocated $30 million for a new Mideast radio network aimed at Arab youth. The network will feature Arab and Western pop music, and one of its goals is to curb anti-American feelings. In the communication age, states have yet another diplomatic instrument.

Economic Statecraft

States use more than words to exercise power. States may use economic statecraft—both positive and negative **sanctions**—to try to influence other states.[12] Positive sanctions involve offering a "carrot," enticing the target state to act in the desired way by rewarding moves made in the desired direction. The assumption is that positive incentives will lead the target state to change its behavior. Negative sanctions, however, may be more the norm: threatening to act or actually taking actions that punish the target state for moves made in the direction not desired. The goal of using the "stick" (negative sanctions) may be to punish or reprimand the target state for actions taken or may be to try to change the future behavior of the target state. Table 5.1 provides examples of positive and negative sanctions used in economic statecraft.

A state's ability to use these instruments of economic statecraft depends on its power potential. States with a variety of power sources have more instruments at their disposal. Clearly, only economically well-endowed countries can grant licenses, offer investment guarantees, grant preferences to specific countries, house foreign assets, or boycott effectively. Radicals often point to this fact to illustrate the hegemony of the international capitalist system.

Diplomacy and Human Security: A View from Canada

All states use diplomacy to stake their positions internationally. Depending on their role in the international system, states may choose to emphasize certain diplomatic approaches or specialize in certain functions to differentiate themselves internationally. Canada has adopted this approach.

Former Prime Minister Pierre Trudeau once remarked that for Canada, living on the northern border of the United States is "like sleeping with an elephant. No matter how friendly and even tempered the beast . . . one is affected by every twitch and grunt."[a] Hence, Canadian diplomacy is generally supportive of the United States. Canada's membership in the Group of Eight (G8) industrialized powers, and its participation in NATO operations (Kosovo and Afghanistan) and U.S.-led coalitions (Korea and 1991 Gulf War) confirm this observation.

Canada has sometimes found a particular diplomatic approach or theme which serves to differentiate it from the United States and reflect distinct Canadian values. During the Cold War, Canada sent peacekeeping troops to every U.N. operation, which reflected the country's strong support for multilateral institutions. Even after the end of the Cold War, Canada adopted a special role: training peacekeepers from developing countries, setting up command structures, and providing communication facilities for multilateral peacekeeping operations.

In the 1990s, this policy solidified into what is called "niche diplomacy." Niche diplomacy involves concentrating resources into a few specialized areas in which Canada can play an effective role in influencing others to adopt its desired outcomes. Canada has used this diplomatic tool to promote "human security" through initiatives like the Ottawa Convention in 1997, which outlawed antipersonnel land mines and expressed support for human rights. Former foreign affairs minister Lloyd Axworthy is largely responsible for this human security approach, providing leadership in international humanitarian affairs and hosting the first conference leading to the Kyoto Protocol on global warming. This approach to diplomacy, relying on soft power resources, was concurrent with dramatic cuts in Canada's hard power capability.

During the 1990s, military spending in Canada decreased and the size of its military forces was cut. September 11, 2001, and the 2006 plots to carry out terrorism in Ottawa and Toronto have led to a reevaluation of that choice. Defense expenditures were increased, and intelligence cooperation with the United States expanded as Canada recognized that its security, borders, and economy were interdependent with the United States. Yet while Canada supported the U.S. invasion of Afghanistan in 2001 and sent provincial reconstruction teams and special operations officers there in 2005, Canada opposed the 2003 Iraqi operation, making a strategic choice. Despite the changes in the security environment, Canada has continued to push for initiatives in human security, addressing issues such as child soldiers, women's rights, and global warming.

For Critical Analysis

1. To what extent does Canada's relationship with the United States influence its foreign policy strategies?
2. What are the characteristics of the issues on which Canada chooses to focus its niche diplomacy?

[a]Pierre Elliott Trudeau, "On Relations with the U.S.," Address to the National Press Club, Ottawa, Canada, March 26, 1969.

TABLE 5.1

Types of Sanctions in Economic Statecraft		
Type	**Sanction**	**Example**
Positive	Give the target state the same trading privileges given to your best trading partner (most-favored-nation [MFN] status) as incentive for policy change.	U.S. granted MFN status to China, in spite of that country's poor human rights record.
	Allow sensitive trade with target state, including militarily useful equipment.	France and Germany export equipment to Iran, even though Iran's government is hostile to the West.
	Give corporations investment guarantees or tax breaks as incentives to invest in target state.	U.S. offered insurance to U.S. companies willing to invest in post-apartheid South Africa.
	Allow importation of target state's products into your country at best tariff rates.	Industrialized states allow imports from developing countries at lower tariff rates.
Negative	Freeze target state's assets.	U.S. froze Iranian assets during 1979 hostage crisis; U.N. froze Libyan assets 1993–99; U.N. froze Afghanistan's assets under Taliban 1999–2001.
	Blacklist target state.	Arab states blacklisted companies that conducted business in Israel.
	Boycott goods and services of target states.	South Africa was boycotted for apartheid policy in 1970s and 1980s; exports of dual-use technologies were prohibited to Iraq, Iran, Syria, Libya, North Korea, Sudan in the 1990s and after because of their support of terrorism; air links with Libya were canceled 1992–99 because of its support of terrorism.
	Sanction one or all products of target state.	Iraq was forbidden to sell oil internationally 1991–2003 as punishment for the 1991 Gulf War; U.N. sanctions were imposed against Haiti 1990, 1993–94 to try and overthrow the military government there; Arab League has imposed sanctions on Israel since 1948.

While radicals deny it, liberals argue that developing states do have some leverage in economic statecraft in special circumstances. If a state or group of states controls a key resource of which there is limited production, their power is strengthened. Among the primary commodities, only petroleum has this potential, and it gave the Arab members of the Organization of Petroleum Exporting Countries (OPEC) the ability to impose oil sanctions on the United States and the Netherlands when those two countries strongly supported Israel in the 1973 Arab-Israeli War.

South Africa illustrates a case of relative success in the use of economic sanctions. When positive sanctions in the form of the Reagan administration's "constructive engagement" policy failed to work, the U.S. Congress approved harsh sanctions against South Africa's apartheid regime in 1986, over a presidential veto. Under the Comprehensive Anti-Apartheid Act, the United States joined with other countries and the United Nations, which had already imposed economic sanctions. In 1992, the white-controlled South African regime announced a political opening that led to the end of apartheid and majority rule. Most commentators conclude that sanctions probably had an important effect on the regime to change policy. In fact, the 1990s has been referred to as the sanctions decade.[13]

In general, however, economic sanctions have not been very successful. In the short term, the public often rallies around a leader when threatened from outside. States gradually make economic changes to compensate for the sanctioning. Over the long term, it is difficult to maintain international cohesion, because states imposing the sanctions find it ultimately advantageous to bust the sanction, thereby gaining economically.

Increasingly since the mid-1990s, states have imposed so-called smart sanctions, including freezing assets of governments and/or individuals and imposing commodities sanctions (oil, timber, diamonds). Targeting has involved not just "what" but also "who," as the international community has tried to affect specific individuals and rebel groups, reduce ambiguity and loopholes, and avoid the high humanitarian costs of general sanctions. With these modifications, liberal theorists continue to place special emphasis on the diplomatic, economic, and less coercive avenues of power, since they view power as multidimensional. Realist theorists believe it is necessary in exercising power to resort to or threaten to use force on a more regular basis.

The Use of Force

Force (and the threat of force) is another critical instrument of statecraft and is central to realist thinking. Similar to economic statecraft, force or its threat may be used either to get a target state to do something or to undo something it has done—compellence—or to keep an adversary from doing something—deterrence.[14] Liberal theorists are more apt to advocate compellent strategies, moving cautiously to deterrence, whereas realists promote deterrence.

With the strategy of **compellence,** a state tries, by threatening to use force, to get another state to do something or to undo an act that it has undertaken. The prelude to the 1991 Gulf War serves as an excellent example: The United States, the United Nations, and coalition members tried to get Saddam Hussein to change his actions with the compellent strategy of escalating threats. Iraq's invasion of Kuwait was initially widely condemned, and then formal U.N. Security Council measures gave multilateral legitimacy to the condemnation. Next, Iraq's external economic assets were frozen and economic sanctions were imposed. Finally, U.S. and coalition military forces were mobilized and deployed, and specific deadlines were given for Iraq to withdraw from Kuwait. During each step of the compellent strategy of escalation, one message was communicated to Iraq: withdraw from Kuwait or more coercive actions will follow. Similarly, the Western alliance sought to get Serbia to stop abusing the human rights of Kosovar Albanians and to withdraw its military forces from the region. Compellence was also used before the 2003 Iraq war, when the United States and others threatened Saddam Hussein that if certain actions were not taken, then war would follow. Threats began when George W. Bush labeled Iraq a member of the "axis of evil"; they escalated when the United Nations found Iraq to be in material breach of a U.N. resolution. Then in March 2003, Great Britain, one of the coalition partners, gave Iraq ten days to comply with the U.N. resolution. And on March 17, the last compellent threat was issued: Bush gave the Baathist regime forty-eight hours to leave Iraq as its last chance to avert war. In all of these cases, it was necessary to resort to an invasion because compellence via an escalation of threats failed. Note that compellence ends once the use of force begins.

With the strategy of deterrence, states commit themselves to punishing a target state if the target state takes an undesired action. Threats of actual war are used as an instrument of policy to dissuade a state from pursuing certain courses of action. If the target state does not take the undesired action, deterrence is successful and conflict is avoided. If it does choose to act despite the deterrent threat, then the first state will presumably deliver a devastating blow.

Since the advent of nuclear weapons in 1945, deterrence has taken on a special meaning. Today if a state chooses to resort to violence against a nuclear state, there is the possibility that nuclear weapons will be launched against it in retaliation. If this happens, the cost of the aggression will be unacceptable, especially if both states have nuclear weapons, in which case the viability of both societies will be at stake. Theoretically, therefore, states that recognize the destructive capability of nuclear weapons and know that others have a **second-strike capability**—the ability to retaliate even after an attack has been launched by an opponent—will refrain from taking aggressive action, using its **first-strike capability.** Deterrence is then successful.

For either compellence or deterrence to be effective, states have to lay the groundwork. They must clearly and openly communicate their objectives and capabilities, be willing to make good on the threats or to fulfill the promises, and have the capacity to follow through with their commitments. In short, a state's credibility is essential for compellence and deterrence. Yet this is not a one-sided, unilateral process; it is a strategic interaction where the behavior of each is determined not only by one's own behavior, but by the actions and responses of the other.

Compellence and deterrence can fail, however. If compellence and deterrence fail, states may go to war, but even during war, states have choices. They choose the type of weaponry (nuclear or nonnuclear, strategic or tactical, conventional or chemical and biological), the kind of targets (military or civilian, city or country), and the geographic locus (city, state, region) to be targeted. They may choose to respond in kind, to escalate, or de-escalate. In war, both implicit and explicit negotiation takes place, over both how to fight the war and how to end it. We will return to a discussion of war in Chapter 8.

Thinking About Choices: Game Theory

Force and economic instruments are the major techniques states have at their command to translate power potential into power. Economic and military-strategic theorists have developed ways to analyze more systematically the choices states make and the probable outcomes. This method is called **game theory.** Game theory assumes that each state is a unitary actor with one national interest and has a unique set of options and stipulated payoffs associated with each of the options. The game is about strategic interaction and the interdependence of individual strategies.

Recall from Chapter 3 the discussion of the prisoner's dilemma. In that situation, two prisoners were each given the option of confessing to a particular crime but would not know the choice made by the other prisoner. The choices and outcomes in this situation are illustrated in the two-by-two matrix in Figure 5.2. The payoff numbers in the matrix are arbitrary, but they denote the magnitude of the potential gains or losses: the greater the number, the more favorable the payoff. The goal of each prisoner is to avoid the worst possible outcome, and neither prisoner knows which option the other will choose. Suppose you are prisoner 1: according to the matrix in Figure 5.2, your potential payoffs are (clockwise from the upper-left cell) -1, -10, -8, and 0. The worst possible payoff to you is -10, which you would get if you did not confess and prisoner 2 did. Thus to avoid this worst possible outcome, you decide to confess, limiting your potential payoffs to 0 or -8 but avoiding the worst possible, -10. The situation is exactly the same from the perspective of prisoner 2. The solution to the game, then, is that both prisoners confess—an outcome that is neither the best nor the worst for both players. This solution is a safer solution for both players but not the optimum one, where both individuals

FIGURE 5.2

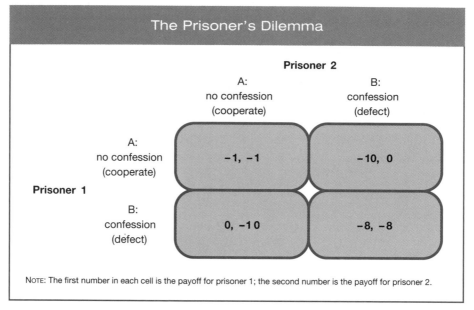

The Prisoner's Dilemma

	Prisoner 2	
	A: no confession (cooperate)	B: confession (defect)
Prisoner 1 A: no confession (cooperate)	−1, −1	−10, 0
B: confession (defect)	0, −10	−8, −8

NOTE: The first number in each cell is the payoff for prisoner 1; the second number is the payoff for prisoner 2.

cooperate. In this game, there is a disincentive for the individual or the state to cooperate, though cooperation may occur over time, as the result of repeated interaction.

Not all games are prisoner's dilemmas. Game theory can also be used in situations where one player wins and the other loses, zero-sum games. In military confrontations, one side wins and the other loses, or in international crises, one state may win (power or prestige), while the other may lose (power or face). Games may also be non-zero sum with many players. In these situations, some of the parties may win, while others may lose. There are elements of both cooperation and conflict. In general, international relations is best conceptualized as a non-zero-sum game with many players, engaged in repeatedly over an extended time period.

There are advantages to using game theory as a simplification of the complex choices states make. Game theory forces both analysts and policymakers to examine assumptions systematically, helping to clarify the choices available and offering possibilities that may not have otherwise been explored. It helps the analyst and the policymaker to see not just their own state's position but also where the other state may stand. It permits simplicity; choices are seen as interdependent.

Yet there are also clear limitations to game theory. Game theory makes some critical assumptions: it assumes a unitary state, in which internal factors play little role in determining a state's preferences. It assumes that the unitary state acts rationally, that states choose the best overall option available. It gives arbitrary payoff structures in advance, whereas in reality states may not know the relative values attached to their various choices or those of the other side. It assumes that the game occurs one time, although most realize that much of international relations is really an extended set of games between the same actors. Thus, the outcome of multiple iterations—in which knowing the choice an actor made at one point in time helps each side to predict the other's choice at a subsequent time period—may be quite different from the one-time encounter. All of these criticisms are key points made by neoliberal institutionalists.

Democracy and Foreign Policy

Although all states use diplomacy, economy, and force to conduct foreign policy, do policy choices vary by type of government? Specifically, do democratic states conduct foreign policy and make policy choices that are any different from the choices and policies made by authoritarian states and leaders? We might expect that in democratic states, the intangible sources of power—national image, public support, and leadership—may matter more since leaders are responsible to the public through elections. If true, then is the foreign policy behavior of democratic states any different from the behavior of nondemocratic or authoritarian states?

The question has occupied philosophers, diplomatic historians, and political scientists for centuries. In *Perpetual Peace* (1795), Immanuel Kant argued that the spread of democracy would change international politics by eliminating war. He reasoned that the public would be very cautious in supporting war since they, the public, are apt to suffer the most devastating effects. Thus, leaders will act in a restrained fashion and tend to abstain from war because of domestic constraints.[15] Since Kant's time, other explanations have been added to the democratic peace hypothesis. Perhaps democracies are just more satisfied with the status quo and unwilling to support change. Perhaps democracies are just more likely to be allies of each other since they share similar values. Many of these ideas found resonance with Woodrow Wilson, a major advocate of the democratic peace.

Political scientists have developed an extensive research agenda related to the democratic peace hypothesis. Are democracies more peaceful than nondemocracies? More specifically, do democracies fight each other less than nondemocracies do? Do democracies fight nondemocracies more than they fight each other? Gathering data on different kinds of warfare over several centuries, researchers have addressed these sets of questions. One study has confirmed the hypothesis that democracies do not go to war against one another: since 1789 no wars have been fought strictly between independent states with democratically elective governments. Another study has found that wars involving democracies have tended to be less bloody but more protracted, although between 1816 and 1965, democratic governments were not noticeably more peace-prone or passive.[16] But the evidence is not that clear-cut and explanations are partial. Why are states in the middle of transitions to democracy more prone to conflict? How can we explain that when democratic states have not gone to war, it may have had little to do with their democratic character?

Why have some of the findings on the democratic peace been divergent? Even within a single research program there may be serious differences in conclusions, based on the assumptions made by researchers and the methods used. Scholars who use the behavioral approach themselves point to some of the difficulties. Some researchers analyzing the democratic peace use different definitions of the key variables—democracy and war; for example, some researchers distinguish between liberal democracies (for example, the United States and Germany) and illiberal democracies (Yugoslavia in the late 1990s). Also, the data for war would be different if wars with less than 1,000 deaths were included, as they are in some studies. And other studies of the democratic peace examine different time periods. Such differences in research protocol might well lead to different research findings. Yet even with these qualifications, the basic finding from the research is that democracies do not engage in militarized disputes against each other. That finding *is* statistically significant; that is, it does not occur by random chance. Overall, democracies are not more pacific than nondemocracies; democracies just do not fight *each other*. In fact, autocracies are just as peaceful with each other as are democracies, so that one could also talk of an autocratic peace.

Models of Foreign-Policy Decisionmaking

How are specific foreign-policy decisions actually made? Do democracies make foreign-policy choices differently from nondemocracies? Do realists, liberals, and radicals view the decisionmaking process differently?

The Rational Model

Most policymakers, particularly during crises, and most realists begin with the rational model, in which foreign policy is conceived of as actions chosen by the national government that maximize its strategic goals and objectives. The state is assumed to be a unitary actor with established goals, a set of options, and an algorithm for deciding which option best meets its goals. The process is relatively straightforward, as shown in Figure 5.3. Taking as our case the 1996 incident in which China was testing missiles by launching

FIGURE 5.3

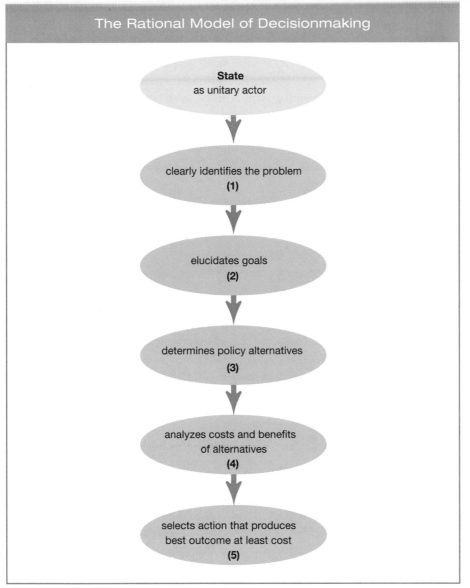

The Rational Model of Decisionmaking

State
as unitary actor

clearly identifies the problem
(1)

elucidates goals
(2)

determines policy alternatives
(3)

analyzes costs and benefits
of alternatives
(4)

selects action that produces
best outcome at least cost
(5)

them over Taiwan, a rational approach would view Taiwan's decisionmaking process about how to respond in the following manner (the numbers correspond to the numbered steps in Figure 5.3):

1. The People's Republic of China is testing missiles over Taiwan, in direct threat to the latter's national security and just prior to Taiwan's first democratic election.

2. Both Taiwan and its major supporter, the United States, have as their goal to stop the firings immediately.

3. The Taiwanese have several options: do nothing; wait until the end of the Taiwanese elections, hoping that the Chinese will then stop; issue diplomatic protests; bring the issue to the U.N. Security Council; threaten or conduct military operations against China by bombing its missile sites or mounting a land invasion; or threaten or use economic statecraft (cut trade, impose sanctions or embargoes).

4. The Taiwanese government analyzes the benefits and costs of these options. Mounting an invasion, for example, may eliminate the problem but will likely result in the destruction of Taiwan, an unacceptable side effect.

5. Taiwan, with U.S. support, chooses as a first step diplomatic protest, in the hope that the antagonistic firing will cease after the election. Doing nothing clearly would have suggested that the missile testing was acceptable, which it was not. Military action against China was too extreme, with possibly disastrous consequences.

In times of crisis, when decisionmakers are confronted by a surprising, threatening event and have only a short time to make a decision about how to respond, then using the rational model as a way to assess the other side's behavior is an appropriate choice. If a state knows very little about the internal domestic processes of another state—as the United States did vis-à-vis mainland China during the era of Mao Zedong—then decisionmakers have little alternative but to assume that the other state will follow the rational model. Indeed, most U.S. assessments of decisions taken by the Soviet Union during the Cold War, in the absence of better information, were based on a rational model: the Soviet Union had a goal, its alternatives were clearly laid out, and decisions were taken to maximize its achievement of its goal. Only since the opening of the Soviet governmental archives following the end of the Cold War

THEORY IN BRIEF

The Realist Perspective on State Power and Policy

Nature of state power	Emphasis on power as key concept in international relations; geography, natural resources, population especially important
Using state power	Emphasis on coercive techniques of power; use of force acceptable
How foreign policy is made	Emphasis on rational model of decisionmaking; unitary state actor assumed
Determinants of foreign policy	Largely external / international determinants

have historians found that, in fact, the Soviets had no concrete plans for turning Poland, Hungary, Romania, or other East European states into communist dictatorships or socialist economies, as the United States believed. The Soviets appear to have been guided by events happening in the region, not by a specific rational plan or ideology.[17] The United States was incorrect in imputing the rational model to Soviet decisionmaking, but in the absence of complete information, this was the least risky approach: the anarchy of the international system means that a state assumes one's opponent engages in rational decisionmaking.

The Bureaucratic/Organizational Model

Not all decisions occur during crises and not all decisions are taken with so little knowledge of domestic politics in other countries. So foreign policy decisions may be products of either subnational governmental organizations or bureaucracies (departments or ministries of government). **Organizational politics** emphasizes the standard operating procedures and processes of an organization. Decisions arising from organizational processes depend heavily on precedents; major changes in policy are unlikely. Conflicts can occur when different subgroups within the organization have different goals and procedures.

Bureaucratic politics, on the other hand, occurs among members of the bureaucracy representing different interests. Decisions determined by bureaucratic politics flow from the pull and haul, or tug-of-war, among these departments, groups, or individuals. In either political scenario, the ultimate decision depends on the relative strength of the individual bureaucratic players or the organizations they represent (see Figure 5.4).

Trade policy provides a ripe area to see the bureaucratic/organizational model of decisionmaking at work. For example, South Korean agricultural markets were traditionally closed to foreign imports. This closure was designed to protect South Korean producers of major agricultural products, including rice, beef, and tobacco. In the 1980s, pressure from the United States to open these markets grew. The South Korean Ministry of Agriculture, Forestry, and Fisheries strongly opposed the opening of agricultural markets, arguing that South Korean farmers would be put out of work. But the Ministry of Finance and the Ministry of Trade and Industry were concerned about retaliatory measures that the United States might take against South Korean manufacturers entering the U.S. market. Policy change resulted from the pull and haul among these various ministries. The Ministry of Agriculture capitulated on tobacco, opening the market to full liberalization, but for rice, whose producers were the strongest and the best organized politically, movement toward liberalization was very slow.

FIGURE 5.4

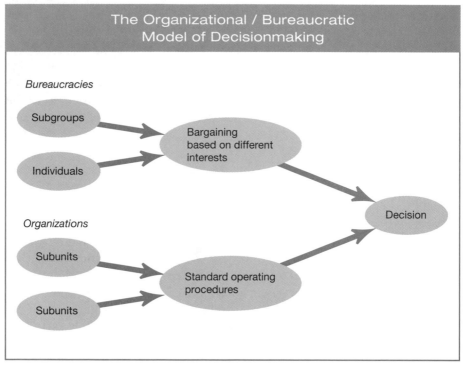

The Organizational / Bureaucratic
Model of Decisionmaking

Bureaucracies

Subgroups

Individuals

Bargaining based on different interests

Decision

Organizations

Subunits

Subunits

Standard operating procedures

Noncrisis situations, like the South Korean foreign-trade-policy issue just described, are apt to reflect the bureaucratic/organizational model. When time is no real constraint, informal bureaucratic groups and departments have time to mobilize. They hold meetings, hammering out positions that satisfy all the contending interests. The decisions arrived at are not always the most rational ones; rather they are the decisions that **"satisfice"**—satisfy the most different constituents without ostracizing any.

Liberals especially turn to this model of decisionmaking behavior in their analyses, since for them the state itself is only the playing field; the actors are the

THEORY IN BRIEF

The Liberal Perspective on State Power and Policy

Nature of state power	Multiple power sources; tangible and intangible sources
Using state power	Broad range of power techniques; preference for noncoercive alternatives
How foreign policy is made	Organizational / bureaucratic and pluralist models of decisionmaking
Determinants of foreign policy	Largely domestic determinants

FIGURE 5.5

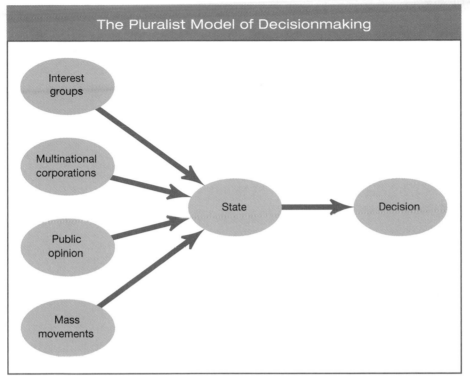

The Pluralist Model of Decisionmaking

competing interests in bureaucracies and organizations. The model is most relevant in large, democratic countries, which usually have highly differentiated institutional structures for foreign-policy decisionmaking and where responsibility and jurisdiction are divided among a number of different units. For example, most foreign-trade decisions made by the United States, Japan, or the governments of European Union countries closely approximate the bureaucratic/organizational model. But to use this model in policy-making circles to analyze or predict other states' behavior or to use it to analyze decisions for scholarly purposes, one must have detailed knowledge of a country's foreign-policy structures and bureaucracies. In the absence of such information and in a crisis situation where policy must be determined quickly, the rational model is the best alternative.

The Pluralist Model

The **pluralist model,** in contrast to the other two alternatives, attributes decisions to bargaining conducted among domestic sources—the public, interest groups, mass movements, and multinational corporations (see Figure 5.5). In noncrisis situations and on particular issues, especially economic ones, societal groups may play very important roles. No one doubts the power of the rice farmer lobbies in both Japan and South Korea in preventing the importation of cheap, U.S.-grown rice. No one disputes the success of French wine-growers in preventing the importation of cheap Greek or Spanish wines by publicly dumping their product for media attention. No one denies the power of U.S. shoe manufacturers in supporting restrictions on the importation of Brazilian-made shoes into the United States, despite U.S. governmental initiatives to allow imports of products from developing countries.

Societal groups have a variety of ways of forcing decisions in their favor or constraining decisions. They can mobilize the media and public opinion, lobby the government agencies responsible for making the decision, influence the appropriate representative bodies (the U.S. Congress, the French National Assembly, the Japanese Diet), organize transnational networks of people with comparable interests, and, in the case of high-profile heads of multinational corporations, make direct contacts with the highest governmental officials. The decision made will reflect these diverse societal interests and strategies—a result that is particularly compatible with liberal thinking. The movement to ban land mines in the 1990s is an example of a societally based pluralist foreign-policy decision, a process reflecting democratic practices.

Both realists and liberals acknowledge that states have real choices in foreign policy, no matter which model explains the behavior; radicals, however, see fewer real choices. In the radical view, capitalist states' interests are determined by the structure of the international system and their decisions are dictated by the economic imperatives of the dominant class. Internal domestic elites have been co-opted by international capitalists like multinational corporations.

Each alternative model offers a simplification of the foreign-policy decisionmaking process. Each provides a window on how groups (both governmental and nongovernmental) influence the foreign-policy process. But these models do not provide answers to other critical issues. They do not tell us the content of a specific decision or indicate the effectiveness with which the foreign policy was implemented.

TABLE 5.2

Challenges to State Power	
Forces	**Effects on the State**
Globalization—political, economic, cultural	Undermines state sovereignty; interferes with state exercise of power
Transnational crime	State is unable to curb due to expansion of communication networks
Transnational movements	
Religious/ideological	Seek loyalty and commitment of individuals beyond the state; want to transform the ideology of the state
Political	Change state behavior on a specific problem or issue
Ethnonational movements	Seek own state; attempt to replace current government with one representing the interests of the movement

Challenges to the State

The state, despite its centrality, is facing challenges from the processes of globalization, religiously and ideologically based transnational movements, and ethnonational movements (see Table 5.2). As Jessica Matthews succinctly explains in her seminal *Foreign Affairs* article of 1997, there has been a power shift: "The steady concentration of power in the hands of states that began in 1648 with the Peace of Westphalia is over, at least for a while."[18]

Globalization

Externally, the state is buffeted by **globalization,** growing integration of the world in terms of politics, economics, communications, and culture, a process that increasingly undermines traditional state sovereignty. Politically, the state is confronted by globalizing issues—environmental degradation and disease—which governments cannot manage alone. Such issues require unprecedented political cooperation, as illustrated by the 2003 SARS (Severe Acute Respiratory Syndrome) threat, when the governments of the developed world had to respond to a growing epidemic in China, where national authorities did not have the capacity to address the issue. More and more, such cooperative actions require states to compromise their sovereignty. Economically, states and financial markets are increasingly tied inextricably together; multinational corporations and the internationalization of production and consumption make it ever more difficult for states to regulate their own economic policies. Culturally, new and intrusive technologies—e-mail, fax machines, direct satellite broadcasting, worldwide television networks such as CNN—increasingly undermine the state's control over information and hence its control over its citizenry. Countries such as Saudi Arabia and others in the Persian Gulf region have fought losing battles trying to "protect" their populations from crass Western values transmitted through modern media. China, too, is losing the battle to limit information coming into the country via the Internet. As Jessica Matthews explains, "The most powerful engine of change in the relative decline of the state and the rise of non-state actors is the computer and telecommunications revolution, whose deep political and social consequences have been almost completely ignored. . . . In every sphere of activity, instantaneous access to information and the ability to put it to use multiplies the number of players who matter and reduces the number who command great authority."[19]

Transnational Crime

Nowhere is this challenge to the state more evident than in the rise of transnational crime—illicit activities made easier by globalization. Growing in value, extending in scope, and becoming highly specialized, these activities have been facilitated by multiple transportation routes, rapid communication, and electronic financial networks. Transnational crime has led to the accelerating movement of illegal drugs, counterfeit goods, smuggled weapons, laundered money, trade in body parts, and trafficking in poor and exploited people. Organized around flexible networks, circuitous trafficking routes, and lubricated by electronic transfer of funds, transnational crime has created new businesses while distorting national and regional economies. States and governments are largely incapable of responding: rigid bureaucracies, laborious procedures, interbureaucratic fighting, and corrupt officials undermine states' efforts. In fact, some states—such as China, North Korea, and Nigeria—actively participate in these illicit activities or do nothing to stop them because key elites are making major profits. In short, most states are failing in the battle to control and punish the transgressors, undermining their own sovereignty.[20]

Transnational Movements

Other products of globalization and now political forces that in their own right challenge the state are **transnational movements,** particularly religious and ideological movements. In Christendom, the main movements are Pentecostalism and Evangelicalism. Now 400 million strong, and expanding rapidly in the developing world, these movements reject secularism and attempt to turn political social, and individual loyalties away from the state and toward religious ideas. These movements are antisecular and antimodern. Members of Christian cults, however, have posed serious problems for state authority. One such group, The Covenant, the Sword, and the Arm of the Lord, is examined in Jessica Stern's revealing book, *Terror in the Name of God*.[21] The cult began as a commune, with members living under primitive conditions and sharing Bible readings and prayer, but the group gradually cut themselves off from the outside world. They came to believe that Zionists, socialists, communists, and others had taken over the United States, as exemplified in the U.N., the IMF, and the Council on Foreign Relations—all indications of Satan's power. Joining forces with other right wing groups, they planned—as directed by God—to poison residents in American cities and to destroy the so-called Zionist Occupied Government. Although federal authorities foiled the plot, the group has since joined with Identity Christianity, the major group of the racist right wing. Among its adherents were Timothy McVeigh, responsible for the Oklahoma City Federal Building bombing in 1995.

States are also confronted with **Islamic fundamentalism.** While Islamic fundamentalists come from many different countries and support different strategies for reaching their end goal, believers are united by wanting to change states and societies by basing them on the ideas contained in the texts of Islam. This movement presents both a basic critique of what is wrong in many secular states, both Christian and Islamic, and solutions that call for radical state transformation. Islamic fundamentalists see a long-standing discrepancy between the political and economic aspirations of states and the actual conditions of uneven economic distribution and rule by corrupt elites. Some advocate violence as the means to overthrow these corrupt rulers and to fight for their Palestinian brethren, who they believe have been wronged by Israel and its Western supporters; others suggest that change can occur without the use of violence.

The fight by the Afghans and their Islamic supporters against the Soviet Union in the 1980s proved to be a galvanizing event for the movement of Islamic fundamentalism. It brought together religiously committed yet politically and economically disaffected young Islamists from all over the world; fighting the "godless" enemy forged group cohesion; and fighting the better-equipped Soviet military allowed them to hone their guerrilla tactics. These *mujahideen* (holy warriors) gained confidence by beating the Soviets into retreat. When they returned to their homelands in Saudi Arabia, Egypt, and other parts of the Middle East, they were imbued with a mission—to wage *jihad* (holy war) against what they view as illegitimate regimes. During the fight in Afghanistan, Osama bin Laden, a Saudi national, emerged as a charismatic leader. When the Taliban assumed power in Afghanistan in

1996, bin Laden and what remained of the *mujahideen* formed Al Qaeda. Yet, as we shall see in Chapter 8, Al Qaeda is just one of many Islamic fundamentalist groups, although its successful terrorist attacks on September 11, 2001, have made it the most well known. Although Islamic fundamentalism represents only a small proportion of the over 1 billion Muslims worldwide, it is still a powerful transnational movement and a challenge to states from the Philippines and Indonesia, to Nigeria and Algeria, to Saudi Arabia and Iran. As terrorist attacks in Israel, Europe, Asia, and the United States show, these areas, too, are the targets of Islamic fundamentalists. These attacks have led many to believe what one well-known political scientist, Samuel Huntington, predicted in the mid-1990s: that the next great international conflict would be a "clash of civilizations" arising from underlying differences between Western liberal democracy and Islamic fundamentalism.[22] Huntington's argument resonates in many parts of the world in the twenty-first century.

Not all transnational movements pose such direct challenges to the state. Indeed, many such movements, rather than forming around major cleavages such as religion or ideology as discussed above, develop around progressive goals such as the environment, human rights, and development, or around conservative goals such as opposition to abortion, family planning, or immigration. Often organized around nongovernmental organizations that frame the issue and mobilize resources, these social movements want change, developing new approaches to problems and seeking to push governments to take action, but these movements are generally not undermining state sovereignty.

Ethnonational Movements

Another dramatic challenge to the state is found in **ethnonational movements.** More than 900 million people belong to 233 national subgroups around the world. The demands from these ethnic groups are not new; after all, World War I was fought over such ethnic demands. Yet, the end of the Cold War and the demise of multiethnic states like the Soviet Union and Yugoslavia, along with the communications revolution of fax and Internet, have led to increasing demands by ethnonational movements.

Ethnonationalist movements identify more with a particular culture than with a state. Having experienced discrimination or persecution, many of these groups are now taking collective action in support of national self-determination. As United Nations adviser Nicholas Kittrie has written, "Who is to tell the Bosnians, the Palestinians, Kurds, Druze, Scots, Basques, Quebecois and Bretons that they are not a people and are not entitled to self-determination?"[23]

Kashmir, 2005

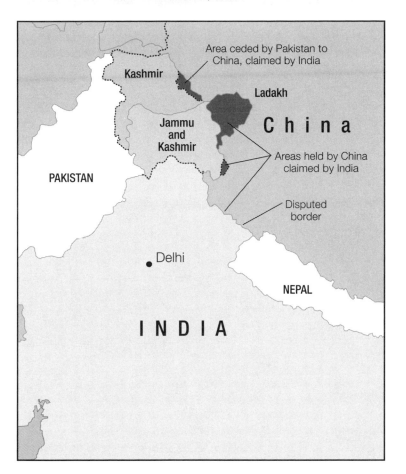

NOTE: The Line of Control separates the two sides in the Kashmir conflict.

Yet not all ethnonationalists want the same thing. A few seek separation from the state, preferring to forge their own destiny in a new, independent state. Some prefer **irredentism**—a policy of not just breaking away from an established state but joining with fellow ethnonationalists in other states and creating with them another state or joining with another state that is populated by fellow ethnonationalists. Others seek solutions in federal arrangements, hoping to win guarantees of autonomy within an established state, and still others seek not much more than official recognition of their unique status, including the right to use their national language and practice their own religion.

One of the more complex ethnonational movements involves Kashmir, a mountainous area at the intersection of India, Pakistan, and China, and

TABLE 5.3

Ethnonational Challengers	
State	**Ethnonational Groups**
Indonesia	Timorese, Papuans, Moluccans
Malaysia	Peoples of Sarawak and Sabah
Spain	Basques
People's Republic of China	Tibetans
Nigeria	Yorubas, Ibos
Burundi, Rwanda	Hutus, Tutsis
Syria, Iraq, Iran, Turkey	Kurds
Moldova	Ukranians, Russians
Serbia, Macedonia	Albanians
Lebanon	Maronites, Palestinians
Mexico, Guatemala	Mayans, Zapotecs, Mixes
Burma, Thailand	Karens
Canada	Quebecois
India	Kashmiris
Afghanistan	Pashtuns, Hazaras, Tajiks, Uzbeks, Turkmens
Georgia	Abkhaz, Ossetes

Kashmiris, a people who are overwhelmingly Muslim but who have traditionally been ruled by Hindus. When India (dominated by Hindus) and Pakistan (dominated by Muslims) separated into two independent states in 1947, the maharaja, Hari Singh, opted to join India, much to the displeasure of the majority population who wanted national affiliation with Pakistan. In 1947–48 and again in 1965, India and Pakistan fought over the territory, which has been punctuated ever since by tensions and periodic skirmishes. A Line of Control (LOC) was reestablished in 1972, dividing Kashmir into India-administered Kashmir to the east and south, with 9 million people, and Pakistan-administered Kashmir to the north and west, with 3 million people. Besides the rival claims between India and Pakistan, since 1989 a growing violent separatist movement has fought against Indian rule in Kashmir. The most prominent separatist group is the pro-Pakistani Hizbul Mujahideen, seeking union with Pakistan. The largest pro-independence group is the Jammu and Kashmir Liberation Front, but its influence has been declining. The Kashmiri ethnonational conflict has been particularly difficult because its factions are not only fighting for control of territory but are also tied into the larger conflict between India and Pakistan. In 2003, India and Pakistan signed a cease-fire along their borders in Kashmir and established diplomatic ties. Yet, violence in the region has continued, and the 2005 earthquake centered in the Pakistan-administered region of Kashmir has turned international efforts to relief and reconstruction.

Some of these ethnonational challenges lead to civil conflict and even war, as the case of Kashmir illustrates. Political scientist Jack Snyder has identified the causal mechanism whereby ethnic nationalists challenge the state on the basis of the legitimacy of their language, culture, or religion. Elites within these ethnonational movements, particularly when countervailing institutions are weak, may be able to incite the masses to war.[24] Table 5.3 lists some of the ethnonational challengers in the world today.

THEORY IN BRIEF
Contending Perspectives on State Power and Policy

	Liberalism / Neoliberal Institutionalism	Realism / Neorealism	Radicalism / Dependency Theory
Nature of state power	Multiple power sources; tangible and intangible sources	Emphasis on power as key concept in international relations; geography, natural resources, population especially important	Economic power organized around classes
Using state power	Broad range of power techniques; preference for noncoercive alternatives	Emphasis on coercive techniques of power; use of force acceptable	Weak having few instruments of power
How foreign policy is made	Organizational / bureaucratic and pluralist models of decisionmaking	Emphasis on rational model of decision-making; unitary state actor assumed	States having no real choices; decisions dictated by economic capitalist elites
Determinants of foreign policy	Largely domestic determinants	Largely external / international determinants	Largely external determinants; co-opted internal elements

In Sum: The State and Challenges Beyond

The centrality of the state in international politics cannot be disputed. In this chapter, the state has been conceptualized according to the contending theoretical perspectives. We have looked inside the state to describe the various forms of state power. We have discussed the ways that states are able to use power through the diplomatic, economic, and coercive instruments of statecraft. We have explored the question of whether certain kinds of governments—democracies, in particular—behave differently from nondemocracies. We have disaggregated the subnational actors within the state to identify different models of foreign-policy decisionmaking. And we have examined the ways in which globalization, transnational crime, transnational movements, and ethnonationalist movements pose threats to state sovereignty and to the stability of the international system. Such movements, however, depend on individuals; it is individuals who lead the challenge. Some are elites who are charismatic and powerful leaders in their own right. Some are part of a mass movement. It is these individuals to whom we now turn.

Notes

1. James N. Rosenau, *Turbulence in World Politics: A Theory of Change and Continuity* (Princeton, N.J.: Princeton University Press, 1990), 117–18.
2. Minxin Pei, "The Paradoxes of American Nationalism," *Foreign Policy*, no. 134 (May–June 2003), 31–37.
3. See Martha Finnemore, *National Interests in International Society* (Ithaca, N.Y.: Cornell University Press, 1996), Chap. 1.
4. Stephen D. Krasner, *Defending the National Interest: Raw Materials Investments and U.S. Foreign Policy* (Princeton, N.J.: Princeton University Press, 1978).
5. Alfred T. Mahan, *The Influence of Seapower upon History 1660–1783* (Boston: Little, Brown, 1897).
6. Halford Mackinder, "The Geographical Pivot of History," *Geographical Journal* 23 (April 1904), 434.
7. Andrew Mack, "Why Big Nations Lose Small Wars: The Politics of Asymmetric Conflict," *World Politics* 27:2 (January 1975), 175–200.
8. Robert D. Putnam, "Diplomacy and Domestic Politics: The Logic of 2-Level Games," *International Organization* 42:3 (Summer 1988), 427–69.
9. Ibid., 434.
10. Raymond Cohen, *Negotiating across Cultures: Communication Obstacles in International Diplomacy* (2nd ed., Washington, D.C.: U.S. Institute of Peace, 1997).
11. Karen A. Mingst and Craig P. Warkentin, "What Difference Does Culture Make in Multilateral Negotiations?" *Global Governance* 2:2 (May 1996), 169–88.
12. David A. Baldwin, *Economic Statecraft* (Princeton, N.J.: Princeton University Press, 1985).

13. David Cortright and George A. Lopez, *The Sanctions Decade: Assessing UN Strate gies in the 1990s* (Boulder, Colo.: Lynne Rienner, 2000); and also by the same authors, *Sanctions and the Search for Security* (Boulder, Colo.: Lynne Rienner, 2002).

14. Thomas C. Schelling, *Arms and Influence* (New Haven, Conn.: Yale University Press, 1966).

15. Immanuel Kant, *Perpetual Peace: A Philosophical Sketch* (1795), reprinted in *Kant Selections*, ed. Lewis White Beck (New York: Macmillan Co., 1988).

16. See, for example, William J. Dixon, "Democracy and the Peaceful Settlement of International Conflict," *American Political Science Review* 88 (1994), 14–32; and Joe D. Hagan, "Domestic Political Systems and War Proneness," *Mershon International Studies Review* 38:2 (October 1994), 183–207.

17. Norman M. Naimark, *The Russians in Germany: A History of the Soviet Zone of Occupation, 1945–1949* (Cambridge, Mass.: Harvard University Press, 1995).

18. Jessica Matthews, "Power Shift," *Foreign Affairs* 76:1 (January–February 1997), 50.

19. Ibid., 50–51.

20. See Moises Naim, *Illicit: How Smugglers, Traffickers, and Copycats Are Hijacking the Global Economy* (New York: Doubleday, 2005).

21. Jessica Stern, *Terror in the Name of God: Why Religious Militants Kill* (New York: HarperCollins, 2003), 9–31.

22. Samuel P. Huntington, *The Clash of Civilizations and the Remaking of World Order* (New York: Simon and Schuster, 1996).

23. Nicholas Kittrie, "Absolutist vs. Pluralist Legitimacy: The New Cold War," *New Perspectives Quarterly* 13:1 (Winter 1996), 57.

24. Jack Snyder, *From Voting to Violence: Democratization and Nationalist Conflict* (New York: Norton, 2000).

The Individual

- *Which individuals matter in international relations?*
- *What psychological factors have an impact on elites making foreign-policy decisions?*
- *What roles do other private individuals play in international relations?*
- *What roles do mass publics play in foreign policy?*
- *According to the various theoretical perspectives, how much do individuals matter?*

International relations certainly affects the lives of individuals, as discussed in Chapter 1. But individuals are not merely passive agents for actions taken by the state or for events emerging out of the structure of the international system. Individuals are actors, too, and as such represent the third level of analysis. Individuals head governments, multinational corporations, and international bodies. Individuals fight wars and make the daily decisions that shape the international political economy.

Recall the possible explanations given in Chapter 3 for why the United States invaded Iraq in 2003. One explanation pointed to the beliefs of President George W. Bush and his security advisers and to their response to Saddam Hussein, his personal characteristics, and his advisers. Clearly, one group of individuals that makes a difference is leaders. But individuals holding more informal roles can also have significant influence, as can the mass public.

Foreign-Policy Elites: Individuals Who Matter

Do individuals matter in the making of foreign policy? Liberals are particularly adamant that leaders do make a difference. Whenever there is a leadership change in a major power, like the United States or Russia, speculation always arises about possible changes in the country's foreign policy. This

reflects the general belief that individual leaders and their personal characteristics do make a difference in foreign policy, and hence in international
relations. Ample empirical proof has been offered for this position. For
instance, in March 1965 Nicolae Ceauşescu became the new leader of the
Communist party of Romania. During his twenty-two years as Romania's
head of state, the course of Romanian security policy changed significantly,
reflecting the preferences and skills of Ceauşescu himself. Romania's security
policy became more independent of the Soviet Union, often in defiance of that
larger and more powerful neighbor. Much to the Soviets' disdain, Romania
maintained diplomatic relations with Israel following the Arab-Israeli War of
1967. That same year, Romania established diplomatic relations with West
Germany before the Soviet Union had agreed to reconciliation with the West.
Ceauşescu strongly denounced the Warsaw Pact invasion of Czechoslovakia
in 1968, and soon thereafter he strengthened ties to another maverick Eastern European state, Yugoslavia. Romania's voting pattern in the U.N. General
Assembly increasingly deviated from that of the Soviet Union as Romania
moved closer to countries in the nonaligned movement (those states purposely unallied with either the United States or the Soviet Union). Ceauşescu
maintained close ties to China despite the latter's increasingly hostile relations with the Soviet Union. In short, Ceauşescu, a strong leader, significantly
changed Romania's foreign policy, moving it in a direction that deviated
from the preferences of its closest ally.

The example of the Soviet leader Mikhail Gorbachev also illustrates the
fact that leaders can cause real change. Soon after coming to power in 1985,
Gorbachev asked penetrating questions about the failures of the Soviet Union
in Afghanistan and examined the reasons for the dismal performance of the
Soviet economy. He began to frame the problems of the Soviet Union differently, identifying the Soviet security problem as part of the larger problem of
weakness in the Soviet economy. Through a process of trial and error, and by
living through and then studying failures, Gorbachev came to a new concep-
tualization of the Soviet security problem. He determined that the economic
system had to be reformed in order to improve the country's security. In initiating that policy change, he needed to decide when and how change would
happen, and how far it would go. Gorbachev's leadership made a difference
in starting and sustaining broad economic reform in the Soviet Union,
although he eventually lost power.

Individual elites are also important in constructivist thinking. Constructivists attribute the policy shift in the Soviet Union to its "New Thinking"
not only to the change in calculations made by Gorbachev himself but
more subtly to the change caused by the policy entrepreneurs, the networks
of Western-oriented reformists and international affairs specialists who

promoted new ideas. To constructivists like Robert Hermann, this is the relevant explanation for the monumental changes in the Soviet Union.[1]

For realists, individuals are of little importance. Their position comes from the realist assumption of a unitary actor. Thus, states are not differentiated by their government type or personalities or styles of leaders in office but by the relative power they hold in the international system. Morgenthau explained as follows:

> The concept of national of national interest defined as power imposes intellectual discipline upon the observer, infuses rational order into the subject matter of politics, and thus makes the theoretical understanding of politics possible. On the side of the actor, it provides for rational discipline in action and creates the astounding continuity in foreign policy which makes American, British, or Russian foreign policy appear as an intelligible, rational continuum, by and large consistent with itself, regardless of the different motives, preferences, and intellectual and moral qualities of successive statesmen.[2]

Yet foreign policy is not always the same, as liberals and constructivists acknowledge. *Glasnost* and *perestroika* were introduced in the Soviet Union beginning in 1986, Romania did carve a foreign-policy niche independent of the Soviet Union during the 1970s, and Cuba and the United States, once allies, did become mortal enemies in the 1960s. What caused these changes? Were individuals responsible for them, or did individual leaders just happen to be the right (or wrong) person at the time? Given the same situation, would different individuals have made different decisions, thus charting a different course through international relations?

Two questions are most pertinent to determining the role of individuals in international relations: When are the actions of individuals likely to have a greater or lesser effect on the course of events? And under what circumstances do different actors (in terms of their personal characteristics) behave differently?

The Impact of Elites: External Conditions

An individual's actions affect the course of events when at least one of several factors is present (see Figure 6.1). When political institutions are unstable, young, in crisis, or collapsed, leaders are able to provide powerful influences. Founding fathers, be they the United States's George Washington, Kenya's Jomo Kenyatta, India's Mohandas Gandhi, Russia's Vladimir Lenin, or the Czech Republic's Vaclav Havel, have a great impact because they lead in the

FIGURE 6.1

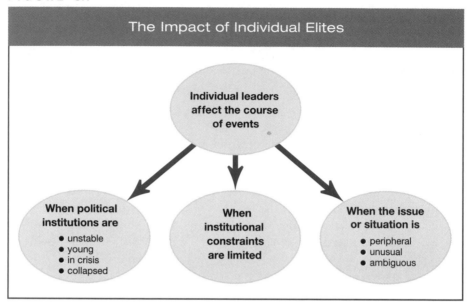

The Impact of Individual Elites

Individual leaders affect the course of events

When political institutions are
- unstable
- young
- in crisis
- collapsed

When institutional constraints are limited

When the issue or situation is
- peripheral
- unusual
- ambiguous

early years of their nation's lives, when institutions and practices are being established. Adolf Hitler, Franklin Roosevelt, and Mikhail Gorbachev had more influence precisely because their states were in economic crises when they were in power.

Individuals also affect the course of events when they have few institutional constraints. In dictatorial regimes, top leaders are relatively free from domestic constraints such as societal inputs and political opposition, and thus are able to chart courses and implement foreign policy relatively unfettered. In democratic regimes, too, occasionally top decisionmakers are able to change policy in a dramatic fashion. For example, U.S. president Richard Nixon in 1972 was able to engineer a complete foreign-policy reversal in relations with the People's Republic of China, secretly sending his top foreign-policy adviser, Henry Kissinger, for several meetings with Chinese premier Chou En-lai and his advisers. These moves were an unexpected change, given Nixon's Republican party affiliation and prior anticommunist record. Bureaucratic and societal constraints mattered little, even in such a relatively open democracy.

The specifics of a situation also determine the extent to which individuals matter. Decisionmakers' personal characteristics have more influence on outcomes when the issue is peripheral rather than central, when the issue is not routine—that is, standard operating procedures are not available—or when the situation is ambiguous and information is unclear. Crisis situations, in particular, where information is in short supply and standard operating procedures inapplicable, create scenarios in which a decisionmaker's personal characteristics count most. Such a scenario arose during the Cuban missile crisis, when President John F. Kennedy's personal openness to alternatives and attention to group dynamics paid off.

The Impact of Elites: The Personality Factor

Even among elite leaders working amid similar external conditions, some individuals seem to have a greater impact on foreign policy than others; this leads us to examine both the personal characteristics that matter and the thought processes of individuals.

Political psychologist Margaret Hermann has found a number of personality characteristics that affect foreign-policy behaviors. Since top leaders do not generally take personality tests, Hermann used a different research strategy. She systematically collected spontaneous interviews and press conferences with eighty heads of state holding office in thirty-eight countries between 1959 and 1968. From these data, she found key personality characteristics that she felt influence a leader's orientation toward policy.[3] Those characteristics are listed in the top section of Figure 6.2.

These personality characteristics orient an individual's view of foreign affairs. Two orientations emerge from the personality traits. One group, leaders with high levels of nationalism, a strong belief in their own ability to control events, a strong need for power, low levels of conceptual complexity, and high levels of distrust of others, tend to develop an independent orientation to foreign affairs. The other group, leaders with low levels of nationalism, little belief in their ability to control events, a high need for affiliation, high levels of conceptual complexity, and low levels of distrust of others, tended toward a participatory orientation in foreign affairs. (The bottom of Figure 6.2 illustrates these orientations.) Then Hermann tested whether these personal characteristics and their respective orientations related to both the foreign-policy style and behavior of the leaders.

Both Hermann and subsequent researchers using the same schema have found that they did. For example, one study considered the personality characteristics of Tony Blair using Hermann's categories to organize Blair's foreign-policy answers to questions posed in the House of Commons.[4] The researcher found Blair had a high belief in his own ability to control events and a high need for power, accompanied by a low conceptual complexity. These personality findings go a long way in explaining British foreign policy toward the Iraq war, a policy that many in the government and the British public opposed. Thus, even in democracies, where institutional constraints

FIGURE 6.2

Personality Characteristics of Individual Leaders

Personality Characteristics of Leaders

Nationalism: strong emotional ties to nation; emphasis on national honor and dignity

Perception of control: belief in ability to control events: high degree of control over situations; governments can influence state and nation

Need for power: need to establish, maintain, and project power or influence over others

Need for affiliation: concern for establishing and maintaining friendly relationships with others

Conceptual complexity: ability to discuss with other people places, policies, ideas in a discerning way

Distrust of others: feelings of doubt, uneasiness about others; doubt motives and actions of others

Foreign Policy Orientations

Independent leader:......... high in nationalism

high in perception of control

high in need for power

low in conceptual complexity

high in distrust of others

Participatory leader:......... low in nationalism

low in perception of control

high in need for affiliation

high in conceptual complexity

low in distrust of others

SOURCE: Margaret G. Hermann, "Explaining Foreign Policy Behavior Using the Personal Characteristics of Political Leaders," *International Studies Quarterly* 24:1 (March 1980), 7–46.

are high, individual personality characteristics influence foreign-policy orientation and behavior.

University of South Carolina professor Betty Glad has developed a profile of former president Jimmy Carter that suggests how his personality characteristics played a key role in influencing the course of U.S. policy during the 1979–81 hostage crisis, which began when Iranian militants kidnapped more than sixty Americans and held them for more than a year. Carter personalized the hostage taking. He was humiliated, obsessed, wanting above all to have *his* decisions vindicated. After an attempted helicopter rescue mission failed, he rationalized the failure as a "worthy effort," feeling that some action was better than nothing. Glad points to Carter's personality characteristics:

> Carter's subsequent difficulty in admitting that he made mistakes in this situation was based on his more general need to be right. He had always had difficulty in learning from his mistakes. In this instance the psychic costs to the United States of its importance in a crisis upon which the entire people and government focused for several months, as well as the political price Carter had to pay for that fixation, would make it particularly difficult for him to see where he had gone wrong.[5]

Personality characteristics affect the leadership of dictators more than that of democratic leaders because of the absence of effective institutional checks, as Glad has also investigated. She analyzed the personalities of tyrants—those who rule without attention to law, who capitalize on grandiose self-presentations and projects, look for every advantage, and utilize cruel, often extreme tactics. Comparing Hitler, Stalin, and Saddam Hussein, she labels them as having malignant narcissism syndrome. Glad explains how "project over-reach and creation of new enemies leads to increasing vulnerability, a deepening of the paranoiac defense, and volatility in behavior."[6] North Korean leader Kim Jong Il ("Dear Leader") and his father, Kim Il Sung ("Great Leader"), exhibit some of these same characteristics. Kim Il Sung erected more than 34,000 monuments to himself during his fifty-year rule, and his photo was prominently displayed in buildings and other public places. Kim Jong Il expresses his megalomania with gigantic orchestrated pictures of himself, spending millions of dollars on spectacles of historical themes while more than a million of his people are starving. These characteristics can be linked to policy choices. Dismissing the starvation of his people as not his fault, Kim Jong Il merely fired the minister of agriculture. One former CIA psychiatrist has suggested that Kim Jong Il is self-absorbed, lacks an ability to empathize, and is capable of "unconstrained aggression." "Dear Leader," he warns, "will use whatever aggression is

The Individual: Hugo Chávez of Venezuela

Leaders are usually more complex than the simplistic labels that are attached to them: "good" or "bad," "weak" or "strong," "democrat" or "tyrant." President Hugo Chávez of Venezuela is one such leader: he is a complicated individual who supports populist domestic policies and revolutionary policies abroad.

President Hugo Chávez is a charismatic, democratically elected authoritarian who presides over a "competitive autocracy." After a failed coup attempt in 1992, he decided the way to win power was through the ballot box. Chávez was elected in 1998, running on a campaign platform that exploited Venezuela's discontent with existing political parties and the economic system. Inspired by Fidel Castro, Simon Bolivar, and other Latin American revolutionaries, Chávez has adopted a style and policies that put Venezuela on a different course.

Arguing that the model of economic development imposed on Latin American governments by the United States has failed, Chávez calls for a new "socialism of the twenty-first century." He has spent large amounts of money on social programs—housing, health care, food subsidies. In 2004 state spending increased by more than 30 percent. And in the last two years, Chávez has moved $15 billion from central bank reserves to a fund for domestic projects. Government authorities assert that this spending has led to significant economic gains for the masses. The economy is strong and almost $5 billion of the country's foreign debt has been paid off. A recent Latinobarometro survey found that among Latin American respondents in eighteen countries, those in Venezuela rank themselves as the most satisfied.

During his tenure, Chávez has effectively been able to exercise his democratic authority by reducing the size of the political center and opposing but not banning political opposition. He lavishes his supporters with gifts and withholds resources from those who oppose him. He has broadened popular political participation while asserting increased control over the judiciary, the institution that supervises elections, and the oil industry. Chávez remains popular, especially among the poor, and continues to win elections.

Chávez's anti-imperial and anti-American rhetoric also makes him extremely popular in Latin America as a whole, inspiring other left-leaning leaders in the region with his brand of democratically legitimized authoritarianism. His well-publicized visits to Cuba, to be at the bedside of the ailing Fidel Castro, and to Bolivia and Peru have included offers of foreign aid and strengthened rising leftist movements. Chávez has also forged relationships with other oil-producing countries, visiting and defending both Iranian and Libyan policies and opposing the imperialistic policies of the United States.

For Critical Analysis

1. Is it personality or policies that have made Chávez popular and powerful? Using Herman's personality characteristics, how would you classify Chávez?
2. How has the person of Chávez augmented the power of the Venezuelan state?

necessary, without qualm of conscience, be it to eliminate an individual or to strike at a particular group."[7]

Personality characteristics, then, partly determine what decisions individual leaders make. But those decisions also reflect the fact that all decisionmakers are confronted with the task of putting divergent information into an organized form.

Individual Decisionmaking

The rational model of decisionmaking that we discussed earlier suggests that the individual possesses all the relevant information, stipulates a goal, examines the relevant choices, and makes a decision that best achieves the goal. In actuality, however, individuals are not perfectly rational decisionmakers. Confronted by information that is neither perfect nor complete, and often overwhelmed by a plethora of information and conditioned by personal experience, the decisionmaker selects, organizes, and evaluates incoming information about the surrounding world.

A variety of psychological techniques are used by individuals to process and evaluate information. In perceiving and interpreting new and oftentimes contradictory information, individuals rely on existing perceptions, often based on prior experiences. Such perceptions are the "screens" that enable individuals to process information selectively; these perceptions have an integrating function, permitting the individual to synthesize and interpret the information. And they serve an orienting function, providing guidance about future expectations and expediting planning for future contingencies. If those perceptions form a relatively integrated set of images, then they are called a **belief system.**

International relations scholars have devised methods to test the existence of elite images, although research has not been conducted on many individuals, for reasons made obvious below. Duke University professor Ole Hosti systematically analyzed all of the publicly available statements of Secretary of State John Foster Dulles concerning the Soviet Union during the years 1953–54. From the 434 documents surveyed, Hosti singled out 3,584 of Dulles's assertions about the Soviet Union. His research showed convincingly that Dulles held a very specific and unwavering image of the Soviet Union, one focused on atheism, totalitarianism, and communism. To Dulles, the Soviet people were good, but their leaders were bad; the state was good, the Communist party bad. This image was unvarying; the character of the Soviet Union in Dulles's mind did not change. Whether this image gleaned from Dulles's statements affected U.S. decisions during the period cannot be stated with certainty. He was, after all, only one among a group of top leaders. Yet a plethora of decisions taken during that time are consistent with the image.[8]

Political scientists Harvey Starr and Stephen Walker both completed similar empirical research on Henry Kissinger.[9] Elucidating Kissinger's operational code (the rules he operated by) from his scholarly writings, Walker found that the conduct of the Vietnam War, orchestrated in large part by Kissinger between 1969 and 1973, was congruent with the premises of his operational code and his conception of mutually acceptable outcomes. He wanted to negotiate a mutual withdrawal of external forces and to avoid negotiating about the internal structure of South Vietnam. He used enough force, applied in combination with generous peace terms, so that North Vietnam was faced with an attractive peace settlement versus unpalatable alternatives—stalemate or escalation.

These elite mindset studies were possible because the particular elites left behind extensive written records from before, during, and after they held key policymaking positions. Since few leaders leave such a record, however, our ability to empirically reconstruct elite images, perceptions, or operational codes is limited, as is our inability to state with certainty their influence on a specific decision.

Information-Processing Mechanisms

One's image and perception of the world are continually bombarded by new, sometimes overwhelming, and often discordant information. Images and belief systems, however, are not generally changed, and almost never are they radically altered. Thus, individual elites utilize, usually unconsciously, a number of psychological mechanisms to process the information that forms their general perceptions of the world. These mechanisms are summarized in Table 6.1.

First, individuals strive to be **cognitively consistent,** ensuring that images hang together consistently within their belief systems. For example, individuals like to believe that the enemy of an enemy is a friend and the enemy of a friend is an enemy. Because of the tendency to be cognitively consistent, individuals select or amplify information that supports existing beliefs and ignore or downplay contradictory information. For example, because both Great Britain and Argentina were friends of the United States prior to their war over the Falkland/Malvinas Islands in 1982, U.S. decisionmakers denied the seriousness of the conflict at the outset. The United States did not think that its friend, the "peaceful" Britain, would go to war with Argentina over a group of barren islands thousands of miles from Britain's shores. The United States underestimated the strength of public support for military action in Britain, as well as misunderstood the precarious domestic position of the Argentinian generals trying to bolster their power by diverting attention to a popular external conflict.

Elites in power also perceive and evaluate the world according to what they have learned from past events. They look for those details of a present episode that look like a past one, perhaps ignoring the important differences. This is often referred to as the **evoked set.** During the 1956 Suez crisis, for instance, British prime minister Anthony Eden saw Egyptian president

TABLE 6.1

Psychological Mechanisms Used to Process Information		
Technique	**Explanation**	**Example**
Cognitive consistency	Tendency to accept information that is compatible with what has previously been accepted, often ignoring inconsistent information. Desire to be consistent in attitude.	Just prior to the Japanese attack on Pearl Harbor, military spotters saw unmarked planes approaching the island. Not believing the evidence, they discounted the intrusions.
Evoked set	Tendency to look for details in a present situation that are similar to information gleaned from past situations. Leads one to conclusions that are similar to those of the past.	U.S. decisionmakers during the Vietnam War saw the Korean War as a precedent, although there were critical differences.
Mirror image	Tendency of individuals and groups to see in one's opponent the opposite of characteristics seen in oneself. Opponent is viewed as hostile and uncompromising, while one's self is viewed as friendly and compromising.	During the Cold War, both U.S. elites and masses viewed the Soviet Union in terms of their own mirror image: the United States was friendly, the Soviet Union hostile.
Groupthink	Tendency for small groups to form a consensus and resist criticism of that core position, often disregarding contradictory information.	During the U.S. planning for the Bay of Pigs operation against Cuba in 1961, opponents were ostracized from the planning group.
Satisficing	Tendency for groups to search for a "good enough" solution, rather than an optimal one.	Decision of NATO to bomb Kosovo in 1999 in an attempt to stop the ethnic cleansing against the Albanian Kosovars, rather than send in ground troops.

Gamal Abdel Nasser as another Hitler. Eden recalled Prime Minister Neville Chamberlain's failed effort to appease Hitler with the Munich agreement in 1938 and thus believed that Nasser, likewise, could not be appeased.

Individual perceptions are often shaped in terms of **mirror images:** while considering one's own action good, moral, and just, the enemy is automatically found to be evil, immoral, and unjust. Mirror imaging often exacerbates conflicts, making it all the more difficult to resolve a contentious issue.

These psychological mechanisms that we have discussed so far affect the functioning of both individuals and small groups. But small groups themselves also have psychologically based dynamics that undermine the rational model. The psychologist Irving Janis called this dynamic **groupthink.** Groupthink, according to Janis, is "a mode of thinking that people engage in when they are deeply involved in a cohesive in-group, when members' strivings for unanimity override their motivation to realistically appraise alternative courses of action."[10] The dynamics of the group, which include the illusion of invulnerability and unanimity, excessive optimism, the belief in their own morality and the enemy's evil, and pressure placed on dissenters to change their views, leads to groupthink. During the Vietnam War, for example, a top group of U.S. decisionmakers, unified by bonds of friendship and loyalty, met in what they called the Tuesday lunch group. In the aftermath of President Lyndon Johnson's overwhelming electoral win in 1964, the group basked in self-confidence and optimism, rejecting out of hand the pessimistic information about North Vietnam's military buildup. When information mounted about the increasing casualties suffered by the South Vietnamese and the Americans, the group pulled even more tightly together; as the external stress intensified, the group further closed ranks, its members taking solace in the security of the group. New information was inserted only into old perceptions; individuals not sharing the group's thinking were both informally and formally removed from the group, as their contradictory advice fell on deaf ears.

Participants in small groups, then, are apt to employ the same psychological techniques, like the evoked set and the mirror image, to process new incoming information at the individual level. But additional distorting tendencies affect small groups, such as the pressure for group conformity and solidarity. Larger groups seeking accommodation look for what is possible within the bounds of their situation, searching for a "good enough" solution, rather than an optimal one. Herbert Simon has labeled this trait satisficing.[11]

These tendencies confirm again that the rational model of decisionmaking may be incomplete, contrary to the expectations of realist theory. Yet top leaders—with their various personality characteristics and often inaccurate perceptions—do influence foreign policy. It is not just the tyrants (Germany's Adolf Hitler, North Korea's Kim Jong Il, Uganda's Idi Amin, the Central African Republic's Jean Bokassa, or Cambodia's Pol Pot), but also the visionaries (Tanzania's Julius Nyerere, India's Mohandas Gandhi, South Africa's Nelson Mandela) and the political pragmatists (Great Britain's Margaret Thatcher, the Philippine's Corazon Aquino, Russia's Vladimir Putin) who make a difference on the basis of their roles and positions.

A few of the top leaders who make a difference represent the international community rather than the state. The eight individuals who have served as secretary-general of the United Nations are one such group. Their personalities and interpretations of the U.N. Charter, as well as world events, have combined to increase the power, resources, and importance of the position and of the United Nations. Yet how they have used the position has depended largely on their individual characteristics.

After the devastating reigns of corrupt authoritarian leaders such as Saddam Hussein in Iraq, Mobutu Sese Seko in Congo (formerly Zaire), and Robert Mugabe in Zimbabwe, whose people have been held unwitting hostage, some pundits and politicians have suggested that "bad" or "corrupt" leaders should be removed by the international community.[12] That debate brings up numerous normative and pragmatic issues for students of international relations.

Private Individuals

While leaders holding formal positions have more opportunity not only to participate in but to shape international relations, private individuals can and do play key roles. Private individuals, independent of any official role, may by virtue of circumstances, skills, or resources carry out independent actions in international relations. Less bound by the rules of the game or by institutional norms, such individuals engage in activities in which official representatives are either unable or unwilling to participate. The donations by Microsoft founder Bill Gates and his wife, Melinda, to global vaccination, immunization, and AIDS programs is one such example.

In the area of conflict resolution, for instance, private individuals increasingly play a role in so-called **track-two diplomacy.** Track-two diplomacy utilizes individuals outside of governments to carry out the task of conflict resolution. High-level track-two diplomacy has met with some success. In the spring of 1992, for example, Eritrea signed a declaration of independence, seceding from Ethiopia after years of both low- and high-intensity conflict. The foundation for the agreement was negotiated in numerous informal meetings in Atlanta, Georgia, and elsewhere between the affected parties and former president Jimmy Carter, acting through the Carter Center's International Negotiation Network at Emory University. In the fall of 1993, the startling framework for reconciliation between Israel and the Palestine Liberation Organization was negotiated through track-two informal and formal techniques initiated by Terje Larsen, a Norwegian sociologist, and Yossi Beilin of the opposition Labor party in Israel. A series of preparatory negotiations was

P O L I C Y
D E B A T E

Should "bad" or "corrupt" leaders be forcibly removed by the international community?

YES:

◆ Removal of "bad" leaders by the international community potentially averts war and continued humanitarian abuses, saving lives and money in the long term.

◆ Forcible removal of leaders not only punishes those individuals but serves as a deterrent to the behavior of other leaders.

◆ International intervention to remove tyrannical leaders reinforces universal respect for international law and for the promotion of democracy internationally.

◆ Under the principle of universal jurisdiction by the international community over the criminal acts of individuals, there is legal precedent for the removal of leaders from office.

NO:

◆ Removal of leaders from office by the international community undermines traditional notions of sovereignty and noninterference in the domestic affairs of states.

◆ Deciding which leaders are so dangerous to the state and the international community is a highly charged political question, subject to abuse and unfair selectivity.

◆ There is a contradiction between the international community's responsibility to ensure international peace and security and the decision to use force, coercion, or even assassination to remove a corrupt leader.

conducted over a five-month period in total secrecy. Beginning unofficially, the talks gradually evolved into official negotiations, building up trust in an informal atmosphere and setting the stage for an eventual agreement.[13]

Such high-level track-two diplomatic efforts are not always well received. For example, Jimmy Carter's eleventh-hour dash in 1994 to meet with North Korea's Kim Il Sung to discuss the latter's nuclear buildup was met by a barrage of probing questions. Was the U.S. government being preempted? For whom did Carter speak? Could the understandings serve as the basis of a formal intergovernmental agreement? Despite the misgivings and the eventual unraveling of North Korean promises, Carter received the Nobel Peace Prize in 2002 for this and other efforts to promote peace around the world.

Other types of track-two diplomacy involve a more lengthy process, a sustained dialogue. In some cases, unofficial individuals from different international groups are brought together in small problem-solving workshops in order to develop personal relationships and understandings of the problems from the perspective of others. It is hoped that these individuals will then seek to influence public opinion in their respective states, trying to reshape, and often rehumanize, the image of the opponent. This approach has been used to address the conflict between Protestants and Catholics in Northern Ireland and the Arab-Israeli dispute. Problem-solving workshops have been conducted over two decades and cooperative activities encouraged.

Other private individuals have played linkage roles between different countries. Armand Hammer, a U.S. corporate executive, was for years a private go-between for the Soviet Union and the United States. His long-standing business interests in the Soviet Union and his carefully nurtured friendships with both Soviet economic and political leaders and U.S. officials provided a channel of communication at a time when few informal contacts existed between the two countries. In the immediate aftermath of the 1986 Chernobyl nuclear plant explosion, Hammer convinced Gorbachev to accept U.S. medical personnel and expertise. Similarly, during the Vietnam War, Ross Perot, a private citizen and entrepreneur, organized rescue efforts on behalf of U.S. prisoners of war.

Sometimes individuals are propelled into the international arena by virtue of their actions: A. Q. Khan, who ran a blackmail operation in nuclear components; the actress Jane Fonda, who illegally visited North Vietnam during the 1960s and questioned the morality of the United States's war against Vietnam; Olympic athletes who defect from their countries, thus calling attention to the abuses of repressive regimes; Kenya's Nobel Prize–winner Wangari Maathai who promoted that country's Green Belt movement; Aziza Hussein, whose tireless efforts to change family law in Egypt later propelled her to the presidency of the International Planned Parenthood Federation; financier George Soros, who uses his private fortune to support democratization initiatives in the states of the former Soviet Union; Nobel Prize–winner Aung San Sun Kyi, who has led the public campaign against the military rulers of Myanmar. Individuals, acting alone, can make a difference; they can significantly influence international relations. Yet more often than not, these individual stories are not what we typically have in mind when we think of international diplomacy.

Alternative critical and postmodernist approaches are attempting to draw mainstream theorists' attention to these other stories, because they, too, are part of the fabric of international relations. Feminist writers in particular have sought to bring attention to the role of private individuals and especially women. Political scientist Cynthia Enloe, in *Bananas, Beaches, and Bases,* shows strikingly how "the personal is international" by documenting the many ways that women influence international relations. She points to women in economic roles participating in the international division of labor, as seamstresses, light-industry "girls," nannies, Benetton models. She also identifies women more directly involved in foreign policy—the women living around military bases, diplomatic wives, domestic servants, and women in international organizations.[15] Theirs are the untold stories of marginalized groups that critical theorists, postmodernists, and constructivists are increasingly bringing to light.

Mass Publics

Mass publics have the same psychological tendencies as elite individuals and small groups. They think in terms of perceptions and images, they see mirror images, and they use similar information-processing strategies. For example, following the seizure of the U.S. embassy in Iran in November 1979, public-opinion surveys showed the prevalence of mirror images. The majority of U.S. respondents attributed favorable qualities to the United States and its leader and unfavorable ones to Iran and its leader. The United States was strong and brave; Iran, weak and cowardly. The United States was deliberate and decisive; Iran, impulsive and indecisive. President Carter was safe; the Ayatollah Khomeini, dangerous; Carter, humane; Khomeini, ruthless. In a relatively short period of time, under crisis conditions, the public's perception of Iran had crystallized. Yet whether this had an impact on top decision-makers is unclear.[16] President Carter focused almost exclusively on the hostages, becoming obsessed with his mission of freeing them. But was this because of the public attention being paid to the hostages? Or did Carter's personality characteristics predispose him to focus so exclusively and so passionately on the hostages?

The influence that mass publics do have on foreign policy can be explained in three ways. First, it can be argued that elites and masses act the same because they share common psychological and biological characteristics. Second, the masses have opinions and attitudes about foreign policy and international relations, both general and specific, that are different from those of the elites. If these differences are captured by public-opinion polls, will the elites listen to these opinions? Will policy made by the elites reflect the public's attitudes? The third possibility is that the masses, uncontrolled by formal institutions, may occasionally act in ways that have a profound impact on international relations, regardless of anything that the elites do. These three possibilities are illustrated in Figure 6.3.

FIGURE 6.3

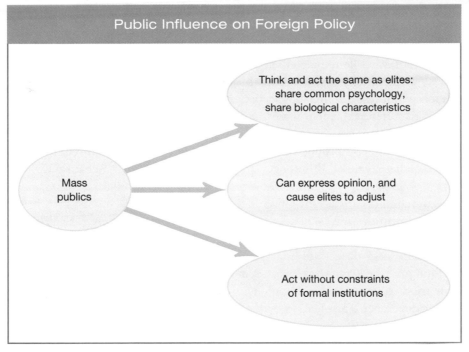

Public Influence on Foreign Policy

Mass publics

Think and act the same as elites: share common psychology, share biological characteristics

Can express opinion, and cause elites to adjust

Act without constraints of formal institutions

Elites and Masses: Common Traits

Some scholars argue that there are psychological and biological traits common to every man, woman, and child and that societies reflect those characteristics. For example, individuals, like animals, are said to have an innate drive to gain, protect, and defend territory—the "territorial imperative." This, according to some, explains the preoccupation with defending territorial boundaries, such as Britain's determination in 1982 to defend its position on the Falkland Islands, a desolate archipelago 8,000 miles from Britain's shores. Individuals and societies also share the frustration-aggression syndrome: when societies become frustrated, just as with individuals, they become aggressive. Frustration, of course, can arise from a number of different sources—economic shocks such as those Germany suffered after World War I or those Russia experienced in the 1990s, or failure to possess what is felt to be rightfully one's own, as with the Palestinian claim to territory of the Israeli state.

The problem with both the territorial imperative and the frustration-aggression notion is that even if all individuals and societies share these innate biological predispositions, not all leaders and all peoples act on these predispositions. So general predispositions of all societies or the similarities in predispositions between elites and masses cannot explain the extreme variation found in individual behavior.

Another possibility is that elites and masses share common traits differentiated by gender. Male elites and masses possess characteristics common to each other, while female elites and masses share traits different from the males'. These differences can explain political behavior. While there is considerable interest in this possibility, the research is sketchy. One much-discussed difference is that males, both elites and masses, are power seeking, whereas women are consensus builders, more collaborative, and more inclined toward compromise. One study, for example, sees the direct implications of these gender differences for peace negotiations. Because women often come to the negotiating table with experience in civic activism, non-governmental organizations, and citizen-empowering movements, they bring different attitudes and skill-sets to the table. Drawing on this research, the European Union (EU) has mandated that 40 percent of all peacekeeping, reconciliation, and peace-building posts by given to women, and the United Nations and the Organization of Security and Cooperation in Europe have both tried to include more women in peace processes, in anticipation that gender differences may lead to better outcomes.[17]

If there are differences in male and female attitudes and behavior, are these differences rooted in biology or are they learned from the culture? Most feminists, particularly the constructivists, contend that these differences are socially constructed products of culture and can thus be reconstructed over time. Yet, once again, these general predispositions, whatever their origin, cannot explain extreme variation in individual behavior.

The Impact of Public Opinion on Elites

Publics do have general foreign-policy orientations and specific attitudes about issues that can be revealed by public-opinion polls. Sometimes these attitudes reflect a perceived general mood of the population that leaders can detect. President Johnson probably accurately gauged the mood of the U.S. people toward the Vietnam War when he chose not to run for reelection in 1968. President George H. W. Bush was able to capitalize internationally on the positive public mood in the aftermath of victory in the 1991 Gulf War, although the domestic effect was short lived; he did not win reelection. Even leaders of authoritarian regimes pay attention to dominant moods, since these leaders also depend on a degree of legitimacy.

More often than not, however, publics do not express one dominant mood; top leaders are usually confronted with an array of public attitudes. These opinions are registered in elections, but elections are an imperfect measure of public opinion since they merely select individuals for office—individuals who share voters' attitudes on some issues but not on others.

Occasionally and quite extraordinarily, the masses may vote directly on an issue with foreign-policy significance. For example, following the negotiation of the 1992 Maastricht Treaty, which detailed closer political cooperation among members of the European Union (EU), some states used popular referendums to ratify the treaty. At first, the Danish population defeated the referendum, thus choosing not to join the EU, despite the fact that the measure had support from most societal groups. Subsequently, the referendum was approved. The Norwegian public chose by a referendum to remain outside of the EU, another rare instance of direct public input on a foreign-policy decision. Similarly, in 2002 the Swiss people voted to join the United Nations. In 2005, both French and Dutch voters failed to approve the referendum on the European Union Constitution.

In most democratic regimes, public-opinion polling, a vast and growing industry, provides information about public attitudes. The European Union, for example, conducts the Eurobarometer, a scientific survey of public attitudes on a wide range of issues in EU countries. Because the same questions are asked during different polls over time, both top leaders in member states and the top leadership of the EU have sophisticated data concerning public attitudes. But do they make policy with these attitudes in mind? Do elites change policy to reflect the preferences of the public?

Evidence from the United States suggests that elites do care about the preferences of the public, although they do not always directly incorporate those attitudes into policy decisions. Presidents care about their popularity because it affects their ability to work; a president's popularity is enhanced if he or she follows the general mood of the masses or fights for policies that are generally popular. Such popularity gives the president more leeway to set a national agenda. But mass attitudes may not always be directly translated into policy. For example, opinion polls suggest that U.S. elites, including top decisionmakers, are more supportive of an activist international agenda and of free trade and less supportive of economic protectionism than the mass public is. Thus, elite-made policy is not a direct reflection of public attitudes; the relationship between elite and mass public opinion is a complex one.

Mass Actions by a Leaderless Public

The mass public does not always have articulated opinions, nor is it always able to vote at the polls. Nor are groups of elites always able to control events. At times, the masses, essentially leaderless, take collective actions that have significant effects on the course of world politics.

Individuals act to improve their own political and economic welfare. An individual alone making such decisions usually will not impact international relations. However, when hundreds or even thousands of individuals act, the repercussions can be dramatic. It was the individual acts of thousands fleeing East Germany that led to the construction of the Berlin Wall in 1961. Twenty-eight years later, it was the spontaneous exodus of thousands of East Germans through Hungary and Austria that led to the tearing down of the wall in 1989. The spontaneous movement of "boat people" fleeing Vietnam and the ragged ships leaving Cuba and Haiti for the U.S. coast resulted in changes in U.S. immigration policy. The spontaneous mass uprising against Philippine president Ferdinand Marcos in 1986 signaled the demise of his regime. The "Velvet Revolution" of the masses in Czechoslovakia in the 1990s brought the end of the communist regime in that country. Iranian students marching against the regime, likewise, seek more social and economic freedom and an end to religious rule.

The scenario of dramatic changes initiated by the masses is vividly illustrated by the "people's putsch" during October 2000 against Yugoslavian leader Slobodan Milošević. After thirteen years of rule, people from all walks of Serbian life joined seven thousand striking miners, crippled the economic system, blocked transportation routes, and descended on Belgrade, the capital. Aided by new technology such as the cell phone, they were able to mobilize citizens from all over the country, driving tractors into the city, attacking the parliament, and crippling Milošević radio and TV stations. As *Time* reported, "Years of pent-up frustration under Milošević blighting misrule had finally erupted in a tumultuous showdown, as each new success taught Serbs to see they had the power to change their future. The revolution ran at cyberspeed from the disputed election two weeks ago, ending victoriously in the dizzying events of one day. Just like that, the Serbs took back their country and belatedly joined the democratic tide that swept away the rest of Eastern Europe's communist tyrants a decade ago."[18]

The people's revolution in Serbia against Milošević (the "Bulldozer Revolution") has proven to be a blueprint for action in other states of the post-communist world. In Georgia, in 2003, the "Rose Revolution" brought to power President Mikheil Saakashvili, and a dynasty was broken. In the Ukraine in 2004, after seventeen days of demonstrations in bitter cold, opposition leader Viktor Yushchenko won a hotly contested election in the "Orange Revolution." In March 2005, the old-style dictator of Kyrgyzstan was forced to flee to Moscow after holding power since the independence of that tiny republic in Central Asia in the "Tulip Revolution." While these events were vivid illustrations of the power of the masses and of mass communications, the immediate outcomes could not have been anticipated. The struggle in each state to develop institutions and find legitimate leaders is an ongoing process.

In Sum: How Much Do Individuals Matter?

For liberals, the actions of individuals matter. Individual elites can make a difference: they have choices in the kind of foreign policy they pursue and therefore can affect the course of events. Thus, we need to pay attention to personality characteristics and understand how individuals make decisions, how they employ various psychological mechanisms to process information, and how these processes impact individual and group behavior. Mass publics matter to liberals because liberals believe they help formulate the state's

---

THEORY IN BRIEF

Contending Perspectives on the Individual

	Liberalism / Neoliberal Institutionalism	Realism / Neorealism	Radicalism / Dependency Theory
Foreign-policy elites	Significant impact on international relations through choices made and personality factors	Constrained by anarchic international system and national interests	Constrained by international capitalist system
Private individuals	Secondary role, but may be involved in two-track diplomacy and may fund important initiatives	Actions of private individuals only have effect in aggregate, as reflected in national interest	Individual capitalists may be influential
Mass publics	May affect international relations through mass actions that pressure state decisionmakers	Actions may be reflected in national interest	Agents of potential change

interests. Private individuals also matter, although they are clearly of secondary importance even in liberal thinking. Only in more recent postmodernist and constructivist scholarship, especially in feminist scholarship, have private individuals' stories found salience.

Constructivists do see individuals as important. Individuals form collective identities; elites can serve as key policy entrepreneurs who can promote change through ideas.

Realists and radicals do not recognize the importance of individuals as independent actors in international relations. They see individuals as primarily constrained by the international system and by the state. To realists, individuals are constrained by an anarchic international system and by a state seeking to project power consonant with its national interest. Similarly, radicals see individuals only as members of a class often misled or deluded by elites of the international capitalist system and within a state driven by economic imperatives. In neither case are individuals believed to be sufficiently unconstrained to be considered a level of analysis on the same plane as either the international system or the state.

Individuals and states are not only important in themselves. They form into groups and operate internationally in both international organizations and nongovernmental organizations, within a framework of international law. We turn to these actors in the next chapter.

Notes

1. Robert G. Herman, "Identity, Norms, and National Security: The Soviet Foreign Policy Revolution and the End of the Cold War," in *The Culture of National Security: Norms and Identity in World Politics*, ed. P. J. Katzenstein (New York: Columbia University Press, 1996), 271–316.
2. Hans J. Morgenthau, *Politics among Nations* (brief ed. rev. Kenneth W. Thompson; New York: McGraw-Hill, 1993), 5.
3. Margaret G. Hermann, "Explaining Foreign Policy Behavior Using the Personal Characteristics of Political Leaders," *International Studies Quarterly* 24:1 (March 1980), 7–46.
4. Stephen Benedict Dyson, "Personality and Foreign Policy: Tony Blair's Iraq Decisions," *Foreign Policy Analysis* 2:3 (July 2006), 289.
5. Betty Glad, "Personality, Political, and Group Process Variables in Foreign Policy Decision Making: Jimmy Carter's Handling of the Iranian Hostage Crisis," *International Political Science Review* 10 (1989), 58.
6. Betty Glad, "Why Tyrants Go Too Far: Malignant Narcissism and Absolute Power," *Political Psychology* 23:1 (2002), 6.
7. Jerold Post quoted in Peter Carlson, "The Son Also Rises," *Washington Post National Weekly Edition*, May 26–June 1, 2003, 10–11.

8. Ole Holsti, "The Belief System and National Images: A Case Study," *Journal of Conflict Resolution* 6 (1962), 244–52.

9. Harvey Starr, *Henry Kissinger: Perceptions of International Politics* (Lexington, Ky.: University Press of Kentucky, 1984); and Stephen Walker, "The Interface between Beliefs and Behavior: Henry Kissinger's Operational Code and the Vietnam War," *Journal of Conflict Resolution* 21:1 (March 1977), 129–68.

10. Irving L. Janis, *Victims of Groupthink: A Psychological Study of Foreign-Policy Decisions and Fiascoes* (Boston: Houghton Mifflin, 1972), 9.

11. Herbert Simon, "A Behavioral Model of Rational Choice," in *Models of Man: Social and Rational,* ed. Herbert Simon (New York: John Wiley, 1957).

12. Anne-Marie Slaughter, "Mercy Killings," *Foreign Policy,* no. 134 (May–June 2003), 72–73.

13. David Makovsky, *Making Peace with the PLO: The Rabin Government's Road to the Oslo Accord* (Boulder, Colo.: Westview, 1996).

14. For excellent case studies of South Africa and Tajikistan dialogues, see Harold Saunders, *Politics Is about Relationships* (New York: Palgrave, 2005).

15. Cynthia H. Enloe, *Bananas, Beaches, and Bases: Making Feminist Sense of International Politics* (Berkeley: University of California Press, 1990).

16. Pamela Johnston Conover, Karen A. Mingst, and Lee Sigelman, "Mirror Images in Americans' Perceptions of Nations and Leaders during the Iranian Hostage Crisis," *Journal of Peace Research* 17:4 (1980), 325–37.

17. Swanee Hunt and Cristina Posa, "Women Waging Peace," *Foreign Policy,* no. 124 (March/June 2001), 38–47.

18. Johanna McGeary, "The End of Milošević," *Time,* October 16, 2000, 60.

Intergovernmental Organizations, Nongovernmental Organizations, and International Law

- *Why do intergovernmental organizations form?*
- *What have intergovernmental organizations like the United Nations contributed to international peace and security?*
- *How has the European Union changed over time?*
- *What roles are played by nongovernmental organizations?*
- *What is the role of international law in international relations?*
- *How do international relations theorists see intergovernmental organizations, nongovernmental organizations, and international law?*

States and individuals are not the only actors in international politics. **Intergovernmental organizations (IGOs)** and **nongovernmental organizations (NGOs)** also play a role in the international system. In this chapter we examine these actors, their historical development and functions, and their role in international relations. We also trace the development of international law. These actors and the international legal framework are key to understanding the liberal view of international politics in particular. We explore the strengths and weaknesses of liberal approaches to these elements of international relations and examine realist, radical, and constructivist responses.

Intergovernmental Organizations

The Creation of IGOs

Why have states chosen to organize themselves collectively? Responses to this question revolve around three major theories about the formation and development of intergovernmental organizations: federalism, functionalism, and collective goods.

FEDERALISM

◆ War is caused by individual states exercising sovereignty.

◆ Peace will be achieved if states transfer sovereignty to a higher federal body.

◆ In a federal system, states will be joined together and sovereignty transferred to the collectivity.

◆ In a federal system, the root cause of war has been eliminated.

Federalism

Jean-Jacques Rousseau expanded on the ideas of his predecessors in support of a united Europe. Rousseau reasoned that war was the product of the sovereign relationship among states and that peace could be attained if states gave up their sovereignty and invested it in a higher, federal body. Thus, Rousseau, in his *Project towards a Perpetual Peace,* proposed that states establish "such a form of federal government as shall unite nations by bonds similar to those which already unite their individual members and place the one no less than the other under the authority of the law."[1] Federalism suggests that states join together with other states, each surrendering some pieces of sovereignty. A diminution of sovereignty, or a pooling of sovereignty to a higher unit, it is believed, will help eliminate the root cause of war—military competition among sovereign states. That is the main intention of federalists in international relations.

Many of the specific schemes for federalism have focused on Europe. Indeed, one of the first proposals for European cooperation after World War II was that for the European Defense Community, which would have placed the military under community control, thus touching at the core of national sovereignty. This revolutionary proposal was defeated by the French Parliament, however, in 1954. Having been invaded by Germany twice in the twentieth century, the French were unwilling to place their security in the hands of an untested supranational body.

Functionalism

Functionalists believe that IGOs form for very different reasons. This viewpoint is best articulated by the scholar David Mitrany in *A Working Peace System*: "The problem of our time is not how to keep the nations peacefully apart but how to bring them actively together."[2] Thus, he proposed that units "bind together those interests which are common, where they are common, and to the extent to which they are common."[3] Like the federalists, the functionalists also want to eliminate war. However, they believe that the root cause of war is economic deprivation and disparity, not the fact that sovereign states each have military capability. Furthermore, functionalists believe that states are not suitable units to resolve these problems.

Functionalists promote building on and expanding the habits of cooperation nurtured by groups of technical experts, outside of formal state channels.

They believe that eventually, those habits will spill over into cooperation in political and military affairs, as functional experts lose their close identification with the state and develop new sets of allegiances to like-minded individuals around the globe. Along the way, functionalists believe, the economic disparities will be eliminated and war will therefore be less likely.

In Focus

FUNCTIONALISM

◆ War is caused by economic deprivation.

◆ Economic disparity cannot be solved in a system of independent states.

◆ New functional units should be created to solve specific economic problems.

◆ People will develop habits of cooperation, which will spill over from economic cooperation to political cooperation.

◆ In the long run, economic disparities will lessen and war will be eliminated.

The route of the European Union, the major European IGO, was a functionalist one. Its architect, Jean Monnet, believed that the weakened forces of nationalism could in the long run be further undermined by the logic of economic integration. Beginning with the creation of the European Coal and Steel Community (the predecessor of the European Economic Community [EEC]), he proposed cooperative ventures in nonpolitical issue areas, which, according to Mitrany, would spill over from the economic area to issues of national security. But Europe did not support all the functionalists' views, as discussed below.

At the core, functionalists, like federalists, are liberals in the idealist fashion. But whereas federalists place their faith in formal institutions to help curb states' appetites, functionalists believe that individuals can change and that habits of cooperation will develop if given sufficient time.

Collective Goods

The third theoretical perspective suggests that IGOs develop for quite different reasons. Biologist Garrett Hardin in "The Tragedy of the Commons" tells the story of a group of herders who share a common grazing area. Each herder finds it economically rational to increase the size of his own herd, allowing him to sell more in the market. Yet if all herders follow what is individually rational behavior, then the group loses: too many animals graze the land and the quality of the pasture deteriorates, which leads to decreased output for all. As each person rationally attempts to maximize his own gain, the collectivity suffers, and eventually all individuals suffer.[4]

What Hardin describes—the common grazing area—is a **collective good.** The grazing area is available to all members of the group, regardless of individual contribution. The use of collective goods involves activities and choices that are interdependent. Decisions by one state have effects for other states; that is, states can suffer unanticipated negative consequences as a result of the actions of others. In the international case, the decision by wealthy countries to continue the production and sale of chlorofluorocarbons affects all countries through long-term depletion of the ozone layer. With collective goods, market mechanisms break down. Alternative forms of management are needed.

Hardin proposed several possible solutions to the tragedy of the commons. First, use coercion. Force nations or peoples to control the collective goods. States, for example, could force people to limit the number of children they have in order to prevent a population explosion that harms the environment by drawing heavily on scarce natural resources. Second, restructure the preferences of states through rewards and punishments. Offer positive incentives for states to refrain from engaging in the destruction of the commons; tax or threaten to tax those who fail to cooperate, say, by making it cheaper for a polluter to treat pollutants than to discharge them untreated. Third, alter the size of the group. Smaller groups can more effectively exert pressure, since violations of the commons will be more easily noticed. Small groups can also mobilize collective pressure more effectively. China's population policy of one child per couple is administered at the local level, by individuals residing on the same street, in the same apartment building, or in the workplace. Close monitoring by these individuals, coupled with strong social pressure, is more apt to lead to compliance with the one-child policy. These alternatives can be achieved through organizations.

Each of these theoretic approaches has its own shortcomings. States may be unwilling to weaken their sovereignty by turning control over to a federal body, as federalists advocate. The question of the composition of the governing body also arises: who would exert control? And what instruments would the governing body have at its disposal? It is unclear precisely how such bodies would prevent war. Federalists struggle with these issues.

Economic disparity, the focus of functionalists, is unlikely to be the main cause of war. Furthermore, habits of cooperation do not inevitably spill over into other issue areas. Individuals are often unwilling to shift loyalties beyond or outside of the nation-state. Despite the successes of the EU, the functionalists still are faced with these realities.

In Focus

COLLECTIVE GOODS

◆ Collective goods are available to all members of the group regardless of individual contributions.

◆ Some activities of states involve the provision of collective goods.

◆ Groups need to devise strategies to overcome problems of collective goods caused by the negative consequences of the actions of others—the "tragedy of the commons."

◆ Strategies include use of coercion, changing preferences such as by offering positive incentives to refrain from engaging in an activity, and altering the size of the group to ensure compliance.

Collective goods theorists likewise confront practical difficulties. Not all international problems are collective goods problems. But for those problems that are, how can the number of participants be altered if, indeed, the problem is international in scope?

The Roles of IGOs

Intergovernmental organizations, such as the United Nations, the World Bank, and the International Civil Aviation Organization, can play key roles at each level of analysis, as highlighted in Table 7.1.[5] In the international system, IGOs contribute to habits of cooperation; through IGOs, states become socialized to regular interactions, a development that functionalists advocate. Such regular interactions occur between states in the United Nations. Some programs of IGOs, such as the International Atomic Energy Agency's nuclear monitoring program, establish regularized processes of information gathering, analysis, and surveillance that are particularly relevant to collective goods theory. Some IGOs, such as the World Trade Organization, develop procedures to make rules, settle disputes, and punish those who fail to follow the rules. Other IGOs conduct operational activities that help to resolve major substantive international problems, such as the transmission of communicable diseases, decolonization, economic disparity, and weapons proliferation. Some IGOs also play key roles in international bargaining, serving as arenas for negotiating and developing coalitions. They facilitate the formation of transgovernmental and transnational networks composed of both subnational and nongovernmental actors. And IGOs may be the place where major changes in the international distribution of power are negotiated.

IGOs, along with states, often spearhead the creation and maintenance of international rules and principles based on their common concerns. They establish expectations about behavior of other states. These have come to be known generally as **international regimes.** Charters of IGOs incorporate the norms, rules, and decisionmaking processes of regimes. By bringing members of the regime together, IGOs help to reduce the incentive to cheat and enhance the value of a good reputation. The principles of the international human rights regime, for example, are articulated in a number of international treaties, including the Universal Declaration of Human Rights. Some IGOs, like the United Nations (through its Office of the High Commissioner for Human Rights) and the European Union, institutionalize those principles into specific norms and rules. They establish processes designed to monitor states' human rights behavior and compliance with human rights principles. These same organizations provide opportunities for different members of the regime—states, other IGOs, NGOs, and individuals—to meet and evaluate their efforts.

TABLE 7.1

Roles of Intergovernmental Organizations		
Level	**Role**	**Example**
In the international system	Contribute to habits of cooperation.	Work within U.N. system and specialized agencies.
	Engage in information–gathering, surveillance.	World Bank gathers economic statistics; International Atomic Energy Agency monitors movement of nuclear materials across state boundaries.
	Aid in dispute settlement.	Dispute settlement procedures within the World Trade Organization or the International Court of Justice.
	Conduct operational activities.	Immunization campaigns for childhood diseases of the World Health Organization; refugee camps run by U.N. High Commissioner for Refugees.
	Serve as arena for bargaining.	European Council of Ministers, forums for different ministers to meet and negotiate.
	Lead to creation of international regimes.	International trade regime and international food regime.
With respect to states	Used by states as instrument of foreign policy.	Nordic states use U.N. to distribute international development assistance.
	Used by states to legitimate foreign policy	U.S. legitimates military action in Korea and in first Gulf war through U.N.
	Enhance information available to states.	Small states use in absence of extensive bilateral diplomatic network.
	Punish states for acting in certain ways.	Sanctions against South Africa, Rhodesia, Iraq, Serbia, and Iran.
With respect to individuals	Place where individuals can be socialized to international norms.	U.N. and EU delegates learn diplomatic norms.
	Place where individuals become educated about national similarities and differences.	Participants are educated at international meetings.

For states, IGOs enlarge the possibilities for foreign-policy making and add to the constraints under which states operate and especially implement foreign policy. States join IGOs to use them as instruments of foreign policy. The IGOs may serve to legitimate a state's viewpoints and policies; thus, the

United States sought the support of the Organization of American States during the Cuban missile crisis. The IGOs increase the information available about other states, thereby enhancing predictability in the policymaking process. Small states, in particular, use the U.N. system to gather information about the actions of others. Some IGOs, like the U.N. High Commissioner for Refugees and UNICEF, may be used to conduct specific activities. These functions are compatible with or augment state policy.

But IGOs also constrain states. They constrain or affect member states by setting international and hence national agendas and forcing governments to make decisions; by encouraging states to develop specialized decisionmaking and implementing processes to facilitate and coordinate IGO participation; and by creating principles, norms, and rules of behavior with which states must align their policies if they wish to benefit from their membership. Both large and small states are subject to such constraints. For example, members of the U.N. General Assembly have at times set the international agenda to the displeasure of the United States, forcing the United States to take a stand it would not have taken otherwise. Small states, likewise, have to organize their foreign-policy apparatus to address issues discussed in IGOs.

IGOs also affect individuals by providing opportunities for leadership. As individuals work with or in IGOs, they, like states, may become socialized to cooperating internationally.

Not all IGOs perform all of these functions, and the manner in and extent to which each carries out particular functions varies. Clearly the United Nations has been given an extensive mandate to carry out many of the functions. Yet the United Nations itself is a product of a historical process, an evolution that permits it to play its designated roles.

The United Nations

Basic Principles and Changing Interpretations

The United Nations was founded on three fundamental principles (see Table 7.2). Yet over the life of the organization, each of these principles has been significantly challenged by changing realities.[6]

First, the United Nations is based on the notion of the sovereign equality of member states, consistent with the Westphalian tradition. Each state—the United States, Lithuania, India, or Suriname, irrespective of size or population— is legally the equivalent of every other state. This legal equality is the basis for each state having one vote in the General Assembly. However, the actual inequality of states is recognized in the veto power given to the five permanent members of the Security Council (China, France, Russia, the United Kingdom, and the United States), the special role reserved for the wealthy

Roots of Contemporary International Organization and Law

Ancient times	Treaties concluded between city-states and communities (e.g., Mesopotamia, 3000 B.C.)
Greek and Roman eras	Development of different kinds of laws governing states, citizens, and aliens
Middle Ages	Under authority of Catholic Church, canon law applies to all believers
Seventeenth and eighteenth centuries	Hugo Grotius (1583–1645) writes that international relations is based on the rule of law, making him the father of international law; European writers like Émeric Crucé (1590–1648) and Abbé de Saint-Pierre (1658–1743) propose that European states meet to discuss conflicts and make plans for a court and league of states
Nineteenth century	Concert of Europe: major European powers use multilateral diplomacy to settle problems and coordinate actions, giving special status to great powers; formation of public international unions to address problems of commerce and communications (e.g., Universal Postal Union, 1864; International Telegraphic Union, 1865)
Late nineteenth and early twentieth centuries	Development of international legal institutions resulting from conferences in The Hague, Netherlands; both small states and non-European states join with European powers to develop dispute-settlement mechanisms
1918	U.S. president Woodrow Wilson calls for a general association of states in his "Fourteen Points" address to the U.S. Congress
1920	Treaty of Versailles is entered into force, and League of Nations is established; International Labor Organization and Permanent Court of International Justice are also established
1945	Representatives of fifty states meet in San Francisco and conclude U.N. Charter
1946	League of Nations transfers all assets to the United Nations

states in budget negotiations, and the weighted voting system used by the World Bank and the International Monetary Fund.

Second is the principle that only international problems are within the jurisdiction of the United Nations. Indicative of the Westphalian influence,

TABLE 7.2

U.N. Principles and Contemporary Realities	
Principles	**Changing Realities**
Sovereign equality of states.	Increasing number of members, including micro- and ministates that contribute little but still have equal votes in the General Assembly.
Only international problems are within U.N. jurisdiction.	Expansion of what is considered international because of changes in transportation, technology, and communication. For example, refugees can easily cross borders, leading states to initiate humanitarian intervention without the consent of other states involved.
Primarily concerned with international peace and security.	Broadened view of security, to include economic and environmental security; international intervention to manage economic instability and to protect from environmental pollution.

the U.N. Charter does not "authorize the United Nations to intervene in matters which are essentially within the domestic jurisdiction of any state" (Article 2, Section 7). Over the life of the United Nations, the once-rigid distinction between domestic and international issues has weakened and led to an erosion of sovereignty. Global telecommunications and economic interdependencies, international human rights, election monitoring, and environmental regulation are among the developments infringing on traditional areas of domestic jurisdiction and hence on states' sovereignty. War is increasingly civil war, which is not legally under the purview of the United Nations. Yet because international human rights are being abrogated, because refugees cross national borders, and because weapons of war are supplied through transnational networks, such conflicts are increasingly viewed as international, and the United Nations is viewed by some as the appropriate venue for action.

This has led to a growing body of precedent for humanitarian intervention without the consent of the host country. This was exercised in Somalia, where there was no central government to give consent to the U.N. humanitarian relief operations in 1992, and led to debate over whether intervention should occur in Darfur to stop the atrocities, even though the Sudanese government objects, as discussed in Chapter 8.

The third principle is that the United Nations is designed primarily to maintain international peace and security. This has meant that states should refrain from the threat or the use of force, settle disputes by peaceful means, as detailed at the Hague conferences, and support enforcement measures.

While the foundations of both the League of Nations and the United Nations focused on security in the realist, classical sense—protection of national territory—the United Nations is increasingly confronted with demands for action to support a broadened view of security. Operations to feed the starving populations of Somalia and Rwanda or to provide relief in the form of food, clothing, and shelter for Kurds fleeing to the mountains of northern Iraq or to Kosovars forced out of their homes are examples of this broadened notion of security—**human security.** Expansion into these newer areas of security collides head-on with the domestic authority of states, undermining the principle of state sovereignty. The United Nations's founders recognized the tension between the commitment to act collectively against a member state and the affirmation of state sovereignty. But they could not foresee the dilemmas that changing definitions of security would pose.

Structure

The structure of the United Nations was developed to serve the multiple roles assigned by its charter, but incremental changes in the structure have accommodated changes in the international system, particularly the increase in the number of states. The central U.N. organs comprise six major bodies, as shown in Table 7.3.

The power and prestige of these various organs has changed over time. The **Security Council,** responsible for ensuring peace and security and deciding enforcement measures, was very active during the 1940s. As the Cold War hardened between East and West, use of the Security Council diminished because of the Soviet Union's frequent use of the veto to block action. With the demise of the Cold War, the Security Council has again grown in power. The number of annual official Security Council meetings has risen and the number of annual resolutions passed increased. This heightened activity reflects the absence of Cold War hostility and the declining exercise of the veto by the five permanent members.

The **General Assembly,** with its growth in membership from 51 to 192, permits debate on any topic under its purview. The bulk of the work of the General Assembly is done in six functional committees: Disarmament and Security; Economic and Financial; Social, Humanitarian, and Cultural; Political and Decolonization; Administrative and Budgetary; and Legal. Debate on resolutions emerging from the committees is organized around regionally based voting blocs, member states using their one vote to coordinate positions and build support for them. Since the end of the Cold War, the General Assembly's work has been increasingly marginalized, as the epicenter of U.N. power has shifted back to the Security Council and a more active Secretariat, much to the dismay of the states in the **Group of 77,** the coalition of developing states.

Over the years, the Secretariat has expanded to employ over 7,000 individuals, with continuing efforts to reduce that number. The role that the secretary-general plays has expanded significantly. Having few formal powers,

TABLE 7.3

Principal Organs of the United Nations		
Organ	**Membership and voting**	**Responsibilities**
Security Council	15 members; 5 permanent with veto; 10 rotating on substantive issues	Peace and security: identifies aggressor; decides on enforcement measures
General Assembly	192 members; each state has one vote; work in 6 functional committees	Debates any topic within charter's purview; admits states; elects members to special bodies
Secretariat, headed by secretary-general	Secretariat of 7,500; secretary-general elected for 5-year renewable term by General Assembly and Security Council	Secretariat: gathers information, coordinates and conducts activities Secretary-general: chief administrative officer, spokesperson
Economic and Social Council (ECOSOC)	54 members elected for 3-year terms	Coordinates economic and social welfare programs; coordinates action of specialized agencies (FAO, WHO, UNESCO)
Trusteeship Council	Originally composed of administering and nonadministering countries; now made up of 5 great powers	Supervision has ended; proposals have been floated to change function to that of forum for indigenous peoples, NGOs, or nation building
International Court of Justice	15 judges	Noncompulsory jurisdiction on cases brought by states and international organizations

the authority of the secretary-general depends on persuasive capability and an aura of neutrality. With this power, the secretary-general, especially in the post–Cold War era, can potentially forge an activist agenda, as Secretary-General Kofi Annan did until his retirement in 2006. In 1998, at the request of members of the Security Council, he traveled to Baghdad to negotiate a compromise between Iraq and the United States over the authority, composition, and timing of U.N. inspection teams searching for nuclear, biological, and chemical weapons in Iraq. The secretary-general's negotiated compromise averted a showdown between the two powers at the time. Annan continued to play a mediator role between Iraq and the rest of the international community. He also implemented significant administrative and budgetary reforms within the organization and worked hard to establish a better relationship with the United States, especially the U.S. Congress, a key body in authorizing funding. Annan used the office to push other initiatives, including the international response to the AIDS epidemic and the promotion of better relations between the private sector and the United Nations. Considered a highly visible secretary-general, he was awarded the Nobel Peace Prize in 2001. No wonder the process to elect a successor in 2006 was such a contentious one, leading to the selection of Ban-Ki-Moon of the Republic of Korea.

Throughout the United Nations, when one organ has expanded in importance, others have diminished, most notably the Economic and Social Council (ECOSOC) and the Trusteeship Council, albeit for very different reasons. ECOSOC was originally established to coordinate the various economic and social activities within the U.N. system through a number of specialized agencies. But the expansion of those activities and the increase in the number of programs has made ECOSOC's task of coordination a problematic one. In addition to covering such broad issues as human rights, the status of women, population and development, and social development, ECOSOC is charged with coordinating the work of the family of U.N. specialized institutions (discussed later). In contrast, the Trusteeship Council has worked its way out of a job. Its task was to supervise decolonialization and to phase out trust territories placed under U.N. guardianship during the transition from colonies to independent states. Thus, the very success of the Trusteeship Council has meant its demise.

Key Political Issues

The United Nations has always mirrored what was happening in the world, and the world has, in turn, been shaped by the United Nations and its organs. The United Nations played a key role in the decolonization of Africa and Asia. The U.N. Charter endorsed the principle of self-determination for colonial peoples, and former colonies such as India, Egypt, Indonesia, and the Latin American states seized on the United Nations as a forum to push the agenda of decolonization. By 1960, a majority of the United Nation's members favored decolonization, and U.N. resolutions condemned the continuation of colonial rule and called for annual reports on the progress toward independence of all remaining territories. The United Nations was key to the legitimation of the new international norm that colonialism and imperialism are unacceptable state policies. By the mid-1960s, most of the former colonies had achieved independence with little threat to international peace, and the United Nations had played a significant role in this transformation.

The emergence of the newly independent states transformed the United Nations and international politics more generally. These states formed a coalition of the South, or Group of 77—developing states whose interests lie in economic development, a group often at loggerheads with the developed countries of the North. The split between the North and the South became the basis for the call by the Group of 77 for a New International Economic Order, described in Chapter 9. The North-South conflict continues to be a central feature of world politics and of the United Nations.

Peacekeeping

Of the issues the United Nations confronts none is as vexing as peace and security. During the Cold War, the structure of the Security Council (requiring unanimity among the five permanent members) prevented the United Nations from playing a major role in issues directly affecting those members. A new approach labeled peacekeeping evolved as a way to limit the scope of conflict and prevent it from escalating into a Cold War confrontation. Peacekeeping operations fall into two types, or generations. In **traditional peacekeeping,** multilateral institutions such as the United Nations seek to contain conflicts between two states through third-party military forces. Ad hoc military units, drawn from the armed forces of nonpermanent members of the U.N. Security Council (often small, neutral members), have been used to prevent the escalation of conflicts and to keep the warring parties apart until the dispute can be settled. Invited in by the disputants, the troops operate under U.N. auspices, supervising armistices, trying to maintain cease-fires, and physically interposing themselves in a buffer zone between warring parties. Table 7.4 lists some of these traditional U.N. peacekeeping operations.

In the post–Cold War era, U.N. peacekeeping has expanded to address different types of conflicts and to take on new responsibilities. Whereas traditional peacekeeping activities primarily address interstate conflict, **complex peacekeeping** activities respond also to civil war and ethnonationalist conflicts in states that have not requested U.N. assistance. To deal with these new conflicts, peacekeepers have taken on a range of both military and nonmilitary functions. Militarily, they have aided in the verification of troop withdrawal (the Soviet Union from Afghanistan) and have separated warring factions until the underlying issues could be settled (Bosnia). Sometimes resolving underlying issues has meant organizing and running national elections, such as in Cambodia and Namibia; sometimes it has involved implementing human rights agreements, such as in Central America. At other times U.N. peacekeepers have tried to maintain law and order in failing or disintegrating societies by aiding in civil administration, policing, and rehabilitating infrastructure, as in Somalia, East Timor, and Afghanistan. (This is often referred to as **nation-building.**) And peacekeepers have provided humanitarian aid, supplying food, medicine, and a secure environment in part of an expanded version of human security in Africa. Table 7.5 lists some representative cases of complex peacekeeping operations.

Complex peacekeeping has had successes and failures, as illustrated by the two African cases of Namibia and Rwanda. Namibia (formerly South-West

TABLE 7.4

Traditional Peacekeeping Operations			
Operation	**Location**	**Duration**	**Strength**
UNTSO (U.N. Truce Supervision Organization)	Egypt, Israel, Jordan, Syria, Lebanon	June 1948–present	572 military observers
UNEF I (First U.N. Emergency Force)	Suez Canal, Sinai Peninsula	Nov. 1956–June 1967	3,378 troops
ONUC (U.N. Operation in the Congo)	Congo	June 1960–June 1964	19,828 troops
UNFICYP (U.N. Peacekeeping Force in Cyprus)	Cyprus	March 1964–present	917 uniformed personnel
UNEF II (Second U.N. Emergency Force)	Suez Canal, Sinai Peninsula	Oct. 1973–July 1979	6,973 troops
UNDOF (U.N. Disengagement Observer Force)	Syrian Golan Heights	June 1974–present	1,048 troops, 57 military observers
UNMEE (U.N. Mission in Ethiopia and Eritrea)	Ethiopia/Eritrea border	Sept. 2000–present	2,063 troops, 222 military observers
UNIFIL (U.N. Interim Force in Lebanon)	Southern Lebanon	New mandate Aug. 2006–present	10,326 troops, 53 military observers

SOURCE: United Nations.

Africa), a former German colony, was administered by South Africa following the end of World War I. Over the years, pressure was exerted on South Africa to relinquish control of the territory and grant Namibia independence. As long as Soviet-backed Cuban troops occupied neighboring Angola, South Africa refused to consider change, citing security concerns. Finally in 1988, Cuba and Angola agreed to a withdrawal of Cuban troops as part of a regional peace settlement that included Namibian independence. The United Nations established a major peacekeeping operation in the region, which supervised the cease-fire, monitored the withdrawal of South African forces, oversaw the civilian police force, secured the repeal of discriminatory legislation, arranged for the release of political prisoners, and created conditions for free and fair elections. The U.N. Transition Assistance Group in Namibia (UNTAG) played a vital role in managing the move from war to a cease-fire and then to independence. The operation in Namibia became the model for U.N. complex

TABLE 7.5

	Complex Peacekeeping Operations		
Operation	**Location**	**Duration**	**Strength**
UNTAG (U.N. Transition Assistance Group)	Namibia, Angola	April 1989–March 1990	70 military observers
UNPROFOR (U.N. Protection Force)	Former Yugoslavia (Croatia), Bosnia, Macedonia	March 1992–Dec. 1995	30,500 troops and civilians
UNTAC (U.N. Transition Authority in Cambodia)	Cambodia	Feb. 1992–Sept. 1993	15,900 troops, 3,600 police, 2,400 civilians
UNOSOM I, II (U.N. Operation in Somalia)	Somalia	Aug. 1992–March 1995	28,000 troops, 2,800 civilians
MONUC (U.N. Mission in Democratic Republic of Congo)	Congo	1999–present	16,700 troops, 734 military observers
UNMIK (U.N. Interim Administration Mission in Kosovo)	Kosovo	1999–present	Details, see www.unmikonline.org
UNMISET and UNMIT (U.N. Missions in East Timor)	Timor-Leste	2002–present	1,588 troops, 1,608 police, and 1,200 civilians

SOURCE: United Nations.

peacekeeping and nation-building in Cambodia in the early 1990s and in East Timor in the late 1990s.

But not all U.N. peacekeeping operations have been successful. Rwanda is an example of where a limited U.N. peacekeeping force proved to be insufficient and where genocide subsequently escalated as the international community watched and did nothing. Rwanda and neighboring Burundi have seen periodic outbreaks of devastating ethnic violence between Hutus and Tutsis since the 1960s. In the 1990s, intermittent fighting once again broke out. A 1993 peace agreement called for a U.N. force (the U.N. Assistance Mission in Rwanda [UNAMIR]) to monitor the cease-fire. Yet less than a year later, large-scale violence erupted following the death of the Rwandan president in a plane crash, with Hutu extremists in the Rwandan military and police slaughtering minority Tutsis, resulting in 750,000 Tutsi deaths in a ten-week period. UNAMIR was not equipped to handle the crisis, and despite its commander's call for more troops, the U.N. Security Council failed to respond until it was too late. While UNAMIR did establish a humanitarian protection zone and provided security for relief-supply depots and escorts for aid convoys, peacekeeping failed disastrously.

Enforcement and Chapter VII

Since the end of the Cold War, the Security Council has intervened in situations deemed threatening to international peace and security as authorized in Chapter VII of the U.N. Charter. That provision enables the Security Council to determine threats to peace and acts of aggression and take enforcement measures (economic sanctions, military force) to restore international peace. Previously, such actions had only been invoked two times, the United Nations preferring the more limited traditional peacekeeping. Enforcement of Chapter VII includes the use of economic, diplomatic, and financial sanctions, as well as direct military action, to prevent or deter threats to international peace or to counter acts of aggression. The 1991 Gulf War was an enforcement action under Chapter VII. The Security Council authorized members "to use all necessary means," a mandate that led to direct military action by the multinational coalition under U.S. command. Economic sanctions against Iraq during the 1990s were also enforcement actions under Chapter VII, as were the disarmament provisions overseen by the U.N. Special Commission for the Disarmament of Iraq and the International Atomic Energy Agency (IAEA), one of the United Nations' specialized agencies.

In 2002, the United States went to the Security Council seeking Chapter VII enforcement against Iraq again, claiming that Iraq was in material breach of its obligations under previous U.N. resolutions. The Security Council was divided, with the United States and Great Britain supporting enforcement and France, Russia, and China opposing the action. When the stalemate solidified, the United States chose not to return to the Security Council to seek formal authorization for the use of force. Thus, the U.S.-led coalition in the 2003 Iraq war was not authorized by the United Nations, leading many to ponder whether the United Nations is still a relevant player in international politics.

Reform: Success and Stalemate

Faced with escalating demands and saddled with structures that no longer reflect the power realities of the international system, the United Nations has been confronted with persistent calls for reform. Although many reforms have been undertaken, the challenges remain critical. Because amending the charter is difficult—requiring ratification of two-thirds of the members, including all five permanent members of the Security Council—most reforms have been undertaken without actually amending the charter.

In response to criticisms of the size of the Secretariat, its number has been reduced by 4,000. To address management problems publicized in the Oil-for-Food scandal, when U.N. officials were accused of taking bribes and

POLICY DEBATE

In the aftermath of the 2003 Iraq war, is the United Nations still a relevant actor in world politics?

YES:

◆ The United States and Great Britain, having engaged in the Security Council debates about how to deal with Iraq, recognized the organization's legitimacy and sought its approval.

◆ U.N. procedures succeeded: hegemonic powers were not able to get the other members of the Security Council to support measures that they opposed.

◆ After the war was concluded, the United States and Great Britain showed deference to Security Council debates about the lifting of sanctions against Iraq and conceded that the United Nations should be involved in rebuilding Iraq and in conducting elections, suggesting the continuing relevance of the United Nations in world politics.

◆ NATO similarly engaged in enforcement action against Kosovo in 1999 without U.N. Security Council authorization, and that action did not result in long-term damage to either NATO or the United Nations.

◆ In the long run, the United Nations will still be needed to address many peace and security and economic development issues, and the fact that the war in Iraq was unauthorized will not detract from the necessity of such U.N. involvement.

NO:

◆ The fact that the United States and its coalition partners had to resort to the use of force against Iraq shows both the ineffectiveness of U.N.-backed economic sanctions and the ineffectiveness of the U.N. weapons inspection teams.

◆ Failure of the U.N. Security Council to act shows the politicized infighting and posturing of that body, confirming that the United Nations is unable to secure consensus.

◆ Failure of the United Nations to act illustrates how rogue states and leaders can take shelter within the rigid legalisms of the U.N. Charter and thereby thwart interference in their domestic affairs, defeating the very purpose of the United Nations.

◆ The Iraq case affirms the realist proposition that strong and powerful states can chart their own course of action without being constrained by the international community.

showing favoritism in awarding contracts for Iraq, new financial accountability mechanisms have been put in place and internal oversight has been established. To address newer issues, structures have been created or reorganized, including the High Commissioner for Human Rights in 1997 and the

Counter-Terrorism Committee in 2001 to help countries become more effective in addressing terrorism. To manage peacekeeping operations more efficiently, the Department of Peacekeeping Operations has been expanded, military staff have been added from the troop-contributing countries, and strategic deployment stocks and rapid deployment teams organized. In 2006, a new Peacebuilding Commission was formed to systematically address post-conflict recovery, whose mandates included monitoring economic stabilization and building government capacity. U.N. economic development activities have become more coordinated with U.N. Houses in recipient countries, providing a focal point for activities. And a new body formed in 2002 began the practice of bringing the heads of twenty-eight U.N. programs and agencies together, including the World Bank, International Monetary Fund, and World Trade Organization—a step that has been on the agenda for decades.[7]

In 2005, at the occasion of the United Nations's sixtieth birthday, one major reform emerged: Security Council reform. This is critical because it relates to the legitimacy of the Security Council's role in enforcement with the use of force. The five permanent members of the Council, the victors of World War II and their veto power over substantive issues, is an anachronism. Europe is overrepresented; China is the only developing country and only Asian member; both Germany and Japan contribute more financially to the organization than the other four permanent members do. Virtually all agree that membership should be increased. But there agreement ends. What other countries should be admitted? Germany, Japan, and/or Italy? India, Pakistan, South Africa, and/or Nigeria from the developing world? Argentina or Brazil? Should the new members have the veto? Should the differentiation between permanent and nonpermanent membership be maintained? In the 2005 session, contending proposals were discussed, but no agreement was reached. After all, reform begins and ends with states.

A Complex Network of Intergovernmental Organizations

The central organs of the United Nations discussed above are only a small part of the U.N. system of organizations. Today, there are nineteen specialized agencies formally affiliated with the United Nations, each a reflection of functionalist thinking. These organizations have separate charters, memberships, budgets, and secretariats. They also focus on different issues and therefore have their own respective constituencies. They include the World Health Organization, the Food and Agriculture Organization, and the International Monetary Fund and World Bank. While each reports to the ECOSOC, none can be instructed by it or by the General Assembly. In addition, there are other intergovernmental organizations not affiliated with the United Nations, including the World Trade Organization and the Organization of Petroleum Exporting Countries, as well as a plethora of regional and

TABLE 7.6

Representative International and Regional Organizations	
U.N. Specialized Agencies	**Independent Organizations**
World Health Organization	Organization of Petroleum Exporting Countries
Food and Agriculture Organization	World Trade Organization
International Labor Organization	Organization of Islamic Conference
International Atomic Energy Agency	North Atlantic Treaty Organization
World Bank Group	
International Monetary Fund	
International Atomic Energy Agency	
Regional Organizations	**Subregional Organizations**
European Union	Nordic Council
Organization for Security and Cooperation in Europe	European Free Trade Association
African Union	Economic Community of West African States
Organization of American States	Mercosur
Arab League	Gulf Cooperation Council

subregional organizations like the African Union, the Organization of American States, and the Common Market for Eastern and Southern Africa, with representative examples listed in Table 7.6.

The European Union—Organizing Regionally

Regional organizations also play an increasingly visible role in international relations. But none has been as visible, as strong, or as copied as the European Union. The idea of a united Europe goes back centuries. Plans presented by Immanuel Kant and Jean-Jacques Rousseau were filled with ideas on how to unite Europe.[8] After World War I, idealists dreamed that a united Europe could have forestalled the conflagration. World War II only intensified these sentiments. Hence, after that war, some theorists and political leaders, both functionalists and federalists, began earnest discussion. No one at the time could have envisioned that a union in 2007 would bring together 500 million citizens in 27 countries, allowing them to travel freely with a burgundy EU passport, enjoying a $13.4 trillion economy, and many of them (13) using a common currency, the euro.

Historical Evolution

The impetus for the creation of the European Union came not only from the direct wartime experience, but also from the threat that remained. Urged on by the United States, an economically strong Europe (made possible by the reduction of trade barriers) knew it would be better equipped to counter the threat of the Soviet Union if it integrated. Europe also understood that if the Germans were enmeshed in such agreements, they would pose less of a threat to other states. Of course, U.S.-based multinational corporations would also benefit from an expanded market. Thus, security threats, economic incentives, and a post-war vision all played a role in the drive of political elites for European integration.[9]

The European Coal and Steel Community, placing Franco and German coal and steel production under a common "High Authority," represented the first step toward realizing this idea. Although Germany was treated as an equal, its key economic sector supporting the arms industry was brought into a community with five other member states. The functionalist experiment was so successful in boosting coal and steel production that states agreed to expand cooperation under the European Atomic Energy Community and the European Economic Community. Thus the Treaties of Rome, signed in 1957, committed the six states to create a common market—removing restrictions on internal trade, imposing a common external tariff, reducing barriers to movement of people, services, and capital, and establishing a common agricultural and transport policy. In 1968, two years ahead of schedule, most of the goals had been achieved.

New policy areas were gradually brought under the umbrella of the community, including health, safety, and consumer standards. As success in these areas waxed and waned, and economic stagnation hindered progress, action was taken. The first initiative was expanding the size of the community—the so-called widening process. The original six members were joined by three others in 1973, and then five successive enlargements followed, the most recent in 2007, resulting in the 27-state membership. The enlargements have quadrupled membership and increased the influence of the organization, as well as complicated the decisionmaking.

In 1987, the most important step was taken in deepening the integration process—the signing of the Single European Act (SEA), which established the goal of completing a single market by the end of 1992. This meant a complicated process of removing the remaining physical, fiscal, and technical barriers to trade; harmonizing national standards of health; varying levels of taxation; and eliminating the barriers to movement of peoples. New environmental and technological issues were also addressed. Three thousand specific measures were needed to complete the single market.

Even before that was completed, the Maastricht Treaty was signed in 1992. The European Community became the **European Union** (EU). Members

Expansion of European Union, 1952–2007

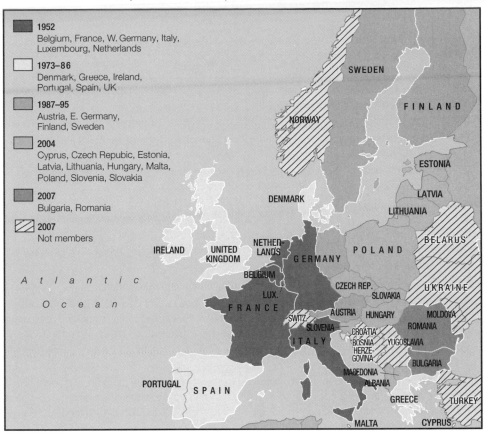

1952
Belgium, France, W. Germany, Italy, Luxembourg, Netherlands

1973–86
Denmark, Greece, Ireland, Portugal, Spain, UK

1987–95
Austria, E. Germany, Finland, Sweden

2004
Cyprus, Czech Repubic, Estonia, Latvia, Lithuania, Hungary, Malta, Poland, Slovenia, Slovakia

2007
Bulgaria, Romania

2007
Not members

committed themselves to not only an economic union, but a political one, including the establishment of common foreign and defense policies, a single currency, and a regional central bank. Five years later, in 1997, the Amsterdam Treaty was signed, making some changes to the previous treaties, including granting more power to the European Parliament but generally putting more emphasis on the rights of individuals, citizenship, justice, and home affairs.

The increased power of the EU has not been without its opponents. After the Maastricht Treaty, for example, the United Kingdom opted out of the monetary union and some social commitments. The Danish public rejected the treaty the first time, reversing itself a year later. The French electorate approved it by only a slim margin. These events signaled to European leaders that while the European public supports the idea of economic and political cooperation, they also fear a diminution of national sovereignty and are reluctant to surrender their democratic rights by placing more power in the hands of bureaucrats and other nonelected elites.

TABLE 7.7

Significant Events in the Formation and Expansion of the European Union	
Year	**Event**
1952	European Coal and Steel Community created by Belgium, France, Italy, Luxembourg, Netherlands, and West Germany.
1954	French National Assembly rejects proposal to form the European Defence Community.
1957	Treaty of Rome establishes the European Economic Community (EEC) and the European Atomic Energy Community, comprising same six members.
1968	Customs union is completed; all internal customs, duties, and quotas are removed and common external tariff is established.
1973	EEC is joined by Denmark, Ireland, and the United Kingdom.
1975	Lomé Convention between the EEC and 46 developing countries in Africa, the Caribbean, and the Pacific signed.
1979	High-level negotiations on European Monetary System are completed; first direct elections to the European Parliament.
1981	Greece joins the EEC; European political cooperation is extended.
1986	Passage of the Single European Act designed to ensure faster decisions; more attention to environmental and technological issues; list of measures compiled that need to be taken before achieving single market in 1992; Spain and Portugal join the EEC.
1990	West and East Germany reunited after fall of Berlin Wall; larger Germany maintains EEC membership.
1992	Maastricht Treaty completed, committing members to political union, including the establishment of a common foreign and defense policy, a single currency, and a regional central bank; name changed to European Union (EU); controversial referendums held in several countries.
1995	Austria, Finland, and Sweden join EU.
1997	Treaty of Amsterdam extends competence on Justice and Home Affairs, defines European citizenship.
1999	Common monetary policy and single currency (the euro) launched.
2002	Euro in circulation.
2004	Ten new members join in 2004; European Constitution negotiated.
2005	French and Dutch publics reject the proposed constitution; on-going discussions.
2007	Bulgaria and Romania join EU.

The debate over the proposed European Constitution brought these issues to a head. Pushed forward by political leaders, the European Constitution was signed by the heads of state in 2004. The constitution brings together the many treaties and agreements; it specifies the powers of the EU and the role of the EU institutions. It also incorporates the Charter of

TABLE 7.8

Principal Institutions of the European Union		
Institution	**Membership and Voting**	**Responsibilities**
European Commission	27 members, 4-year terms plus 23,000 support staff (Eurocrats)	Initiates proposals; guardians of treaties; executes policies
Council of Ministers	Ministers of member states; unanimity or qualified majority	Legislates; sets political objectives; coordinates; resolves differences
European Parliament	785 members, divided among members; elected every 5 years by citizens; organized around political parties	Legislates; approves budget; supervises executive
European Council	Heads of government; summit meetings twice yearly	Key body for EU initiatives
Economic and Social Committee	344 members drawn from economic/social interest groups; represents employers, employees, others	Consultative role; platform for civil society; forwards opinions to other institutions
European Court of Justice	Judges and advocates-general; appointed by states for 6-year terms	Adjudicates disputes on EU treaties; ensures uniform interpretation of EU laws; advisory opinions to states

Fundamental Rights. But the document requires ratification by all member states. In 2005, two states dealt a serious blow to the constitution, the Dutch and French electorate rejecting the document in respective referendums. Although thirteen other states have ratified the new constitution, including Italy, Greece, and Spain, the process is stalled while EU decisionmakers decide on whether to modify the original text, adopt separate portions of the text, or begin negotiations again. Among the controversial parts are the arrangements for the various EU institutions.

Structure

Table 7.8 provides the basic information about the EU's decisionmaking bodies, membership, voting, and responsibilities. Just as power has shifted between the U.N. organs, so, too, has power shifted in the EU. Initially, power resided in the Commission, which is designed to represent the interests of the community as a whole. While each state is entitled to one member, commission members are expected to be impartial and are not national representatives. Each is responsible for a particular policy area, known as a directorate-general, which, in turn, is divided into a directorate that covers a specific part of a policy area. For much of its history, the Commission has played this engine role, with the Council of Ministers ratifying, modifying, or vetoeing proposals, even though the Commission formally reports to the Council. Increasingly, the Council, with a weighted voting system, has assumed more power; some policy decisions in foreign and security affairs, immigration and taxation, even require unanimous support.

The increasing power of the European Parliament is also another change. Since the mid-1980s, it has gained a greater legislative and supervisory role. Because members are elected by universal suffrage, the body represents an element of democratic accountability not found in the other institutions. So, too, has the power of the European Court of Justice expanded. Since 1954, it has heard over 9,000 cases and issued more than 4,000 judgments. These rulings include both the court advising national courts on matters relating to EU law and direct actions requiring states or EU institutions to fulfill their obligations under the treaties.

Policies and Problems

The EU has moved progressively into more policy areas, from trade and agriculture (discussed in Chapter 9), to transport, competition, social policy, monetary policy, to the environment, justice, and common foreign and security policy. Among the many controversial issues has been the failed effort to develop a common European foreign and security policy. The split between those who supported the United States's Iraq policy (Great Britain and Spain) and those who opposed it (Germany and France) is suggestive. The difficulties in security policy have had repercussions in other arenas, and the war against terrorism has brought into question key EU policies, including open borders versus the security threats resulting from the absence of border controls, and the commitment to human rights versus the increased call for limitations on immigration and on revising the rights of aliens. Thus, disputes over deepening continue to be vexing. Should current members continue to deepen the range of cooperation? Should members try to reduce the tensions that develop when members split over foreign policy?

Equally as problematic are the issues surrounding widening. Should the EU continue to expand its membership by reaching out to the newly democratic states of Eastern Europe and the former Soviet Union? How rapidly can these new members come to adhere to the 80,000 pages of EU law and regulations in effect? How will the special concessions these countries won affect the functioning of the Union? Can Turkey, the first state with a majority Muslim population, eventually meet the criteria for membership: stable democratic institutions, a functioning market, and a capacity to meet union obligations? Will the EU governing institutions be able to change? So far, the debate over the European Constitution suggests that the answers will not be easy ones.

Nongovernmental Organizations

The world of intergovernmental organizations is becoming inextricably linked with nongovernmental organizations. NGOs, like IGOs, are increasingly recognized as influential actors in world politics. Today, over 250 million people are reached by NGOs. They distribute over $7.2 billion in aid and over 50 percent of World Bank projects are disbursed through NGOs.

NGOs are generally private, voluntary organizations whose members are individuals or associations that come together to achieve a common purpose. They are incredibly diverse entities, ranging from entirely local and/or grassroots organizations to those organized nationally and transnationally. Some are entirely private, that is, funding comes only from private sources, while others rely partially on government funds or aid-in-kind. Some are open to mass membership; others are closed member groups or federations. These differences have led to an alphabet soup of acronyms specifying types of NGOs. These include GONGOs (government-organized NGOs), BINGOs (business and industry NGOs), DONGOs (donor-organized NGOs), and ONGOs (operational NGOs), to name a few.

The number of NGOs has grown dramatically, although estimates vary enormously. The *Yearbook of International Organizations* identifies about 6,000 nongovernmental organizations that have an international dimension either in terms of their membership or their commitment to conduct activities in several states. Exclusively national NGOs may number upwards of 26,000. Grassroots local NGOs may number in the millions. Their numbers are rising exponentially.[10]

The Growth of NGO Power and Influence

Although NGOs are not new actors in international politics, they are of growing importance.[11] Historically, the antislavery campaign was one of the earliest NGO-initiated efforts to organize transnationally to ban a morally unacceptable practice. Its genesis lay in societies established in the 1780s dedicated to the abolition of slavery in the United States, England, and France. The group was strong enough to force the British Parliament in 1807 to forbid the slave trade for British citizens. In 1815, at the Congress of

Vienna and in the Treaty of Ghent, the international community considered again the abolition of the slave trade and reaffirmed that these practices were inhumane and unjust. While NGOs took the first steps toward enforcing the principles, they were not strong enough to succeed. Successful enforcement did not come until almost a century later.

NGOs organizing on behalf of peace and noncoercive methods of dispute settlement also appeared during the 1800s, as did the International Committee of the Red Cross, which advocated for humanitarian treatment for wounded soldiers, and international labor unions fighting for better working conditions. These same groups were instrumental in the first half of the twentieth century in lobbying for a "league of nations" and the International Labor Organization, and subsequently in supporting the establishment of the United Nations and the related agencies protecting different groups of people, including refugees (U.N. High Commissioner for Refugees) and women and children (UNICEF), among others. During this time, a variety of internationally relevant issues came to the attention of NGOs, and they worked both through states and established international groups to bring these issues to the international agenda.

During the 1970s, as the number of NGOs grew, networks and coalitions were formed among various groups, and by the 1990s these NGOs were able to effectively mobilize the mass public and influence international relations. A number of factors explain the remarkable resurgence of NGO activity and their increased power as an actor in international politics. First, the issues seized on by NGOs have been increasingly viewed as interdependent, or globalizing, issues—issues states cannot solve alone and whose solutions require transnational and intergovernmental cooperation. Airline hijackings of the 1970s; acid rain pollution and ocean dumping of the 1970s and 1980s; and global warming, land mines, and the AIDS epidemic of the 1990s are examples of issues that require international action and are "ripe" for NGO activity. Some of these issues have been increasingly viewed as human security issues, an argument many NGOs have promoted. Second, global conferences became a key venue for international activity beginning in the 1970s, each designed to address one of the globalizing issues—the environment (1972, 1992), population (1974, 1984), women (1975, 1985, 1995), and food (1974, 1996, 2002). A pattern emerged that NGOs organize separate but parallel conferences on the same issues. This creates opportunities for NGO representatives not only to network with each other and form coalitions on specific issues but to lobby governments and international bureaucrats. In some cases, those linkages between the governmental and nongovernmental conferees enhance the power of the latter. Third, the ending of the Cold War and the expansion of democracy in both the former communist world and developing countries have provided an unprecedented political opening for NGOs into parts of the world before untouched by NGO activity. Finally, the communications revolution also partly explains the rise of NGOs. The communications revolution, first fax, then the Web and e-mail, has enabled NGOs to communicate with core constituencies, build coalitions with other like-minded groups, and generate mass support. They can disseminate information rapidly, recruit new members, launch publicity campaigns, and encourage individuals to participate in ways unavailable two decades before. NGOs are the beneficiary of these changes and have been able to capitalize on them to increase their own power.

Functions and Roles of NGOs

NGOs perform a variety of functions and roles in international relations. They act as advocates for specific policies and offer alternative channels of political participation, as Amnesty International has done through its letter-writing campaigns on behalf of victims of human rights violations. They mobilize mass publics, as Greenpeace did in saving the whales (through international laws limiting whaling) and in forcing the labeling of "green" (non–environmentally damaging) products in Europe and Canada. They distribute critical assistance in disaster relief and to refugees, as Médecins Sans Frontières (Doctors without Borders), World Catholic Relief, and Oxfam have done in Somalia, Yugoslavia, Rwanda, and Sudan. They are the principal monitors of human rights norms and environmental regulations and provide warnings of violations, as Human Rights Watch has done in China, Latin America, and elsewhere.

NGOs are also the primary actors at the grassroots level in mobilizing individuals to act. For example, during the 1990 meeting to revise the 1987 Montreal Protocol on Substances That Deplete the Ozone Layer, NGOs criticized U.N. Environmental Program secretary-general Mostafa Tolba for not advocating more stringent regulations on ozone-destroying chemicals. Friends of the Earth International, Greenpeace International, and the Natural Resources Defense Council held press conferences and circulated brochures to the public, media, and officials complaining of the weak regulations. The precise strategy of each group varied. Friends of the Earth approached the matter analytically, while Greenpeace staged a drama to show the effects of environmental degradation. But the intent of each was the same—to focus citizen action on strengthening the Montreal Protocol. By publicizing inadequacies, NGOs force discussion both within states and between states in international forums.

Nowhere has the impact of NGOs been felt more strongly than at the 1992 U.N. Conference on the Environment and Development (UNCED) in Rio de Janeiro. NGOs played key roles in both the preparatory conferences and the Rio conference itself, adding representation and openness (or "transparency") to the process. For the first time, they made statements from the floor during official working group and plenary meetings. They drafted informational materials, which were circulated on tables inside meeting rooms for easy access by government delegations. They scrutinized working drafts of U.N. documents, reviewing and passing on comments to influential officials and delegates. They spoke up to support or oppose specific phrasing. The UNCED provided extensive opportunities for NGO networking. More than four hundred environmental organizations were accredited at the conference, including not only traditional, large, well-financed NGOs, such as the World Wildlife Fund, but also those working on specific issues and those with grassroots origins in developing countries, many of which were poorly financed and had had few previous transnational linkages.

The persistence of the NGOs paid off. Agenda 21, the official document produced by the conference, recognized the unique capabilities of NGOs and recommended their participation at all levels from policy formulation and decisionmaking to implementation. What began as a parallel informal process of participation within the U.N. system evolved into a more formal role, a role replicated at the 1994 International Conference on Population and Development in Cairo and at the 1995 Fourth World Conference on Women in Beijing.

NGOs also play unique roles at the national level. In a few unusual cases, NGOs take the place of states, either performing services that an inept or corrupt government is not doing or stepping in for a failed state. Bangladesh hosts the largest NGO sector in the world, a response in part to that government's failure and the failure of the private for-profit sector to provide for the poor. Thus, NGOs have assumed responsibility in education, health, agriculture, and microcredit, originally all government functions. The failed state of Somalia has also witnessed an explosion of NGO activity, performing vital economic functions that the government is ill equipped to handle, a situation that has led some commentators to suggest that Somalia has governance without a government. Other NGOs are working to change various countries' public institutions, the Muslim Brotherhood in Egypt being a salient example. This nonviolent group dating back to 1928 has had a long confrontational relationship with the Egyptian government and seeks first social justice and then the implementation of *sharia* (Islamic law).

Yet NGOs seldom work alone. The communications revolution has served to link NGOs with each other, formally and informally. The Muslim Brotherhood, for example, maintains close connections with groups considered more militant, such as Hamas, and is active in several Middle Eastern countries and in Europe. Increasingly, NGOs are developing regional and global networks through linkages with other NGOs, like that which the Women's Environment and Development Organization has forged among its 283 worldwide member organizations. These networks and coalitions create multilevel linkages between different organizations, each of which retain its separate organizational character and membership, but through the linkages enhance each other's power. These networks have learned from each other, just as constructivists would have predicted. Environmentalists and women's groups have studied human rights campaigns for guidance in building international norms. Women's groups used the language of human rights to mainstream women's rights in the 1990s; environmentalists seeking protection of spaces for indigenous peoples also increasingly use the language of human rights.

We usually associate NGOs with humanitarian and environmental groups working for a greater social, economic, or political good, but NGOs may also be formed for malevolent purposes, the Mafia, international drug cartels, and even Al Qaeda being prominent examples. The Mafia, traditionally located in Italy, but with networks in Russia, Eastern Europe, and the Americas, is engaged in numerous illegal business practices, including money laundering, tax evasion, and fraud. International drug cartels, many with origins in Colombia, function with suppliers in such far-reaching states as Peru, Venezuela, Afghanistan, and Myanmar, while maintaining links with middlemen in Nigeria, Mexico, and the Caribbean, in order to deliver illegal drugs to North America and Europe. Their illegal activity is calculated to be $400 billion annually, or 8 percent of world trade. What these NGOs share is a loose form of networks working across national boundaries, moving illicit goods and services in international trade. Their leadership is dispersed and their targets ever changing, making their activities particularly difficult to contain.

Al Qaeda, too, represents such an NGO—decentralized, dispersed, with individuals deeply committed to a cause, even at the price of death, and able and willing to take initiatives independent of a central authority. The organization has changed and expanded its goals over time, which has enabled it to recruit members willing to die for diverse causes. Osama bin Laden has forged broad links and alliances with various groups. Like all NGOs, Al Qaeda has benefited from new communications technologies, using the World Wide Web to collect information and train individuals, and e-mail to transfer funds and communicate messages, all virtually untrackable.[12] Opponents of Al Qaeda and these other NGOs are waging a different battle, a war on organized crime, a war on drugs, and a war against terror.

The Power of NGOs

What gives NGOs the ability to play such diverse roles in the international system? What are their sources of power? NGOs rely on soft power, meaning credible information, expertise, and moral authority that attracts the attention and admiration of governments and the public. This means that NGOs have resources such as flexibility to move staff rapidly depending on need, independent donor bases, and links with grassroots groups that enable them to operate in different areas of the world. This very flexibility enables them to create networks to increase their power potential, banding together with other like-minded NGOs and forming coalitions to push their respective agendas. And the new communication technologies have facilitated this networking and coalition-building source of NGO power.

NGOs have distinct advantages over individuals, states, and intergovernmental organizations. They are usually politically independent from any sovereign state, so that they can make and execute international policy more rapidly and directly, and with less risk to national sensitivities, than IGOs can. They can participate at all levels, from policy formation and decision-making to implementation, if they choose. Yet they can also influence state behavior by initiating formal, legally binding action; pressuring authorities to impose sanctions; carrying out independent investigations; and linking issues together in ways that force some measure of compliance. Thus, NGOs are versatile and increasingly powerful actors.

The Limits of NGOs

NGOs lack traditional forms of power. Except for some of the malevolent groups, they do not have military or police forces as governments do, and thus they cannot command obedience through physical means.

Most NGOs have very limited economic resources since they do not collect taxes as states do. Thus the competition for funding is fierce; NGOs sharing the same concerns—for example, human rights organizations—often compete for the same donors. There is a continuous need to raise money, leading some NGOs to find new causes to expand their donor base. To expand their resources, NGOs increasingly rely on governments, an alternative that comes with its own set of limitations. If NGOs choose to accept state assistance, then their neutrality and legitimacy is potentially compromised. They may be forced to continually report "success" in order to renew the financing, even though success may be difficult to prove or even be an inaccurate description of reality. In short, there is a competitive "scramble" among NGOs for resources.[13]

Do most NGOs succeed in accomplishing their task? This is difficult to evaluate because the NGO community is itself diverse; there is no single agenda, and NGOs are often working at cross-purposes, just like states. Groups can be found on almost any side of every issue, resulting in countervailing pressures. And some people are beginning to question whether certain activities undertaken by NGOs, which have been traditionally viewed as supportive of the common good—providing refugee camps, feeding starving children—may, in the long run, result in prolonging conflicts or leading to other unexpected even dysfunctional outcomes.[14]

Finally, in a world that is increasingly viewed as democratic, are NGOs appropriate? To whom are NGOs accountable if their leaders are not elected? How is transparency maintained when there is no publicly accountable mechanism? Do NGOs reflect liberal values? No wonder there has been a backlash against NGOs in some states.

International Law

Since the beginning of the new millennium, international law has captured the headlines more than perhaps at any other time. In the aftermath of 9/11, the U.S. military actions in Afghanistan and Iraq, and mounting humanitarian crises, international treaties have become well-known documents: the Geneva Conventions (technically the Geneva Convention for Victims of War, 1949), the Convention Against Torture (the U.N. Convention Against Torture and Other Cruel, Inhuman or Degrading Treatment or Punishment, 1984, 1987), and the Genocide Convention (Convention on the Prevention and Punishment of Genocide, 1948). Debate has raged over the definitions of terms: torture, genocide, terrorism, enemy combatants, enemy detainees, rendition. NGOs, like the International Committee of the Red Cross and Human Rights Watch, once known to only a few, have attained international recognition. Thus, understanding the characteristics of international law and its limitations is all the more urgent.

International Law and Its Functions

International law consists of a body of both rules and norms regulating interactions among states, between states and IGOs, and in more limited cases among IGOs, states, and individuals. Laws serve several purposes: setting a body of expectations, providing order, protecting the status quo, and legitimating the use of force by a government to maintain order. Law provides a mechanism for settling disputes and protecting states from each other. It serves ethical and moral functions, aiming in most cases to be fair and equitable and delineating what is socially and culturally desirable. These norms demand obedience and compel behavior.

At the state level, law is hierarchical. Established structures exist for both making law (legislatures and executives) and enforcing law (executives and judiciaries). Individuals and groups within the state are bound by law. Because of a general consensus within the state on the particulars of law, there is widespread compliance with the law. It is in the interest of everyone

Nongovernmental Organizations: Views from the Former Soviet States

While the power of NGOs has grown in many countries, that power has led to a back-lash in other states. Nowhere is this more true than in post–Cold War Russia and other former Soviet states. Decisionmakers in these countries fear NGOs for the power they have exerted and policies they have promoted, like democratization and support for human rights. Thus, these states have often taken measures to limit NGO activities.

In 2006 Russia adopted a law that severely limits the operations of NGOs. This followed similar initiatives taken by other countries in the region. In 2005, the president of Uzbekistan, Islam Karimov, ordered the closing of most of the NGOs operating in the country. In Belarus President Aleksandr Lukashenko outlawed all forms of civil society and external aid. In Tajikistan, all foreign embassies and organizations must report any involvement with local media, NGOs, and political parties.

These reactions follow several years during which NGOs in these struggling democracies have come under increasing criticism. With over 300,000 NGOs operating in Russia, the government has increasingly denied entry to individuals working for NGOs, closed NGO offices, conducted long audits, and questioned the organizations' tax-exempt status. The Russians consider the NGOs' criticism of the government to be tarnishing to Russia's reputation abroad and a cause of civil strife. These recipients of foreign funds are seen as acting against the interests of the Russian state. The recent law gives enhanced power to the Ministry of Justice to register NGOs, audit their finances, and effectively determine which activities they can carry out. With full implementation, Russia will be able to control what occurs within its sovereign borders.

Leaders suspect that the democratic revolutions of Georgia, Ukraine, and Kyrgyzstan were financed by groups such as the U.S.-based National Democratic Institute, the International Republican Institute, Freedom House, and the Open Society Institute. The 2005 revolution in Kyrgyzstan, for example, is largely attributed to the publication of photos of President Askar Akayev's mansion in a Kyrgyz newspaper that was printed on a press financed by the United States. Widespread riots followed and the unpopular president fled to Moscow.

American-financed NGOs promoting democracy or human rights are viewed as advocating regime change or reflecting U.S. government policy, rather than an independent position. American NGO credibility is also weakened by the United States' diminished status as a symbol for human rights and democracy. Opponents of these NGOs point to torture in American-run prisons and renditions to foreign territories, asking what right the United States and its state-supported NGOs have to promote so-called political and civil unrest in Russia and other states? The governments of these states cannot accept interference from the agents of an imperialistic state that tortures people abroad.

For Critical Analysis

1. Are NGOs that advocate democracy interfering with established governments and undermining state sovereignty?
2. How might realists and radicals justify the states' opposition to foreign-financed NGOs?

that order and predictability be maintained. But if law is violated, the state authorities can compel violators to judgment and use the instruments of state authority to punish wrongdoers.

In the international system, authoritative structures are absent. There is no international executive, no international legislature, and no judiciary with compulsory jurisdiction. So is there international law, given the absence of a sovereign body with enforcement power and the inability to compel compliance with effective physical coercion? Legal scholar Christopher C. Joyner argues "yes": binding legal rules are created, states recognize their obligations, and resorting to force is not necessary for the international legal system to operate. After all, "international legal rules obtain their normative force not because any superior power or world government prescribes them but because they have been generally accepted by states as rules of conduct, with the expectation that states will follow suit."[15]

Liberals acknowledge that law in the international system is different from that in domestic systems. To them, international law not only exists, but it has an effect in daily life. As political scientist Louis Henkin explains,

> If one doubts the significance of this law, one need only imagine a world in which it were absent. . . . There would be no security of nations or stability of governments; territory and airspace would not be respected; vessels could navigate only at their constant peril; property—within or without any given territory—would be subject to arbitrary seizure; persons would have no protection of law or diplomacy; agreements would not be made or observed; diplomatic relations would end; international trade would cease; international organizations and arrangements would disappear.[16]

We turn now to an assessment of the ways that international law is similar to and different from national law.

The Sources of International Law

International law, like domestic law, comes from a variety of sources (see Figure 7.1). Virtually all law emerges from custom. Either a hegemon or a group of states solves a problem in a particular way; these habits become ingrained as more states follow the same custom, and eventually the custom is codified into law. For example, Great Britain and later the United States were primarily responsible for developing the law of the sea. As great seafaring powers, each state adopted practices—rights of passage through straits, methods of signaling other ships, conduct during war, and the like—that became the customary law of the sea and were eventually codified into law.

FIGURE 7.1

Sources of International Law

Custom

Treaties

International law

Authoritative bodies

Courts (international, national, and local)

The laws protecting diplomats and embassies, likewise, emerged from long-standing customs.

But customary law is limited. For one thing, it develops slowly; British naval custom evolved into the law of the sea over several hundred years. Sometimes customs become outmoded. For example, the 3-mile territorial extension from shore was established because that was the distance a cannonball could fly. Eventually law caught up with changes in technology, and states were granted a 12-mile extension of territory into the ocean. Furthermore, not all states participate in the making of customary law, let alone give assent to the customs that have become law through European-centered practices. And the fact that customary law is initially uncodified leads to ambiguity in interpretation.

International law also comes from treaties, the dominant source of law today. Treaties, explicitly written agreements among states, number more than 25,000 since 1648 and cover all issues. Most judicial bodies, when deciding cases, look to treaty law first. Treaties are legally binding: only major changes in circumstances give states the right not to follow treaties they have ratified.

International law has also been formulated and codified by authoritative bodies. Among these bodies is the U.N. International Law Commission, composed of prominent international jurists. That commission has codified much customary law: the Law of the Sea (1958), the Vienna Convention of the Law of Treaties (1969), and the Vienna Conventions on Diplomatic Relations (1961) and on Consular Relations (1963). The commission also drafts new conventions for which there is no customary law. For example, laws on product liability and on the succession of states and governments have been formulated in this way, then submitted to states for ratification.

Courts are also sources of international law. Although the International Court of Justice (ICJ), with its fifteen judges located in The Hague, the Netherlands, has been responsible for some significant decisions, the ICJ is basically a weak institution, for several reasons. First, the court actually hears very few cases; between 1946 and 2006, the ICJ has had 112 contentious cases brought before it and has issued 25 advisory opinions, although since the end of the Cold War its caseload has increased. Ever since the small developing country Nicaragua won a judicial victory over the United States in 1984, developing countries have shown greater trust in the court. Although procedures have changed to speed up the lengthy process, the court's noncompulsory jurisdiction provision still limits its caseload. Both parties must agree to the court's jurisdiction before a case is taken. This stands in stark contrast to domestic courts, which enjoy compulsory jurisdiction. Accused of a crime, you are compelled to judgment. No state is compelled to submit to the ICJ. Second, when cases are heard, they rarely deal with the major controversies of the day, such as the war in Vietnam, the invasion of Afghanistan, or the unraveling of the Soviet Union or of Yugoslavia. Those controversies are political and outside of the court's reach. But interstate boundary disputes are major issues on the court's agenda. Third, only states may initiate proceedings; individuals and nongovernmental actors like multinational corporations cannot. Hence, with such a limited caseload concerning few fundamental issues, the court could never be a major source of law. In contrast, the European Court of Justice of the European Union is a significant source of European law. It has a heavy caseload, covering virtually every topic of European integration.

National and even local courts are also sources of international law. Such courts have broad jurisdiction; they may hear cases occurring on their territory in which international law is invoked or cases involving their own citizens who live elsewhere, and they may hear any case to which the principle of universal jurisdiction applies. Under **universal jurisdiction,** states may claim jurisdiction if the conduct of a defendant is sufficiently heinous to violate the laws of all states. Several states claimed such jurisdiction as a result of the genocide in World War II and more recently for war crimes in Bosnia, Kosovo, and Rwanda. In the European Union, national and local courts are a vital source of law. A citizen of an EU country can ask a national court to invalidate any provision of domestic law found to be in conflict with provisions of the EU treaty. A citizen can also seek invalidation of a national law found to be in conflict with self-executing provisions of community directives issued by the EU's Council of Ministers. Thus, in the European system, national courts are both essential sources of European community law and enforcers of that law.

Enforcement of International Law

A key trend now clear in the new millennium has been the expansion of the international judiciary, motivated by the idea of individual responsibility for war crimes and crimes against humanity. The idea is not new. After World War II, the Nuremberg and Tokyo trials punished individuals for war crimes, but because these trials were the victor's punishment of the vanquished, they were not seen as precedents. Following the atrocities in Yugoslavia, Rwanda, and later East Timor, the United Nations established two ad hoc criminal tribunals, the International Criminal Tribunal for the Former Yugoslavia, in 1993, and the International Criminal Tribunal for Rwanda, in 1994. These ad hoc tribunals approved by the U.N. Security Council have developed procedures to deal with the myriad of issues involved in these cases, including jurisdiction, evidence, sentencing, and imprisonment. Among the accused on trial was former Serbian president Slobodan Milošević, until his death in 2006, and among those sentenced are a number of Rwandan officials, including the former prime minister, Jean Kambanda. Because of the need to establish procedures and the difficulty of finding those accused, the trials have been subject to criticism.

In light of the difficulties with the ad hoc tribunals, in 1998, states under U.N. auspices concluded the statute for the International Criminal Court (ICC), an innovative court having both compulsory jurisdiction and jurisdiction over individuals. Four types of crimes are covered: genocide (attacking a group of people and killing them because of race, ethnicity, or religion); crimes against humanity (murder, enslavement, forcible transfer of population, torture), war crimes, and crimes of aggression (undefined). No individuals (save those under eighteen years of age) are immune from jurisdiction, including heads of states and military leaders. The ICC functions as a court of last resort, hearing cases only when national courts are unwilling or unable to deal with prosecuting grave atrocities.

In 2003, the eighteen justices of the ICC were installed, and work began. Pending cases all concern crimes committed in African countries. With the exception of Darfur, most of the cases have attracted little international attention. Yet the ICC is controversial. Widely hailed by many, including a broad-based coalition of over one thousand NGOs, supporters see the court as

essential for establishing international law and enforcing individual accountability for actions taken during conflict. Others, including the United States,
China, India, and Turkey, are critical. Specifically, the United States objects to
provisions of the statute that might make U.S. military personnel or the U.S.
president subject to ICC jurisdiction, believing that the United States has
"exceptional" international responsibilities as a hegemon that should make its
military and leaders immune from the ICC's jurisdiction. The United States
objects more generally on the grounds that the ICC infringes on U.S. sovereignty. The controversy continues, while the ICC proceeds despite the United
States's refusal to sign the treaty.[17]

With weak authoritative structures at the international level, like the
International Court of Justice and the nascent International Criminal Court,
why do most states obey international law most of the time? The liberal
response is that states obey international law because it is right to do so.
States want to do what is right and moral, and international law reflects what
is right. To liberals, individual states benefit from doing what is right and
moral, and all states benefit from living in an ordered world where there are
general expectations about other states' behavior. States want to be looked on
positively, according to liberal thinking. They want to be respected by world
public opinion, and they fear being labeled as pariahs and losing face and
prestige in the international system.

Should states choose not to obey international law, other members of the
international system do have recourse. A number of the possibilities are self-
help mechanisms that realists rely on:

- Issue diplomatic protests, particularly if the offense is a relatively
  minor one.
- Initiate reprisals, actions that are relatively short in duration and
  intended to right a previous wrong.
- Threaten to enforce economic boycotts or impose embargoes on both
  economic and military goods if trading partners are involved.
- Use military force, the ultimate self-help weapon.

But liberals contend, rightly in many cases, that self-help mechanisms of
enforcement from one state alone are apt to be ineffective. A diplomatic
protest from an enemy or a weak state is likely to be ignored, although a
protest from a major ally or a hegemon may carry weight. Economic boycotts
and sanctions by one state will be ineffective as long as the transgressor state
has multiple trading partners. And war is both too costly and unlikely to lead
to the desired outcome. In most cases, then, for the enforcement mechanism
to be effective, several states have to participate. To be most effective, all

states have to join together in collective action against the violator of international norms and law. In the view of liberals, states find protection and solace in collective action and in collective security.

Realist Views of International Organization and Law

Realists are skeptical about international law, intergovernmental organizations, and nongovernmental organizations, though they do not completely discount their place. Recall that realists see anarchy in the international system, wherein each state is forced to act in its own self-interest and obliged to rely on self-help mechanisms. International law purportedly creates some order, as many realists acknowledge. But why do states choose to comply with these norms? The realist answer to this question is different from the response of the liberals. Realists contend that compliance occurs not because the norms are good and just in themselves but because it is in the state's self-interest to comply. States benefit from living in an ordered world, where there are some expectations about other states' behavior. A constant fear of infringement on territory and insecurity for their population is costly for states, in terms of both the economic cost of having to prepare for every possible contingency and the psychological cost of anxiety and fear. It is in the self-interest of most states to have their territory and airspace respected, to have their vessels free to navigate international waters, and to enjoy the secure procedures of diplomatic relations and international trade. Yet realists also know that states can opt out of following international law, and for the more powerful, there is little other states can do.

Realists are also skeptical about international organizations, both IGOs and NGOs, as independent actors. IGOs are controlled by states, and states often prefer weak organizations. For example, realists point to the failure of the council of the League of Nations to act when Japan invaded Manchuria in 1931 and its slow response to the Italian invasion of Ethiopia in 1935. These failures confirm the fundamental weaknesses of the League and of its collective approach to punishing aggressors. Without the great powers to support the League's principles, especially its commitment to prevent war, the institution's power and legitimacy deteriorated. Realists likewise do not put much faith in the United Nations. They can legitimately point to the Cold War era, when the Security Council proved impotent in addressing the conflict between the United States and the Soviet Union. And the failure in 2003 of the United Nations to enforce Security Council resolutions against Iraq is another reminder of the organization's weakness and supposed irrelevance.

In the state-centric world of the realists, NGOs are generally not on the radar screen at all. After all, most NGOs exist at the beck and call of states; it is states that grant them legal authority, and it is states that can take away that authority. To realists, NGOs are not an independent actor.

Realists recognize that international law and international organizations have the potential to provide an alternative to states' utilizing self-help alternatives. It may be in states' self-interest to utilize these institutions. Yet they do not. States are uncertain whether such institutions will function as planned. There is an element of mistrust. They are skeptical about whether long-term gains can be achieved. Realists doubt that collective action is possible and believe states will refuse to rely on the collectivity for the protection of individual national interests.

The Radical View of International Organization and Law

Radicals in the Marxist tradition are also very skeptical about international law, IGOs, and many NGOs, albeit for very different reasons from those of the realists. Radicals see contemporary international law and organization as the product of a specific time and historical process, emerging out of eighteenth-century economic liberalism and nineteenth-century political liberalism. Thus, international law primarily comes out of Western capitalist states and is designed to serve the interests of that constituency. International law is biased against the interests of socialist states, the weak, and the unrepresented.

Similarly, IGOs, most notably the League of Nations, the United Nations, and the United Nations's specialized agencies, were designed to support the interests of the powerful. According to radicals, those institutions have succeeded in sustaining the powerful elite against the powerless mass of weaker states. For example, international legal principles, like the sanctity of national geographic boundaries, were developed during the colonial period to reinforce the claims of the powerful. Attempts to alter such boundaries are, according to international law, wrong, even though the boundaries themselves may be unfair or unjust. Radicals are quick to point out these injustices and support policies that overturn the traditional order. Thus, from their viewpoint, the actions by the United Nations following the Iraqi invasion of Kuwait in 1990, including a series of resolutions condemning Iraq and imposing sanctions on that country, were designed to support the position of the West, most notably the interests of the hegemonic United States and its capitalist friends in the international petroleum industry. To radicals, the U.N.-imposed sanctions provide an excellent example of hegemonic interests injuring the marginalized—Iraqi men, women, and children striving to eke out meager livings. Radicals also view the NATO actions in Kosovo as another example of hegemonic power harming the poor and disenfranchized.

THEORY IN BRIEF

Contending Perspectives on International Organization and Law

	Liberalism / Neoliberal Institutionalism	Realism / Neorealism	Radicalism / Dependency Theory
Intergovernmental organizations	Important independent actors for collective action	Skeptical of their ability to engage in collective action	Serve interests of powerful states; biased against weak states and the unrepresented
Nongovernmental organizations	Increasingly key actors that represent different interests and facilitate collective action	Not independent actors; power belongs to states; any NGO power is derived from states	Represent dominant economic interests; unlikely to effect major political or economic change
International law	Key source of order in the international system; states comply because law assures order	Acknowledges that international law creates some order, but stresses that states comply only when it is in their self-interest; states prefer self-help	Skeptical because origins of law are in Western capitalist tradition; international law only reaffirms claims of the powerful

To most radicals, the lack of representativeness and the lack of accountability of NGOs are key issues. Most radicals see the world of NGOs based in the North as dominated by members of the same elite who run the state and international organizations. They see NGOs as falling under the exigencies of the capitalist economic system and as captive to the dominant interests of that system. Only a few NGOs, according to radicals, have been able to break out of this mold and develop networks enabling mass participation designed to change the fundamental rules of the game. After all, radicals desire major political and economic change in favor of an international order that distributes economic resources and political power more equitably. Contemporary international law and organizations are not the agents of such change.

The Constructivist View of International Organization and Law

Constructivists place critical importance on institutions and norms.[18] Both international governmental organizations and nongovernmental organizations can be norm entrepreneurs that socialize and teach states new norms. Those norms may change state preferences, which, in turn, may influence state behavior. Constructivists acknowledge that new international institutions have been developing at a rapid rate and are taking on more tasks. But, they warn, with such international authority, international institutions may become dysfunctional, serving the interests of international bureaucrats.

Law plays a key role in constructivist thinking, not because law establishes precise rules, but because it reflects changing norms. Thus, both adherents of customary international law and constructivists see the critical role such norms play in providing shared expectations about appropriate state behavior. Over time, those norms are internalized by states themselves, they change state preferences, and shape behavior. A number of key norms are of particular interest to constructivists. Multilateralism, the practice of joining with others in making decisions, is one such norm. Occurring both outside and within formal organizations, participants learn the value of the norm. By participating multilaterally, states have also learned other norms, including the emerging prohibition against the use of nuclear weapons, the norm of humanitarian intervention, or the increasing attention to human rights norms. Yet just as these norms and ideas affect state behavior, states also participate in shaping the norms and practice. Each of these norms is discussed in coming chapters. Thus, with the steady expansion of international institutions and international law and influence, constructivists have an active research agenda.

In Sum: Do Intergovernmental Organizations, Nongovernmental Organizations, and International Law Make a Difference?

Realists remain skeptical about the utility of intergovernmental organizations, nongovernmental organizations, and international law. In the view of many realists (though not all), they are but reflections of state power and hence have no independent identity or role in international relations. Radicals, too, view international organizations and law with skepticism. Radicals see them as mere reflections of political and economic hegemony. In contrast, liberals and constructivists are convinced that IGOs, NGOs, and international law matter in international politics, albeit with a different emphasis. To liberals, these organizations and international law do not replace states as the primary actors in international politics, although in a few cases they may be moving in that direction; but they do provide alternative venues, whether intergovernmental or private, for states themselves to engage in collective action and for individuals to join with other like-minded individuals in pursuit of their goals. They permit old issues to be seen in new ways, and they provide a venue to discuss the new globalizing issues and an arena for action. To constructivists, the emphasis is on how changing norms and institutions shape issues. We analyze the substantive issues in international relations in the next three chapters.

Notes

1. Jean-Jacques Rousseau, "Extrait du projet de paix perpétuelle," from *Ouevres complètes bibliothèque de la pleiade* III (Paris, 1760), 564, as translated and quoted in Torbjörn L. Knutsen, *A History of International Relations Theory* (Manchester, Eng.: Manchester University Press, 1997), 120.
2. David Mitrany, *A Working Peace System* (London: Royal Institute of International Affairs, 1946), 7.
3. Ibid., 40.
4. Garrett Hardin, "The Tragedy of the Commons," *Science* 162 (December 13, 1968), 1243–48. See also Mancur Olson, Jr., *The Logic of Collective Action: Public Goods and the Theory of Groups* (New York: Schocken, 1968).
5. Margaret P. Karns and Karen A. Mingst, "The United States and Multilateral Institutions: A Framework," in *The United States and Multilateral Institutions: Patterns of Changing Instrumentality and Influence*, ed. Margaret P. Karns and Karen A. Mingst (Boston: Unwin Hyman, 1990), 1–24.
6. See Karen A. Mingst and Margaret P. Karns, *The United Nations in the 21st Century* (3rd ed.; Boulder, Colo.: Westview, 2007).
7. United Nations, *A More Secure World: Our Shared Responsibility*. Report of the Secretary-General's High-level Panel on Threats, Challenges and Change (New York: UN, 2004), www.un.org/secureworld/.
8. Immanuel Kant, "Idea for a Universal History from a Cosmopolitan Point of View" (1784), reprinted in *Kant Selections*, ed. Lewis White Beck (New York: Macmillan Co., 1988); and Jeans-Jacques Rousseau, "State of War," "Summary," and "Critique of Abbé Saint-Pierre's Project for Perpetual Peace," in *Reading Rousseau in the Nuclear Age*, trans. and ed. Grace G. Roosevelt (Philadelphia: Temple University Press, 1990), 185–229.
9. This section draws on Margaret P. Karns and Karen A. Mingst, *International Organizations: The Politics and Processes of Global Governance* (Boulder, Colo.: Lynne Rienner, 2004), Chap. 5.

10. For specific case studies, see Ann M. Florini, ed., *The Third Force: The Rise of Transnational Society* (Washington, D.C.: Carnegie Endowment for International Peace, 2000); Michael Edwards and John Gaventa, *Global Citizen Action* (Boulder, Colo.: Lynne Rienner, 2001); and Sidney G. Tarrow, *The New Transnational Activism* (Cambridge, UK: Cambridge University Press, 2005).

11. This section on NGOs draws on Karns and Mingst, *International Organizations,* Chap. 6.

12. Jessica Stern, "The Protean Enemy," *Foreign Affairs* 82:4 (July–August 2003), 27–40.

13. See Alexander Cooley and James Ron, "The NGO Scramble: Organizational Insecurity and the Political Economy of Transnational Action," *International Security* 27:1 (Summer 2002), 5–39.

14. For example, see Fiona Terry, *Condemned to Repeat? The Paradox of Humanitarian Action* (Ithaca, N.Y.: Cornell University Press, 2002); and David Kennedy, *The Dark Side of Virtue: Reassessing International Humanitarianism* (Princeton, N.J.: Princeton University Press, 2004).

15. Christopher C. Joyner, *International Law in the 21st Century: Rules for Global Governance* (Lanham, Md.: Rowman & Littlefield, 2005), 6.

16. Louis Henkin, *How Nations Behave: Law and Foreign Policy* (2d ed.; New York: Columbia University Press, 1979), 22.

17. See Bartram S. Brown, "Unilateralism, Multilateralism, and the International Criminal Court," in *Multilateralism and U.S. Foreign Policy: Ambivalent Engagement,* ed. Stewart Patrick and Shepard Forman (Boulder, Colo.: Lynne Rienner, 2002), 323–44; and Henry A. Kissinger, "The Pitfalls of Universal Jurisdiction," *Foreign Affairs* 80:4 (July–August 2001), 86–97.

18. For pathbreaking theoretical and empirical work, see Martha Finnemore, *National Interests in International Society* (Ithaca, N.Y.: Cornell University Press, 1996) and *The Purpose of Intervention: Changing Beliefs about the Use of Force* (Ithaca, N.Y.: Cornell University Press, 2003); Michael Barnett and Martha Finnemore, *Rules for the World: International Organizations in Global Politics* (Ithaca, N.Y.: Cornell University Press, 2004); and Margaret E. Keck and Kathryn Sikkink, *Activists beyond Borders: Advocacy Networks in International Politics* (Ithaca, N.Y.: Cornell University Press, 1998).

War and Strife

⑧

■ *What makes security a preeminent value?*

■ *How do the levels of analysis help us to explain the causes of war?*

■ *Is general war becoming obsolete? Why?*

■ *What are the characteristics of asymmetric warfare?*

■ *How is terrorism of the last decade different from earlier forms of terrorism?*

■ *When is a war just? How can we fight justly?*

■ *How is insecurity managed in the world of the liberals?*

■ *How are realist approaches to managing insecurity different from those of the liberals?*

Among the numerous issues engaging the actors in international relations, war is the oldest, the most prevalent, and in the long term, the most salient. War has been the subject of historians for centuries, beginning with Thucydides' *History of the Peloponnesian War* to Carl von Clausewitz's *On War*. Following World War I, it was war and its aftermath (the creation of the League of Nations) that led American diplomatic historians and legal scholars to create a new discipline called International Relations. Prominent scholars in the field have addressed many of the critical and vexing issues. This attention to war and security is clearly warranted: of all the values, security comes first; all other competing values—good government, economic development, human rights, clean environment, quality health—presuppose a basic level of security. Consider the difficulties the United States has had in Iraq reviving the economy, establishing legal authority, and guaranteeing a new level of human rights. All these activities have proved problematic in the absence of basic security.

Yet history suggests that security has not always been attainable. There have been approximately 14,500 armed struggles throughout history, with about 3.5 billion dying either as a direct or indirect result. In the contemporary era (since 1816), there have been between 224 and 559 international and intrastate wars, depending on how war is defined. After the horrific great wars of the twentieth century and a slight rise in the number of wars in the following decades, a new trend has emerged: the incidence of war has declined since 1991. Both the number and intensity of war has dropped by one-half in the subsequent fifteen years. The number of battlefield deaths has dropped by 80 percent.[1] Yet, as it should be, international relations theorists continue to analyze why international and intrastate conflicts occur. This chapter analyzes that critical issue.

Theorists are also concerned with the alternatives to war. How can security be assured short of war? In ancient Greece, when Melos was physically surrounded by the fleet of its archenemy Athens, Melos had few alternatives. It could appeal to a distant ally—another city-state, whose interests may have been fundamentally different from those of Melos—or it could rely on its own resources—its military strength and the men and women of Melos. Just as Melos was ultimately responsible for its own security, so, too, are states in an anarchic system. This is similar to the position of each prisoner in the prisoner's dilemma game described in Chapters 3 and 5; fearing the worst possible outcome, each player confesses to ensure himself a better outcome. There is no incentive to cooperate. Likewise, states, fearing the worst possible outcome—other states' amassing more and better armaments than they have—choose to arm. The people of Melos, each prisoner, and states all rely on self-help.

Yet ironically, if a state prepares to protect itself, if it takes self-help measures—building a strong industrial base, constructing armaments, mobilizing a military—then other states become less secure. Their response is to engage in similar activities, increasing their own level of protection but leading to greater insecurity on the part of others. This situation is known as the **security dilemma:** in the absence of centralized authority, one state's becoming more secure diminishes another state's security. As political scientist John Herz describes, "Striving to attain security from attack, [states] are driven to acquire more and more power in order to escape the power of others. This, in turn, renders the others more insecure and compels them to prepare for the worst. Since none can ever feel entirely secure in such a world of competing units, power competition ensues, and the vicious circle of security and power accumulation is on."[2] The security dilemma, then, results in a permanent condition of tension and power conflicts among states.

But is self-help the only alternative? How can states mitigate the effects of the security dilemma? How can insecurity be managed short of war? This chapter introduces the prominent approaches.

The Causes of War

Why do wars break out? An analysis of any war—Vietnam, Angola, Cambodia, World War II, or the Franco-Prussian War—would find a variety of reasons for the outbreak of violence. Kenneth Waltz in *Man, the State, and War* posits that the international system is the primary framework of international relations.[3] But that framework exists all the time, so to explain why sometimes wars occur and sometimes they do not, we also need to consider the other levels of analysis. Characteristics of individuals, both leaders and the masses, and the internal structure of states are some of the forces that operate within the limitations of the international system. Waltz finds that all three levels of analysis can be applied to explain the causes of war.[4]

The Individual: Realist and Liberal Interpretations

Both the characteristics of individual leaders and the general attributes of people (discussed in Chapter 6) have been blamed for war. Some individual leaders are aggressive and bellicose; they use their leadership positions to further their causes. Thus, according to some realists and liberals, war occurs because of the personal characteristics of major leaders. It is impossible, however, to prove the veracity of this position. Would past wars have occurred had different leaders—perhaps more pacifist ones—been in power? We can only speculate.

If it is not the innate character flaws of individuals that cause war, is there a possibility that leaders, like all individuals, are subject to misperceptions? According to liberals, misperceptions by leaders—seeing aggressiveness where it may not be intended, attributing the actions of one person to a group—can lead to the outbreak of war. Historians have typically given a key role to misperceptions. There are several types of misperceptions that may lead to war. One of the most common is exaggerating the hostility of the adversary, believing that the adversary is more hostile than it may actually be or that the adversary has greater military or economic capability than it actually has. This miscalculation may lead a state to respond, that is, take actions like building up its own arms, which, in turn, may be viewed as hostile activities by its adversary. Misperceptions thus spiral, potentially leading to war. The events leading up to World War I are often viewed as a conflict spiral, caused by misperceived intentions and actions of the principal protagonists. We can only speculate.

If not because of the leaders, perhaps characteristics of the masses lead to the outbreak of war. Some realist thinkers—St. Augustine and Reinhold Niebuhr, for example—take this position. St. Augustine wrote that every act is an act of self-preservation on the part of individuals. For Niebuhr the link goes even deeper; the origin of war resides in the depths of the human psyche.[5] This approach is compatible with that of sociobiologists who study animal behavior. Aggressive behavior is adopted by virtually all species to ensure survival; it is biologically innate. Yet this view does not explain subtle differences among species; some do engage in cooperative behavior. And human beings are seen by many as an infinitely more complex species than animal species. If true, these presumptions lead to two possible alternative assessments, one pessimistic and the other optimistic. For pessimists, if war is the product of innate human characteristics or a flawed human nature, then there is no reprieve; wars will inevitably occur all the time. For optimists, if war, or aggression, is innate, the only hope of eliminating war resides in trying to fundamentally alter human nature.

Yet war does not, in fact, happen all the time; it is the *unusual* event, not the norm. So characteristics inherent in all individuals cannot be the only cause of war. Nor can the explanation be that human nature has, indeed, been fundamentally changed, since wars *do* occur. Most experiments aimed at changing mass behavior have failed miserably, and there is no visible proof that fundamental attitudes have been altered.

Thus the individual level of analysis is unlikely to provide the only cause of war, or even the primary one. Individuals, after all, are organized into societies and states.

State and Society: Liberal and Radical Explanations

A second level of explanation suggests that war occurs because of the internal structures of states. States vary in size, geography, ethnic homogeneity, and economic and political preferences. The question, then, is how do the characteristics of different states affect the possibility of war? Which state structures are most correlated with the propensity to go to war?

State and society explanations are among the oldest. Plato, for example, posited that war is less likely where the population is cohesive and enjoys a moderate level of prosperity. Since the population would be able to thwart an attack, an enemy is apt to refrain from coercive activity. Many thinkers during the Enlightenment, including Kant, believed that war was more likely in aristocratic states.

Drawing on the Kantian position, liberals posit that republican regimes (ones with representative government and separation of powers) are least likely to wage war; that is the basic position of the theory of the democratic peace introduced in Chapter 5. Democracies are pacific because democratic norms and culture inhibit the leadership from taking actions leading to war. Democratic leaders hear from multiple voices that tend to restrain decisionmakers and therefore lessen the chance of war. Such states provide outlets for individuals to voice opposing viewpoints, and structural mechanisms exist for replacing war-prone or aggressive rulers. To live in such a state, individuals learn the art of compromise. In the process, extreme behavior like waging war is curbed and is engaged in only periodically and then only if necessary to make a state's own democracy safe.

Other liberal tenets hold that some types of economic systems are more war prone than others. Liberal states are also more apt to be capitalist states whose members enjoy relative wealth. Such societies feel no need to divert the attention of the dissatisfied masses to an external conflict; the wealthy masses are largely satisfied with the status quo. Furthermore, war interrupts trade, blocks profits, and causes inflation. Thus, liberal capitalist states are more apt to avoid war and to promote peace.

But not every theorist sees the liberal state as benign and peace loving. Indeed, radical theorists offer the most thorough critique of liberalism and its economic counterpart, capitalism. They argue that capitalist liberal modes of production inevitably lead to competition between the two major social classes within the state, the bourgeoisie and the proletariat, for both economic dominance and political leadership. This struggle leads to war, both internally and externally, as the state dominated by the entrenched bourgeoisie is driven to expand the engine of capitalism at the expense of the proletariat and for the economic preservation of the bourgeoisie.

In this view, conflict and war are attributed to the internal dynamics of capitalist economic systems. Capitalist systems stagnate and slowly collapse in the absence of external stimulation. Three different explanations have been offered for what happens to capitalist states and why they must turn outward. First, the English economist John Hobson claimed that the internal demand for goods will slow down in capitalist countries, leading to pressures for imperialist expansion to find external markets to sustain economic growth. Second, to Lenin and others, the problem is not one of underdemand but one of declining rates of return on capital. Capitalist states expand outward to find new markets; expanding markets increase the rates of return on capital investment. Third, Lenin and many twentieth-century radicals pointed to the need for raw materials to sustain capitalist growth; external suppliers are needed to obtain such resources. So according to the radical view, capitalist states inevitably expand, but radical theorists disagree among themselves on precisely why expansion occurs.

While radical interpretations help explain colonialism and imperialism, the link to war is more tenuous. One possible link is that capitalist states spend not only for consumer goods but also for the military, leading inevitably to arms races and eventually war. Another link points to leaders who, in order to avert domestic economic crises, resort to external conflict.

This is called **diversionary war.** Such behavior is likely to provide internal cohesion at least in the short run. For example, there is considerable evidence to support the notion that the Argentinian military used the Falkland/Malvinas conflict in 1982 to rally the population around the flag and draw attention away from the country's economic contraction. Still another link suggests that the masses may push a ruling elite toward war. This view is clearly at odds with the liberal belief that the masses are basically peace loving. Adherents of this view point to the Spanish-American War of 1898 as an example where the public might have pushed the leaders into aggressive action.

Those who argue that contests over the structure of states are a basic cause of war have identified another explanation for the outbreak of some wars. Numerous civil wars have been fought over which groups, ideologies, and leaders should control the government of the state. The United States's own civil war (1861–65) between the North and the South, Russia's civil war (1917–19) between liberal and socialist forces, China's civil war (1927–49) between nationalist and communist forces, and the civil wars in Vietnam, Korea, the Sudan, and Chad—each pitting north versus south—are poignant illustrations. In many of these cases, the struggle among competing economic systems and among groups vying for scarce resources within the state illustrates further the proposition that internal state dynamics are responsible for the outbreak of war. The United States's civil war was not just over which region should control policy but over a belief by those in the South that the government inequitably and unfairly allocated economic resources. China's civil war pitted a wealthy landed elite supportive of the nationalist cause against an exploited peasantry struggling, often unsuccessfully, for survival. And the ongoing Sudanese civil war pits an economically depressed south against a northern government that poured economic resources into the region of the capital. Yet in virtually every case, neither characteristics of the state nor the state structures were solely responsible for the outbreak of war. State structure is embedded in the characteristics of the international system.

The International System: Realist and Radical Interpretations

To realists, the anarchic international system is governed only by a weak overarching rule of law, which is easily dispensed with when states determine it is in their self-interest to do so. States themselves are the final authorities and the ultimate arbiters of disputes; herein resides sovereignty. Such an anarchic system is often compared to a state of nature, after Hobbes's characterization. The international system is equivalent to a state of war, where there are no enforcement instruments to make states cooperate. Thus, it is states that, when feeling threatened, decide to go to war against other, similarly situated states. And the inexorable logic of the security dilemma makes such perceptions of insecurity all the more likely. War breaks out, then, according to realists, because of the anarchic structure of the international system. War in such a system is the logical course of action to take. After all, states must protect themselves. A state's security is ensured only by its accumulating military and economic power. One state's accumulation makes other states less secure, according to the logic of the security dilemma.

In an anarchic system, there may be few rules about how to decide among contending claims. One of the major categories of contested claims is territory. For thousands of years, the Jewish and Arab dispute has rested on competing territorial claims to Palestine; in the Horn of Africa, the territorial aspirations of the Somali people are disputed; and in the Andes, Ecuador and Peru have competing territorial claims. According to the international-system-level explanation, there are no authoritative and legitimized arbiters of such disputes over territorial claims. John Mearsheimer calls this the "911 problem—absence of central authority, to which a threatened state can turn for help."[6]

Neither is there an effective arbiter of competing claims on self-determination. Who decides whether the Chechen, Bosnian, or Quebecois claims for independence are legitimate? Who decides whether Kurdish claims against Turkey and Iraq are worthy of consideration? Absent an internationally legitimized arbiter, authority is relegated to the states themselves, with the most powerful ones often becoming the decisive, interested arbiters.

In actuality, there are several realist variants attributing war to the anarchic nature of the international system. One system-level explanation for war, represented in the work of Kenneth Organski, is power transition theory. To Organski and his intellectual heirs, it is not just the inequality of capabilities among states that leads to war; it is *changes* in state capabilities that lead to war. War occurs when a dissatisfied challenger state begins to attain the same level of capabilities as the hegemon. The challenger will launch a war to solidify its position. Power transition theorists find that war can be explained by a challenger approaching the power of the dominant hegemon, as illustrated in the Franco-Prussian War (1870–71), the Russo-Japanese War (1904–5), and the two world wars.[7]

A variant derived from power transition theory is that war is caused by the changing distribution of power among states that occurs because of uneven rates of economic development. George Modelski and William Thompson find regular cycles of power transitions since 1494. There are one-hundred-year cycles between hegemonic wars, wars that fundamentally alter the structure of the international system. Hegemonic wars create a new

TABLE 8.1

Causes of War by Level of Analysis	
Level	**Cause**
Individual	Aggressive characteristics of leaders Misperceptions by leaders Attributes of masses (innate behavior or flawed character) Communications failure
State / society	Liberal capitalist states according to radicals Nonliberal / nondemocratic states according to liberals Domestic politics, scapegoating Struggle between groups for economic resources Ethnonational challengers
International system	Anarchy Lack of an arbiter Prominence of long cycles of war and peace Power transitions Aggressiveness of the international capitalist class

hegemonic power; its power waxes and wanes, a struggle follows, and a new hegemon assumes dominance. The cycle begins once again.[8]

To radicals, as well, the international system structure is responsible for war. Dominant capitalist states within the international system need to expand economically, leading to wars with developing regions over control of natural resources and labor markets, or with other capitalist states over control of developing regions. The dynamic of expansion inherent in the international capitalist system, then, is the major cause of wars, according to radical thinking. Both the realist and radical reliance on one level of explanation may be overly simplistic. In actuality, most wars are caused by the interaction between various factors at different levels of analysis. Iraq's invasion of Kuwait in 1990 and the civil wars resulting from the breakup of Yugoslavia in 1995 provide examples of why wars occur. A list of these general causes is given in Table 8.1.

The Case of Iraq's Invasion of Kuwait

In August 1990, Iraq invaded and successfully annexed Kuwait. Between August and November of that year, the U.N. Security Council approved twelve successive resolutions in an effort to secure Iraqi withdrawal. January 15, 1991, was set as the deadline for Iraq's compliance, but Iraq did not comply.

On January 16, 1991, a U.S.-led multinational coalition launched a war against Iraq using 500,000 land, sea, and air forces. Air attacks, followed by ground combat, pushed Iraq's troops out of Kuwait, and forty-two days later a cease-fire was accepted by both sides.

Why did Iraq invade Kuwait? Can the explanation be found by examining the personality characteristics of Saddam Hussein? Because he controlled the state as an authoritarian leader and because his advisers were unlikely to support differing views, Saddam's individual characteristics, including his basic insecurity and his ruthless techniques, were not easily countered. Did he miscalculate or misinterpret U.S. ambassador April Gillespie's prior statements supporting Iraqi intentions in the region? Did he miscalculate Saudi Arabia's response in permitting U.S. forces on Arab territory? These are individual-level explanations.

Or was Iraq just acting in its own national interest? Iraq had historic claims on the territory (and oil fields) in what is now contemporary Kuwait. During the nineteenth century, this land had been a part of the southern Iraqi province of Basra. Iraq felt that the land had been illegally seized during British occupation around World War I. Thus, no Iraqi government had ever legally recognized Kuwait as a separate state. Given this historical claim, was it not in the vital interest of Iraq to secure its rightful land in the Persian Gulf? The fact that Kuwait has approximately 9 percent of the world's known oil reserves strengthened the economic dimension of Iraq's national interest justification. Was it not also in the national interest to guarantee more oil resources, since Iraq's national economic development demanded such enormous expenditures? After all, Iraq's 1980–88 war with Iran had reduced oil revenues, and Kuwait had refused to increase oil outflow within OPEC to make up for that decline in revenue. And, Iraq argued, Kuwait was pumping too much oil out of the fields near the territorial border. These explanations encompass the state level of analysis.

But not all authoritarian leaders choose to use military force to invade a tiny neighbor, because of their own national interest. So why did Iraq invade? International-level explanations are relevant. Perhaps Saddam calculated that his actions would not elicit a military response from the international community. The United Nations Security Council had rarely been able to muster a united front among the permanent five members. The Council's repeated threats did not appear credible. Was not the international community preoccupied with other more important events, including the unraveling of the Soviet Union? And Iraq felt the Arab League would be unlikely to condemn actions by a fellow Arab state. These are possible explanations at the international level of analysis.

Why did the United States and its coalition partners respond with military force? Was this just a manifestation of the New World Order, in which the major powers, as well as many of the developing states, united against an aggressor state on behalf of a tiny, largely defenseless neighbor? Or was the United States acting on behalf of its own national interest? Kuwait's oil resources (and also neighboring Saudi Arabia's) were crucial to the United States. These resources had to be kept under the control of friendly powers. In addition, the United States felt that Iraq must be ousted from Kuwait and punished for its aggressive action. Or did the U.S. stance just support the beck and call of the international petroleum companies whose power was threatened by Iraq's takeover of Kuwait? Clearly all three levels of analysis are critical for explaining the cause of war.

The Case of Yugoslavia

Are these causes of interstate wars equally as relevant for civil conflicts? Yugoslavia illustrates how individual-, state-, and international-level explanations are also useful for civil wars. The case also shows how what began as an intrastate war quickly became internationalized. Slovenia and Croatia, two of Yugoslavia's republics, declared independence in 1991; Bosnia-Herzegovina and Macedonia followed a year later. Shortly thereafter, a Serb minority group within Bosnia announced the formation of the Serb Republic of Bosnia-Herzegovina, and war began in Bosnia. A three-year war followed, displacing 4.3 million people and leaving 200,000 individuals dead. The Dayton Accord ended the fighting in 1995. Why did war break out?

Beginning in the late 1980s, first as leader of the Serbian Communist party and then as president of Yugoslavia, Slobodan Milošević began to push an extreme form of Serbian nationalism, a change from the multiethnic Yugoslavia that had been the foundation of the country since World War II under its leader Marshal Tito. Milošević revived the idea of a Greater Serbia, using the media to promote hypernationalism. He replaced leaders in the republics with people sharing similar views. These actions provoked separatist movements in the various republics. When the ethnically homogeneous Slovenia declared independence, that act did not lead to a violent response. But that was not true in the other provinces, where the various ethnic groups contended for power: Serbs versus Croats in Croatia; Serbs versus Macedonians in Macedonia; and in Bosnia, the most heterogeneous province, with 31 percent Serbs, 44 percent Muslim, and 17 percent Croats. Fighting was particularly fierce in this region, where Bosnian Serbs, aided militarily by the rump Yugoslavia (composed of Serbia and Montenegro), attacked Muslim villages, shelled the city of Sarajevo, and drove hundreds of thousands from their homes.

States outside of Yugoslavia fueled the fire—Germany by prematurely recognizing the new states of Croatia and Slovenia, thus legitimizing the notion of a divided Yugoslavia; Russia and France by supporting old Serb allies; and Middle Eastern states by publicly siding with the Bosnian Muslims in their struggle against Christian Croat and Serb forces. Many would-be international arbiters—the European Union, the Conference on Security and Cooperation in Europe, the U.N. secretary-general and his special representative—tried to help settle the dispute, but none of them was effective or was recognized as legitimate by all the contending parties. U.N. peacekeepers were called in, to be replaced by a NATO Implementation force under the 1995 Dayton Peace Accord. Joining with NATO were a panoply of NGOs.

The central Yugoslavian conflict also involved another territory, Kosovo, the southern province and the historic "homeland" of the Serbs, which in 1974 was granted the status of an autonomous province within the Serbian republic of Yugoslavia. Kosovo had an ethnic majority of Albanians and a Serbian minority, and in the early 1980s, the majority began demonstrating for full republic status within Yugoslavia. However, Milošević stripped Kosovo of its autonomy, leading to multiple riots and threats to government rule. Following the imposition of martial law, the backlash escalated, and in 1996 the Kosovo Liberation Army (made up of Albanian Kosovars) emerged; by 1998 it had seized control of 40 percent of the countryside. When the Serbs countered with massive force against the rebel forces, U.N. resolutions ordered the cessation of conflict, but neither side was willing to accept a settlement. Hence, in March 1999, prompted by reports of human rights abuses, NATO forces began bombing Yugoslavian targets. The bombing continued until June 1999, when NATO and Yugoslavian military authorities signed an agreement on the withdrawal of Yugoslavian security forces from Kosovo. Since 1999, the U.N. Interim Administration in Kosovo (UNMIK) has assumed civil functions responsible for law and order, human rights, and refugees. That role may be ending as Kosovo inches toward independence.

Explanations for the outbreak of war in Yugoslavia can be seen at each level of analysis. *Individual leaders,* particularly Serbian leader Slobodan Milošević, were able to stoke in the Serb masses an ultranationalism that threatened other groups in the Yugoslav federation, including the Albanians in Kosovo. The masses were ripe for such action, in part because of a history of past injustices, including atrocities committed against the Serbs by the Croats during World War II. *State and societal organization* exacerbated the situation. The Serbs felt themselves in an inferior economic position to their Croat and Slovenian neighbors to the north. And when those two provinces, Croatia and Slovenia, proclaimed independence—recognized by several European powers—the stage was set for an international conflict. Muslims in multiethnic Bosnia and in Kosovo also felt that they were victims of centuries of economic discrimination, and they positioned themselves as an ethnonational challenger for control of the Bosnian state and the territory of Kosovo.

No effective international arbiter existed in the *international system* to settle these competing claims. In the face of this anarchy, both the European organizations (the EU and the CSCE) and the United Nations, and eventually NATO, inserted their multilateral presence.

Thus, each of the three levels of analysis helps us understand why war broke out both in Iraq and in the former Yugoslavia. Waltz was perhaps correct that the characteristics of the international system—the general state of anarchy, the lack of an accepted arbiter—provide the general explanation, but to understand the particulars, we need to delve into state and society and the individual levels of analysis.

Categorizing Wars

Once the decision has been made to go to war, to aggress against a foe or to support an ally, decisionmakers are still faced with a variety of options for how to proceed. The nineteenth-century Prussian general Carl von Clausewitz, in *On War*, describes the political nature of these decisions: "War is not merely a political act, but also a real political instrument, a continuation of political commerce, a carrying out of the same by other means."[9] The most significant decisions to be made are about what kind of war will be fought—a decision often dictated by long-range goals—and what kind of weapons will be used.

International relations scholars have developed numerous classification schemes to categorize wars. These classifications include general war and limited war.

General War

General war is armed conflict involving massive loss of life and widespread destruction, usually with many participants, including multiple major powers. These wars are fought for many reasons: to conquer and occupy enemy territory; to take over the government and/or to control the economic resources of an opponent. Wars may also be fought over conflicts of ideas (communism vs. capitalism; democracy vs. authoritarianism) or religion (Catholic vs. Protestants; Shiites vs. Sunni Muslims; Hindu vs. Islam). To accomplish the goal of prevailing military over the opponent(s), decisionmakers utilize all available weapons of warfare and target both civilian and military sites. The Thirty Years War (1618–48), the longest general war ever, involved numerous great powers (Britain, France, Hapsburgs/Austria, Netherlands, Spain, Sweden) and resulted in over 2 million battlefield deaths. A half-century later, the War of the Spanish Succession (1701–14) pitted most of the same powers against each other and ended in over 1 million deaths, and at the end of that century, the Napoleonic Wars resulted in over 2.5 million battle deaths. For much of the eighteenth and nineteenth centuries, wars between great powers were common.

World War I and World War II were critical turning points in making general war a policy option, with the same great powers (Britain, France, Austria/Hungary [in WWII, Germany], Japan, Russia/the Soviet Union, and the United States) fighting and resulting in 7.7 million and 13 million deaths, respectively. With industrialization, these wars involved most of the respective societies. The battlefield included not just military combatants, but also the people working in the factories making the armaments, as well as civilians growing the food.

Since the end of World War II, however, general wars, particularly large-scale wars between the great powers, have become less frequent; the number of countries participating in such wars has fallen; and the length of time such wars last has shortened. This has led several political scientists to speculate whether or not extremely costly general wars like World Wars I and II are events of the past.

John Mueller, for example, argues that such wars have become obsolete. Among the reasons he cites are the memories of the devastation of World War II, the postwar satisfaction of the great powers with the status quo, and the recognition that any war among the great powers could escalate, either nuclear or not, to a level that would become too costly.[10] Robert Jervis has broadened the analysis and offered an explanation embedded in the notion of a security community that combines thinking drawn from the various theoretical perspectives. In the security community composed of the United States, West Europe, and Japan, war is unthinkable. Realists explain the security community as arising from American hegemony; U.S. military spending is greater than the combined spending of the next eight countries; there are no viable rivals. That dominance is magnified by the effect of nuclear weapons and by the continued recognition that all-out general war would be unwinnable and hence irrational, just as Mueller posits. The liberal explanation is based on the democratic peace argument. Not only are democracies unlikely to go to war against each other, but that effect becomes magnified if they are interdependent economically and if they share membership in international organizations. And constructivists posit that the explanation rests not with material conditions (American hegemony or interdependency) but with individuals increasingly "socialized into attitudes, beliefs, and values that are conducive to peace."[11] As Jervis explains, "The destructiveness of war, the benefits of peace, and the changes in values interact and reinforce each other."[12]

Civil wars have not decreased as precipitously as general war. Civil wars include wars between factions within a state over control of territory; establishment of a government, for control of a "failed state" (Somalia or Liberia);

ethnonationalist movements seeking greater autonomy or secession (Chechens in Russia, Tamils in Sri Lanka); or wars between ethnic, clan, or religious groups for control of the state (Colombia, Peru, Algeria, Rwanda). The American civil war and the Russian civil war are prime examples. The various actors—states, substate actors, and transnational actors—possess enhanced war-making potential, with the ability to purchase weapons through the expanding international arms trade.

Although some civil wars remain contained within state boundaries, increasingly civil wars are international. The repercussions of civil wars are felt across borders, as refugees from civil conflicts flow into neighboring states and funds are transferred out of the country. States, groups, and individuals from outside of the warring country become involved, funding particular groups, selling weapons to various factions, and diplomatically supporting one group over another. Thus, few civil wars are really solely domestic; they are often international events. While a few civil wars become general, most can be categorized as limited war.

Limited War

Wars can be classified as **limited wars** on the basis that the objective is not surrender and occupation of enemy territory. The Korean War and the 1991 Gulf War are excellent examples of wars fought for limited goals. In the first case, the goal was to prevent the Chinese-backed Korean army from taking over the peninsula and then to push back China. The goal was not to take over China. In the second case, the goal was to free Kuwait from the Iraqi occupation forces. Like the Chinese, the Iraqi troops were pushed behind a line across which the victorious forces chose not to pass. In limited wars, not all available armaments are unleashed. In these two cases, conventional weapons of warfare were used—tanks, foot soldiers, aircrafts, and missiles— but despite their availability, nuclear weapons were not deployed. There is no better illustration of limited war than the long-standing Arab-Israeli dispute described in Chapter 2 and debated in Chapter 5. Israel has fought against its neighbors, Egypt, Syria, Jordan, and Lebanon, as well as Palestinians on the West Bank and Gaza. The wars have blown "hot" and "cold." Both sides have employed a variety of the techniques described below.

Whereas the number of general wars have declined precipitously, limited wars and particularly civil wars that are limited in nature have not. In the century between 1816 and the end of World War I, there were about fifty civil wars, while the decade of the 1990s alone saw about 195 civil wars. Two-thirds of all conflicts since World War II are civil wars, which can usually be categorized as limited.

These wars share several characteristics. They often last a long time, even decades, with periods of fighting punctuated by periods of relative calm.

Whereas the goals may be relatively limited—secession, group autonomy—the human costs are high. Both combatants and civilians are killed and maimed; food supplies are interrupted; diseases are spread as health systems suffer; money is diverted from constructive economic development to purchasing armaments; and generations of people grow up knowing only war.

The African continent provides numerous examples of these limited civil wars; most conflicts are now concentrated there. Ethiopia's war with two of its regions (Ogaden and Eritrea) lasted decades, as did the civil war between the north and south in both Sudan and Chad. Liberia and Sierra Leone, likewise, have also been sites of civil conflict where various factions, guerrilla groups, paramilitary groups, and mercenaries fought for control of a territory where, until recently, no government existed. Some wars are relatively new in origin. In 2002, for example, civil war erupted in Côte d'Ivoire following an army mutiny in that country by individuals from ethnic groups in the north of the country, representatives of Muslim groups. Long seen as one of the most politically stable and economically strong countries, Côte d'Ivoire is now engaged in a war that pits a poorer Muslim north against a richer Christian south whose leaders have been well entrenched for years. The conflict, like many of Africa's conflicts, has spilled over into neighboring countries, as migrants working in the country have fled, trade routes have been disrupted, and xenophobia has expanded across already porous and often disputed borders.

In virtually all these cases, the civil wars have been facilitated by the availability of small arms, the recruitment of child soldiers, and financing from illicit commodity trades (diamonds, oil). In all these cases, too, the human rights abuses and humanitarian crises have captured media attention, but not the political commitment or financial resources of the international community.

With the increased destructiveness of modern warfare, limited war has become the only option. Yet wars are fought using different approaches and a variety of weapons.

How Wars Are Fought

Conventional Means

Throughout most of human history, wars were fought through conventional means, using the technologies available at the time. Weapons of choice ranged from swords and shields, to gunpowder and cannons, to the professional armies fielding infantry and riding in tanks, navies using specialized ships, and air forces flying fixed-wing aircraft. Such weapons are utilized to defeat the enemy on the territorial battlefield.

Beginning in the 1980s, two major changes occurred that have impacted conventional warfare. First have been changes in technology that have made weapons and delivery systems more capable of precise targeting, increased miniaturization—which enables combatants to conceal supplies—and lighter-weight weapons capable of being manned by children. Second has been the increasing magnitude of the international armaments market and its wider geographic scope. Every imaginable weapon is for sale, supplied by multiple producers. Although 75 percent of the cost of arms is spent by the developed countries, the escalating number of deliveries to the developing countries (77 percent of all arms delivered) reveals a truly international market in conventional weapons. The number of small weapons in the hands of Iraqis, Somalians, and Liberians has surprised even those versed in the international arms trade, even though only 3 percent of small arms worldwide are in the hands of governments, the military, or police. Thus, it is not surprising that combatants have a variety of lethal conventional weapons at their disposal.

Weapons of Mass Destruction

The dropping of the atomic bomb over Hiroshima and Nagaski in 1945 had an immediate and dramatic impact on war-fighting capability. The destructiveness of the weapon, its capacity to kill hundreds of thousands without discrimination, and its long-lasting effects stemming from radiation ushered in the nuclear age. Both the United States and the Soviet Union during the Cold War constructed bigger and more lethal weapons, developing more accurate delivery systems, ballistic missiles, and cruise missiles, each capable of reaching around the world and killing the population many times over. This mutual assured destruction (or, ironically, MAD) led the major antagonists to eschew fighting directly using nuclear weapons, but rather fighting through proxies using conventional weapons, as discussed in Chapter 2.

The fact that nuclear weapons have never been employed in war except against Japan has led to a controversial debate about the effects of nuclear weapons on the decision to wage war. Has the very existence of nuclear weapons increased the probability that an all-out war will occur at some point? After all, a country having a nuclear advantage may be able to achieve all their objectives in short-order. So are nuclear weapons a destabilizing influence in the long run? Or have nuclear weapons actually insured the peace—their very destructiveness making rational decisionmakers less likely to resort to their use? Can nuclear weapons then become a stabilizing force in the world? Scott Sagan and Kenneth Waltz debated these issues in the 1980s and renewed the debate in the beginning of the twenty-first century after traditional rivals India and Pakistan had each acquired a nuclear capability. Waltz argues that "more may be better," that a slow proliferation of nuclear weapons means that states are enhancing their capability, making it more likely that potential enemies will refrain from action. Sagan disagrees, arguing that the proliferation of nuclear weapons is more apt to lead to a failure in deterrence or an accidental war.[13] This debate over the threat posed by the possession of nuclear weapons has gained a new saliency as the technology to build nuclear weapons has proliferated. The tangled web of the Pakistani official Ali Khan providing parts of nuclear technology, from Europe to Pakistan and then North Korea, has led many to question the stabilizing effect of proliferation.

Chemical and biological weapons, together with nuclear weapons comprise the more general category of **weapons of mass destruction** (WMD). Chemical and biological weapons have existed for many more years than nuclear weapons have; mustard gas proved very lethal during World War I and led the international community to ban its use. Although surreptitious testing and use of such weapons have persisted, their lack of an efficient delivery system has not made them a weapon of choice. However, as with nuclear weapons, what has changed is the possibility that such weapons can find their way into the hands of terrorists, nonstate actors, or even rogue states.

It was the possibility that Saddam Hussein was developing weapons of mass destruction that led to the 2003 U.S. invasion. And it is the realization that Iran is developing uranium enrichment capacity and that North Korea has tested nuclear weapons that has led to some of the most contentious political conflicts of the new millennium. Even when the 2007 negotiations over the issue appear to have reached a compromise in the North Korean case, implementation is fraught with difficulties.

Asymmetric Warfare

Asymmetric warfare is a type of warfare that undercuts an important proposition of both conventional warfare and nuclear war: that conventional weapons and nuclear confrontations are more likely to occur among states with rough equality of military strength that utilize similar strategics and tactics. If one party is decidedly weaker, the proposition goes, they are unlikely to resort to war. Asymmetric warfare, by contrast, is warfare conducted between parties of unequal strength. The weaker party seeks to neutralize its opponent's strengths, including its technological superiority, by exploiting that opponent's weaknesses.[14]

One strategy of asymmetric warfare is **guerrilla warfare** ("little war" in Spanish). There, the weaker party may often utilize a willing (or unwilling) civilian population to provide supplies like food and shelter and to gather

Going Nuclear: A View from Iran

In recent years, no decision has been as controversial as the decision to go nuclear. The debates over nuclear programs in India, Pakistan, North Korea, and Iran have centered on what this decision means, the reasons for the decision, and how it relates to international law. Iran defends its decision to go nuclear on several grounds.

At the United Nations General Assembly in 2005, Iranian President Mahmoud Ahmadinejad stated it was his country's "inalienable right" to acquire nuclear technology. Indeed, under the terms of the Nuclear Nonproliferation Treaty of which Iran is a party, states have the "inalienable right to develop research, production and use of nuclear energy for peaceful purposes without discrimination." According to the Iranian government, the country's significant deposits of petroleum and natural gas will diminish, and it must be prepared to use alternative energy resources, including nuclear power. Thus research on a centrifuge to speed enrichment is necessary. Attempts by the United Nations to block Iran's efforts with limited economic sanctions in 2006 are seen by the Iranian government as part of an Anglo-American plot to keep Iran from developing economically.

Some Iranian officials also point to legitimate security threats that might lead Iran to push for more than just the right to develop nuclear-fuel-production capabilities—the country may assert its right to make the leap to developing nuclear bombs. Iran is located near to its traditional enemies Israel (which has nuclear capacity) and Iraq, which fought a decade-long war against Iran in the 1980s. Shiite Iran also has unstable relations with many of the Persian Gulf states who have large, sometimes unhappy Shiite minorities. On the country's western border is Turkey, a NATO member and close American ally with economic and political ties with Israel, and on its eastern border is Sunni Pakistan, another nuclear power and ally of the United States.

The Iranian decision to make the leap to nuclear weaponry has been propelled by the actions of the United States, which has been Iran's enemy since the 1950s. The preemptive U.S. attack against Iraq in 2003 reflected the American position that Iraq was part of the "axis of evil," a group which also included Iran and North Korea. The fact that Iran has long been considered a potential target by American war planners causes further anxiety. Iran's movement to develop a nuclear weapons program could serve as a major deterrent to the United States, decreasing the likelihood that the United States will forcibly promote regime change in Iran. American intervention in Iranian domestic affairs would be unacceptable to virtually every sector within Iran.

The domestic population strongly supports Iran's nuclear program. Iranians see the program as a symbol of the revival of Persian pride, a move to reclaim the country's former greatness, and a reflection of pride in the 1979 revolution. To supporters of the revolution, Iran represents the forces of good and the United States the forces of evil. Nuclear weapons represent the power necessary to drive America out of the region and secure a leadership position in the world for Iran.

For Critical Analysis

1. *Would Iran's acquisition of nuclear weapons make the region safer or would it further destabilize the region?*
2. *Based on the theory of deterrence, could the United States deter Iran should it acquire nuclear weapons? Could Iran deter the United States? How critical are Iran's intangible sources of power?*

intelligence where they have no such capability. To overcome larger forces, guerrilla fighters may rely on hit-and-run tactics, inflicting casualties again and again, until a war of attrition wears down the enemy. The weaker side then chooses to avoid any direct confrontation, but instead tries to limit the operations of the opponent until the other is exhausted. These were the tactics used by the Algerians against the French in the 1950s, by the Vietcong and the North Vietnamese against the United States in the 1960s and early 1970s, by the *mujahideen* in Afghanistan against the Soviet Union in the 1980s, and by the Taliban against coalition forces in Afghanistan.

Guerilla wars may be a prelude to an insurgency—a widespread rebellion against a government or an occupying power. The goal of insurgents is to "liberate" areas and control an area for its own purposes. Many have debated whether the conflict in Iraq after 2004 is a guerrilla war, fought by a small dedicated group; an insurgency, with widespread opposition to American occupation; or a civil war between two groups fighting for control of the central government. In any case, asymmetric wars involve using a strength that the adversary lacks, or threatening those elements of society that the defender holds dear, including power plants or water supplies. It may include using the enemy's own system against it—be it a fluid financial system to fund terrorist activities or an open travel and visa system that permits easy entry for foreigners.

Terrorism

Techniques used in asymmetric wars may include terrorist attacks against an adversary's population, such as those Al Qaeda carried out against U.S. embassies in Africa in 1998, against cities on U.S. soil in 2001, the bombing of the Madrid rail station in 2004, and the London subway attack in 2005. **Terrorism** is a particular kind of asymmetric warfare that has increasingly become a major international security threat.

Terrorism involves four major elements: (1) premeditation, the decision by a perpetrator to commit an act to instill terror or fear in others; (2) motivation or a cause, whether it be political, religious, or economic; (3) targets, usually noncombatants, such as political figures, bureaucrats, or innocent bystanders; and (4) secretiveness, where perpetrators belong to clandestine groups or are secretly sponsored by states.[15]

Terrorism has a long history. During Greek and Roman times, terrorist acts were often carried out by individuals against a ruler. During the Middle Ages, groups perpetuated violence against other groups, while during the French Revolution, acts of terrorism were sponsored by the state itself. Organized state terrorism used against a state's own citizens reached its zenith in Nazi Germany and the Soviet Union under Joseph Stalin.

Terrorists began to use aircraft hijackings in the 1970s to project their message. For example, in December 1973, Arab terrorists killed thirty-two people in Rome's airport during an attack on a U.S. aircraft. Hostages were taken in support of the hijackers' demand for the release of imprisoned Palestinians. In 1976, a French plane with mostly Israeli passengers was hijacked by a Middle Eastern organization and flown to Uganda, where the hijackers threatened to kill the hostages unless Arab prisoners in Israel were released. In the aftermath of a number of such high-profile cases, the international community responded by signing a series of international agreements designed to tighten airport security, sanction states that accept hijackers, and condemn state-supported terrorism. The 1979 International Convention against the Taking of Hostages is a prominent example of such an agreement.

Much of the recent terrorist activity has its roots in the Middle East—in the Palestinians' quest for self-determination and their own internal conflicts over strategy, in the hostility among various Islamic groups toward Western forces, and in the resurgence of Islamic fundamentalism. Among the groups with roots in the Middle East are Hamas, Hezbollah, and Palestine Islamic Jihad. Since September 11, 2001, Al Qaeda has been the most publicized. A shadowy network of Islamic fundamentalists from many countries, including countries outside of the Middle East, Al Qaeda, led by Osama bin Laden, is motivated by its desire to install Islamic regimes in the Middle East, support Islamic insurgencies in Southeast Asia, and punish the United States for its support of Israel and for its tight linkages with corrupt regimes in the Middle East.

But terrorism also has a long history in other parts of the world, reflecting diverse, often multiple, motivations. Some groups represent extreme religious positions, like the Irish Republican Army, protector of Northern Irish Catholics in their struggle against Protestant British rule. Hindu-Muslim rivalry in India has led to numerous terrorist incidents. Other groups seek territorial separation or autonomy from a state. The Basque separatists (ETA) in Spain, Tamil Tigers in Sri Lanka, Abu Sayyaf Group in the Philippines, and Chechen groups in Russia are all excellent examples.

Since the 1990s, terrorism has taken a new turn.[16] The acts have become more lethal. In the 1990s, almost one-quarter of terrorist attacks resulted in deaths, whereas in the 1970s, about 17 percent of terrorist attacks killed someone. Until 2000, the worst loss of life came from the 1985 bombing of an Air India flight in which 329 people were killed. That changed dramatically on September 11, 2001, when over 3,000 civilians died and $80 billion in economic losses were incurred. The choice of weapons used by terrorists has become more diverse. AK-47s, sarin gas, shoulder-fired missiles, anthrax, backpack explosives, and airplanes as missiles have all been utilized; many of

TABLE 8.2

Terrorist Organizations		
Group	**Location**	**Characteristics and attacks**
Al Qaeda	Formerly in Afghanistan; now dispersed throughout Afghanistan, Pakistan, Iran, Indonesia	Formed by Osama bin Laden in the late 1980s among Arabs who fought the Soviets in Afghanistan; responsible for the bombings in Africa (1998), Yemen (2000), U.S. (2001), Spain (2004), Great Britain (2005), India (2006).
Hamas (Islamic Resistance Movement)	Israel, West Bank, Gaza Strip	Its leader signed bin Laden's 1998 *fatwa* calling for attacks on U.S. interests; elected in 2006 as governing authority in Gaza.
Hezbollah (Party of God)	Lebanon	Also known as Islamic Jihad; often directed by Iran and suspected in the bombing of the U.S. embassy and marine barracks in Beirut in 1983; dominates Lebanon politically; fights against Israel.
Palestinian Islamic Jihad	Israel, West Bank, Gaza Strip, Jordan, Lebanon, Syria	Committed to the creation of an Islamic Palestinian state; conducts suicide bombings against Israel and opposes Arab governments considered tainted by secularism.
Euzkadi Ta Askatasuna: Basque Fatherland and Liberty (ETA)	Spain, primarily autonomous regions in north	Separatists, involved in bombings, assassinations of government officials, violence against civilians; 2006 ceasefire, but broke later that year.
Communist Party of Philippines/ New People's Army (CPP/ NPA)	Northern, rural Philippines, cells in Manila and other metropolitan centers	Opposes U.S. military presence; NPA targets U.S. personnel if in NPA areas
Revolutionary armed forces of Colombia (FARC)	Colombia, with some activities in neighboring Brazil, Venezuela, Panama	Bombings, murder, kidnapping, extortion, narcotrafficking against Colombian officials; Marxist

Is religious fundamentalism, particularly Islamic fundamentalism, the next great threat to international security?

YES:

◆ Islamist militants have been able to coordinate and advance anti-Western, antisecular political agendas in various regions, resulting in regional instability.

◆ Islamic fundamentalism is a countervailing force to Western power and influence in the world and hence is a threat to international security.

◆ Islamic fundamentalists are able to carry out high-impact violence, coordinated for simultaneity and initiated by networks of leaderless cells, making their attacks hard to deter or defend against by conventional means and thus posing an as-yet unstoppable security threat.

◆ Islamic fundamentalists are able to draw various other terrorist organizations, rogue states like Iran and Iraq, and religious fanatics into widespread networks that are hard to contain or detect and thus threaten international stability.

NO:

◆ The threat of the spread of weapons of mass destruction is the greatest threat to international security. The dispute between India and Pakistan, each of which has nuclear weapons, and the dispute between North Korea and its Asian neighbors over the North Korean nuclear weapons program threaten to destabilize these two regions; it is these threats that should most concern us.

◆ Ethnic conflicts and conflicts over power and resources pose greater threats to international security than does Islamic fundamentalism.

◆ The international community's war against terror and against the forces of Islamic fundamentalism is increasingly successful, as networks have been broken up and access to financing denied; hence, the threat is under control.

these weapons are easily available today. The infrastructure used to support terrorism has also become more sophisticated. It is financed through money-laundering schemes and illegal criminal activities. Training camps attract not just young, single, and educated potential terrorists, but also older, better educated individuals who are increasingly willing to commit suicide to accomplish their objectives.

The groups practicing terrorism are more wide-ranging, from nationalists and neo-Nazis, to religious, left-wing, and right-wing militants. Sponsorship of terrorist groups by states, state-sponsored terrorism, is increasingly common. North Korea, Iran, Iraq, Syria, Libya, Sudan, and Cuba have all been singled out as state sponsors of terrorism. And terrorists are increasingly launching attacks in developing countries: Turkey, Morocco, Indonesia, India, Kenya, and Pakistan are all examples.

Responding to terrorist activity has become increasingly difficult, because most perpetrators have networks of supporters in the resident populations. Protecting populations from random acts of violence is an almost impossible task, given the availability of guns and bombs in the international marketplace and the necessity, at least in Western democratic states, of balancing civil and human rights with antiterrorist legislation. Pressure is very strong because people worry disproportionately about terrorism, even though it kills a relatively small number of people. Despite better devices for detection, committed individuals or groups of terrorists are difficult to deter. Indeed, such individuals may become heroes in the community—one person's terrorist is another person's freedom fighter.

The international community has taken action against terrorists first by creating a framework of international rules dealing with terrorism, including twelve conventions that address such issues as punishing hijackers and those who protect them; protecting airports, diplomats, and nuclear materials in transport; and blocking the flow of financial resources to global terrorist networks. Steps have also been taken by individual states to increase state security, such as in the United States through passage of the controversial USA PATRIOT Act; to support counterintelligence activities; and to promote cooperation among national enforcement agencies in tracking and apprehending terrorists. States that have been seen as supporting terrorists, or not taking effective enforcement measures, have been sanctioned by other states. Libya, Sudan, Afghanistan, Syria, Iran, and Iraq are prominent examples.

The Just War Tradition

Should states go to war? If war is generally viewed as an illegal and immoral act, are there any conditions when resorting to war is acceptable? What constitutes an appropriate justification to enter into war, *Jus ad bellum?* And what constitutes moral and ethical conduct once the decision has been made to go to war, *Jus in bello?* Normative political theorists draw our attention to the classical **just war tradition.** Although a Western and Christian doctrine dating from medieval times, just war theory draws on ancient Greek philosophy and precepts found in the Koran. As developed by St. Augustine, Thomas Aquinas, Hugo Grotius, and more recently by the political philosopher Michael Waltzer, just war theory asserts that there are several criteria that can make the decision to enter a war a just one.[17] There must be a just cause (self-defense or the defense of others, or a massive violation of human rights) and a declaration of intent by a competent authority (which since the formation of the United Nations has been interpreted to mean the Security Council). The leaders need to have the correct intentions, desiring to end abuses and establish a just peace, and have exhausted all other possibilities for ending the abuse, employing war as a last resort. Forces need to be rapidly removed after the humanitarian objectives have been secured. Because states choose war for a variety of reasons, however, it may not always be easy to assess the justness of a particular cause or of particular intentions.

The just war tradition also addresses conduct in war. Combatants and noncombatants must be differentiated, with the latter protected from harm as much as possible. The violence used needs to be proportionate to the ends to be achieved. Undue human suffering should be avoided at all costs and particularly heinous weapons not employed. Because mustard gas caused particularly cruel deaths during World War I, it was subsequently outlawed, thus providing the basis for future chemical and biological warfare conventions. Many of the extended norms of the just war tradition were codified in the four 1949 Geneva Conventions and two additional protocols concluded in 1977. These are designed to protect civilians, prisoners of war, wounded soldiers, as well as to ban particular methods of war and certain weapons that cause unnecessary suffering.

Just war is an evolving practice. The successful International Campaign to Ban Landmines (ICBL), launched in 1992 by a group of NGOs, including Vietnam Veterans of America and the International Red Cross, and finalized in 1999, outlawed the use, production, stockpiling, and sale of antipersonnel land mines. The campaign successfully argued that land mines have a particularly cruel impact on noncombatants, harming innocents, especially children, even after war has ended. The success of the ICBL, recognized by the awarding of the Nobel Peace Prize to its coordinator, Jody Williams, in 1997, may be attributed in part to the framing of the issue as a humanitarian one. Large stockpiles (34 million mines) have been destroyed by 61 states, casualties have been significantly reduced, and over $1.4 billion has been contributed to the task of further mine clearing and to aid victims.[18]

There is a growing pressure on scholars and statesmen to act in accord with just war principles. The level of discussion in the general media on the question before and during the 2003 Iraq war suggests that the prohibitions are taken seriously and failures to follow them are increasingly met by criticism.

The Debate over Humanitarian Intervention

No issue emerging from the just war tradition has been more critical or controversial than the debate over **humanitarian intervention.** Just war tradition asserts that military intervention by states or the international community may be justified if there have been massive violation of human rights. Yet that position directly contradicts the hallmark of the Westphalian tradition, that is, respect for state sovereignty. Throughout history, military intervention was on behalf of humanitarian causes, but it was used selectively: in the nineteenth century, Europeans used military force to protect Christians in Turkey and the Middle East, though they chose not to protect other religious groups and they did not intervene militarily to stop slavery, though they prohibited their own citizens from participating in the slave trade.[19]

Since the end of World War II, the notion has emerged that all human beings are in need of protection—not just a particular group—and that states have an obligation to intervene, a **responsibility to protect.** The belief gained even greater prominence in the 1990s. The idea is that in the case of massive violation of human rights and when domestic avenues for redress have been exhausted and actions by other states might reasonably end the abuse, states should interfere in the domestic affairs of the state where the abuse is occurring. If one's own state does not provide such protection, then it is the obligation of others to protect and intervene, as necessary. As two U.N. officials put it, this "marks the coming of age of the imperative of action in the face of human rights abuses, over the citadels of state sovereignty." Yet as the same two writers warn, it can also serve as "a pretext for military intervention often devoid of legal sanction, selectively deployed and achieving only ambiguous ends."[20]

But questions remain: How massive do the violations of human rights have to be to justify intervention? Who decides when to respond to the abuses? Can states be using the excuse of humanitarian intervention to achieve other goals? Is it an obligation to intervene militarily in these humanitarian emergencies?

Given their colonial experiences, many Asian and African countries are skeptical about altruistic claims by Western countries. Other states like Russia and China have insisted that for a claim of humanitarian intervention to be legitimate, it must be authorized by the U.N. Security Council. Thus, when Western states sought military intervention in Kosovo, Russia opposed the measure and the Western powers turned to the North Atlantic Treaty Organization. The United States opposed increased use of the military to protect civilians in Rwanda in 1993–94 despite the genocide, having suffered humiliation in Somalia several years earlier. Thus, only a small military contingent from the African Union has been mobilized for the Darfur region, despite

400,000 deaths and the culpability of the Sudanese government. In the Dar-fur case, other national interests have been deemed more vital (China's access to Sudanese oil; Russia's export arms market; U.S. preoccupation with Iraq and the war on terror) than support for humanitarian intervention.

So while there is an emergent norm in support of humanitarian interven-tion, it is still the subject of debate. Because states will never intervene in all situations of humanitarian emergencies, state sovereignty remains intact. But when there are widely recognized gross violations and when military inter-vention does not conflict with other national interests, then humanitarian intervention is seen as a justified use of force.

Approaches to Managing Insecurity

Disparity in power between states, the inability to know the intentions of states and individuals, and the lack of an overarching international authority means that states are continuously confronted by the need to manage their insecurity. The need to manage insecurity is made more urgent by the recent proliferation of military weapons and increases in military spending, in each case a growth trend proportionately greater than the growth of either popula-tion or the economy. Proliferation of weapons through international trade has enhanced the capacity of both developed and developing states, as well as nonstate groups, to fight, and subsequently has dispersed military capacity throughout the world in the form of nuclear, conventional, and small-arms weapons.

Four approaches to managing insecurity are well tested. Two of these approaches reflect the liberal theoretical perspective and thus focus largely on multilateral responses by groups of states acting to coordinate their policies. The other approaches reflect realist thinking, requiring individual states them-selves to maintain an adequate power potential. Liberals and realists support different policy responses to arms proliferation, the resulting security dilemma, and managing insecurity more generally, as illustrated in Figure 8.1.

Liberal Approaches: Collective Security and Arms Control/Disarmament

Liberal approaches to managing the security dilemma call on the interna-tional community or international institutions to coordinate actions in order to manage power.

The Collective Security Ideal

Collective security is captured in the old adage "one for all and all for one." Based on the proposition that aggressive and unlawful use of force by any

FIGURE 8.1

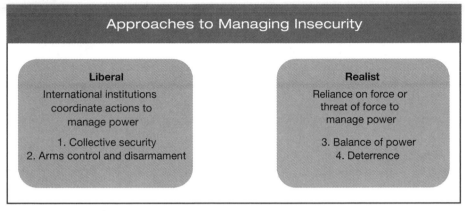

Approaches to Managing Insecurity

Liberal

International institutions coordinate actions to manage power

1. Collective security
2. Arms control and disarmament

Realist

Reliance on force or threat of force to manage power

3. Balance of power
4. Deterrence

state against another must be stopped, collective security posits that such unlawful aggression will be met by united action: all (or many) other states will join together against the aggressor. Potential aggressors will know this fact ahead of time and thus will choose not to act.

Collective security makes a number of fundamental assumptions.[21] One assumption is that although wars can occur, they should be prevented, and they are prevented by restraint of military action. In other words, wars will not occur if all parties exercise restraint. Another assumption is that aggressors—no matter who they are, "friends or foes"—should be stopped. This assumption presumes that the aggressor can be identified easily by other members of the international community. (In some conflicts, it is difficult to differentiate between the aggressor and the victim.) Collective security also assumes moral clarity: the aggressor is morally wrong because all aggressors are morally wrong, and all those who are right must act in unison to meet the aggression. Finally, collective security assumes that aggressors know that the international community will act to punish an aggressor.

Of course, the underlying hope of collective security proponents is compatible with the logic of deterrence (a realist strategy). If all countries know that aggression will be punished by the international community, then would-be aggressors will refrain from engaging in aggressive activity. Hence, states will be more secure with the belief that would-be aggressors

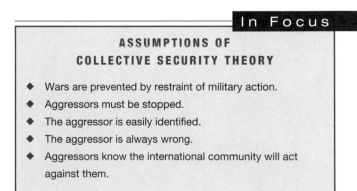

In Focus

ASSUMPTIONS OF COLLECTIVE SECURITY THEORY

◆ Wars are prevented by restraint of military action.

◆ Aggressors must be stopped.

◆ The aggressor is easily identified.

◆ The aggressor is always wrong.

◆ Aggressors know the international community will act against them.

will be deterred by the prospect of united action by the international community. But for collective security to work, the threat to take action must be credible and there must be cohesion among all the potential enforcers.

Collective security does not always work. In the period between the two world wars, Japan invaded Manchuria and Italy overran Ethiopia. In neither case did other states act as if it were in their collective interest to respond. Were Manchuria and Ethiopia really worth a war? In this instance, collective security did not work because of a lack of commitment on the part of other states and an unwillingness of the international community to act in concert. In the post–World War II era, collective security could not work because of fundamental differences in both state interests and ideologies. Agreement among the most powerful states was virtually impossible. And a collective security response against one of the five permanent members of the U.N. Security Council—the United States, the Soviet Union, Great Britain, France, or China—was impossible due to the veto power that each held. Two major alliance systems—the North Atlantic Treaty Organization (NATO) and the Warsaw Pact—arrayed states into two separate camps. States dared not engage in action against an ally or a foe, even if that state was an aggressor, for fear of embarking on another world war.

Collective security is also likely to be unworkable because of the problematic nature of its assumptions. Can the aggressor always be easily identified? Clearly not. In 1967 Israel launched an armed attack against Egypt: this was an act of aggression. The week before, however, Egypt had blocked Israeli access to the Red Sea. Clearly that, too, was an act of aggression. Twenty years earlier the state of Israel had been carved out of Arab real estate. That, too, was an act of aggression. Many centuries before, Arabs had ousted Jews from the territory they inhabited, also an aggressive action. So who is the aggressor? Furthermore, even if an aggressor can be identified, is that party always morally wrong? Collective security theorists argue, by definition, yes. Yet trying to right a previous wrong is not necessarily wrong; trying to make just a prior injustice is not always unjust. Like the balance of power, collective security in practice supports the status quo at a specific point in time.

Arms Control and Disarmament

Arms control and general **disarmament** schemes have been the hope of many liberals over the years. The logic of this approach to security is straightforward: fewer weapons means greater security. By regulating the upward spiral of arms proliferation (arms control) and by reducing the amount of arms and the types of weapons employed (disarmament), the costs of the security dilemma are reduced.

During the Cold War, many arms control agreements were negotiated to reduce the threat of nuclear war. For example, in the 1972 Treaty on the Limitation of Antiballistic Missile Systems (ABM treaty), both the United States and the Soviet Union agreed not to use a ballistic missile defense as a shield against a first strike by the other. The Strategic Arms Limitations Talks in 1972 and 1979 (SALT I and SALT II, respectively) put ceilings on the growth of both Soviet and U.S. strategic weapons. However, due to the Soviet invasion of Afghanistan in 1979, the second SALT treaty was never ratified by the U.S. Senate. The Treaty on the Nonproliferation of Nuclear Weapons (NPT) was negotiated in 1968 at the United Nations in response to the Cuban missile crisis.

Table 8.3 lists some of the important arms control agreements negotiated to date. Most of these treaties, be they bilateral or multilateral, call for individual states to reduce either the number or the type of armaments already deployed. A few are designed to halt the spread of particular weapons to states that do not yet have them; a few provide verification mechanisms to monitor whether the terms of the treaty are being met. Nevertheless, virtually all arms control treaties are fraught with difficulties.

The NPT provides both a positive and a negative example of the impact of such treaties. The NPT spells out the rules of **nuclear proliferation** since 1970. In the treaty, signatory countries without nuclear weapons agree not to acquire or develop them, while states with nuclear weapons promise not to transfer the technology to nonnuclear states and to eventually dismantle their own. Like many of the arms control treaties, however, a number of key nuclear states and threshold nonnuclear states (i.e., states that probably have or could quickly assemble nuclear weapons) remain outside the treaty, including Cuba, India, Israel, and Pakistan. During the 1990s, three states that previously had nuclear weapons programs—South Africa, Brazil, and Argentina—dismantled their programs and became parties to the treaty, along with three other states—Belarus, Kazakhstan, and Ukraine—that gave up nuclear weapons left on their territory after the dissolution of the Soviet Union. The International Atomic Energy Agency (IAEA), a U.N.-based agency established in 1957 to disseminate knowledge about nuclear energy and promote its peaceful uses, is the designated guardian of the treaty. The IAEA created a system of safeguards, including inspection teams that visit nuclear facilities and report on any movement of nuclear material, in an attempt to keep nuclear material from being diverted to nonpeaceful purposes and to ensure that states that signed the NPT are complying. Inspectors for IAEA visited Iraqi sites after the 1991 Gulf War and North Korean sites in the mid-1990s. Their purpose in the first case was to verify that illegal materials had been destroyed and, in the

TABLE 8.3

Representative Arms Control Agreements since 1959

Agreement	Signed by	Provisions	Year
Antarctic Treaty	43 states	Prohibits all military activity in Antarctic area.	1959
Partial Nuclear Test Ban Treaty	154 states	Prohibits nuclear explosions in the atmosphere, in outer space, and underwater.	1963
Outer Space Treaty	127 states	Prohibits all military activity in outer space, including on the moon and other celestial bodies.	1967
Treaty of Tlatelolco	33 states	Prohibits nuclear weapons in Latin America.	1967
Nuclear Nonproliferation Treaty (NPT)	188 states	Prohibits acquisition of nuclear weapons by nonnuclear nations and commits nuclear states to negotiations for general and complete nuclear disarmament.	1968
Strategic Arms Limitation Treaty (SALT)	U.S., U.S.S.R.	Limits deployment of antiballistic missile systems to two sites in each country. Reduced to one site by 1974 agreement.	1972
SALT I: Interim Offensive Arms Agreement	U.S., U.S.S.R.	Provides for freeze on aggregate number of fixed land-based ICBMs and SLBMs.*	1972
Biological Weapons Convention	155 states	States agree not to develop, produce, acquire biological agents or toxins, as well as weapons or means of delivery.	1975
South Pacific Nuclear-Free Zone Treaty	18 states	Bans testing, manufacture, acquisition, stationing of nuclear weapons in the South Pacific.	1985
Confidence- and Security-Building Measures and Disarmament in Europe	54 states	Requires notification of military movements and maneuvers, observers, and inspection.	1986
Intermediate-Range Nuclear Forces (INF) Treaty	U.S., U.S.S.R.	Eliminates all missiles with range between 500 and 5,500 kilometers.	1987
Conventional Armed Forces in Europe (CFE) Treaty	30 states	Sets specific limits on NATO and former members of Warsaw Pact for tanks, other armored vehicles, artillery, combat helicopters, and aircraft.	1990
Strategic Arms Reduction Treaty (START) I	U.S., U.S.S.R. (now Russia, Belarus, Kazakhstan, Ukraine)	Reduces number of U.S. and former Soviet strategic nuclear warheads by approximately one-third; makes Russia, Belarus, Ukraine, and Kazakhstan responsible for carrying out former U.S.S.R. treaty obligations.	1991

Agreement	Signed by	Provisions	Year
Open Skies Treaty	34 states	Creates a regime for confidence-building and stability of arms control, by allowing observational flights by unarmed reconnaissance aircraft over signatory states.	1992
START II	U.S., Russia	Reduces the number of deployed U.S. and Russian strategic nuclear warheads by the year 2003; bans multiple-warhead land-based missiles.	1993
Chemical Weapons Convention (CWC)	178 states	Bans the use, production, development, and stockpiling of chemical weapons within 10–15 years of treaty's entry into force.	1993
U.N. Registration of Conventional Arms	97 states	Requires that states submit information on seven categories of major weapons exported or imported during prior year.	1993
Wassenaar Arrangement on Export Controls for Conventional Arms and Dual-Use Goods and Technologies	40 states	Regulates transfer of dual-use technologies.	1995
ASEAN Nuclear-Weapon-Free Zone Treaty	10 states	Creates nuclear-free zone in Southeast Asia.	1996
African Nuclear-Weapon-Free Zone Treaty (Treaty of Pelindaba)	45 states	Creates nuclear-free zone in Africa.	1996
Comprehensive Test Ban Treaty (CTBT)	176 states	Bans testing of nuclear weapons.	1996
Antipersonnel Landmines Treaty	149 states	Bans production and export of land mines.	1999
Inter-American Convention on Transparency in Conventional Weapons Acquisitions	34 states	Requires Organization of American States (OAS) members to report export and import of weapons.	1999
Treaty between U.S. and Russian Federation on Strategic Offensive Reductions (Moscow Treaty)	U.S., Russia	Limits operationally deployed strategic warheads to 1,700–2,200; no verification; no time limit.	2003

*ICBM = intercontinental ballistic missile; SLBM = submarine-launched ballistic missile.

second case, to confirm that nuclear materials in that country were being used for nonmilitary purposes only.

The end of the Cold War and the dismemberment of the Soviet Union have resulted in major new arms control agreements, as Table 8.3 shows. More arms control agreements between the United States and Russia and its successor states are likely, as the latter are forced by economic imperatives to reduce their military expenditures. Yet the logic of arms control agreements is not impeccable. Arms control does not eliminate the security dilemma. You can still feel insecure if your enemy has a bigger or better rock than you do. And as realists would argue, state policy toward such agreements is never assured. Verification is spotty and difficult to monitor. That is one reason why the United States is not party to some of the treaties. Witness the North Korean case. In 1994, the United States and North Korea signed the Agreed Framework. North Korea agreed to stop its nuclear weapons program in exchange for a U.S. package deal of energy supplies, light-water reactors, and security guarantees. The framework collapsed in 2002. North Korea announced it was pulling out of the Nuclear Nonproliferation Treaty in response to U.S. decisions to halt shipments of fuel oil supporting North Korea's electric grid. In response to North Korea's resumption of the Yongbyon nuclear reactor used to process weapons-grade nuclear material, the United States and Japan halted aid shipments.

In 2003, North Korea publicly admitted that it was building a nuclear-weapons program and three years later tested both long- and short-range missiles, causing great consternation in the region and in the United States. Is North Korea using nuclear weapons to further destabilize an already volatile region? Or is North Korea bargaining for more aid in return for promising to halt its nuclear-weapons program? The agreement brokered in 2007 as a result of negotiations conducted among the six parties—North Korea, China, Japan, the United States, South Korea, and Russia—indicates that North Korea would close its main nuclear reactor in exchange for a package of fuel, food, and other aid. Threatening nuclear proliferation as a coercive measure to secure aid creates an intriguing new security twist.

Complete disarmament schemes as envisioned by utopian liberal thinkers are unlikely, given how risky such a scheme would be. Unilateral disarmament would place the disarmed state in a highly insecure position and cheaters could be rewarded. But incremental disarmament, such as represented by the Chemical Weapons Convention (CWC), which bans the development, production, and stockpiling of chemical weapons, remains a possibility, although the increasing sophistication and miniaturization of chemical and biological weapons makes them difficult to detect, so that it is hard to guarantee compliance. Liberals place their faith, however, in international institutions like the IAEA to monitor adherence to such limited disarmament schemes.

Realist Approaches: Balance of Power and Deterrence

As mentioned earlier, realist approaches to managing security place less faith in the international community and more faith in individual state power.

Balance of Power

In Chapter 4, we saw that a balance of power is a particular configuration of the international system. But theorists use the terms in other ways as well. So *balance of power* may refer to an equilibrium between any two parties, and *balancing power* may describe an approach to managing power and insecurity. The latter usage is relevant here.

Balance-of-power theorists posit that, to manage insecurity, states make rational and calculated evaluations of the costs and benefits of particular policies that determine the state's role in a balance of power. Should we enlarge our power by seeking new allies? Is our enemy (or friend) altering the balance of power to our detriment? What can we do to make the balance of power shift in our favor? By either explicitly or implicitly asking and responding to such questions, states minimize their insecurity by protecting their own interests. All states in the system are continually making choices to increase their own capabilities and to undermine the capabilities of others, and thereby the balance of power is maintained. When that balance of power is jeopardized, insecurity leads states to pursue countervailing policies.[22]

Alliances represent the most important institutional tool for enhancing one's own power and meeting the perceived power potential of one's opponent. If a state is threatening to achieve a dominant position, the threatened state will join with others against the threat. This is external balancing. Formal and institutionalized military alliances play a key role in maintaining a balance of power, as the NATO and Warsaw Pact alliances did in the post–World War II world. States may also engage in internal balancing, increasing their own military and economic capabilities to counter potential threatening enemies.

A balance of power operates at both the international and regional levels. At the international level during the Cold War, for instance, a relative balance of power was maintained between the United States and the Soviet Union. If one of the superpowers augmented its power through the expansion of its alliances or through the acquisition of more deadly, more effective armaments, the other responded in kind. Absolute gains were not as critical as relative gains; no matter how much total power one state accrued, neither state could afford to fall behind the other. Gaining allies in the uncommitted part of the Third World, through foreign aid or military and diplomatic intervention, was one way to ensure that the power was balanced. To not maintain the power balance was too risky a strategy; national survival was at stake.

Balances of power among states in specific geographic regions are also a way to manage insecurity. In South Asia, for example, a balance of power works to maintain peace between India and Pakistan, a peace made more durable by the presence of nuclear weapons, according to realist thinking. In East Asia, Japan's alliance with the United States creates a balance of power vis-à-vis China. In the Middle East, the balance of power between Israel and its Arab neighbors continues. In some regions a complex set of other balances has developed: between the economically rich, oil-producing states of Saudi Arabia and the Persian Gulf and the economically poor states of the core Middle East; between Islamic militants (Iran, Libya), moderates (Egypt, Tunisia), and conservatives (Saudi Arabia). With the breakup of the Soviet Union, the newly independent states of Central Asia are struggling for position within a newly emerging regional balance of power.

Realist theorists assert that the balance of power is the most important technique for managing insecurity. It is compatible with the nature of man and that of the state, which is to act to protect one's self-interest by maintaining one's power position relative to others. If a state seeks preponderance through military acquisitions or offensive actions, then war against that state is acceptable under the balance-of-power system. But if all states act similarly, the balance can be preserved.

A major limitation of the balance-of-power approach, however, is its inability to manage security during periods of fundamental change. A balance-of-power approach supports the status quo. When change occurs, how should other states respond? Fundamental change occurred at the end of the Cold War, for example, with the dismemberment of the Soviet Union and the dissolution of the Warsaw pact alliance. A balance-of-power strategy would have suggested that the United States also reduce its power potential, particularly its military capability, since the military of its rival had been impaired. Yet such a rational response is not only politically difficult to make, but also wrong in the view of offensive realists. Fear of a resurgence of power from the opponent, fear of a return to the old order, and pressure from domestic constituencies to maintain defense spending and employment all make dramatic changes in policy difficult to accommodate.

Balance of power is especially problematic during periods of transition. The end of the Cold War represents such a transition, and it has dramatically affected the role of NATO, the major Western alliance formed after World War II to counter the threat posed by the Soviet Union. With the disintegration of the Soviet Union as a state and the end of communist leadership in it and neighboring states, some scholars predicted the imminent demise of NATO. What happened is not the organization's demise but its reconfiguration both in terms of the tasks undertaken and in terms of the expansion of its membership.

With the bloody civil war in Yugoslavia and attendant refugee crises in Europe, NATO increasingly took on peacekeeping and stabilization roles in Bosnia. Then in 1999, NATO undertook its largest military operation (since its creation in 1949) in Operation Allied Force, the air war over Serbia. Without U.N. authorization, NATO forces conducted a seventy-eight-day air war against the Federal Republic of Yugoslavia to halt attacks against ethnic Albanians in the Serbian province of Kosovo. The war resulted in a popular uprising and the attendant overthrow of the Serbian leadership, the extradition of Serbian strongman Slobodan Milošević to the Hague War Crimes Tribunal, and the petition by Serbia to join NATO's Partnership for Peace.

Since the global war against terrorism began in September 2001, NATO has tried to position itself in the new security environment.[23] NATO has enhanced its operational capabilities to keep up with technology, created a rapid reaction force to respond to crises, and streamlined the military command structure. It has employed forces "out of area"—outside Europe, in Afghanistan—and has practiced for operations in Africa. Its members have helped train the Iraqi military, although the organization has not joined in the U.S.-led coalition in Iraq.

NATO membership has also expanded as its tasks have diversified. In 1997, the first wave of new members, including Poland, Hungary, and the Czech Republic, were admitted. It has proven a more difficult task than anticipated to convince these states to make necessary defense reforms, increase defense expenditures, and modernize equipment and training. These new members were to be contributors to enhanced security in the region, not just the recipients of a security umbrella. Yet despite these problems, a second wave of members was admitted in 2003 that included Estonia, Latvia, Lithuania, Slovakia, Slovenia, Romania, and Bulgaria, bringing the total NATO membership to twenty-six, along with twenty-six Partnership for Peace member states and seven Mediterranean Dialogue states. This round of admission was a reaction to the war on terror, a search by the United States and others for dependable allies where bases could be maintained at a cheaper cost and where greater proximity to the Middle East could be achieved. The newer NATO members could curry favor with the United States and did not have to make reforms to be admitted to the organization.

During most of the 1990s, Russia opposed NATO enlargement, seeing its old allies coming under the NATO auspices. Expansion of the alliance itself was viewed as a potential military threat. Yet in the aftermath of 9/11 and the newest explosion of membership, Russian opposition has softened, as they realized that these newest members were turning NATO into a kind of "toothless lion." And Russia still has military bases in locations such as Georgia, Ukraine, Moldova, Armenia, Tajikistan, and Kyrgyzstan.

To most member states, particularly the United States, expansion was seen as a natural consequence of winning the Cold War, establishing a new post–Cold War security order, and more recently, trying to respond to new security threats posed by terrorism. Realists see NATO expansion as a means to achieve relative gains over Russia and further enhance Western security. Liberals view expansion as a means to strengthen democracy in former communist states and bring institutional stability to areas threatened with crises. NATO has worked closely with Russia to convince it that NATO's expansion is not an offensive threat and has institutionalized dialogue with Russia on key NATO issues that pertain to Russia's own security.

Deterrence: Balance of Power Revisited

The goal of deterrence, like that of the balance of power, is to prevent the outbreak of war. Deterrence theory posits that war can be prevented by the *threat* of the use of force. The United States, in its 2002 National Security Strategy made the threat very explicit for those who may pursue global terrorism. The United States writes that it will defend "the United States, the American people, our interests at home and abroad by identifying and destroying the threat before it reaches our border. . . . We will not hesitate to act alone, if necessary, to exercise our right of self-defense by acting preemptively against such terrorists, to prevent them from doing harm against our people and our country."

Deterrence theory as initially developed is based on a number of key assumptions.[24] First and most important is the realist assumption of the rationality of decisionmakers. Rational decisionmakers are assumed to want to avoid resorting to war in those situations in which the anticipated cost of the aggression is greater than the gain expected. Second, it is assumed that nuclear weapons pose an unacceptable level of destruction, and thus that decisionmakers will not resort to armed aggression against a nuclear state. Third, the theory assumes that alternatives to war are available to decisionmakers irrespective of the situation. Thus, under deterrence, war will not occur and insecurity is reduced, as long as rational decisionmakers are in charge, the threat is sufficiently large, and other nonmilitary options are available.

For deterrence to work, then, states must build up their arsenals in order to present a credible threat. Information regarding the threat must be conveyed to the opponent. Thus, knowing that an aggressive action will be countered by a damaging reaction, the opponent will decide, according to deterrence theorists, not to resort to force and thereby destroy its own society.

In Focus

ASSUMPTIONS OF DETERRENCE THEORY

◆ Decisionmakers are rational.

◆ The threat of destruction from warfare is large.

◆ Alternatives to war are available.

As logical as deterrence sounds and as effective as it seemed during the Cold War—after all, there was no nuclear war between the superpowers—the very assumptions on which deterrence is based are troublesome. Are all top decisionmakers rational? Might not one individual or a group of individuals risk destruction, deciding to launch a first strike? Might some states be willing to sacrifice a large number of people, as Germany's Adolf Hitler, Iran's Ayatollah Khomeini, and Iraq's Saddam Hussein were willing to do in the past? How do states convey to a potential adversary information about their own capability? Why not bluff or lie, to feel more secure? The Soviet Union tried this, placing missiles in Cuba, and almost caused a nuclear confrontation with the United States. For states without nuclear weapons, or for nuclear-weapons states that are launching an attack against a nonnuclear state, the costs of war may be acceptable: their own society may not be threatened with destruction. In such cases, deterrence will fail.

The security environment makes deterrence even more problematic in the new millennium. First, the rise of terrorism conducted by nonstate actors organized in horizontal networks decreases the possibility that deterrence will work. Nonstate actors do not hold territory; the threat to destroy such territory cannot be a potent deterrent. And flexible networks, spread over different geographic areas, rather than an organizational hierarchy located within a particular state, make eliminating those networks more difficult. The increasing willingness of some groups to use suicide terrorism to achieve their objectives guarantees that deterrence will be less effective. Deterrence depends on the calculation that significant loss of life is unacceptable; suicide terrorists are willing to sacrifice their own lives and are therefore not easily deterred.[25]

Second, the changed security environment is one in which the United States is approaching nuclear primacy.[26] It may be possible for the United States to destroy the long-range nuclear arsenals of both Russia and China with a first strike. This has occurred because of the improvements in the U.S. nuclear capacity, including the ability to track submarines and mobile missiles, the declining capability of the Russian military, and the slow pace of China's modernization. In fact, China has no long-range bombers and no advanced warning system. So U.S. primacy may prevent other states from acting against America, but it may not serve to restrain U.S. actions. Some states worry that the United States may be emboldened to use a preemptive nuclear strike.

So, can the traditional liberal or realist approaches to managing insecurity be effective in the new security environment of the new millennium? There does not appear to be sufficient consensus to make collective security viable; globalization of markets and miniaturization of weapons has made verifiable arms-control increasingly difficult to implement. Balance of power may not operate in periods of international system change. Deterrence cannot work against a preeminent hegemon unless the hegemon itself exercises self-restraint. Deterrence cannot be effective against terrorists who feel they have nothing to lose. Despite this pessimistic assessment, the fact is all kinds of wars have declined in number. The state system is more secure, although the daily headlines and news reports suggest otherwise.

A Changing View of International Security

Traditionally, international security has meant states' security and the defense of states' territorial integrity from external threats or attack. Over time this definition has broadened to include not only interstate wars, but also intrastate conflicts. In both situations, conflicts arise not only over control of territory, but control over government and ideas. Typically, it has been government officials, in democracies acting in consultation with the society, and the military who are responsible for national security and provide humanitarian intervention. This has been the major focus of our chapter.

But a new trend is occurring more and more: outsourced security—from the government to private security firms.[27] Names as obscure as Executive Outcomes, Blackwater, Eric, Sandline, Alpha, BDM, COFRAS, and Southern Cross represent new actors in security. These contracting private companies perform diverse tasks: servicing military airplanes and ships, providing food for armies, protecting high-profile officials, guarding and interrogating prisoners of war, training troops, and sometimes carrying out low-intensity military operations on behalf of the client. These "soldiers"—the mercenaries of the twenty-first century—come from all over the world—from the Ukraine to Fiji, Australia to Chile, many of the players former government military personnel. And they serve in locations from Sierra Leone to Sri Lanka and Bosnia to the Democratic Republic of the Congo and East Timor.

Data on private security are difficult to obtain. But recent estimates put the annual market revenue over $100 billion, a figure that is projected to double by 2010. There are unconfirmed reports of over 100,000 private security forces in Iraq in 2006, coming from more than eighty companies.

What are the problems—logistic, legal, and ethical—emerging from this trend? Are these people merely mercenaries acting out of pecuniary self-interest? Or are they pragmatically solving problems that the military could not otherwise solve? Do they save the military money through competitive bidding? Where are their loyalties? To what state or what ideology do they belong? What is their relationship with the organized military? Can they be accountable for actions taken in war? In other words, does *jus in bello* also apply to these forces? Should they be used by the international community for U.N.-mandated peacekeeping?

In the waning years of the twentieth century, another change has occurred that concerns who or what should be protected. Should only states be protected? Or should individuals be protected as well, not only from inter-state rivalries but from failures of their own government to protect life, property, and ideas? That states and the international community have the obligation, indeed the responsibility, to protect human beings, even if it means intervention into the affairs of another state is the norm of humanitarian intervention.

But what should the individual be protected against? Should protection include more than protection against the physical violence typically associated with interstate conflict, civil war, genocide, nuclear weapons, or terrorism discussed in this chapter? Or should the concept of security be broadened? In 2004, the U.N. High-level Panel on Threats, Challenges, and Change identified additional threats to security and labeled them human security, a term that has increasingly been used since the early 1990s. Should individuals be protected from deleterious effects of economic globalization or from poverty? Should they be protected from infectious diseases and environmental degradation? It is to the economic issues that we now turn.

Notes

1. Data on war frequency and number of deaths can be found in several, sometimes divergent, sources. These include Quincy Wright, *A Study of War,* 2 vols. (Chicago: University of Chicago Press, 1942; rev. ed., 1965); J. David Singer and Melvin Small, *The Wages of War, 1816–1965: Statistical Handbook* (New York: Wiley, 1972); Jack S. Levy, *War in the Modern Great Power System, 1495–1975* (Lexington, Ky.: University Press of Kentucky, 1983); Ruth Leger Sivard, *World Military and Social Expenditures, 1996* (Washington, D.C.: World Priorities, 1996); and Recent Trends in Human Security Centre, The Human Security Report 2005, available at www.humansecurityreport.info.

2. John Herz, "Idealist Internationalism and the Security Dilemma," *World Politics* 2:2 (January 1950), 157–80.

3. Kenneth N. Waltz, *Man, the State, and War* (New York: Columbia University Press, 1954).

4. For a more comprehensive approach, see Jack S. Levy, "The Causes of War: A Review of Theories and Evidence," in *Behavior Society and Nuclear War*, vol. 1, ed. Philip E. Tetlock et al. (New York: Oxford University Press, 1989), 209–333.

5. St. Augustine, "Confessions" and "City of God," in *Great Books of the Western World*, vol. 18, ed. Robert Maynard Hutchins (Chicago: Encyclopedia Britannica, 1952, 1986); and Reinhold Niebuhr, *The Children of Light and Children of Darkness* (New York: Scribner, 1945).

6. John J. Mearsheimer, *The Tragedy of Great Power Politics* (New York: Norton, 2001), 32.

7. A. F. K. Organski, *World Politics* (New York: Knopf, 1958), Chap. 12; and A. F. K. Organski and Jacek Kugler, *The War Ledger* (Chicago: University of Chicago Press, 1980).

8. George Modelski and William R. Thompson, "Long Cycles and Global War," in *Handbook of War Studies*, ed. Manus I. Midlarsky (Boston: Unwin Hyman, 1989).

9. Carl von Clausewitz, *On War*, ed. with an introduction by Anatol Rapoport (Middlesex, Eng.: Penguin Books, 1968), 119.

10. John Mueller, "The Essential Irrelevance of Nuclear Weapons: Stability in the Postwar World," *International Security* 13:2 (Fall 1988), 55–79, and *Retreat from Doomsday: The Obsolescence of Major War* (New York: Basic Books, 1989). See also Gregg Easterbrook, "The End of War?" *The New Republic* (May 30, 2005), 18–21.

11. Robert Jervis, "Theories of War in an Era of Leading Power Peace," *American Political Science Review* 96:1 (March 2002), 11.

12. Ibid, 9.

13. Scott D. Sagan and Kenneth N. Waltz, *The Spread of Nuclear Weapons: A Debate Renewed* (New York: Norton, 2003).

14. Andrew Mack, "Why Big Nations Lose Small Wars: The Politics of Asymmetric Conflict," *World Politics* 27:2 (January 1975), 175–200.

15. Paul R. Pillar, *Terrorism and U.S. Foreign Policy* (Washington, D.C.: Brookings Institution Press, 2001), 13–14.

16. See, for example, Dan Caldwell and Robert E. Williams Jr., *Seeking Security in an Insecure World* (Lanham, Md.: Rowman & Littlefield, 2006); and Walter Enders and Todd Sandler, "Distribution of Transnational Terrorism among Countries by Income Class and Geography after 9/11," *International Studies Quarterly* 50:2 (June 2006), 367–68.

17. For contemporary views, see Michael Waltzer, *Just and Unjust Wars* (New York: Basic Books, 1977).

18. See Ramesh Thakur and William Maley, "The Ottawa Convention on Landmines: A Landmark Humanitarian Treaty in Arms Control?" *Global Governance* 5:3 (July–September 1999), 273–302.

19. Martha Finnemore, *The Purpose of Intervention: Changing Beliefs about the Use of Force* (Ithaca, N.Y.: Cornell University Press, 2003), 52–84.

20. Shashi Tharoor and Sam Daws, "Humanitarian Intervention: Getting Past the Reefs," *World Policy Journal* 18:2 (Summer 2001), 23.

21. For a complete treatment, see Inis Claude, *Power and International Relations* (New York: Random House, 1962), 94–204.

22. Hans J. Morgenthau, *Politics among Nations: The Struggle for Power and Peace* (4th ed.; New York: Knopf, 1967), 161–215.

23. Zoltan Barany, "NATO's Post–Cold War Metamorphosis: From Sixteen to Twenty-Six and Counting," *International Studies Review* 8:1 (March 2006), 165–78.

24. See Glenn Snyder, *Deterrence and Defense* (Princeton, N.J.: Princeton University Press, 1961); and Alexander L. George and Richard Smoke, *Deterrence in American Foreign Policy: Theory and Practice* (New York: Columbia University Press, 1974).

25. For a sophisticated analysis of suicide terrorism, see Robert A. Pape, "The Strategic Logic of Suicide Terrorism," *American Political Science Review* 97:3 (August 2003), 343–61.

26. Keir A. Lieber and Daryl G. Press, "The Rise of U.S. Nuclear Primacy," *Foreign Affairs* 85:2 (March/April 2006), 42–54.

27. Deborah Avant, "The Privatization of Security and Change in the Control of Force," *International Studies Perspectives* 5 (2004), 153–57, and *The Market for Force: The Consequences of Privatizing Security* (Cambridge, UK: Cambridge University Press, 2005).

International Political Economy

9

- *What are the core concepts of economic liberalism?*
- *What roles have multinational corporations played in expanding economic liberalism?*
- *What roles have the major international economic institutions played in the post–World War II era?*
- *How do the views of mercantilists/statists and radicals differ from economic liberals?*
- *What are characteristics of the new thinking about economic development?*
- *What are the similarities and differences between the regionalism of the European Union and NAFTA?*
- *How is energy interdependence an economic and political issue?*
- *What are the arguments of the antiglobalization movement?*

From World War II to the early 1960s, international relations centered on issues of war and peace, where the nation-state was the primary actor in an international political system. In the 1960s and 1970s, changes took place that led to a surge of interest in a second issue, the international political economy. International political economics is the study of the interrelationship between politics and economics and between states and markets. It also examines how politics can be used to achieve economic goals, and how economic instruments are utilized for political purposes.

The increasing importance of the international political economy stems from several trends. First, economic transactions among states, including trade, investment, and lending have been rising dramatically. The number of interactions among states has grown both in absolute terms and as a share of total economic activity. Second, there has been increasing expectations about the responsibilities of national governments for economic policies. Citizens expect their governments not only to have political objectives, but to formulate economic and social policy objectives as well. Third, as these economic issues become the subject of public discussion, they become more transparent to individuals and groups that are potentially affected by the decisions; hence, the outcomes are more controversial and therefore more politicized.

These changes have been facilitated by a number of key technological transformations that began in the 1800s (transoceanic telegraphic cables and phone service), expanded during the 1900s (transoceanic airplane service, satellite communication), and then accelerated during the late twentieth century into the twenty-first century with the advent of the World Wide Web, cell phones, and virtual instantaneous communication among peoples as well as movement of money around the world. These developments have led most commentators to conclude that the twenty-first-century international political economy can best be described as the century of economic globalization, that is, the broadening and thickening of economic ties among states, international organizations, and individuals.

In *The Lexus and the Olive Tree*, Thomas Friedman defines globalization as "the inexorable integration of markets, nation-states and technologies to a degree never witnessed before in a way that is enabling individuals, corporations and nation-states to reach around the world further, faster, deeper and cheaper than ever before."[1] Power is wielded by the Electronic Herd—the Intels, Ciscos, and Microsofts. The state has decreasing control. In his subsequent book, *The World Is Flat*, Friedman describes another wave of globalization where technology (digitalization, interoperability), open sources (Wikipedia), outsourcing of jobs, offshoring (moving companies to new locations), and supply chaining (efficient tracing of products) have all converged to create a new political economy, the flat world, "as the world starts to move from a primarily vertical—*command and control*—system for creating value to a more horizontal—*connect and collaborate*—value-creation model. . . ." As he asserts, this affects everything, including what role government has to play.[2]

This chapter discusses the roots of economic globalization found in economic liberalism, its theoretical underpinnings, its core concepts, and the roles of both the multinational corporations and the Bretton Woods institutions in the expansion of economic liberalism. We then turn to alternative perspectives on the international political economy, namely mercantilism (or its contemporary variant, statism) and radicalism.[3] Although economic liberalism may now be triumphant in the twenty-first century, both perspectives are found in contemporary policies and offer powerful critiques. Three major issues emerging from economic globalization are explored: global inequalities, or the continuing gap between the developed and the developing world; the tension between regionalism and economic globalization; and the implications of economic interdependence in energy.

Economic Liberalism

While economic globalization has emerged full bloom in the twenty-first century, its roots can be found in the writings of the eighteenth-century British economist Adam Smith. Smith began with the notion that human beings act in rational ways to maximize their self-interest.

When individuals act rationally, markets develop to produce, distribute, and consume goods. These markets enable individuals to carry out the necessary transactions to improve their own welfare. Market competition, when there are many competing buyers and sellers, ensures that prices will be as low as possible. Low prices result in increased consumer welfare. Thus, in maximizing economic welfare and stimulating individual (and therefore collective) economic growth, markets epitomize economic efficiency.

For markets to function most efficiently, economics and politics must be separated as much as possible; that is, markets must be free. Although government should provide basic order in society, its institutions should largely be developed to facilitate the free flow of trade and to maximize economic intercourse, which in the long term will guarantee both optimum prices (equilibrium) and economic stability. Thus, in contrast to the statist view that politics determines economics, liberals see economics as determining politics, though ideally the two should be kept separated as much as possible.

At the international level, if national governments and international institutions encourage the free flow of commerce and if they do not interfere in the efficient allocation of resources provided by markets, then increasing interdependence among economies will lead to greater economic development for all states involved.

Multinational corporations (MNCs) play a key role as engines of this growth. To economic liberals, MNCs are the vanguard of the liberal order. They are "the embodiment par excellence of the liberal ideal of an interdependent world economy. [They have] taken the integration of national economies beyond trade and money to the internationalization of production. For the first time in history, production, marketing, and investment are being organized on a global scale rather than in terms of isolated national economies."[4] For liberals, MNCs represent a positive development: economic improvement is made through the most efficient mechanism. MNCs invest in capital stock worldwide, they move money to the most efficient markets, and they finance projects that industrialize and improve agricultural output. MNCs are the transmission belt for capital, ideas, and economic growth. In the liberal idea, MNCs should act independently of states, perhaps replacing states in the long term. There is little need to control or regulate their behavior because the market self-regulates.

While the institution itself is not new—the Greek, Phoenician, and Mesopotamian traders were its ancient forerunners, as were the British East

India Company, the Hudson Bay Company, and the Dutch East India Company in the seventeenth and eighteenth centuries—after World War II, the trend toward larger companies conducting business in different states accelerated, a trend led by U.S.-based MNCs.

Although there are over 63,000 MNCs, with over 820,000 foreign affiliates, employing 90 million people, MNCs are, in fact, concentrated. The top one thousand of these MNCS account for more than 80 percent of the world's gross product. Before World War II, most MNCs were in manufacturing (General Motors, Ford, Toyota, Sony, Siemens, Nestlé, Bayer), and currently, they are prominent in financial services (Citigroup, ICI, Bank of America, Deutsche Bank, Fuji Bank). Very little economic activity originates in the developing countries; most comes from the Western industrialized countries and a handful of Asian and Latin American states, including China, Malaysia, Hong Kong, South Korea, Singapore, Brazil, and Mexico.

MNCs take many different forms, ranging from companies that participate only in direct importing and exporting, to those making significant investments in a foreign country, to those buying and selling licenses in foreign markets, to others engaging in contract manufacturing (permitting a local manufacturer in a foreign country to produce their products), and to still others opening manufacturing facilities or assembly operations in foreign countries.

Whatever the specific form that their business takes, all MNCs choose to participate in international markets for a variety of reasons. They seek to avoid tariff and import barriers, as many U.S. firms did in the 1960s when they established manufacturing facilities in Europe to circumvent the external barriers of the newly established European Economic Community. They may seek to reduce transportation costs by moving facilities closer to consumer markets. Some MNCs are able to obtain incentives like tax advantages or labor concessions from host governments; these incentives can cut production costs and increase profitability. Others go abroad in order to meet the competition and the customers, capitalize on cheaper labor markets (e.g., U.S. firms operating in Mexico or Romania), or obtain the services of foreign technical personnel (e.g., computer firms in India). Note that these reasons are based in economics. Rationales based on political policies of the host state may also play a role. MNCs may move abroad to circumvent tough governmental regulations at home, be they banking rules, currency restrictions, or environmental regulations. In the process, MNCs become not only economic organizations but political ones, potentially influencing the policies of both home and host governments.

Some liberal economists go further than extolling the economic benefits of liberalism or the virtues of MNCs. They see a positive relationship between the international liberal economy and war and peace. We saw one aspect of this view in our discussion of the democratic peace in Chapter 5. Norman

Angell, recipient of the Nobel Peace Prize in 1933, argued in favor of stimulating free trade among liberal capitalist states, in the belief that enhanced trade would be in the economic self-interest of all states. But more than that, Angell argued that national differences would vanish with the formation of an international market. Interdependence would lead to economic well-being and eventually to world peace; war would become an anachronism.[5] While not all liberals agree with this formulation, eco-

THEORY IN BRIEF	
Economic Liberalism	
Views of human nature	Individuals act in rational ways to maximize their self-interest
Relationship between individuals, society, state, market	When individuals act rationally, markets are created to produce, distribute, and consume goods; markets function best when free of government interference
Relationship between domestic and international society	International wealth is maximized with free exchange of goods and services; on the basis of comparative advantage, international economy gains

nomic liberalism does suggest specific economic policies (open markets, free trade, free flow of goods and services). They also posit that government's role should be limited to protecting property rights through a functioning legal system. Under this formulation, international competition is viewed as healthy and desirable, though it may not inevitably lead to peaceful interactions.

Key Concepts in Liberal Economic Theory

Liberal economics is based on the recognition that states differ in their resource endowments (land, labor, and capital). Under these conditions, worldwide wealth is maximized if states engage in international trade. The British economist David Ricardo (1772–1823) developed a theory that states should engage in international trade according to their **comparative advantage.** That is, states should produce and export those products which they can produce most efficiently, relative to other states. Because each state differs in its ability to produce specific products—because of differences in the natural resource base, labor force characteristics, and land values—each state should produce and export that which it can produce relatively most efficiently and import goods that other states can produce more efficiently. Thus, gains from trade are maximized for all.

Consider the production of cars and trucks in the United States and Canada. The United States can produce both cars and trucks using fewer workers than Canada, making production less expensive in the United States.

Under the principle of *absolute* advantage, the United States would manufacture both cars and trucks and export both to Canada. However, under *comparative* advantage, each country should specialize; the United States should produce the car, where it has a relative advantage in production, and Canada, the truck. By trading cars for trucks, each country gains by specialization. Each state minimizes its opportunity cost. Each gives up something to get something else. The United States gives up the production of trucks for more car production; Canada gives up the production of cars in favor of more truck production. Each gains by shifting resources to manufacturing more of the commodity produced most efficiently and by trading for the other commodity. Liberal economics states that under comparative advantage, production is oriented toward an international market. Efficiency in production is increased and worldwide wealth maximized.

In liberal economic thinking, national currencies, like goods and services, should be bought and sold in a free market system. In such a system of *floating exchange rates*, the market—individuals and governments buying and selling currencies—determines the actual value of one currency as compared with other currencies. Just as for a tangible good, there is a supply and demand for each national currency, and the prices of each currency constantly adjust according to market supply and demand. According to liberal thinking, floating exchange rates will lead to market equilibrium, in which supply equals demand.

Yet, in neither international trade nor international finance have liberal economic policies been consistently implemented. With respect to trade, governments often restrict free trade in order to achieve objectives other than economic efficiency. For example, they impose tariffs or quotas on imported goods to create new revenue or to protect domestic materials for national security reasons. They protect home industries from competition to lessen the effects of economic adjustment on individuals or groups such as laborers in a certain industry or producers of a specific agricultural crop. These protectionist measures benefit some domestic groups over other groups and over international efficiency.

With respect to financial transactions, too, currency exchange rates have not always been allowed to float freely. After World War II, a system of fixed exchange rates was established, whereby many currencies were supported by government commitments to keep them at specific values. In other words, currencies were pegged at a fixed exchange rate. This was revised in 1976 when the International Monetary Fund formalized the system of floating exchange rates, a policy more consistent with economic liberalism. Yet few anticipated how that modification would result in uncertainty and high market volatility. So governments still intervene in currency markets, by changing the interest rates that they pay, in order to regulate supply and demand.

Governments themselves buy and sell currency to quell the effects of speculation by private investors. Or they may even form a "basket" of currencies
whose exchange rates float together, as practiced in the early years of the
European Economic Community.

Much of the post–World War II economic controversies over trade and
finance have been precisely over this issue: the desire to achieve an open,
economically liberal system versus domestic pressures to protect home markets and to prevent destabilizing market volatility.

Roles of the International Economic Institutions

Economic liberalism described above has been supported by the establishment and expansion of the Bretton Woods institutions, the intergovernmental organizations set up at the end of World War II.

The World Bank, the International Monetary Fund (IMF), and to a lesser
extent the General Agreement on Tariffs and Trade (GATT)—now the World
Trade Organization (WTO)—have all played and continue to play key roles in
the expansion of economic liberalism, namely the notion that economic stability and development are best achieved when trade and financial markets
flow with as few restrictions as possible (see Figure 9.1). From their incep-
tion in Bretton Woods, New Hampshire, in 1944, the policies of these intergovernmental organizations have reinforced this philosophy.

The World Bank—Stimulating Economies

The **World Bank** was designed initially to facilitate reconstruction in
post–World War II Europe, hence its formal name: the International Bank for
Reconstruction and Development. During the 1950s, the World Bank shifted
its primary emphasis from reconstruction to development. It generates capital funds from member-state contributions and from borrowing in international financial markets. Like all banks, its purpose is to loan these funds,
with interest, and in the case of the World Bank, to loan them to states for
their economic development projects. Its lending is designed not to replace
private capital but to facilitate the use of private capital. Over the years, a
high proportion of the World Bank's funding has been used for infrastructure
projects, including hydroelectric dams, basic transportation needs such as
bridges and highways, and agribusiness ventures.

To aid in meeting the needs of developing countries, the International
Finance Corporation (IFC) and the International Development Association
(IDA) were created in 1956 and 1960, respectively. The IDA provides capital
to the poorest countries, usually in the form of interest-free loans. Repayment schedules of fifty years theoretically allow the developing countries
time to reach economic takeoff and sustain growth. Funds for the IDA need

FIGURE 9.1

The International Economic Institutions

World Bank
Loans funds to states proposing economic development projects

International Finance Corporation (IFC)
Provides loans to promote growth of private enterprises in developing countries

International Development Association (IDA)
Provides interest-free loans to the poorest countries

Multilateral Investment Guarantee Agency (MIGA)
Encourages the flow of private equity capital to developing countries

International Monetary Fund (IMF)
Original purpose was to guarantee exchange-rate stability. Purpose is to act as lender of last resort to keep debtor countries from collapsing

International Trade Organization
(was not formed)

General Agreement on Tariffs and Trade (GATT)
Series of multilateral trade negotiations designed to stimulate trade by lowering trade barriers

World Trade Organization (WTO)
Replaced GATT as forum for negotiating new trade agreements. Includes stronger dispute-settlement procedures

At the Bretton Woods Conference in July 1944, world leaders agreed to create three institutions to facilitate worldwide economic coordination and development. Two of these institutions—the World Bank and the International Monetary Fund—were created shortly after the conference. Although the third institution proposed at Bretton Woods—the International Trade Organization—was never created, the principles behind it were later incorporated in the General Agreement on Tariffs and Trade, which in 1995 became the World Trade Organization. The latter is not technically part of the Bretton Woods institutions.

to be continually replenished by major donor countries. The IFC provides loans to promote the growth of private enterprises in developing countries. In 1988, the Multilateral Investment Guarantee Agency (MIGA) was added to the World Bank group. This agency's goal—to augment the flow of private equity capital to developing countries—is met by insuring investments against losses. Such losses may result from expropriation, government currency restrictions, and civil war or ethnic conflict.

The World Bank has changed its orientation over time without undermining its commitment to liberal economics.[6] During the 1950s and 1960s, the bank, like other development institutions and major donors such as the United States, adopted a strategy for development emphasizing large infrastructure such as dams, electric power, and telecommunications. In the 1970s, the bank, realizing that not all groups were benefiting from the infrastructure approach, began to fund projects in health, education, and housing, designed to improve the economic life of the poor. During the 1980s, the bank shifted toward reliance on private-sector participation to meet the task of restructuring economies and reconstructing states torn apart by ethnic conflict. In the 1990s, **sustainable development,** an approach to economic development that incorporates concern for renewable resources and the environment (see below), became part of the bank's repertoire, as pushed by the 1992 U.N. Conference on Environment and Development in Rio de Janeiro. Of these various changes, the bank's support of private-sector participation in reconstruction and development has been the most profound. When areas of the economy are privatized, the government's fiscal burden is reduced, and state spending can then increase in education and health. This approach to economic growth has become known as the **Washington Consensus,** a version of liberal economic ideology. Its adherents hold that only with correct economic policies, including privatization, liberalization of trade and foreign direct investment, government deregulation in favor of open competition, and broad tax reform, will development occur. The bank and its sister institution, the International Monetary Fund, are leaders in pushing for these policies.

The IMF—Stabilizing Economies

From its establishment, the task of the **International Monetary Fund (IMF)** was different: to stabilize exchange rates by providing short-term loans for member states confronted by temporary balance-of-payments difficulties. Originally, the fund established a system of fixed exchange rates and, with the United States, guaranteed currency convertibility. From the 1940s to the 1970s, the United States guaranteed the stability of this system by fixing the value of the dollar against gold, at $35 an ounce. In 1972, however, this system collapsed when the United States announced that it would no longer guarantee a system of fixed exchange rates; today the exchange rates float.

The IMF has been involved in two major issues, the debt problem and the transition from socialist to market economies. The first concerns states that are plagued by persistently high debts and states that are in debt crisis. Since the early 1980s, the IMF has expanded its short-term loan function, providing longer-term loans and bestowing an "international stamp of approval" on other multilateral and bilateral lending as well as on private banks interested in investing in these indebted countries. In return for assistance, the IMF encourages **structural adjustment programs,** requiring countries to institute certain policies or to achieve certain conditions in order to receive IMF assistance and its stamp of approval (see Figure 9.2). During the 1990s, it became apparent that some countries needed more help. So in 1995, the IMF and the World Bank orchestrated a major policy shift under the Heavily Indebted Poor Countries (HIPC) Initiative for forty-one debt-distressed countries. The plan was a historic one, for never before had foreign national debt been canceled or substantially rescheduled. Implementation of the plan and its attendant conditions has been slow and controversial. Continued pressure by supporters of Jubilee Plus and increasing recognition by leading economic powers like the United States and European countries that debt reduction is necessary are behind this change in IMF-led policy toward debt relief. The IMF intervened in countries in crisis, like Mexico, Ecuador, Chile, Argentina, and Brazil in the 1980s and Thailand, Indonesia, and South Korea in the 1990s (the so-called Asian financial crisis), when the global financial structure seemed threatened. Bailout packages were given to affected countries, each accompanied by a set of conditions that the country had to meet. In each case, the controversial objective was to reform statist economies into more market-oriented ones.

The IMF has also played an active role in helping Russia and other former communist countries make the transition to market economies. The IMF's task has been to provide financial resources to make the adjustment more orderly. IMF credits have helped to replenish state reserves, keeping those countries out of major debt. The results have been mixed, with the most advanced economies able to achieve success, liberalizing foreign trade and keeping inflation down. The less-advanced economies, like Russia, have not been as successful.

With such programs initiated by the IMF, the distinction between the IMF and the World Bank has been blurred. Both play key roles in structural-adjustment lending, mutually reinforcing each other, bilateral donors, and international banks. All lenders have been the subject of intense criticism.

FIGURE 9.2

IMF Structural Adjustment Programs

PROFILE

Profile of a Country in Need of Structural Adjustment

- Large balance-of-payments deficit
- Large external debt
- Overvalued currency
- Large public spending and fiscal deficit

GOALS

Typical Goals of Structural Adjustment Programs

- Restructure and diversify productive base of economy
- Achieve balance-of-payments and fiscal equilibrium
- Create a basis for noninflationary growth
- Improve public-sector efficiency
- Stimulate growth potential of the private sector

TYPICAL STRUCTURAL ADJUSTMENT POLICIES

Economic Reforms

- Limit money and credit growth
- Force devaluation of the currency
- Reform the financial sector
- Introduce revenue-generating measures
- Introduce user fees
- Introduce tax code reforms
- Eliminate subsidies, especially for food
- Introduce compensatory employment programs
- Create affordable services for the poor

Trade Liberalization Reforms

- Remove high tariffs
- Rehabilitate export infrastructure
- Increase producers' prices

Government Reforms

- Cut bloated government payroll
- Eliminate redundant and inefficient agencies
- Privatize public enterprises
- Reform public administration and institutions

Private-Sector Policies

- Liberalize price controls
- End government monopolies

Among the critics are those who argue that both the IMF and World Bank have strayed too far from their liberal economic foundations.[7]

In 1994, fifty years after the Bretton Woods meetings that established the two institutions, the "Fifty Years Is Enough" campaign was launched. This campaign united the critics who claimed that the World Bank's commitment to growth had to be replaced by an emphasis on poverty reduction and that its record of support for authoritarian regimes had to be replaced by a commitment to democracy. In the words of one critic, "The World Bank is an old temple of cold warriors; a highly centralized, secretive, undemocratic vestige of another time. Fifty years is enough."[8]

GATT and the WTO—Managing Trade

The third part of the liberal economic order is the **General Agreement on Tariffs and Trade (GATT).** This treaty enshrined important liberal principles:

- Support of trade liberalization, since trade is the engine for growth and economic development
- Nondiscrimination in trade (i.e., most-favored-nation treatment), by which states agree to give the same treatment to all other GATT members as they give to their best (most-favored) trading partner
- Exclusive use of tariffs as devices for protecting home markets
- Preferential access in developed markets to products from the South in order to stimulate economic development in the South
- Support concept of "national treatment" of foreign enterprises

Procedures have put these principles into practice. The GATT established a continual process of multilateral negotiations among those countries sharing major interests in the issue at hand (major producers and consumers of a product, for example); the agreements reached in these negotiations were then expanded to all GATT participants. Individual states could claim exemptions (called safeguards) to accommodate any domestic and balance-of-payments difficulties that might occur because of the resulting trade agreements.

Most of the work of GATT was carried out over the course of eight negotiating rounds—each round progressively cutting tariffs, giving better treatment to the developing countries, and addressing new problems (subsidies and countervailing duties). For example, in the Kennedy Round between 1963 and 1967, tariff cuts averaged 35 percent on $40 billion of trade among sixty-two countries. In the following Tokyo Round (1973–79), 102 states negotiated tariff cuts amounting to again more than 35 percent for $100 billion of trade. In addition, more favorable arrangements were negotiated for developing countries.

The final round, called the Uruguay Round, began in 1986. The Uruguay Round covered new items such as services (insurance), intellectual property rights (copyrights, patents, trademarks), and for the first time agriculture. Previously, agriculture was seen as too contentious an issue, complicated by both U.S. agricultural subsidies and the European Union's protectionist Common Agricultural Policy. Agreement was reached to begin to phase out agricultural subsidies. In late 1994, a four-hundred-page agreement was finally reached, the most comprehensive trade agreement in history, covering paper clips to computer chips. Tariffs on manufactured goods were cut by an average of 37 percent among members. Analysts predicted that global wealth would increase by more than $200 billion per year by 2005 because of the Uruguay Round negotiations.

In 1995, GATT became a formal institution, renaming itself the **World Trade Organization (WTO).** The WTO incorporated the general areas of GATT's jurisdiction, as well as expanded jurisdiction in services and intellectual property. Regular ministerial meetings give WTO a political prominence that GATT lacked. Representing states that conduct over 90 percent of the world's trade, the WTO has the task of implementing the Uruguay Round, serving as a forum for trade negotiations, and providing a venue for trade review, dispute settlement, and enforcement.

Two important procedures were initiated in WTO. First is the Trade Policy Review Mechanism (TPRM), which conducts periodic surveillance of trade practices of member states. Under this procedure there is a forum where states can question each other about trade practices. Second is the Dispute Settlement Body, designed as an authoritative panel to hear and settle trade disputes. With the authority to impose sanctions against violators, the body is more powerful than other economic dispute resolution arrangements.

China's accession to the WTO in 2001, after fifteen years of negotiations has proven to be a complicated issue. During the initial negotiations, China revised its laws to permit foreign ventures in areas previously restricted, leading to a significant inflow of foreign investment. China's membership demands its continuous dismantling of barriers to trade in stages: first, restrictions on foreign law firms were lifted; next, foreign companies are gradually being allowed to provide insurance to Chinese; finally, China has to reduce auto tariffs and other high tariffs. These changes require China to translate WTO rules into domestic legislation; it is estimated that the Chinese legislature will need to amend 570 laws and over 1,000 central government rules and regulations. The WTO, then, is facilitating China's transition to an open-market economy, though the country still has a long way to go to disentangle the government from the economy.[9]

Trade liberalization, the major goal of the WTO, remains controversial. The Doha Round, launched in 2001, illustrates the difficulties. Announced as a "development round," trade liberalization was to help the developing countries correct the inequities of the previous trade agreements. Among the most controversial was agricultural subsidies provided by the governments in the North. The developing countries argued that those subsidies were examples of unfair competition with unsubsidized products. Two years later, in Cancun, a deadlock persisted over the issue. Five years later, another total collapse was narrowly averted when the EU agreed to eliminate farm export subsidies by 2013 and the North agreed to quota-free access to 97 percent of developing country exports to the North. Yet the devil may be in the details; agricultural export subsidies are but a small portion of domestic agricultural subsidies, and developing country exports represent only one-half percent of global exports.

As Benin's chief negotiator Samuel Amehou pessimistically concluded, "In the end, it's business as usual. . . . Where is this 'development' round?"[10] The stalled progress on trade liberalization has caused many states in the global South to target the WTO as too closely aligned with the developed North.

The WTO has also served as a lightning rod for domestic groups from many countries that feel that the organization, a symbol of economic globalization, is usurping the decisions and degrading the welfare of individuals. NGOs are some of the major cities of WTO activities. Some NGOs opposed the idea that the WTO has the power to make regulations and settle disputes in ways that intrude on or jeopardize national sovereignty. Still others fear that promotion of unregulated free trade undermines the application of labor and environmental standards; to them, the WTO privileges economic liberalization over other social values.

To understand fully these criticisms and others, we turn to an analysis of contending approaches to the international political economy, rooted in mercantilism (or statism) and radicalism.

Contending Approaches to the International Political Economy

Mercantilism or Statism

Economic liberalism has not always been the major approach to political economy even though it is clearly triumphant in the twenty-first century. Between the fifteenth and eighteenth centuries in Europe, powerful states were created, dedicated to the pursuit of economic power and wealth. Governments organized their then-limited capabilities to increase the wealth of the country: encouraging exports over imports and industrialization over agriculture, protecting domestic production against competition from imports, and intervening in trade to promote employment.

The early proponents of mercantilism were policymakers themselves. For example, Jean-Baptiste Colbert (1619–83), an adviser to Louis XIV, argued that states needed to accumulate gold and silver to guarantee power and wealth. That meant a strong central government was needed for efficient tax collection and maximization of exports, all geared to guaranteeing military prowess. The United States's first secretary of the treasury, Alexander Hamilton (1757–1804), advocated policies to protect the growth of the state's manufacturers. In his "Report on Manufactures" to Congress in 1791, he supported protectionist policies and investment in inventions. Likewise, Germany's political economist Friedrich List (1789–1846), writing in exile in the United

States, advocated strong government intervention for economic development and government aid to technology, education, and, like Hamilton, to industry. Traditional mercantilists contend that a surplus **balance of payments** is critical to protect the national interest.

A modern version of mercantilism emphasizes the role of the state—hence the term *statism*—and the subordination of all economic activities to the goal of state building, which includes the maintenance of the state's security and military power. With economic policy subservient to the state and its interests, politics determines economics. Thus politics and the state are used to curb man's natural aggressiveness and conflictual tendencies and to make economic policies that enhance state power. This mercantilist-like thinking dominated explanations of the economic success of Japan and the newly industrializing countries of East Asia (South Korea, Taiwan, Thailand, and Singapore). States used their power to harness industrial growth. Consistent with mercantilist logic, states single out certain industries for special tax advantages; they promote exports over imports and encourage education and technological innovations to make their respective economies more competitive internationally.

Statists see the international economic system as anarchic, and therefore as inherently conflictual, just as their realist political counterparts see the international political system. Since all states cannot simultaneously pursue successful statist policies—all states cannot enjoy surpluses—significant economic competition and conflicts, such as massive trading wars, are likely to occur. Each state is continually trying to improve its own economic potential, acting defensively at the expense of other states.

To illustrate the statist perspective, we turn to a description of multinational corporations. According to statists, MNCs at the service of the state can be powerful allies, but when MNCs act contrary to state political interests, they become dangerous agents that need to be controlled by both home and host governments. Prioritizing national economic and political objectives over international economic and political objectives, statists see MNCs as an economic actor to be controlled. So

THEORY IN BRIEF	
The Statist Perspective on the International Political Economy	
Views of human nature	Humans are aggressive; conflictual tendencies
Relationship between individuals, society, state, market	Goal is to increase state power, achieved by regulating economic life; economics is subordinate to state interests
Relationship between domestic and international society	International economy is conflictual; insecurity of anarchy breeds competition; state defends itself

they suggest imposing national controls on MNCs, including denying market entry to some MNCs, using taxing powers to control repatriation of profits, imposing currency controls, and even nationalizing industries. Remember, the key goal for the statist is to ensure that MNCs make economic decisions that are in the home state's national interest.

Radicalism: Marxist and Dependency Alternatives

Radicalism and its various permutations from socialism to communism have clearly had worldwide influence beginning with the mid-nineteenth century. Having seen the deleterious living conditions of the working class during nineteenth-century industrialization and cognizant of the economic chasm between the developed and developing world in the twentieth century, radicals blame the capitalist system under economic liberalism.

A number of core beliefs unite the body of Marxist and neo-Marxist writing, although interpretations vary. First, while individuals may be naturally cooperative, when in society they act in conflictual ways. Second, the main conflict emerges from the competition among groups of individuals, particularly between the owners of wealth and the workers, over the distribution of scarce resources. Third, the state acts to support the owners of the means of production, placing the state and the workers in opposition to each other. Fourth, in these capitalist systems, the owners of capital are determined to expand and accumulate resources at the expense of the working class and those in developing countries. Thus, the international system is basically conflictual.

For radical theorists, particularly dependency theorists, multinational corporations are one of the major culprits exploiting the resources of the poor in favor of the rich. For radicals, MNCs, particularly those from the developed world, perpetuate the dominance of the North and are responsible for the dependency of the South. So whereas economic liberals value the interdependencies that MNCs create, radicals see dependency, exploitation, and even imperialism. Decisions are made in the economic and financial centers of the world—Tokyo, Berlin, New York, Seoul—but the actual work of carrying out these decisions occurs in factories of developing countries. According to radical theorists, then, MNCs embody the same inherent inequality and unfairness of the international economic system.

Radical political economists, including some policymakers in the South, also blame the international economic institutions, particularly the World Bank and the International Monetary Fund, for perpetuating economic inequality by promoting the interests of private international capital. One critic, Michael Goldman in his aptly titled book *Imperial Nature*, suggests that both the bank and the multinational corporations are only profit seekers.[11] Development dollars distributed by the bank bring economic returns to the North only, those rich, developed countries whose firms provide the services for the dams and power plants. And other bank policies that have been rigidly developed without considering local conditions and local knowledge end up disproportionately affecting the disadvantaged sectors of population: the unskilled, the women, and the weak.

Not all radicals are as critical; instead, they suggest reforms to alter the weighted voting system used by the IMF and World Bank and to develop a more inclusive bureaucracy. In the current system, the major donors are guaranteed voting power commensurate with their contributions (the five largest share holders in each institution hold slightly less than 40 percent of the total votes). Reformists believe a more equitable voting structure might lead to the promotion of different policies. And hiring a more diverse group of bureaucrats from the current predominance of economists trained in Western developed countries might bring new innovative solutions to development dilemmas.

Most radicals, however, share the belief that the distribution of international and economic power must significantly be altered if the disadvantaged position of the developing countries is to be improved. States themselves cannot adequately control multinational corporations, because many host-states in the developing world are highly economically dependent on MNCs. The leaders who have the authority to pass appropriate control measures are often coopted by the very same MNCs to be regulated. Thus, radicals have sought international regulations in many forums. These views undergirded much of the thinking and the agenda of the developing countries in the 1960s and 1970s. The New International Economic Order (NIEO), discussed later in this chapter, is one manifestation of such thinking. Yet although these attempts at international regulation have been uniformly unsuccessful, radicals continue to point to MNCs and the international economic institutions as major inhibitors of economic development and as perpetuating global inequality.

THEORY IN BRIEF

The Radical / Marxist Perspective on the International Political Economy

Views of human nature	Naturally cooperative as individuals; conflictual in groups
Relationship between individuals, society, state, market	Competition among groups, particularly between owners of wealth and laborers; conflictual and exploitative
Relationship between domestic and international society	Conflictual relationships because of inherent expansion of capitalism; seeks radical change in international economic system

THEORY IN BRIEF

Contending Perspectives on the International Political Economy

	Statism	Economic Liberalism	Radicalism / Marxism
Views of human nature	Humans are aggressive; conflictual tendencies	Individuals act in rational ways to maximize their self-interest	Naturally cooperative as individuals; conflictual in groups
Relationship between individuals, society, state, market	Goal is to increase state power, achieved by regulating economic life; economics is subordinate to state interests	When individuals act rationally, markets are created to produce, distribute, and consume goods; markets function best when free of government interference	Competition among groups, particularly between owners of wealth and laborers; conflictual and exploitative
Relationship between domestic and international society	International economy conflictual; insecurity of anarchy breeds competition; state defends itself	International wealth is maximized with free exchange of goods and services; on the basis of comparative advantage, international economy gains	Conflictual relationships because of inherent expansion of capitalism; seeks radical change in international economic system

But the radical view does not end there. Marxists also take a normative position that resources must be more equitably distributed both within societies and between societies in the international system. In short, radicals seek system-level change. It is for that reason that radicals are also labeled structuralists. Structure conditions outcomes—radicals believe that the structure at both the international and national levels must be changed.

Because the former Soviet Union both embodied and championed one model of Marxist/socialist thinking on economics, that model was the major competitor of liberal economic thought during the interwar and Cold War periods. The Soviet model emphasized internationally a conflictual system and domestically a system based on central planning and the regulation of all economic activity by the state and on the development of heavy industry at the expense of agriculture and consumer goods.

The anticapitalism and anti-imperialism of Marxism (and of Soviet policies) has had a strong appeal among developing countries, as did the Soviet model of central planning and rapid industrialization. In the late 1950s, a strand of thinking emerged in the writings of Latin American economists who had been influenced by Marxism. As discussed in Chapter 3, this strand is known as dependency theory. Dependency theorists assert that developing countries are in a permanent state of economic dependency on the capitalist states; major change in the international order is the only way to break the dependency.

It is those differences in perspective among economic liberals, statists, and radicals that have led directly to the one major debate in the international political economy: how to bridge the economic development gap, given global inequalities and the realities of economic globalization.

Global Inequalities: The Development Gap

The differences between the North and the South are more than geographic; they often include major differences in the level of economic development and political systems. The North basks in relative wealth, with high consumptive habits, high levels of education and health services, and social welfare nets; the South lies mired in relative poverty, struggling to meet basic caloric needs, with poor educational and health services and no welfare nets to meet the needs of the poorest of the poor. In 2005, the top 25 countries enjoyed GDP per capita of $25,000 or more, while inhabitants in the other 113 countries have GDP per capitas of less than $10,000. In thirty-four countries, that amount is less than $2000, twenty-seven of those states being in Africa. If we view other indicators like the Human Development Index (HDI; illustrated in Table 9.1), the regional differences are also pronounced. Over time, twenty countries have actually suffered reversals of the HDI; thirteen of those countries are in Africa, where AIDS has had such a devastating impact on life expectancy. Caused by many factors—colonialism, earlier industrialization of Europe, geography—this is the development gap.

How to address the gap and one's view of whether the gap is actually being bridged through economic globalization depends, in part, on one's theoretical perspective. Proponents of economic liberalism point to the average per capita incomes in developing countries that have doubled over a fifty-year period, the gross national products (GNPs) of some economies that have grown by more than 500 percent, and the ever increasing share of exports that these same countries enjoy. Their detractors, including many radicals

TABLE 9.1

Human Development Index, 2002

	Life expectancy at birth (in years)	Adult literacy rate (%)	Educational enrollments of school-age population (%)	Real GDP per capita (PPP)*	Human development index (HDI)†
All developing countries	64.6	76.7	60	4,054	.663
Least developed countries	50.6	52.5	43	1,307	.446
Sub-Saharan Africa	46.3	63.2	44	1,790	.465
Industrial countries	78.3	99.3	93	29,000	.935
World	66.9	NA	64	7,804	.729

*PPP is purchasing power parity. It is a way to compare levels of economic data cross-nationally free of price and exchange rate distortions.

†The HDI has three components: life expectancy at birth; educational attainment, comprising adult literacy, with two-thirds weight, and a combined primary, secondary, and tertiary enrollment ratio, with one-third weight; and income. The HDI value for each country indicates how far that country has to go to attain certain defined goals: an average life span of 85 years, access to education for all, and a decent level of income. The closer a country's HDI is to 1.0, the closer it is to attaining those goals.

SOURCE: U.N. Development Programme (UNDP), *Human Development Report,* 2002 (New York: UN Development Programme, 2004).

and those working within the U.N. development community, contend that the gap between the rich and poor is increasing. The share of world income had by the richest 20 percent is 86 percent, while the share of the poorest 20 percent has declined over the years to 1.1 percent of world income. All agree that the gap between rich and poor needs to be narrowed by providing economic growth and development.[12]

A New International Economic Order?

Given the development gap, it is not surprising that the South has sought dramatic changes in the international system. During the late 1960s, the newly named Group of 77, a coalition of countries of the South, adopted the Charter of Algiers, which advocated global economic change. The group brought their demands to a special session of the United Nations in 1974, signaling their call for a New International Economic Order. These demands and the responses by the North reflect strongly the theoretical split between economic liberalism and radicalism over the international political economy.

The South sought changes in five major areas of international economic relations, as shown in the In Focus Box on the right. These proposals are unified by the belief that fundamental change in the international political economy is necessary and that the regulation of both markets (prices, exports) and institutions (donor states, multinational corporations, the World Bank, the IMF)

DEMANDS OF THE SOUTH IN THE NEW INTERNATIONAL ECONOMIC ORDER

◆ *Change the terms of international trade.* Stabilize, then raise the price of exports from the South for primary commodities to keep up with the price of capital goods and finished products imported from the developed North.

◆ *Establish a Common Fund.* Link prices of commodities together in order to establish a joint fund to help countries whose economies have been adversely affected by price declines.

◆ *Regulate multinational corporations.*

◆ *Review the debt burden of the South.* Restructure debt burdens, reduce interest rates, and/or cancel debt.

◆ *Increase foreign aid to the South.*

◆ *Change the structure of the World Bank and the International Monetary Fund.*

is imperative. These demands are consistent with the radical theoretical perspective on the international political economy.

The NIEO record is mixed. The South won some concessions through the 1975 Lomé Convention, which gave countries of the South preferential access to European markets and more favorable terms for commodity price-stabilization plans. Some states of the South were able to reschedule their debts, in part through innovative refinancing plans. However, on most critical issues, the North refused to negotiate concessions. No Common Fund was established. No mandatory code to regulate multinational corporations was negotiated. No widespread debt cancellation was immediately undertaken. No major changes were made in the World Bank or IMF institutional structures.

Of the NIEO issues, only debt renegotiation and cancellation has remained prominent on the international agenda. As explained above, through the efforts of Jubilee 2000 (then Jubilee Plus), the HIPC was initiated, putting into place a plan to relieve debt of the most heavily indebted countries, should they make domestic changes.

By the 1990s, most developing states had embraced economic liberalism and tempered their radical perspectives. In fact, at the eighth UNCTAD meeting in Cartagena, Colombia, in 1992, a broad consensus emerged on the viability of market-oriented economic policies and political pluralism as the foundation for economic development. In view of this ideological and policy change, the confrontational tactics of the past have been replaced by an

emphasis on consensus building and developing appropriate domestic policies, rather than on imposing international regulations, which had been the
cornerstone of the original NIEO proposals.

New Thinking about Economic Development

Acceptance of liberal economics to achieve development was possible
because of four trends. First was the realization of the role that foreign direct
investment from multinational corporations played in economic development. Since the mid-1980s, capital flows to developing countries have
increased dramatically from foreign direct investment and other private
sources, even as official flows from bilateral donors (the United States, Germany, Japan) and multilateral institutions (the World Bank, regional development banks) have declined as a percentage of total capital flows. Indeed,
private international capital between the 1960s and 1980s did provide essential lending to the successful Asian "tigers," including Taiwan and South
Korea, although private capital alone cannot explain their success. Strong
statist policies were able to harness private capital and make it productive.
The infusion of private investment to particular countries—the emerging
economies of China, Brazil, Argentina, Chile, South Korea, Mexico, Singapore, and Thailand—has been substantial, capital that has played a major
role in their economic success.

Yet while most acknowledge the key role played by private capital, critics
from all perspectives realize that some of the most capital-poor parts of the
world received little; Africa, for example received only 4.3 per-cent of private
capital. Thus, the volatility and unpredictability of capital movements makes it unreliable for sustained development in many
parts of the world.[13]

The development community has turned to an alternative
view of development—sustainable development—which was the
second trend. This concept rec-ognized that the South cannot
develop in the same way that Great Britain, the United States, Germany, and other industrialized nations did. Private foreign capital may not be available in many

---

In Focus

OBJECTIVES OF SUSTAINABLE DEVELOPMENT

◆ Reorient the Bretton Woods system to focus on sustainable development.

◆ Reschedule debts in developing countries when they lead
to overexploitation of natural resources.

◆ Create new sources of financing for the global commons,
such as ocean fishing, Antarctica.

◆ Include environmental conditions in international commodity agreements and structural adjustment programs.

◆ Strengthen the U.N. Environmental Program and regional
environmental institutions.

countries; scarce natural resources cannot be exploited as in the past; environmental sustainability must be assured so that growth can be assured for future generations. This means that debts must be rescheduled in the poorest country; that the Bretton Woods institutions must focus on human development—education, health—and not on large projects like dams that harm the environment; and that the targets of development—the people—should have a say in how funds are allocated.

The third trend was the recognition that nongovernmental organizations have an important role to play in development; indeed, they, along with the U.N. World Commission on Environment and Development, were instrumental in shifting the thinking of the development community toward sustainable development. Many NGOs play a direct role, organizing individuals at the grassroots level to carry out locally based projects. Famines and other humanitarian emergencies brought on by civil strife and warfare emergencies in Somalia, the Sudan, Mozambique, and the Democratic Republic of the Congo have been met by NGOs such as World Catholic Relief, Oxfam, and Doctors Without Borders, all delivering food and medical assistance, distributing seeds, drilling wells, and planning local-level projects that they hope will bring economic development.

NGOs often working in networks like the Women's Environment and Development Organization (WEDO) not only organize at the project level but also at the international level to lobby states and international organizations. Although all affiliated NGOs may not always agree on the specifics, WEDO organizes not only around the need to develop environmental programs aimed at assisting women but also on the need to include women as environmental resource managers. This is compatible with the sustainable development perspective, to bring in those groups often left out of the process and to promote their participation.

When a state is either too weak or unwilling to aid in an economic development effort or when international assistance is absent, NGOs can be alternative channels for assistance. One particularly effective effort has been the Grameen Bank in Bangladesh. Created in 1983 by an academic turned banker, Muhammad Yunus (who also won the Nobel Prize in 2006), the bank provides small amounts of capital to people who cannot qualify for regular bank loans. Its founder was convinced that such individuals, particularly women, would benefit from small loans, enabling them to pull themselves out of poverty. Having eventually convinced the government of Bangladesh to provide the seed money, this independent bank began making small loans averaging $100, although many loans were as little as $10 to $20. A typical housing loan is $300. Initially, the client has to recruit five other coborrowers in order to generate local-level

Debt Relief and Poverty Reduction: A View from Uganda

Mired in debt, developing countries have long argued for debt relief or outright cancellation. Developed countries and international economic institutions have been reluctant to grant such relief, claiming that it would undermine the contract between lenders and borrowers, and that debtor countries would be likely to squander the savings. Uganda illustrates a new approach to this dilemma.

Uganda ranks 146 out of 177 countries in the U.N. Human Development Index, with a GDP per capita of $1,390, a life expectancy at birth of 46 years, and an adult literacy rate of 69 percent. The state's potential to eradicate extreme levels of poverty dramatically increased in 2006 because the country was selected as a beneficiary of the International Monetary Fund's debt cancellation program. Under the Heavily Indebted Poor Country initiative (HIPC), $126 million of debt was cancelled, making Uganda the first country to complete the initiative. This long overdue and much needed debt relief, negotiated in response to the Jubilee 2000 debt-relief campaign organized by activists around the world, allows the country to focus its resources on combating disease, and increasing income and standards of living while decreasing its dependency on the donor institutions of the West.

Uganda was able to negotiate debt relief successfully for several reasons. First, President Yoweri Museveni, who is much admired in development circles for his vigorous anti-AIDS strategies, invited both local and international NGOs to play a role in developing debt reduction strategies beginning in the 1990s. Then the government, working with the NGOs through the Uganda Debt Network, helped to achieve sound macroeconomic policies and poverty reduction strategies by slowly decreasing public expenditures. That network also initiated a number of consensus-building activities to campaign for debt relief, including the Jubilee 2000 campaign, and established a Public Information Center to provide electronic and audiovisual information to both the NGOs and the public.

Before a country's debt can be canceled, a Poverty Eradication Action Plan is required by the World Bank and the IMF. Designed to prioritize the major poverty issues and allot appropriate resources to eradicate such problems, the plan includes specific projects—school construction, feeder roads, water systems—that are developed by local communities during the consultative process. Community involvement assures that local needs are met and that the public enjoys "ownership" of the project, increasing the likelihood of success. These projects are financed and implemented with NGO participation, using funds saved by not having to repay the country's debt.

Although the HIPC relieves Uganda of its onerous debt, many challenges lie ahead. AIDS remains an urgent public health issue affecting both quality of life and overall economic productivity. Discriminatory trade rules make it difficult for Uganda to industrialize production, and even the government recognizes ongoing corruption problems. Cancellation of debt does not automatically result in development but it can be a crucial first step in many developing countries.

For Critical Analysis

1. *Why would adherents of liberal economics be likely to oppose debt restructuring?*
2. *Why would radical theorists welcome cancellation of the debt but still be skeptical that poverty can be reduced?*

support. The terms are stiff; interest rates are relatively high and repayment times short.

The Grameen Bank has been a tremendous success. It now has more than two thousand branches, each run as a franchise by staff trained in established branches. Branches borrow money from headquarters at 12 percent interest and lend money at 20 percent, providing to the franchisees considerable opportunity for profit. The bank has provided loans to more than 6.6 million borrowers in 43,000 villages, lending about $30 million per month. Amazingly, its loan recovery rate is 97 percent! Clients for housing loans have a perfect repayment record. Over 58 percent of those borrowing who have been with the bank for five years have risen above the poverty line. The effects are more than economic: In families that have received loans, children go to school, "the nutrition level is better than in non-Grameen families, child mortality is lower and adoption of family-planning practices is higher. All studies confirm the visible empowerment of women."[14]

The fourth trend was the formation of partnerships among the different actors in economic development. In the 1990s, partnerships among the international private sector, donor states, international development and financial institutions, and NGOs became increasingly common. Partnerships are founded on an emerging normative consensus that just as poverty is socially and politically undesirable, so is it also bad for private-sector business. This is the underpinning of the Millennium Challenge Account, a U.S.-financed initiative, introduced in 2002, to target increased financing to countries that are improving their government structures by curbing corruption and supporting the rule of law and human rights. The underlying idea is that only countries with good government structures will be able to attract private investment. With such improvements, both private capital and NGO projects are apt to be more effective.

Is Development Occurring? A Progress Report

Economic globalization is a reality; whether that globalization can bring not only economic benefits but also social and political benefits to all and therefore close the development gap between the developed and developing world is another question. Setting the goals of sustainable development and monitoring the progress have been tasks undertaken by the United Nations. In 2001, the U.N.-sponsored summit set forth eight goals known as the Millennium Development Goals (MDGs). These goals are designed to reduce poverty and promote sustainable human development in direct response to globalization. For each substantive goal (poverty reduction, better education, improved health, environmental sustainability, and global partnerships), there are specific targets, time frames, and performance indicators, with an implementation plan.[15]

The report card shows that the Asian and Pacific countries are on track to meet the development goals. The number of people living in extreme poverty (less than $1 a day) has been cut in half during the 1990s. In South Asia, too, rapid progress is evident. In these two regions, accounting for almost one half of the world's population, the goals of access to drinking water, hunger reduction, and access to sanitation are all on track. Progress in China and India is largely responsible for these positive trends. Yet the projections are less promising in Sub-Saharan Africa. At present rates, several goals will not be achieved until the next century rather than the goal of a decade. And in some areas—hunger, poverty, and access to sanitation—the situation is worsening, and within countries, inequalities are increasing. Radicals see despair in these trends, but liberal economists are hopeful. As world economic growth continues, they assert, interstate inequalities will lessen, and as states develop domestically, while there may be winners and losers in the short term, everyone will benefit in the long term.

Economic Globalization and Regionalism

While economic globalization has emerged as the defining characteristic of the international political economy, regionalism has also been growing. Especially since the 1990s, more regional economic arrangements have been negotiated and those already operational been strengthened. What is the relationship between globalization and regionalism? Is this regionalism another step toward increased, enhanced globalization? When state barriers are removed in favor of regional markets and economies expand, will globalization be enhanced? Or is regionalism a reaction to globalization, an effort by states to become more competitive vis-à-vis other groups or an effort by economic hegemons to maintain their dominant roles? There is no doubt that the establishment of the European Union (discussed in Chapter 6) and accompanying economic integration has had a major impact on the international political economy and has served as a model for other regions.

European Economic Integration

European economic integration was predicated on the notion that the larger market with the free movement of goods and services would permit economies of scale and specialization to stimulate growth; opportunities for investment would be enhanced; and competition and innovation stimulated, all goals compatible with liberal economics. The European Union has proven successful in achieving some of these objectives, creating a single market and developing the monetary union. Yet to achieve the objectives, the EU also relied on protectionist measures.

European economic growth had been sluggish since the mid-1970s, when the United States and Japan were increasingly competitive. To stimulate Europe's growth and hence its international competitiveness, the Single European Act of 1987 accelerated the integration process, setting the goal of achieving a single market by 1992. That involved removing physical, fiscal, and technical barriers to trade and harmonizing national standards. Some parts of that goal were quickly achieved, namely, the elimination of customs barriers. Other areas have proved more problematic, notably the movement of persons. While most countries eliminated passport controls and adopted similar visa rules, recognition of education and professional qualifications has proven a thorny issue. Abolishing technical barriers to trade has also been difficult because of differing health and safety standards, but the process is ongoing, as is the effort to break state monopolies and eliminate state aids to specific sectors. All of these measures are designed to deepen economic integration among member states.

The overall results have been positive, with the growth of all types of economic transactions across state borders deepening integration among the national economies of member states. Exports of goods and services are over one-third of the GDP for the average EU member and between one-fourth to over one-third for even the largest states. For the fifteen countries of the EU (before the recent enlargements), most more than doubled their exports of goods and services between 1960 and 2003, with Great Britain being a dominant exception. Currently, almost 70 percent of total trade in goods is conducted with other EU members. Not only is trade integrated but also capital flows, as cross-border mergers and acquisitions have accelerated. There is a broad consensus that European integration has resulted in greater trade creation and has also had a positive welfare effect on both member and non-member states.[16]

The EU is more than a regional trading area or a single market. During the discussions for the single market, the outlines of a monetary union were negotiated. With monetary stability and a single currency, the union would grow and prosper even more. The European Monetary Union under the Maastricht Treaty called for the establishment of a single currency, the euro, and a common monetary policy. Members who have agreed to these provisions, and not all have, no longer can use exchange rates and interest rates as instruments of economic policy. Whether the creation of the monetary union has stimulated the integration process further is subject to much debate. Yet most agree that the euro has facilitated business transactions and eliminated the uncertainty caused by fluctuations in exchange rates. Thus, through both the single market and a common monetary policy, the EU can voice a unified position in global economic affairs, although they do not always do so. These events have served as an example for other parts of the world to follow suit, as explained below.

The European Union very early recognized, just as international trade negotiators did, that agriculture was different. Agricultural prices dramatically fluctuate with weather and disease, so there has long been a strong incentive to moderate the price fluctuations caused by supply volatility. Foodstuffs are viewed as vital for national security; in emergencies, no state wants its population to depend on others. And in many countries, the well-organized farm sector enjoys disproportionate political power. For all these reasons, the EU adopted the Common Agricultural Policy (CAP). Contrary to the free trade ideology, the EU purchases surplus crops, pays guaranteed prices to farmers, and absorbs the losses if the product cannot be sold on the international market. Farmers are subsidized to the tune of over $45 billion annually, requiring a significant portion of the EU budget. The CAP has proved to be one of the most controversial policies of the EU. Not only has it been a major issue for states seeking membership and wanting their share of the agricultural budget, but it is also a critical issue in multilateral negotiations, since nonmembers will pay more for EU agricultural products.

So, aside from the CAP, have the EU's policies contributed to economic globalization or proved an impediment? Most economists agree that the openness of the European markets has not only benefited Europeans, but has also become increasingly compatible with the goals of the multilateral global system. Indeed, the EU has developed a web of preferential agreements with not only its neighbors (Mediterranean area) and former colonies with shared histories (African countries), but also with other regional trade agreements, including the North American Free Trade Agreement and Mercosur in South America. These actions not only enhance the EU as a global economic power, but also give it strong leverage against U.S. economic hegemony.[17]

One response by other states to the economic power and success of the European Union has been to establish their own regional trading blocs that give their members more favorable access than states outside the bloc have. There has been, in fact, an explosion of such regional trading blocs, with the formation of over 150 in the last fifty years. Among the largest and most successful are the Asia-Pacific Economic Cooperation (APEC), founded in 1989, and the ASEAN Free Trade Area (AFTA), established in 1992. APEC's twenty-one members, including Australia, Canada, Japan, Mexico, and the United States, seek economic cooperation as a counterweight to "Fortress Europe," while AFTA's goal is to attract foreign investment to the region taking advantage of economies of scale. But are the same conditions in Europe—similarity of economic, political, and social systems, a history of post–World War II cooperation, and the development of nascent community political institutions—present in other parts of the world?

The North American Free Trade Agreement

The free trade area negotiated by the United States, Canada, and Mexico in 1994 differs substantially from the European Union and other regional schemes. It comprises one dominant economy and two dependent ones: Mexico's and Canada's combined economic strength is one-tenth that of the United States's. The driving force in NAFTA is not political elites but multinational corporations (MNCs) that seek larger market shares than their Japanese and European competition. The agreement phases out many restrictions on foreign investment and most tariff and nontariff barriers. This has allowed MNCs to shift production to low-wage labor centers in Mexico and to gain economically by creating bigger companies through mergers and acquisitions.

The social, political, and security dimensions we saw in the European Union are absent from NAFTA. Cooperation in trade and investment is not intended to lead to free movement of labor, as championed by the European Union. Quite the opposite; the United States expects that Mexican labor will *not* seek employment in the United States since economic development in Mexico will provide ample employment opportunities. And economic cooperation does not mean political integration in NAFTA. As public questioning of the Maastricht Treaty suggests, even Europe may not be ready for this final step in regional integration. With NAFTA, economic integration is to remain just that—confined to specific economic sectors.

The North American Free Trade Agreement supports the phased elimination over ten years of tariff and nontariff barriers. Specifically, tariffs on over nine thousand categories of goods produced in North America are to be eliminated by 2008. At the same time, NAFTA protects the property rights of those companies making investments in the three countries. Some domestic producers are given special protection, notably the Mexican oil and gas industry and the U.S. shipping industry. The agreement, a five-volume, fifteen-pound document, is clearly detailed and complex. By the year 2000, trade among the three countries had doubled from 1990 levels.

Yet the economic controversies generated by NAFTA continue to be profound, illustrating that the state is not a unitary actor. Labor unions in the United States estimate that between 150,000 to 500,000 workers have lost their jobs to Mexico and that over one-third of those individuals will never receive comparable wages again. Environmental groups in the United States fear free trade with Mexico comes at the expense of the environment, as firms in the United States relocate to Mexico to skirt domestic environmental regulations. They point to the degraded environment of the border regions between the two countries. Canadian labor contends that manufacturing in that country is fast becoming a lost art and that the country is becoming too dependent on exports of natural resources. Others fear that Canadian sovereignty is threatened as economic decisions are taken out of the country, that its national identity is in jeopardy. Mexican supporters point to the fact that Mexican exports have more than doubled those of the rest of Latin America combined, while radical economists argue that NAFTA is yet another example of U.S. expansionism and exploitation of the Mexican workforce.

The NAFTA case suggests that, similar to other regional integration schemes, there will be winners and losers. In NAFTA, agriculture and manufacturing in general may well be the winners. Agricultural markets are better integrated, and consumers enjoy lower prices with virtually all tariffs eliminated. Both Canada and Mexico are now large markets for U.S. agricultural exports, and the share of Canadian exports absorbed by the United States has doubled, while agricultural exports from Mexico have almost tripled. Tariffs on manufactured goods have been almost entirely eliminated. U.S. and Canadian trade has grown by 120 percent, and trade between the United States and Mexico has increased 300 percent since NAFTA. But some manufacturers and some groups of individuals have also been losers, as American jobs are exported to lower-cost locations. Some Mexican workers are the losers, working in environmentally unsafe conditions or losing their jobs to still cheaper production facilities in China. So both radicals and statists have ample examples to support their analysis.

Just as the EU success has led to more liberalized agreements with other regions, so, too, has NAFTA's success led to subregional trade agreements. The Central American Free Trade Association and the Free Trade of the Americas are relevant examples. These developments have led the United States itself to pursue other bilateral free trade agreements or regional agreements beyond NAFTA. Thus, regionalism may well be serving as a stepping stone to increased economic globalization, though the end of the story has yet to be told.

Energy Interdependence

No international economic issue is more illustrative of benefits and liabilities of globalization than energy in the twenty-first century; no economic issue is as politicized as this one. Although it has always been recognized that natural resources are an important ingredient of national power, as explained in

Chapter 5, what has changed is that one natural resource—petroleum—is now the strategic resource of the twenty-first century. While coal supplies are expanding, fossil supplies of conventional oil and natural gas are more limited.

Ever since World War II, the industrialized countries have relied on crude oil as fuel for economic development and growth. For many years, the United States was both the largest producer and largest exporter, while the other developed countries, including Japan and Europe, had few domestic sources, making them dependent on cheap Middle Eastern petroleum. Most developing oil-producing countries with low levels of industrialization had excess capacity and were thus eager to sell. This fundamental interdependency between producers and consumers, between developing countries and industrialized countries, has evolved over time, illustrating the changing reality of globalization.

The Economics of Petroleum

Finding oil deposits, extracting crude, building refining capacity and pipelines are all expensive and economically risky activities. Economists call the responsiveness of supply-and-demand levels to price changes **elasticity.** Thus, in the short term, oil supply is inelastic. New oil supplies will not come online quickly in response to increased demand. In the long term, if demand is high and prices have risen, there will be incentive to find new supplies; that is the logic of liberal economics. But the risks are real. Oil may not be found; many potential substitutes (natural gas, coal, hydropower, uranium) are not directly substitutable and are in themselves supply inelastic, particularly in the short term.

Unlike many other commodities, oil is located only in certain geologic regions of the world, making it more susceptible to political manipulation by those who have control. Over 60 percent of the world's reserves are located in the Middle East, 25 percent of which are in Saudi Arabia, 11 percent in Iraq, and 9 percent in both the United Arab Emirates and Iran. These countries, along with other major producers like Venezuela, Mexico, Kazakhstan, and Azerbaijan, depend on petroleum for their revenue. When prices increase, these same countries benefit from the massive infusion of revenue; they invest in both the domestic economy and in world financial markets, mainly in industrialized countries.

Consuming country demand for petroleum products is largely determined by rates of economic growth, namely industrialization. Thus, demand is not as responsive to price except at very high price levels when demand could shift to substitutes, as explained above. Yet, because of the critical nature of petroleum, virtually all consuming developed countries impose high taxes and/or duties on petroleum products to both limit demand and outlay of foreign exchange and to provide revenue. Multiple economic interdependencies describe the global petroleum market.

The Role of OPEC and the Politics of Oil

The fact that oil is such a valuable economic resource makes it a political asset for producing-states and a vulnerability for consuming-states. The establishment of the Organization of Petroleum Exporting Countries provided momentum for the oil-producing countries to assume greater control over the international oil markets from the multinational corporations (so-called Seven Sisters) that had dominated the production and distribution of oil since the 1930s.

The impetus for OPEC came in 1959 and 1960, when the multinational oil companies acting in unison, but without consultation with oil-exporting countries, reduced average crude prices from 5 to 7 percent to compensate for the world glut in oil. In response to that action, producing states in both the Arab world and Venezuela met for the first time in 1960 to restore prices to former levels and develop plans to unify policies. The Organization of Petroleum Exporting Countries was born.

The 1960s was a period of consolidation for that organization. Both Libya and Algeria became active participants, each country winning significant concessions from the oil companies and thus increasing the revenue from oil exports. Iraq and Iran joined, and the producers in the Gulf region formed their own subgroup, the Organization of Arab Petroleum Exporting Countries. Nigeria and Indonesia became more active participants as their oil production grew. The balance in power was shifting from the multinational oil companies, which still possessed the necessary technology and technical skills, to the oil-exporting states themselves and their state-owned companies. Today OPEC's twelve members produce about 40 percent of the world's oil. But the number of oil producers has expanded from Norway to Mexico, Angola, Azerbaijan, and Russia and these states, sharing 60 percent of the world's production, are not members. Although OPEC or any one producer no longer has the power to control the international oil market, there has been a significant realignment of power.

The structure of the international oil market changed through four oil shocks, each showing the repercussions of globalization. In 1974, the Arab members of OPEC used an embargo to withhold oil from states supporting Israel, causing a significant increase in oil prices (and hence revenues) and a substantial economic disruption in both the United States and the Netherlands, both of which were embargoed. Buoyed by OPEC's success, Southern

producers of other primary commodities joined the bandwagon, forming cartels in copper, tin, cocoa, coffee, and bananas. Although these cartels met
with little success, OPEC members still enjoyed the economic benefits of
their political actions. This first shock brought home to the American policymakers and the public the issue of natural resource interdependence and
potential vulnerability, because Americans were forced to cut back on driving
in order to conserve fuel, were relegated to inconvenient lines at the pump,
and had to pay much higher prices for that privilege.

A second oil shock occurred at the end of the 1970s following the seizure
of power by Islamic fundamentalists in oil-rich Iran. Although Iran
accounted for less than 20 percent of OPEC exports, oil prices dramatically
escalated in the face of the shortage of supply and the possibility that oil
could once again be a political weapon. Panic set in, as import bills for petroleum increased by over 1,000 percent. The outbreak of the Iran-Iraq war in
1980 only exacerbated the situation, destabilizing oil markets further, with a
10 percent drop in world production.

With the 1991 Gulf War, the third oil shock occurred, a short-term dou-
bling of oil prices. Iraq's invasion and occupation of Kuwait cut both Iraq
and Kuwaiti production, and when Iraq burned Kuwait's oil fields in its hasty
retreat, production was cut even more. Similar to the fears of the second
shock, there was also the fear that oil production in Saudi Arabia would be
affected or transportation routes blocked, neither of which actually occurred.
The panic that spread throughout both the international petroleum and international financial markets clearly confirms economic interdependence characteristic of globalization.

While the first three oil shocks emanated from threats to supply princi-
pally in the Middle East, the fourth and most recent oil shock developed from
rapidly changing and unexpected acceleration of demand. Since 2000,
demand for oil has grown by 7 million barrels a day, 2 million barrels of
which are destined for China. The dramatic economic growth in China (and
to a lesser extent, India) has led both countries to seek more oil, which can
only be found in foreign markets. Continued high demand in the United
States, the lack of refinery capabilities to produce the right mixture of products, and supply shortfalls in Venezuela and Iraq are all factors exacerbating
the shortfall, leading to unprecedented price increases. Russia's upsurge in
production—40 percent of the world's total production since 2000—has
helped but proven insufficient at least in the short term. There are various
responses to the latest oil shock: a rush by the oil companies to find new
sources of petroleum; and a push by China and India to find reliable new
suppliers, whether it be in Nigeria, Angola, Sudan, Kazakhstan, or in the
Middle East, therefore putting them in competition with the United States
and Europe.[18] As war continues in the Middle East (whether or not it

involves oil-producers Iraq or Iran or Israel and Lebanon), panic over insta-bility of supply best describes the situation.

These oil shocks have called attention once more to changing economic and political interdependencies. Oil-dependent states vying for oil contracts have changed or modified their political allegiances to enhance their oppor-tunity for a reliable oil supply. For example, after the first oil shock, Japan not only adopted a domestic policy to lessen its dependence on foreign sup-plies, but it shifted political allegiance toward support of the Arab political position in the Middle East in hopes of securing supply routes. Emanating from the fourth oil shock, China has refused to censure Sudan (the third largest producer in Africa) over its policies in Darfur for fear of losing new oil concessions. Some have argued that U.S. intervention in Iraq in 2003 can be partly explained by wanting to assure steady oil supplies from that state and region.

Oil-producing states with a massive increase in oil revenue have found themselves able to pursue domestic policies that are more immune to inter-national influences. For example, the so-called petrostates like Russia, Ka-zakhstan, Nigeria, and even Saudi Arabia have been able to continue repressive antidemocratic domestic practices, knowing that criticism will be muted and consuming states unlikely to initiate sanctions to force destabiliz-ing domestic changes. These same states are able to use oil as a strategic weapon, as Russia did in early 2006 when it cut gas supplies to the Ukraine, after the latter refused to agree to price increases. Supply was restored only after the Ukraine was forced to make concessions. Part of Russia's strategy was to use its oil and natural resources as a wedge to renew its claim as a superpower. Similarly, Venezuela used its petrodollars to pay off Argentina's loans to the IMF to lessen that country's dependence on the U.S.-supported institution. This posture led two commentators to suggest "an emerging 'axis of oil' that is acting as a counterweight to American hegemony on a widening range of issues."[19]

Even international institutions have found it more difficult to utilize their influence in getting the oil-producing states to comply with international agreements. When petroleum was discovered in Chad, the World Bank pro-vided partial funding to build a pipeline that would deliver the product to port, with the proviso that the country use its 40 percent in government rev-enue to improve the life of its 9 million poor citizens. Chad was to be the new model for how oil could be used as an engine of development in Africa. But that experiment has proven short-lived: the promises of the oil-empowered government elites have been broken, with oil-hungry donor states and MNCs seeking security of supplies over other values.

Finally, as oil has become more valuable, it has become a target for groups (both indigenous or international) trying to disrupt established governments, blowing up pipelines, and interrupting supply. Nigerian pipelines, for example, are continually compromised by actions of people located in the Delta region who feel that their development needs are not being met. Similarly, the Iraqi pipelines are the object of terrorist attacks in hopes of further undermining that country's economic recovery and general stability. Al Qaeda and its affiliates have tried to attack Saudi facilities. No wonder the new pipelines across the Caucasus Mountains are in growing need of military protection, as ethnic groups and terrorists find that these lifelines have become new areas of a state's vulnerability. Indeed, the entire oil-supply market chain is vulnerable, another by-product of globalization.

With gradual economic globalization, an integrated market has emerged, linking key producing, consuming states with multinational companies. Shifts in the distribution of power among these primary players have led to the emergence of petroleum as a weapon, with implications for the economic, political, and even strategic decisions that states, international organizations, and even subnational and transnational groups make.

Emerging Challenges to Economic Globalization

In the waning years of the twentieth century, beliefs about economic theory converged. The principles of economic liberalism proved more effective at raising the standard of living for people worldwide. The radical alternatives that were created to foster economic development did not prove viable, even though statist alternatives have remained attractive to some states. This convergence, however, has not meant the absence of conflict over issues in the international political economy.

Economic globalization resulting from the triumph of economic liberalism has been confronted with several challenges. In 1994, an army of peasant guerrillas seized towns in the southern Mexican state of Chiapas to protest against an economic and political system that was viewed as biased against them. The date of the protest coincided with the beginning of NAFTA. Individuals, feeling that economic decisions were beyond their control, protested against the structures of the international market, the state, and economic globalization. This rebellion alerted the world to the challenges of globalization. While NAFTA was designed to promote regional prosperity through trade liberalization, subgroups felt threatened. They were able to tell their side of the story, ironically enough, through the Internet, one of the by-products of the globalization they opposed.

Halfway around the world a few years later, economic globalization was challenged in a different way. In a relatively short period of time, beginning in Thailand in 1997 and spreading to other countries in Asia and beyond, capital flowed out of the region; in 1997, 2 percent of gross domestic product left Thailand, increasing to 5 percent only a year later. Many countries were unable to adjust to the rapid withdrawal of capital. Exchange rates plummeted to 50 percent of precrisis values, stock markets fell 80 percent, and real GDP dropped 4 to 8 percent. Individuals lost their jobs as companies went bankrupt or were forced to restructure. In Southeast Asian countries, South Korea and Taiwan, and spreading to Brazil and Russia, economies that had previously depended on external trade experienced an unparalleled sense of economic vulnerability. Fueled by instantaneous communication, global financial markets capable of moving $1.3 trillion daily, and the power of MNCs, traders, and financial entrepreneurs, economic globalization quickly displayed its pitfalls. The largely unregulated market had melted down, and states and individuals appeared helpless. The repercussions of economic globalization were widely experienced.

States voiced dissatisfaction with some of the solutions and implementation by the international economic institutions. Some groups within the affected countries became the losers, marginalized by structural adjustment programs that did not, they believed, reflect enough local conditions. That view reinforced a position already widely espoused by many developing countries—that these institutions were captive to the interests of the developed world.

The antiglobalization movements have grown, the opposition coming together at annual meetings of the World Trade Organization and, to a lesser extent, at World Bank and IMF meetings, as well as meetings of the G-7/G-8.[20] The demonstrators largely shut down the 1999 WTO's Seattle ministerial meetings—and buoyed by success took similar actions in the streets of Prague, Washington, D.C., and Calgary. Many of these groups had their own agendas—some preferred a return to governance at the local level where jobs could be better protected. Others sought more environmentally friendly conditions for workers; others more labor concessions. Many just wanted these institutions to be totally abolished. But they were all united in their opposition to economic globalization. Even moving the meetings to Doha in 2001, where only a few hundred NGOs were granted visas or to St. Petersburg in 2006, where stricter controls were in place, the views of the antiglobalizers are still making themselves known.

The oil shocks of 2006 reinforced the antiglobalizers' common cause. The fact that livelihoods of individuals are under the "control" of the petrostates or even big multinational oil companies finds resonance in dissatisfaction with economic globalization.

Antiglobalizers have also been stimulated by other unanticipated repercussions resulting from the openness of economic markets. Two trends have become particularly vexing in the twenty-first century. The first concerns the

POLICY DEBATE

Is economic globalization a positive trend for the international community?

YES:

◆ Most political leaders, business leaders, and other elites view economic globalization as positive because it leads to economic growth.

◆ Under economic globalization, economic systems are streamlined and labor and management have to compete globally, resulting in greater economic efficiency.

◆ Increased economic growth occurs with globalization, as trade and employment increases.

◆ Economic globalization means new ideas and technology are rapidly transmitted to states and individuals around the world.

◆ Economic homogenization, a product of economic globalization, is an economic benefit, enabling products to be utilized around the world.

◆ Economic globalization is an inevitable trend—international trade is growing more rapidly than domestic production; hence, policymakers need to embrace and support it.

◆ Economic globalization provides new opportunities for international capitalists to broaden investment and expand businesses to spread risks.

NO:

◆ Economic globalization tears apart communities and states because jobs move to new locales to take advantage of cheaper labor.

◆ Multinational corporations are the main beneficiaries of economic globalization because of increasing profits; ordinary people are not the beneficiaries, as MNCs move jobs to lower wage areas to insure profitability.

◆ Under economic globalization, an economic elite will emerge as most powerful, leaving the rest behind.

◆ Economic globalization leads to rampant materialism antithetical to non-Western cultures; values profit over other human needs.

◆ Communities are unable to adjust to economic globalization; adjustment is not an automatic process.

◆ The more global the market, the less likely individuals will be able to control the devastating effects of the market.

◆ There is no guaranteed redistribution of economic resources to those in need under economic globalization; the strong will benefit more than the weak.

movement of labor. The EU had adopted the goal, at the outset, of free movement of goods, services, *and* labor. Though the latter has not been achieved, the Schengen Accord adopted in 1985 allowed the free movement of nationals from member states who did not have passports and visas. Individuals from non-EU states have found that once they arrive in an EU country, by whatever means, they can move more easily among countries. This has resulted in a flood of illegal aliens seeking better paying jobs in EU countries. This has also led to a new market in illicit labor, trafficking in people, including women and children for the sex trade. Some of those arriving may even be terrorists who seek to conduct illegal activities against a receiving country.

NAFTA and many other regional trading arrangements did not specifically call for mobility of labor; indeed, part of NAFTA's rationale was to improve working conditions in Mexico so that Mexicans would choose NOT to cross into the United States. Yet the U.S./Mexican border remains porous, as Mexican illegals seek better paying jobs in the United States. So the immigration "problem"—the number of illegals and the possibility of receiving those with malevolent intentions—has become a by-product of economic globalization.

A second trend under economic globalization has been labeled the clandestine side of globalization: the rise of illicit markets.[21] This can include the illegal movement of commodities such as arms or even money to evade tariffs and trade restrictions, as well as sanctions. Or it can mean the illegal movement of banned commodities such as drugs, human organs, endangered species, or even protected intellectual property. Thus, states and international organizations seeking the fruits of economic globalization are pitted against market forces that have given rise to undesirable outcomes. These challenges to economic globalization have generated an active debate: is economic globalization a positive trend for the international community?

Globalization is not just a characteristic of the economy. It is also reflected in the issues discussed in the next chapter—health, the environment, and human rights.

Notes

1. Thomas L. Friedman, *The Lexus and the Olive Tree: Understanding Globalization* (New York: Farrar, Straus & Giroux, 1999), 257.
2. Thomas L. Friedman, *The World Is Flat: A Brief History of the Twenty-First Century,* updated and expanded edition (New York: Farrar, Straus & Giroux, 2006), 234.
3. The perspectives are discussed in Robert Gilpin, "Three Models of the Future," *International Organization* 29:1 (Winter 1975), 37–60.
4. Ibid., 39.

5. Sir Norman Angell, *The Great Illusion* (New York: Putnam, 1933).

6. Michelle Miller-Adams, *The World Bank: New Agendas in a Changing World* (London: Routledge, 1999); and Ngaire Woods, *The Globalizers: The IMF, the World Bank and Their Borrowers* (Ithaca, N.Y.: Cornell University Press, 2006).

7. William Easterly, *The White Man's Burden: Why the West's Efforts to Aid the Rest Have Done So Much Ill and So Little Good* (New York: Penguin, 2006); and Joseph E. Stiglitz, *Globalization and Its Discontents* (New York: Norton, 2002).

8. Kevin Danaher, ed., *50 Years Is Enough: The Case Against the World Bank and the International Monetary Fund* (Boston: South End Press, 1994).

9. See Minxin Pei, *China's Trapped Transition: The Limits of Developmental Autocracy* (Cambridge, Mass.: Harvard University Press, 2006).

10. Quoted in Michael Fleshman, "Trade Talks: Where Is the Development?" *Africa Renewal* (April 2006), 16.

11. See Michael Goldman, *Imperial Nature: The World Bank and Struggles for Social Justice in the Age of Globalization* (New Haven, Conn.: Yale University Press, 2005).

12. See Robert Gilpin, *Global Political Economy: Understanding the Economic Order* (Princeton, N.J.: Princeton University Press, 2001).

13. See, for example, Jeffrey Sachs, *The End of Poverty: Economic Possibilities for Our Time* (New York: Penguin, 2005).

14. Muhammad Yunus, quoted in Judy Mann, "An Economic Bridge Out of Poverty: Grameen Bank in Bangladesh Loans Money to Poor Women Who Want to Start Business," *Washington Post*, October 14, 1994, E3. See also Muhammad Yunus, *Banker to the Poor: Micro-Lending and the Battle Against World Poverty* (New York: Public Affairs, 2003).

15. For progress reports broken down by goal and by region, see the United Nations website, www.un.org/millenniumgoals/. See also United Nations, *Human Development Report 2004* (New York: United Nations Development Programme, 2004).

16. Loukas Tsoukalis, "Managing Interdependence: The EU in the World Economy," in *International Relations and the European Union*, Christopher Hill and Michael Smith, eds. (Oxford, Eng.: Oxford University Press, 2005), 232–36.

17. Sophie Meunier and Kalypso Nicolaidis, "The European Union as a Trade Power," in *International Relations and the European Union*, Christopher Hill and Michael Smith, eds. (Oxford, Eng.: Oxford University Press, 2005), 264–65.

18. See Daniel Yergin, "Ensuring Energy Security," *Foreign Affairs* 85:2 (March/April 2006): 69–82; and Richard G. Lugar, "The New Energy Realists," *National Interest* 84 (Summer 2006), 30–33.

19. Flynt Leverett and Pierre Noel, "The New Axis of Oil," *National Interest* 84 (Summer 2006), 62.

20. See Susan Ariel Aaronson, *Taking Trade to the Streets: The Lost History of Public Efforts to Shape Globalization* (Ann Arbor: University of Michigan Press, 2001); and Robin Broad, *Global Backlash: Citizen Initiatives for a Just World Economy* (Lanham, Md.: Rowman & Littlefield, 2002).

21. See Peter Andreas, "Illicit International Political Economy: The Clandestine Side of Globalization," *Review of International Political Economy* 11:3 (August 2004), 642–52; and Moises Naim, *Illicit: How Smugglers, Traffickers, and Copycats Are Hijacking the Global Economy* (New York: Doubleday, 2005).

Globalizing Issues

10

- ■ *What are the critical characteristics of globalizing issues?*
- ■ *What characteristics make AIDS a particularly difficult globalizing issue?*
- ■ *How do the concepts of collective goods and sustainability help us think about environmental issues?*
- ■ *What environmental issues may lead to international conflict?*
- ■ *What are the different generations of human rights?*
- ■ *How can international human rights standards be enforced?*
- ■ *How have the contending theories of international relations been modified or changed to accommodate globalizing issues?*

Today, states are interconnected and interdependent to a degree never previously experienced. Economic globalization discussed in the previous chapter is but one illustration. In this chapter, we introduce three other globalizing issues, specifically health, the environment, and human rights, among a plethora of possible issues. For these issues we show interconnectedness, the interaction among various international actors, and the impacts of these changes on core concepts and on the study of international relations. This provides a framework from which to explore the many other globalizing issues that will affect your lives in the years ahead.

In the twenty-first century, more different kinds of actors than ever participate in international politics, including the state, ethnonational challengers, multinational corporations, intergovernmental organizations, nongovernmental organizations, transnational movements and networks, and individuals. The transition from states being the main actors in international relations to the growing importance of nonstate actors portends a significant power shift. These new actors address a great variety of issues that are substantively and geographically interlinked from the local to the global level. Chapters 8 and 9 introduced two of the core issues—security and the international political economy. These two issues have evolved in new ways. State security is increasingly conceptualized as human security since civil wars and terrorist operations affect combatants and noncombatants alike. The international political economy is just part of the broader process of globalization, dominated by actors other than the state. Economic decisions made by multinational corporations affect national balances of payments and the ability of workers at the local level to hold a job and make a living wage. Issues such as health, the environment, and human rights may be as salient to states and individuals as traditional "guns or butter" issues. Finally, the changes wrought by the global communications and technology revolution lessens the determinacy of geography and undermines the primacy of territorial states. Distance and time are compressed; important issues can be communicated virtually instantaneously around the globe and to the most remote villages of the developing world. The ability of state leaders to manage this flow of information has diminished. One aspect of the sovereignty of the state, namely internal control over its citizens, has eroded.

As a result of these changes, globalizing issues demand further discussion. These issues are not new. Interest at the local and state level in health, the environment, and human rights has been expressed for generations, because these issues touch the quality of people's lives directly. These issues are closely connected to war and strife and political economy. What is new is that there is now *global* interest and action. And these issues are in the forefront in the twenty-first century. How can we think conceptually about globalizing issues? How do these issues crosscut with the traditional issues of security and economics? Who are the various actors with interests? How would a realist, a liberal, a radical, or a constructivist approach these globalizing issues?

Health and Disease—Protecting Life in the Commons

Public health and disease are old issues that have never respected national boundaries. In 1330, the bubonic plague began in China, transmitted from rodents and fleas to humans and then spread among people. Moving rapidly from China to Western Asia and then to Europe, by 1352, the deadly plague had killed one-third of Europe's population, or 25 million people. The epidemic, like others before and after, followed trade routes. During the age of discovery, Europeans carried smallpox, measles, and yellow fever to the distant shores of the Americas, decimating the indigenous populations. Expanding trade and travel in the nineteenth century within Europe and between

Europe and Africa accelerated the spread of deadly diseases like cholera and malaria, leading in 1852 to the first international conference on the subject. Between 1851 and 1903, a series of eleven international sanitary conferences developed procedures to prevent the spread of contagious and infectious diseases, establishing conditions of quarantine. As economic conditions improved and medical facilities expanded, the prevalences of diseases such as cholera, plague, yellow fever, and much later polio declined in the developed world.

Other diseases continued to ravage the developing world, some of them posing a transnational threat. The World Health Organization (WHO), founded as one of the specialized U.N. agencies in 1948, tackled two of the most deadly with its 1955 malaria eradication program and its 1965 smallpox campaign. Malaria eradication proved successful in the United States, the Soviet Union, Europe, and a few developing countries using a combination of the insecticide DDT and new antimalarial drugs. Yet in the developing world, the program failed to curb the disease, as the number of cases of malaria soared in Burma, Bangladesh, Pakistan, India, and much of Africa, where it is still prevalent. Efforts continue in malaria eradication, today focusing on low cost netting to protect sleeping children, the most vulnerable victims. By contrast, the smallpox campaign was a stunning success. When the campaign began, there were an estimated 10–15 million smallpox cases a year, including 2 million deaths and 10 million disfigurements in the developing world. The last reported case of smallpox occurred in 1977.

Buoyed by the success of smallpox eradication, the WHO has tackled polio, a disease that in 1988, when the campaign began, was estimated to paralyze 350,000 children a year. Using an effective and inexpensive vaccine, the WHO, working with state officials, has immunized most of the population, leading to a 99 percent reduction in cases. In 2003, however, there was a polio resurgence when religious authorities in northern Nigeria halted vaccinations. Cases have developed in Nigeria, Namibia, India, and Somalia.

After the widely hailed successes of the eradication of certain transmissible diseases, the international community was caught unawares by the new realities spawned by globalization. Economic and social globalization has had a dramatic effect on the vulnerability of individuals and communities to disease through migration and refugees, air and truck transport, trade, and troop movements. Twenty-first-century mobility has posed major problems for containing outbreaks of newly discovered diseases like Ebola, hantavirus, SARS (severe acute respiratory syndrome), Avian (bird) flu, and HIV/AIDS, as well as for preventing the transmission of older diseases, such as cholera, dengue fever, and typhoid. Of these, none has proven more devastating than AIDS.

A Global View of HIV/AIDS Infection

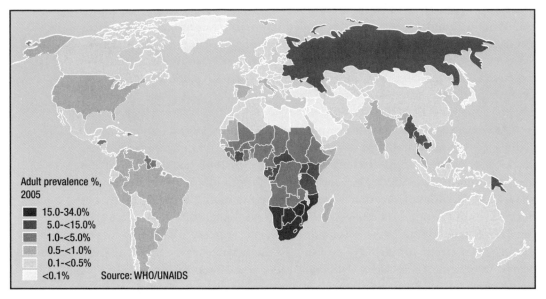

Adult prevalence %, 2005

- 15.0–34.0%
- 5.0–<15.0%
- 1.0–<5.0%
- 0.5–<1.0%
- 0.1–<0.5%
- <0.1%   Source: WHO/UNAIDS

AIDS as a Globalizing Issue

AIDS represents the quintessential globalizing issue. Originally transmitted from animal to man in central Africa, it then spread from individual to individual through the exchange of bodily fluids, and then was carried by those infected to others around the globe as people traveled between states, all long before any symptoms appeared. AIDS has rapidly become a major health and humanitarian problem, with over 3.1 million deaths annually (25 million deaths over the past 25 years) and estimates of between 33 and 46 million individuals living with the disease. AIDS is also an economic issue, disproportionately affecting those in their primary productive years, between 15 and 45. As teachers, workers, military personnel, and civil servants are infected, economic development is stymied, and the viability of the military as an institution threatened. It is also a social issue, as families are torn apart and children are orphaned and left to fend for themselves. These children are often then forced to turn to prostitution or join the military in order to survive. AIDS is a human rights and ethical issue, as well as a security issue. As the independent International Crisis Group has noted, "AIDS can be so pervasive that it destroys the very fiber of what constitutes a nation: individuals, families and communities; economic and political institutions; military and police forces. It is likely then to have broader security consequences."[1] In 2000 the U.N. Security Council identified AIDS as a threat to global security, the first time that health has been so recognized. One of the Millennium Development Goals is to halt and reverse the spread of HIV/AIDS.

Many different actors have responded to the AIDS problem, but individual states are key. Some states and leaders seized on the issue very rapidly, launching major public relations campaigns to inform the population of risky practices leading to transmission of the virus, distributing condoms, and now facilitating the distribution of life-extending drugs. Uganda, Botswana, and Brazil are examples of states that took initiatives very early on, and each has seen the results of its national program as rates of infection have declined. Other states have been very slow to acknowledge the problem. South Africa, India, and China fall into that category. Consistent with a state-centric view of international relations, states are critical actors; without their willingness to act and openness to respond, the programs initiated by the international community cannot penetrate national borders.

Intergovernmental organizations took the leadership role at the early stages. The WHO, for example, took steps to help states create national AIDS programs beginning in 1986. Subsequently, the WHO set the standards for specific levels of care and recommendations for drug treatments, adding antiretroviral drugs to its essential drug list in 2002. Following the WHO's initiative, in 1996, the Joint U.N. Program on HIV/AIDS (UNAIDS) was created, which coordinates cooperative projects among numerous U.N. agencies, including the WHO, the World Bank, the U.N. Development Program, and UNICEF, and is designed to promote joint programs not only among U.N.-based agencies but with NGOs, corporations, and national governments. This is an illustration of the partnership approach described in Chapter 9. At the same time, the United Nations initiated the practice of convening global AIDS conferences every two years to raise awareness and mobilize responses. The Global HIV/AIDS and Health Fund created in 2001 spent $8 billion in 2005.

Many NGOs have been actively involved in the issue, including Médecins Sans Frontières, CARE (Cooperative for Assistance and Relief Everywhere), the International Council of AIDS Service Organizations, and the Global Network of People Living with HIV/AIDS, as well as scores of local NGOs. Some work at the grassroots level, treating victims, helping families and communities survive; while others train health-care workers in AIDS care, so that those workers can then spread out around the world to administer that care.

With the development of antiretrovirals to extend the life of people living with AIDS, the multinational pharmaceutical companies have become a major actor, albeit a controversial one. While these drugs became available for treatment in the developed countries in the mid-1990s, in the developing world, the cost of the drugs of between $10,000 and $15,000 per person annually made that alternative essentially unavailable. But beginning in 1998, Brazilian and

Indian drug companies began manufacturing generics, reducing the cost of the treatment to less than $500 per person annually. This activity was controversial, as the WTO's intellectual property protection rules prohibit internationally traded generics that violate patent restrictions. Brazil took its case to U.N. human rights bodies and to international media, arguing that patients have a human right to treatment. NGOs have led the public campaigns in both the developed and developing countries, charging that pharmaceutical companies essentially withhold treatment from patients because of the prices they charge, dooming them to certain death. On one side of the issue are groups committed to lowering drug prices in order to provide treatment to a larger number of those infected, while on the other are those who simply find the cost too prohibitive in any case and who believe that the available funding should therefore be targeted at changing the behavior among those not yet infected. A compromise of sorts has been reached, with the pharmaceutical companies lowering prices for the developing world and the international community raising funds for a variety of prevention strategies, including antiretroviral treatment.

The major research institutes—the U.S. Centers for Disease Control, the National Institutes of Health, and France's Pasteur Institute—conduct research and aid in global surveillance activities. Many of these activities are supported by private foundations, for example, the Wellcome Trust of Great Britain and the Rockefeller Foundation, neither often thought of as actors in international issues.

No foundation has been more influential in global health than the Bill and Melinda Gates Foundation. Since its establishment in 2000, it has donated about $6 billion to global health causes. Childhood immunization programs have attracted $1.5 billion, with the remainder targeted for AIDS and research on creating better health-delivery systems in developing countries. The 2006 decision by U.S. businessman Warren Buffet to sign over his wealth to the foundation means that the organization will have assets of over $60 billion. With global health and American education as its two priorities, the foundation will direct an unprecedented stream of new revenue toward supporting global health programs.

Individuals like Bill and Melinda Gates and Bono have used their wealth, prestige, and bully pulpit in the fight against AIDS. But there are many others. President Yoweri Museveni of Uganda has played a major role in developing that country's response, as has Peter Mugyenyi, a Ugandan infectious disease expert known for his defiant action in administering cheaper AIDS drugs. In South Africa, it is Zackie Achmat, chairperson of the Treatment Action Campaign, in China, Wan Yan Hai, founder of the Aizhi (AIDS) Action Project in his country. As in other areas of international life, individuals made a difference.

As with other technical issues in international politics, another new group of actors has become increasingly important not only for AIDS and other health-related issues, but critical in international environmental politics as well. That is transnational communities of experts, or **epistemic communities.** Such groups are composed of experts and technical specialists from international organizations, nongovernmental organizations, and state and substate agencies. These communities share expertise as well as a set of beliefs. They share notions of validity and a set of practices organized around solving a particular problem.[2] Members of epistemic communities can influence the behavior of both states and international organizations and have done so on the issue of AIDS.

Beyond AIDS

AIDS is not the only health issue affecting the global community. Other new maladies have developed that infect animals and individuals. Among the most dreaded are the Ebola virus, mad cow disease, and Avian flu, which not only wipe out animals but also can infect humans. Another is SARS, which caused worldwide panic in 2003. In each case, the movement of peoples from the countryside to urban areas, from one urban area to another, and then across national boundaries spreads the disease rapidly to geographic places well beyond its origins. As a result of SARS and the threat of Avian flu, new procedures have been put in place, including both short-term measures (a medical strike force ready in six hours) and long-term ones (train nationals, form regional reporting networks).

Yet health issues include more than the transmission of infectious diseases. Like all globalizing issues, health issues are broader. They involve regulations to insure the quality of pharmaceuticals and to control what many consider to be unhealthy behaviors. While the former is not generally controversial, the latter is. For example, in the early 1970s, health-care workers recognized that bottle-fed babies were dying at higher rates than breast-fed babies because of the use of diluted formula or impure water. An NGO coalition, INFACT, organized boycotts against Nestlé, a major infant formula producer, to push the company to change its marketing strategies. Along with NGOs, the WHO and UNICEF developed a controversial code of conduct regulating the marketing of infant formula. Even more politicized is the issue of tobacco on the WHO agenda, which pits health officials against the power of large and profitable multinational tobacco companies. After years of debate, the WHO's Framework Convention on Tobacco Control was signed in 2003, although its enforcement will pit states against MNCs and states dependent on tax revenue from tobacco companies against health professionals in the coming years.

Increasingly, health is also recognized as a development issue. Economic development and the quality of individual lives cannot change without improvements in health conditions. That is why three of the Millennium Development Goals discussed in Chapter 9 relate to improving health, including reducing child mortality and improving maternal health. The fact that the World Bank during the 1980s became then the largest multilateral financier of health programs in developing countries confirms the health-development connection. The bank uses a sector approach, funding programs to increase the capacity of national and local health facilities. The development gap cannot be breached without attention to health. Even more than a development issue, health more generally is seen in some circles as a human rights issue, just as Brazil argued with respect to access to antiretrovirals. Health is a globalizing issue affecting politics, economics, society, and individuals.

A Theoretical Take

Health is an example of a quintessential functionalist issue. Virtually all agree that prevention of disease is critical and that good health is desired by all. High levels of agreement are found on the need to prevent the spread of infectious diseases and to rely on technical experts (namely, highly regarded and well-trained medical personnel) to carry out the task. Given these two functionalist criteria—a common interest and cooperation among technical experts—it is not surprising that one of the first areas of international cooperation was health. On this issue, liberals, realists, and radicals would all find common ground.

Another feature that all would agree on is the importance of the transnational communities of experts, often a natural outgrowth of functionalist cooperation. From AIDS to SARS, these medical experts, found in both public and private institutions, and making up an epistemic community, have been key actors providing research and policy advice.

Where liberals, realists, and radicals may disagree is on the correct approach to addressing health issues. Liberals, particularly those emerging from an international society perspective, are more apt to focus on international responsibility for dealing with health issues and be willing to utilize all groups possible, including local, substate, state, international, and nongovernmental organizations when appropriate. Realists are more apt to stress individual state responsibility and to acknowledge the importance of health issues when state security is threatened. Radicals see health as yet another issue that illustrates the economic differential between the wealthy developed world and the poor developing world. They may be quicker to point to health inequities exacerbated by exploitative working and living conditions. They would be quick to join in the condemnation of multinational companies that are concerned with bottom-line profits over social and humane objectives.

Radicals would see the reticence of MNCs to provide AIDS antiretrovirals at favorable prices as a confirmation of their viewpoint. Yet health is not the only globalizing issue.

The Environment—Protecting Space in the Global Commons

The environment, likewise, stands out as directly affecting the quality of our individual and collective lives, as well as the political and economic choices we make. A contemporary perspective on the environment confirms that multiple issues of population, natural resources, energy, and pollution are integrally related. Trends in one of these issues affect each of the others. Policy decisions taken to address one issue have impacts on each of the others.

Conceptual Perspectives

Two conceptual perspectives help us think about the suite of environmental issues. These perspectives are not contending approaches; rather they augment each other. First is the notion of collective goods. Collective goods help us conceptualize how to achieve shared benefits that depend on overcoming conflicting interests. How can individual herders in the commons be made not to pursue their own self-interest (increasing grazing on the commons) in the interests of preserving the commons for the collectivity? How can individual contributors to air pollution or ocean pollution be made to realize that their acts jeopardize the very collective good they are utilizing (the air and the ocean)? Collective goods theory provides the theoretical explanation for why there are environmental problems, as well as some ideas on how to address these problems.

The second conceptual perspective is sustainability, as introduced in Chapter 9. How can growth and well-being be achieved simultaneously with environmental protection? Can the policy be implemented without using up the precious capital of the Earth? How can development proceed and the Earth and its resources be maintained? Employing the criterion of sustainability forces individuals to think about policies to promote change that neither damage the environment nor use up finite resources, so that future generations will benefit.

Over time, principles and norms have evolved in customary international law concerning the environment. One core principle is the *no-significant-harm principle,* meaning states cannot initiate policies that cause significant environmental damages to another state. Another is the *good-neighbor principle* of cooperation. Beyond these are "soft law principles," often expressed in conferences, declarations, or resolutions, which although currently nonbinding, often informally describe acceptable norms of behavior. These include the polluter-pays principle, the precautionary principle (action should be taken on the basis of scientific warning and before there is irreversible harm), and the preventive-action principle (states should take action in their own jurisdiction). New emerging principles include the principles of sustainable development and intergenerational equity, both linking economics and the environment to future generations.

International treaties or agreements have also been ratified on numerous environmental issues. As one scholar put it, "the clearest evidence for the ecological trend in world politics is the astonishing array of recent treaties on a host of environmental problems."[3] These include the protection of natural resources such as endangered species of wild fauna and flora, tropical timber, natural waterways and lakes, migratory species of wild animals, and biological diversity in general, as well as protection against polluting, including in marine environments, on land, and in the air. Each of these treaties sets standards for state behavior, and some provide monitoring mechanisms. In doing so, they are very controversial, as they affect core political, economic, and human rights interests.

By studying three key environmental topics, we can see these conflicting interests. While each topic may be treated separately, and often is, they are all three integrally related, and each has global implications.

Population Issues

Recognition of the potential population problem occurred centuries ago. In 1798, Thomas Malthus posited a key relationship. If population grows unchecked, it will increase at a geometric rate (1,2,4,8, . . .), while food resources will increase at an arithmetic rate (1,2,3,4, . . .). Very quickly, he postulated, population increases will outstrip food production. This phenomenon is referred to as the **Malthusian dilemma.** (Although Malthus did not think productivity would keep up with population growth rates, he did acknowledge wars, famine, or moral restraint as a way to check excessive population.[4]) Three centuries later, an independent report (*The Limits to Growth*) issued by the Club of Rome in 1972 systematically investigated the trends in population, agricultural production, natural resource utilization, and industrial production and pollution and the intricate feedback loops that link these trends. Its conclusions were pessimistic: the Earth would reach natural limits to growth within a relatively short period of time.[5]

Neither Malthus nor the Club of Rome proved to be correct. Malthus did not foresee the technological changes that would lead to much higher rates of food production, nor did he predict the **demographic transition**—that popu-

FIGURE 10.1

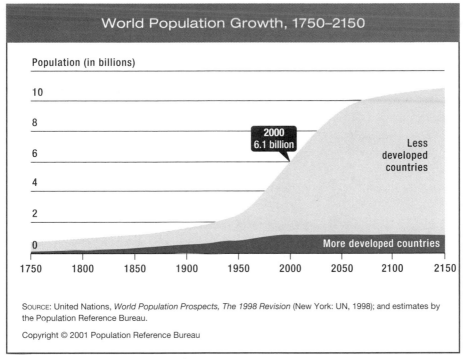

lation growth rates would not proceed unchecked. While improvements in economic development would lead at first to lower death rates and hence a greater population increase, over time, as the lives of individuals improved and women became more educated, birth rates would dramatically drop. As people moved to urban areas, birth rates declined. Likewise, the Club of Rome's predictions proved too pessimistic, as technological change stretched resources beyond the limits predicted in the 1972 report. And the advent of safe, reliable birth control technologies led to a decline in birth rates.

Although Malthus and the Club of Rome missed some key trends, their prediction that population growth rates would increase dramatically has proved correct. Global population growth rates peaked in 1970. Figure 10.1 shows the world population growth line projected over the next hundred years.

Three key observations make these population growth rates all the more disturbing. First, the population increase is not uniformly distributed. The developing world has much higher population growth rates than the developed world. Fertility rates in the developing world have averaged 3.4 children per woman, while in the developed world fertility has declined to 1.6 children per woman as a result of the demographic transition. Thus, there is a significant demographic divide between the rich North with low population growth rates and the poor South with high population growth rates; 98 percent of the growth in the world population is occurring in the developing countries. This divide has politically sensitive consequences, as those in the South, laboring under the burden of the population explosion, attempt to meet the economic consumption standards of the North. Realists fear this could potentially lead to a shift in the states' interests. They will need more food and resources and may seek them at any cost. This could destabilize the balance of power. Both liberals and radicals see this disparity as confirming that the South needs economic development. Narrowing the demographic divide is the best way to close the development gap.

Second, both rapid rates of overall population growth and high levels of economic development mean increased demands for natural resources. For certain countries like China, India, and Bangladesh with large populations already, the problem is severe. In Bangladesh and Nepal, the growing population is forced onto increasingly marginal land. In Nepal, human settlements at higher elevations have resulted in deforestation, as individuals utilize trees for fuel, resulting in hillside erosion, landslides, and other "natural" disasters. In Bangladesh, population pressures have led to settlements on deltas, which are vulnerable to monsoonal flooding, an occurrence that strips the top soil, decreases agricultural productivity, and periodically dislocates millions of individuals.

Accelerating demands for natural resources occur in the developed world as well. As the smaller (even slightly declining) population becomes more economically affluent, there is increasing demand for more energy and resources to support higher standards of living. People clamor for more living space, larger houses, and more highways, creating more demand for energy and resources.

Third, high population growth rates lead to numerous ethical dilemmas for state and international policymakers. How can population growth rates be curbed without infringing on individual rights to procreate? How can the cultural barrier to birth control be overcome? How can the developed countries promote lower birth rates in the developing world without sounding like supporters of eugenics? Can policies be developed that both improve the standard of living for individuals already born and guarantee equally high standards and improvements for future generations?

Population becomes a classic collective goods problem. It is eminently rational for an individual or couple in the developing world to have more children: children provide valuable labor in the family and often earn money in the wage economy, contributing to family well-being. Children are the social safety net for the family in societies where no governmental programs exist. But what is economically rational for the couple is not economically sustainable for the collectivity. The amount of land in the commons shrinks on a per capita basis, and the overall quality of the resource declines. What is economically rational for a family is not environmentally sustainable. The finite resources of the commons over time have a decreasing capacity to support the population.

What actions can be taken with respect to population to alleviate or mitigate the dilemmas just discussed? Biologist Garrett Hardin's solution, using coercion to prohibit procreation, is politically untenable and pragmatically difficult, as China has discovered with its one-child policy. However, that policy has radically altered its demographics. Relying on group pressure to force individual changes in behavior is also unlikely to work in the populous states.[6] Leaving the policy coercion aside, even when individuals may desire smaller families, family planning methods may be unavailable to them. It is estimated that 120 million couples in the developing world want access to such methods and do not have it due to high costs or unavailability. Without access to family planning methods, birth rates will continue to rise, states may be forced to impose coercive restrictions, and abortion rates will rise. What is clear about the population problem is that it is an international one affecting the whole globe. Decisions affect not just states with high rates of population growth but their neighbors, as people on overcrowded land contend for scarce resources and seek a better life in other countries through migration or turn to violence to get more desirable space.

States are not the only actors affected: this issue involves individuals, couples, and communities, along with their deepest-held religious and humanistic values. It also involves the nongovernmental community, those groups like Population Connection or the Population Council that are in the business of trying to change public attitudes about population and procreation, as well as the Catholic Church and fundamentalist Islamic sects that oppose artificial restrictions on the size of families. It involves intergovernmental organizations like the World Bank, charged with promoting sustainable development and yet hamstrung by the wishes of some member states to refrain from directly addressing the population issue. Perhaps most important, the population issue intersects with other environmental issues in an inextricable way. Populations put demands on land use for enhanced agricultural productivity; they need natural resources and energy resources. Thus, ironically, population may well be the pivotal global environmental issue, but it may also be the one that states and other international actors can do the least about.

Natural Resource Issues

The belief in the infinite supply of natural resources was a logical one throughout much of human history, as peoples migrated to uninhabited or only sparsely inhabited lands. Trading for natural resources became a necessary activity as it was recognized that those resources were never uniformly distributed. The belief in the infinite supply of key economic resources was dramatically challenged by radical Marxist thinkers. One of the reasons for imperialism, according to Lenin, was the inevitable quest for sources of raw materials. Capitalist states depended on overseas markets and resources, precisely because resources are unevenly distributed.

In Chapter 9, we explored how oil—one natural resource—is one of the major issues in the contemporary global economy. But just as population pressures and increased per capita consumption has put a squeeze on energy markets, so, too, has water become a globalizing issue.

Freshwater is a key natural resource necessary for all forms of life—human, animal, and plant. Only 3 percent of the Earth's water is fresh, and that supply is one-third lower than in 1970, at the same time that demand is increasing. Agriculture accounts for about two-thirds of the use of water, industry about one-quarter, and human consumption slightly less than one-tenth. It is estimated that by 2025, two-thirds of the world's people will live in countries facing moderate or severe water shortage problems. While most freshwater issues are national problems, increasingly such problems have an international dimension.

Several examples illustrate the international controversies and repercussions. The U.S. use of the Colorado River for irrigation has not only reduced the flow of that river but also diminished the quality of the water that ends up in Mexico, the downstream user. By the time the river crosses the border, the flow is a trickle and is highly saline, driving Mexican agricultural users out of business. U.S. plans to replace a border canal so that it sends water to thirsty San Diego instead has led one newspaper to headline "Border Fight Focus on Water, Not Immigration."[7] Similarly, Israel's control of scarce water on the West Bank has resulted in rationing in neighboring regions. Hence, the World Bank predicts that in the twenty-first century, water could be the major political issue not only between Israel and Jordan, but between Turkey and Syria and between India and Bangladesh.

The story is much the same in Asia, where two upstream countries with relatively poor land, Tajikistan and Kyrgyzstan, are the water source for areas downstream with good land. Under the old system in the Soviet Union, water was freely available for downstream users. Now, there is conflict as water systems are in decay and no new system for water allocation has been developed. In China, water is scarce in the northern cities, and so the country has embarked on a huge plan to rechannel water from the Yangtze basin over three 1,000-mile channels, at an estimated cost of $58 billion. That is more than twice the cost of China's other major water project, the construction of the Three Gorges Dam, the largest construction project ever. The latter is designed to create hydropower. Yet both projects not only come at an enor-

The Environment: A View from Indonesia

Increasing economic growth and raising the living standard of a population can come at the expense of other values, including a commitment to environmental sustainability and improving the quality of people's lives. Indonesia is experiencing firsthand this trade-off between development and environmental quality.

Agricultural production, forestry, and mining are all key sectors in the economy of Indonesia, an archipelago nation of 6,000 islands and 245 million people. Each of these activities is important to the country's economic development—palm oil, timber, and mineral production all employ people and earn precious foreign exchange. Poor people in Indonesia struggle to find suitable land for agricultural production, often squatting on flood plains and building up steep mountains, and they flock to cities whose infrastructure is old and incapable of handling the influx. However, the Indonesian government has limited funds for development, and as foreign-owned companies push for bigger profits, state decisionmakers are unable to enforce existing laws to improve the situation.

Indonesia acknowledges that deforestation is a major problem, with 80 percent of the forestry operations conducted illegally by small landholders tied to multinational corporations. The soil erodes; crops are incapable of regeneration; animal species are lost and biodiversity decreased. The trees harvested, including prized reddish-brown hardwoods called merbau, are replaced by timber plantations and agricultural crops. In many cases, the forests are burned in the process, resulting in forest fires and haze. The fires in 1987, 1994, and 1997–98 caused a cloud of haze over Indonesia, especially on the island of Sumatra, that led to poor air quality, subsequent respiratory illnesses, and a loss of biodiversity and crop productivity. The infamous 1997–98 haze cost Indonesia several billion dollars and was its worst environmental disaster. In late 2005, the haze returned and the wind spread some of it to neighboring Malaysia. The most recent fires were purposely set by the MNCs and local operators to speed the clearing process. Much of the timber grown is shipped to Malaysia and Singapore, and is then manufactured into products to be sold in Taiwan and China.

Mining is also a significant industry in Indonesia. Gold, copper, and coal are mined by several MNCs throughout Indonesia, and are viewed by Indonesian officials as a vital part of the country's economic development. To extract the highest profits, mining companies often disregard environmental protocols, resulting in polluted water, air, and topsoil. In 2004, Indonesia sued the Newmont Mining Corporation, a U.S.-based gold producer, for emitting toxic mercury vapors into the air. In 2006, the company paid Indonesia $30 million in a settlement to compensate for the pollution. That highly publicized case would have to be duplicated many times before significant changes are made in the industry.

Indonesian-based umbrella NGOs, like the Indonesian Network for Forest Conservation and the Indonesian Environmental Network, publicize abuses and institute legal proceedings, frequently teaming with international NGOs like the World Wide Fund for Nature to establish more sustainable environmental initiatives. The environmental cause may benefit from the effects of recent disasters like the 2004 tsunami and flooding in Jakarta in 2007, which may have been worsened by both environmental degradation and poor government economic decisions.

For Critical Analysis

1. How is the Indonesian case a tragedy of the commons? Which of Garrett Hardin's solutions to such a tragedy is possible politically?
2. What other ways can one country's environmental issues have an international impact?

mous financial cost, diverting money from other sources, but are accompanied by detrimental environmental side effects.

Pollution

As pressures on the commons mount, the quality of geographic space diminishes. In the 1950s and 1960s, several events dramatically publicized the deteriorating quality of the commons. Oceanographer Jacques Cousteau warned of the degradation of the ocean, a warning confirmed by the Torrey Canyon oil spill off the coast of England. Rachel Carson's *Silent Spring* warned of the impact of chemicals on the environment.[8] The natural world was being degraded by human activity associated with agricultural and industrial practices. Economic development both in agriculture and industry has negative **externalities**—costly unintended consequences—for everyone, as well as positive effects.

While many of these negative externalities may be local, others have national and international implications. Take the case of energy. To meet the rising demand for oil, the United States and China have turned to the oil sands of Alberta, Canada. Since 2003, it has become economically viable to convert those sands into oil for use as gasoline. MNCs have heavily invested in the operation. Deleterious environmental externalities are, however, becoming evident. The extractive process requires massive withdrawal of water, disturbing the fish populations and adversely affecting water quality. The tailing ponds containing the residues have proliferated, imperiling wildlife; and forests are cut, the same forests that provide carbon sinks to slow down global warming.

Halfway around the world, China's thirst for energy has led to increased coal usage. Coal-burning power plants emit smoot, toxic chemicals, and gases, which, with weather inversions, create air pollution over not only China and neighboring Korea and Japan, but also over the west coast of the United States. These sulfur dioxide emissions carry known health risks, respiratory and heart disease, and certain kinds of cancer.

Nowhere is our globe more affected than by the pollution issues of the twenty-first century: ozone depletion and global warming. Both issues share characteristics in common. They concern pollution in spaces that belong to no one state. They both result from negative externalities associated with rising levels of economic development. They both pit groups of states against each other, and they both have been the subject of highly contested international negotiations.

Thrust onto the international agenda in 1975, the case of ozone depletion illustrates a relative success story with a reversal of the depletion in the ozone layer. States recognized an environmental problem before it became of crisis proportions and reacted with increasingly strong measures. Both the developed and the developing world were involved, with the latter receiving financial aid from the former to finance the change in technology. Substitutes were developed, and MNCS eventually supported the prohibition of chlorofluorocarbons.

The issue of global climate change, or greenhouse warming, has proved more complicated. On the one hand, there are scientific facts that are indisputable. The preponderance of greenhouse gas emissions comes from the burning of fossil fuels in the industrialized countries of the North. But sources are also found in the developing countries, most notably from deforestation of the tropics caused by agriculture and the timber industry, and from rising usage of fossil fuels in China and India. Figure 10.2 shows per capita carbon dioxide emissions by region in the absence of any international agreement.

There are additional data which, while contested in the past, are no longer in dispute. A 2006 report issued by the U.S. National Academy of Sciences concludes that the Earth has been heating up an average of 1 degree in the Northern hemisphere during the last century, much of that during the last two decades. And "human activities are responsible for much of the recent warming." The two greenhouse gases blamed for retaining heat in the atmosphere—carbon dioxide and methane—have experienced sharp spikes after 12,000 years of relative consistency. The scientific community has found the evidence compelling.

There is also an emerging consensus on the effects of global warming. As masterfully illustrated in the documentary film *An Inconvenient Truth*, sea levels are rising, glaciers are melting, hurricanes are strengthening as the oceans warm, and weather patterns are becoming more severe, producing more droughts and more flooding.

While scientists increasingly agree on the problem, politicians and economists have not agreed on the solution. This is not surprising given competing interests from various parties. Industrialized countries seek continued high levels of growth fueled by oil and natural gas, and the South wants to become industrialized and enjoy the consumptive lifestyle, both made possible by oil and gas. So the parties disagree on whether voluntary restraints or market-related responses can be sufficient for both to reach their development objectives and reduce greenhouse emissions. Or are authoritative regulations needed? If regulation is needed, what authority should be invoked—international, state-level, or subnational, even local?

The Kyoto Protocol of 1997 amended a weak 1992 U.N. framework. It provided for stabilizing the concentration of greenhouse gases and delineated international goals for reducing emissions by 2010. Under the protocol, developed countries (including the United States, Europe, and Japan) are

FIGURE 10.2

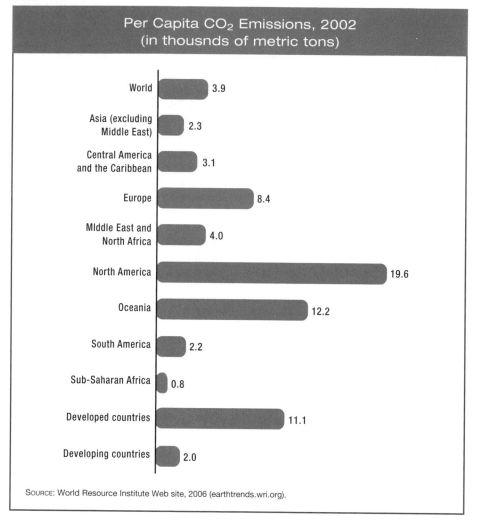

Per Capita CO$_2$ Emissions, 2002
(in thousnds of metric tons)

World	3.9
Asia (excluding Middle East)	2.3
Central America and the Caribbean	3.1
Europe	8.4
Middle East and North Africa	4.0
North America	19.6
Oceania	12.2
South America	2.2
Sub-Saharan Africa	0.8
Developed countries	11.1
Developing countries	2.0

SOURCE: World Resource Institute Web site, 2006 (earthtrends.wri.org).

required to reduce their overall greenhouse gas emissions by at least 5 percent below 1990 levels over the next decade; Japan committed to 6 percent, the United States to 7 percent, and the European Union to 8 percent. In neither the Kyoto Protocol nor the earlier agreement were developing countries included in the emission limitation requirement.

The protocol provides flexibility mechanisms designed to make reaching the emission targets more cost efficient. First, trading of international emission shares is permitted. This allows countries that achieve deeper reductions than their targets to trade their surplus shares to other countries. Second, credits can be earned from "carbon sinks." Since forests absorb the carbon dioxide from the air as they grow and help slow the buildup of the gas in the atmosphere, states can offset the emissions they produce by gaining credits for planting forests. There is debate, however, over whether sinks can be used to meet all or only part of the emission reduction required. Third, joint implementation permits countries to participate in projects for emission reductions and allows each to receive part of the credit. Each mechanism represents a highly complex scientific technique designed to reduce emissions, yet each comes with economic costs that are often difficult, if not impossible, to estimate.

The Kyoto Protocol came into force in 2005, ratified by 156 states representing 55 percent of greenhouse emissions. In the United States, the Bush administration has refused to agree to any binding commitment on emissions, objecting on several grounds. From a pragmatic perspective, the economic costs of moving away from a fossil fuel–based economy are too high; an unacceptable number of jobs would be lost. The developed Northern countries would be forced to comply with restrictions, while the rapidly developing economies like India and China would have fewer restrictions, giving them an unfair economic advantage. From an ideological perspective, the Bush administration opposes international regulations on the issue. Markets—higher prices leading to decreased consumption, and a way to trade emission quotas—will bring about the necessary changes. In particular, the administration opposes international regulations imposed by an unrepresentative and unaccountable body.

Both European states and Japan have signed the protocol and are making efforts to reduce emissions. A Compliance Committee has been established with enforcement tasks; parties found not compliant may not use the flexible mechanisms to offset emission standards. The commitments in the Kyoto Protocol are to expire in 2012, and after a 2005 meeting, all participants have agreed to make new commitments, and both the United States and China have agreed to consider a new climate treaty that includes both states. Since the United States is responsible for 36 percent of the total emissions by industrialized countries, that country's participation is vital. Yet in North America, subnational jurisdictions are leading the charge for policy change. That includes California, the fifth largest economy in the world, and six New England states joined by five Canadian provinces. Each has begun to enact cuts to greenhouse emissions to 1990 levels by 2010.

Whether or not states decide to respond, global warming will continue to be a high-priority agenda item in the twenty-first century.

Environmental NGOs in Action

NGOs have played a vital role in environmental issues since the 1960s. While the number of environmental NGOs has grown, as has the number of NGOs generally, their interests are diverse. On the issue of population, the

Population Connection advocates population limitations, while the Catholic Church opposes artificial birth control. On the issue of natural resources, the Nature Conservancy and the Rainforest Action Network lobby for land protection. The Earth Island Institute and the Global Climate Coalition, the latter an industry-sponsored group against limitations on greenhouse emissions, are concerned with pollution issues.

NGOs perform a number of key functions in environmental affairs. First, they serve as generalized international critics, often using media to publicize their dissatisfaction and to get environmental issues on the international and state agendas. For example, the Rainforest Action Network launched an initiative against Amazon deforestation precipitated by cattle ranching, targeting Burger King for buying the beef. Greenpeace's indictment of Brazil's unsustainable cutting of mahogany trees led that country to stop all shipments until forestry practices could be improved. Second, NGOs may function through intergovernmental organizations, working to change the organization itself. For example, NGOs did this with the International Whaling Commission when they transformed it from a body that limited whaling through quotas into one that banned whale hunting altogether. Third, NGOs can aid in monitoring and enforcing environmental regulations, either by pointing out problems or by actually carrying out on-site inspections. For example, the NGO TRAFFIC, the wildlife trade monitoring program of the World Wildlife Fund and IUCN-The World Conservation Union, is authorized to conduct inspections under the Convention on International Trade in Endangered Species of Wild Fauna and Flora. Fourth, NGOs may function as part of transnational communities of experts, serving with counterparts in intergovernmental organizations and state agencies to try to change practices and procedures of an issue. One such epistemic community formed around the Mediterranean Action Plan of the U.N. Environmental Program. Experts gathered in meetings to discuss ways to improve the sea's water quality, data was shared, and monitoring programs established. These same individuals also became active in domestic bargaining processes, fostering learning among government elites. Finally, and perhaps most important, NGOs can attempt to influence state environmental policy directly, providing information about policy options, sometimes initiating legal proceedings, and lobbying directly through a state's legislature or bureaucracy. For, despite the increased roles for NGOs, it is still states that have primary responsibility for taking action.

A Theoretical Take

What has made many environmental issues so politically controversial at the international level is that states have tended to divide along the developed-developing—North-South—economic axis, although some developed states have been more accommodating than others. To the developed world, many environmental issues stem from the population explosion, a developing world problem. In their view, population growth rates must decline; then pressure on scarce natural resources will decrease, and the negative externality of pollution will diminish. Those in the developed world who have enjoyed the benefits of economic growth and industrialization may now be willing to pay the additional costs for a safe and healthy environment.

States of the developing South perceive the environmental issue differently. These states correctly point to the fact that many of the environmental problems—including the overutilization of natural resources and the pollution issues of ozone depletion and greenhouse emissions—are the result of excesses of the industrialized world. By exploiting the environment, by misusing the commons, the developed countries were able to achieve high levels of economic development. Putting restrictions on developing countries, not allowing them to exploit their natural resources or restricting their utilization of vital fossil fuels, may impede their development. Thus, since the developed states have been responsible for most of the environmental excesses, it is they who should pay for the cleanup.

The challenge in addressing globalizing issues is to negotiate a middle ground that reflects the fact that both sides are, in fact, correct. High population growth rates is a problem in the South—one that will not be alleviated until higher levels of economic development are achieved. And overutilization of natural resources is primarily a problem of the North. Powerful economic interests in the North are constantly reminding us that changes in resource utilization may lead to a lower standard of living. Pollution is a byproduct of both, which in the South tends to be in the form of land and water resource utilization because of excessive population, whereas in the North it stems from the by-products and negative externalities of industrialization. Thus, the environmental issue, more than the other globalizing issues, involves trade-offs with economic interests. Economic security is more likely to lead to environmental security.

Realists, liberals, and radicals do not have the same degree of concern for environmental issues, although each of the perspectives has been modified in response to external changes. Realists' principal emphasis has been on state security, although in some quarters that has recently expanded to include human security. Either version of security requires a strong population base, a nearly self-sufficient source of food, and a dependable supply of natural resources. Making the costs of natural resources or the costs of pollution abatement too high diminishes the ability of a state to make independent decisions. Thus realists fit environmental issues into the theoretical concepts of the state, power, sovereignty, and the balance of power.

Radicals, likewise, are concerned with the economic costs of the environmental problem. Radicals are apt to see the costs borne disproportionately by those in the South and by the poorer groups in the developed North. Neither

FIGURE 10.3

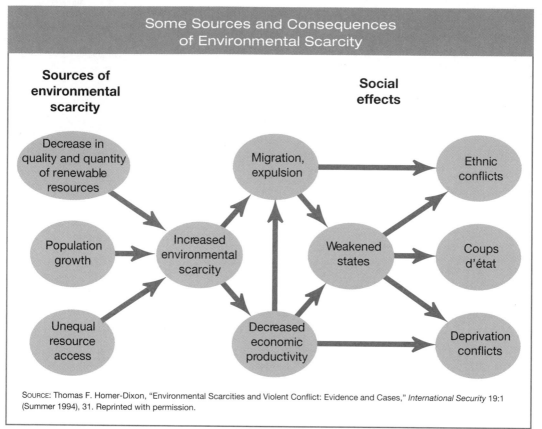

Some Sources and Consequences
of Environmental Scarcity

SOURCE: Thomas F. Homer-Dixon, "Environmental Scarcities and Violent Conflict: Evidence and Cases," *International Security* 19:1 (Summer 1994), 31. Reprinted with permission.

of these burdens is acceptable to most radicals, although there are a few eco-radicals who define sustainability at the level of community.

Both realists and radicals clearly recognize that controversies over natural resources and resource scarcity can lead to violence and even war. Political scientist Thomas Homer-Dixon has proposed one model that directly links the environment to conflict.[9] Figure 10.3 shows these hypothesized relationships. While not all would agree with the lines of causation, they are intellectually provocative and a source of concern for policymakers.

In contrast, liberals have typically seen the environmental issue as appropriate to the international agenda for the twenty-first century. Their broadened view of security, coupled with the credence given to the notion of an international system described as interdependent, perhaps even one so interconnected as to be called an international society, makes environmental issues ripe for international action. Because liberal theory can accommodate a greater variety of different international actors, including nongovernmental actors from global civil society, environmental issues and human rights issues are legitimate, if not key, international issues of the twenty-first century to liberals. Unlike realists and radicals, who fear dependency on other countries because it may diminish state power and therefore limit state action, liberals welcome the interdependency and have faith in the technological ingenuity of individuals to be able to solve many of the natural resource dilemmas.

Constructivists, too, are comfortable with environmental issues as an arena for international action. Environmental issues bring out the salience of discourse. Constructivists are interested in how political and scientific elites define the problem and how that definition changes over time and new ideas become rooted in their belief sets. Constructivists also realize that environmental issues challenge the core concepts of sovereignty. One of the major intellectual tasks for constructivists has been to uncover the roots and practices of sovereignty.[10]

Human Rights—Protecting Human Dignity

The issue of human rights, the treatment of individuals and groups of individuals, has a longer historical genesis than environmental issues, but its global dimension is of more recent vintage. Prior to 1945, relations between a state and the individuals within the state were largely that state's concern. Over these individuals, the state had absolute sovereignty, supreme legal authority. Gradually five exceptions developed. In 1815 the major European powers began to negotiate a treaty, which was finally concluded in 1890, that recognized the obligation of states to abolish the slave trade. But it was not until 1926 that the practice of slavery was abolished by the international community. During the nineteenth century, individuals became entitled to medical treatment by belligerent states during war. In the twentieth century, legal aliens became entitled to minimum civil rights within a state. Laborers achieved some protection under the International Labor Organization, and specific minorities from the vanquished states of World War I were granted nominal international rights by the League of Nations. But the protection of individuals for all other purposes remained solely a state responsibility.[11]

Like the issue of population, the issue of human rights addresses core values over which there are fundamental disagreements—disagreements about what rights should be protected and what the role of the state and the international community should be in the protection of such rights. And realists, liberals, and radicals offer contrasting perspectives.

Conceptualizing Human Rights and the Development of a Regime

Political theorists have long been in the business of conceptualizing human rights. Three different kinds of rights have been articulated. The first group of human rights to be formulated (**first-generation human rights**) was rights possessed by an individual that the state cannot usurp. John Locke (1632–1704), among others, asserted that individuals are equal and autonomous beings whose natural rights predate both national and international law. Public authority is designed to secure these rights. Key historic documents detail these rights, beginning with the English Magna Carta in 1215, the French Declaration of the Rights of Man in 1789, and the U.S. Bill of Rights in the 1791 Constitution. These documents listed rights of the individual that the government could not take away. For example, no individual should be "deprived of life, liberty, or property, without due process of law." Political and civil rights dominate first-generation rights: the right to free speech, free assembly, free press, and freedom of religion. Since these are rights that the government cannot take away, they are referred to as negative rights. To some theorists and to many U.S. pundits, these are the only recognized human rights. First-generation rights are squarely within the liberal tradition and are widely accepted by realists. Even Karl Marx regarded some civil rights as good, though not the emphasis on property rights.

Second-generation human rights developed in large part under the disciples of Marx and other radical socialist thinkers. Marx's concern was for the welfare of industrialized labor. The duty of states is to advance the well-being of its citizens; the right of the citizens is to benefit from these socioeconomic advances. This view emphasizes minimum material rights that the state must provide to individuals. The state has the responsibility to provide for the social welfare of individuals, and thus, individuals have the right to education, health care, social security, and housing, although the amount guaranteed is unspecified. These are referred to as positive rights. Without guarantees of those economic and social rights, political and civil rights are largely meaningless. The Soviet Union and other socialist states in the Cold War Eastern bloc recognized economic and social rights either as just as important as political and civil rights or as more important, as do many social welfare states of Europe today.

Third-generation human rights, a product of late twentieth-century thinking, specify rights for groups. Groups that have rights include ethnic or indigenous minorities within a polity or designated special groups such as women or children. Some theorists have even added group rights to the list of individual human rights: the right to a safe environment, the right to peace and human security, the right to live in a democracy.

Drawing on long religious and philosophical traditions and the three generations of human rights, the U.N. General Assembly approved the Universal Declaration of Human Rights in 1948, a statement of human rights aspirations. Thirty principles incorporating both political and economic rights were identified. These principles were eventually codified in two documents, the International Covenant on Economic, Social, and Cultural Rights and the International Covenant on Civil and Political Rights, approved in 1966 and ratified in 1976. These are together known as the international bill of rights. These rights have been expanded to include special conventions for women and refugees, and to address various kinds of discrimination.

These wide-ranging human rights standards and the variety of actors involved in laying out the principles have led many scholars to conclude that there is an international regime of human rights. The term *regime* refers to agreed-upon rules, norms, and procedures that emerge from high levels of cooperation—beyond the willingness to negotiate internationally and to coordinate policy outcomes on a periodic basis. The notion of a regime suggests that states develop principles about how certain problems should be addressed. Over time, these principles solidify into accepted rules. Such rules and principles may be explicit—as indeed some international law is when it is codified—or they may be implicit. Regimes are "principles, norms, rules, and decision-making procedures around which actors' expectations converge in a given issue area."[12] Whether or not the principles are formalized in an organization or an international treaty, regimes guide state actions. The human rights regime, like other regimes, is comprised of a web of organizations—global and regional, general purpose and specialized, governmental and nongovernmental—that are engaged in activities related to issue areas relevant to the regime. These include not just the U.N. instruments (like the Human Rights Council, the Commission on the Status of Women, and the Office of the High Commissioner for Human Rights), but also the special monitoring committees established under the major international human rights treaties on political and civil rights, social and economic rights, rights of the child, indigenous peoples protection, and racial discrimination. Regional groups have also set standards and developed monitoring and adjudicating bodies, most notably the European Commission of Human Rights and the European Court of Human Rights.

Of the disagreements and controversies within the human rights regime, none has been more salient than the discussion of whether the different conceptions of human rights and the specific protected rights are really universally applicable or not.

Is there a set of rights that should be **universal rights**? There is disagreement. Clearly, some states give priority to one generation of rights over others. Pundits from different regions of the world have argued for **cultural relativism,** that is, that rights are culturally determined, and hence different rights are relevant in different cultural settings. A group of Asian writers, including some in China, Indonesia, Malaysia, Singapore, and Vietnam, have made this argument—that global human rights are a misnomer; human rights are culturally relative. In their view, when regional population and land pressures are so severe, to advocate the rights of the individual over the welfare of the community as a whole is unsound and potentially dangerous. The rights of the individual in first- and second-generation rights may conflict with the collective rights of groups. Asian cultures traditionally give primacy to the latter over the former.[13] Others disagree. The final document of the Vienna World Conference on Human Rights in 1993 asserts, "All human rights are universal, indivisible and interdependent and related." But the practice of human rights remains controversial.

The Human Rights Regime in Action

Over the last fifty years states, intergovernmental organizations, and nongovernmental organizations have helped to set and clarify the standards and norms, as elucidated above. States traditionally have argued that this is primarily the sovereign prerogative of the state, limited only by a state's own constitution. The United States made this argument during the civil rights era of the 1950s and 1960s. Discrimination against African Americans was a U.S. problem to be handled by federal authorities. The People's Republic of China has been one of the more vocal supporters of this point of view, disdainful of any interference in its domestic rights policies, including their treatment of national minorities, prisoners, and political dissidents.

During the twentieth century, with mass communication and the spread of information about how countries were treating their populations, a contending position emerged. That position was based on the realization that how a government treats its own citizens can affect the larger global community. Mistreatment of individuals and minorities can inflame ethnic tensions, causing unrest across national borders. Mistreatment of individuals in one country debases humans everywhere, threatening to undermine the essence of humanity worldwide. The Holocaust, the German Nazi genocide against Jews, gypsies, and countless minorities, brought this issue to the attention of the international community in a way that had not been done previously. Nongovernmental groups participating in the U.N. founding conference in San Francisco pushed for the inclusion of human rights in the new organization's agenda. It was argued that the international community, namely but not exclusively, should assume responsibility for the promotion and encouragement of global human rights standards.

What can the international community actually do? What can the United Nations and other intergovernmental organizations do when they are themselves composed of the very sovereign states that threaten individual rights? The United Nations's activities and the activities of other international organizations concerned with human rights have been confined to several areas.[14] First, the United Nations has been involved in the setting of the international human rights standards articulated in the many treaties, from prohibiting race and gender discrimination, to protecting refugees and children, to proscribing actions during war.

Second, the United Nations and the European Commission on Human Rights have worked to monitor state behavior, establishing procedures for complaints about state practices, compiling reports from interested and neutral observers about state behavior, and investigating alleged violations. Monitoring has generally focused on political rights associated with democracy or on civil rights, rather than on second-generation rights.

NGOs can supplement the activities of intergovernmental organizations, and they have been particularly useful in monitoring activities. Amnesty International, founded in 1961, has become perhaps the most effective human rights monitor. Amnesty International was particularly involved in efforts to end the abuse of human rights in Uruguay and Paraguay, issuing reports of abuses, sending observers to trials, and lobbying governments. It was instrumental in bringing international attention to the Argentinian military abuses involving abductions and disappearances in the early 1980s. Relying on accurate research and modest member contributions, and utilizing publicity, Amnesty International has been able to capitalize on its reputation as an impartial, highly professional, and politically neutral organization. While it originally emphasized the protection of individual political prisoners, the organization has broadened its agenda to include issues where there are systematic patterns of abuses of economic and social rights.

Third, the United Nations has taken measures to promote human rights by assuring fair elections with neutral monitors and providing a focal point for global human rights activity in the person of the High Commissioner for Human Rights. For example, since 1992, the United Nations has provided electoral assistance   election monitors, technical assistance—in over seventy countries. It has actually conducted elections in Namibia, Nicaragua, Cambodia, Eritrea, and Liberia, among others.

Fourth, states and the international community are the primary enforcers of international human rights. States have always been the major enforcers of human rights and remain so. States can use their legal systems, as Spain tried to do to bring the former dictator of Chile, General Augusto Pinochet, to Spain for trial for his abuses against Spanish citizens under the principle of universal jurisdiction. While Spain's attempt failed, Pinochet was ultimately returned to Chile, where he was to stand trial, but poor health and old age intervened (and he has since died). States more commonly use coercive measures such as sanctions or embargoes. Following China's crackdown on dissidents resulting in the Tiananmen Square massacre in June 1989, the United States instituted an arms embargo against China and canceled new foreign aid; it was joined by Japan and members of the European Union. Some estimate that the coercive action may have cost China over $11 billion in bilateral aid over a four year period.

States may also find that positive incentives or engagement may be a better approach to change the human rights practices of another state. Engagement rests on the idea that since states have multiple interests—economic, security, diplomatic, and human rights—linking another issue to human rights may be a way of getting a state to change the latter. For example, a state may be given trade concessions if human rights abuses decline. Linking may work because of the notion that better economic relations and a more open economic system would create domestic pressure for more political freedom, including less-offensive human rights practices. In the China case, after the coercive measures failed to result in major changes, states and the international community turned to engagement. The belief was that if China moved toward a more open economic system, then its human rights record would improve. At this point, the strategy has not brought the anticipated results, although China's human rights abuses have become much more publicized, as the regime is less able to hide its behavior.

U.N. enforcement is also an option. In the case of apartheid—legalized racial discrimination against the majority black population in South Africa and a comparable policy in Southern Rhodesia (now Zimbabwe)—the international community under U.N. authority instituted economic embargoes, seeking to punish those responsible for violating human rights standards and hoping to cause a change in the states' aberrant behavior. While the embargo weakened the minority regimes, the government did not immediately change its human rights policy, nor was the government immediately ousted from power. In a few cases, enforcement action may involve the use of military force. In the case of the humanitarian emergency in northern Iraq after the 1991 Gulf War, as well as in reaction to those in Somalia, Bosnia, and Rwanda, the U.N. Security Council explicitly linked human rights violations to security threats and undertook enforcement action without the consent of the states concerned. Yet the cases where the United Nations can intervene are few. Many states are suspicious of strengthening the United Nation's power to intervene in what many still regard as their domestic jurisdiction.

All of these approaches to human rights enforcement are fraught with difficulties. A state's signature on a treaty is no guarantee of its willingness or ability to follow the treaty's provisions. Monitoring state compliance through self-reporting systems presumes a willingness to comply and to be transparent. Taking direct action by imposing economic embargoes may not achieve the announced objective—change in human rights policy—and may actually be harmful to those very individuals whom the embargoes are trying to help. It has been reported that the international community's economic sanctions against Iraq after the first Gulf War resulted in a lower standard of living for the population and an imposition of real economic hardship on the masses, while the targeted elites remained unaffected. The sanctions did not have the intended affect of securing the elimination of Iraq's weapons of mass destruction.[15]

Even NATO's bombing of Kosovo and Serbia in 1999, designed to stop Serbian atrocities against the Albanian Kosovars and punish the Milošević regime, resulted in unintended Kosovar casualties and increased hardship for all peoples, while the regime went unpunished, at least in the short run. International and national actions on behalf of human rights objectives remains a very tricky business. Use of power, whether hard or soft power, does not always produce the intended result.

While the enforcement of human rights standards by the international community is clearly the exception rather than the norm, important precedents were established in the late twentieth century. Some kind of international action is acceptable, though such actions are not always taken. But the international community may be closer now to saying it has a responsibility, even an obligation, to protect individuals, part of the norm of humanitarian intervention explained in Chapter 8. Most theorists and policymakers agree that genocide should elicit a concerted international response. In the aftermath of the Holocaust, the Convention against Genocide was negotiated. It elucidated clear principles that systematic killing of a group based on race, gender, or ethnicity is prohibited under international law and norms. States have acted to stop genocide, for example, with the NATO-backed coalition organized to stop the ethnic cleansing of Serbs in Kosovo, although the word *genocide* was never used by NATO to describe what was happening. One million Bangladeshis and 2 million Cambodians were killed in the 1970s, and in the 1990s, over 800,000 Rwandans were killed while the world sat back and watched. In the latter case, neither the United Nations nor the United States ever used the word *genocide*, aware that admitting it was genocide would necessitate an international response. Instead, at the outset it was framed as an "ordinary" ethnic conflict; in retrospect, it is clear it was anything but ordinary.

Advocates of each of the three theoretical perspectives might argue for different responses on the part of states. Realists would generally focus on a state's national interest in the situation. If genocide committed by one state jeopardizes another state's national interest, including intruding on its core values, then it should act, in the eyes of realists, although few states are likely to act alone. As former U.S. national security adviser Henry Kissinger has warned, a wise realist policymaker would not be moved by sentiment alone or by personal welfare, but by the calculation of the national interest.[16] But the definition of that national interest may be broad, based on historical tradition or domestic values.

Liberals and radicals would be more likely to advise state intervention in response not only to genocide but also to less dramatic abuses. Liberals' emphasis on individual welfare and on the malleability of the state makes such intrusions into the actions of other states less offensive to them. Like the realists, they may prefer that nongovernmental actors take the initiatives, but they generally see it to be a state's duty to intercede in blatant cases of human rights abuse. Likewise, radicals have few qualms about states' taking such actions. For them, however, the real culprit is the nemesis of an unfair economic system, namely, the international capitalist system, and so the target in their view is much more diffuse. It is critical that intervention be applied without discrimination.

Other Human Rights Actors

Similar to global health and environmental issues, human rights issues involve a multiplicity of actors, not only state actors and international organizations. NGOs have been particularly vocal and sometimes very effective in the area of human rights. Of the over 250 human rights organizations having interests that cross national borders, there is a core group that has been the most vocal and attracted the most attention. It includes Amnesty International (as mentioned above), the International Committee of the Red Cross, Human Rights Watch, and the International Commission of Jurists. These organizations have played a key role in publicizing the issues, including the abuses; in putting pressure on states (both offenders and enforcers); and in lobbying international organizations capable of taking concerted action. The groups have often formed coalitions, leading to advocacy networks and social movements.[17]

The work of human rights NGOs, like environmental NGOs, has become more effective with the use of the Internet and the World Wide Web. Individuals and groups are able to voice their grievances swiftly and to a worldwide audience and to solicit sympathizers to take direct actions, e-mailing individuals and groups who can change the situation. NGOs can disseminate information quickly and to maximum effect. In constructivist discourse, they can aid in the spread of ideas.

Environmentalists and human rights advocates have not been the only groups able to utilize the new technologies effectively. But they, like their counterparts concerned with other issue areas such as gender, labor, and social welfare, have utilized the new communications and, by doing so, have engaged directly and indirectly a larger and more-committed audience.

Women's Rights as Human Rights: The Globalization of Women's Rights

An examination of how women's rights has moved from the national to the international agenda illustrates many of the principles and problems we have just delineated. Women's rights, like other human rights issues, touch directly on cultural values and norms, yet like other human rights issues, they have gradually become a globalizing issue.[18] As a U.N. poster prepared for the Vienna Conference in 1993 headlined: Women's Rights Are Human Rights. This has not always been the case in the eyes of the world.

Evolving Political and Economic Rights

Women first took up the call for political participation within national jurisdictions, demanding their political and civil rights in the form of women's suffrage. Although British and U.S. women won that right in 1918 and 1920, respectively, women in many parts of the world waited until World War II (France, 1944) and after (Greece, 1952; Switzerland, 1971; Jordan, 1974; El Salvador, 1991; and Kuwait, 2006). In some Middle Eastern countries, women still do not have that right or it is limited to local elections. Thus, although the efforts of Eleanor Roosevelt and her Latin American colleagues led to gender's being included in the Universal Declaration of Human Rights (1949), at the time, gender was not yet globally seen as a human rights issue. In the immediate aftermath of the declaration, the priority of the United Nations and its Commission on the Status of Women was on getting states to grant women the right to vote, hold office, and enjoy legal rights, part of first-generation human rights. Specifically, this led to the drafting of the Conventions on the Political Rights of Women in 1952, the Nationality of Married Women in 1957, and the Consent to Marriage in 1962. These actions helped to set the standard for assessing women's political rights. More than a decade later, the 1979 Convention on the Elimination of All Forms of Discrimination Against Women (CEDAW) further articulated the standard, positing not only that discrimination against women in political and public life is illegal, but that so is trafficking in women and prostitution. Although 177 countries have signed the treaty, the United States has not, and the treaty has no system for monitoring or enforcing such rights.

During the 1960s and 1970s, more attention was paid to second-generation human rights—economic and social rights—for women. The development community had believed for many years that all individuals, including women, could participate and benefit equally from the economic development process. Yet, as they began to examine statistics on economic and social issues relevant to women, which were recorded beginning in the 1940s, they found that not to be the case. Esther Boserup's landmark book, *Women's Role in Economic Development*, recorded the finding that as technology improves, men benefit, while women become increasingly marginalized economically. Women would need special attention if they were to become participants in and beneficiaries of development.[19]

The result was the women in development (WID) movement—a transnational movement concerned with the failure of development to make an impact on the lives of the poor and with systematic discrimination against women. These issues developed and expanded over the life of four successive U.N.-sponsored world conferences on women. These conferences, with growing governmental and nongovernmental representation, mobilized women in interlocking networks, enabling them to set a critical economic agenda affecting women, including equal pay remuneration for men and women workers, minimum standards of social security, maternity protection, and nondiscrimination in the workplace. The delegates went further, however, arguing for special programs targeted to benefit women, since economic development was not working for them. The U.N. system responded by establishing programs to train and mobilize women in the development process and to give financial assistance for projects run by women. Virtually all the U.N. specialized agencies, including the World Bank, initiated programs for women's economic enhancement. Today the WID agenda is well integrated in most international assistance programs.

From Political and Economic Rights to Human Rights

By the 1990s, the discussion of women's rights was clearly viewed as one of human rights. This shift was solidified at the 1993 Vienna Conference on Human Rights. As the Vienna Declaration asserted, "The human rights of women and of the girl-child are an inalienable, integral and indivisible part of universal human rights. . . . The human rights of women should form an integral part of the United Nations human rights activities, including the promotion of all human rights instruments relating to women."[20] Included was not only human rights protection in the public sphere (first- and second-generation human rights) but protection against human rights abuses in the private sphere, notably gender-based violence against women. The latter includes violence against women in the family and domestic life; gendered division of labor in the workplace, including work in the informal sector and sexual work; and violence against women in war, particularly rape and torture. In short, violence against women and other abuses in all arenas were identified as breaches of both human rights and humanitarian norms. Their elimination was to be pursued through national and international action.

Three examples illustrate the widespread and often controversial problem of violence against women. The systematic usurpation of women's rights and accompanying violence was an issue in Taliban-run Afghanistan. When the Taliban seized power in 1996, all women's rights were revoked in both the public and private spheres. Women were not permitted to hold jobs or attend school. They were required to wear the burqa, a full-body veil, and to be under the authority of male family members. Violations of the rules resulted in assaults and sometimes death. Led by a secret group, the Revolutionary Association of the Women of Afghanistan (RAWA), in coalition with the U.S.-based Feminist Majority Foundation and over 180 human rights groups, a campaign was launched in international media that focused on the plight of Afghani women. As riveting as the issues were, it took the "war against terrorism" and the U.S. military to oust the Taliban and give Afghani women some rights in the public sphere.

Rape is another example of violence against women. The rape of 2,000 Kuwaiti women by Iraqi soldiers during the 1991 Gulf War, of 60,000 Bosnian women in 1993 by Serb forces, and of 250,000 women in Burundi's and Rwanda's ethnic conflicts in 1993–94 brings home this unique form of violence against women. At the Nuremberg and Tokyo war trials, rape was not brought up as a war crime, even though it was systematically employed during World War II as an instrument of war by states. During the 1990s, rape as a systematic state policy was increasingly viewed as a human rights issue, as NGOs urged the ad hoc international criminal tribunals for Yugoslavia and Rwanda to consider the crime of rape. At the ad hoc tribunal for Rwanda, Rwanda's Jean-Paul Akayesu was accused of gang rape and genocide. In a controversial 1998 decision, the judges issued the unprecedented ruling that rape constitutes not only a crime against humanity but also genocide. The precedent is established, and now, thanks to NGO pressure, the statute for the International Criminal Court includes among crimes against humanity, rape, sexual slavery, and forced prostitution, when such actions are part of a widespread and systematic attack against a civilian population.

Rape is not just a wartime issue. In South Asia and the Middle East, the problem is particularly acute even during peacetime. In some places, rape against women may be seen as an acceptable act of revenge against a prior wrong. The raped women, being dishonored, may be subsequently killed. In other polities, rape may be difficult to prove, as in Pakistan when a woman herself may be convicted of adultery unless four male witnesses corroborate her rape story. Thus, while the act is illegal in virtually every jurisdiction, state authorities in certain countries rarely choose to prosecute. Increasingly, human rights NGOs like Human Rights Watch or Amnesty International bring these cases to the attention of a horrified international community, and public pressure is brought to bear. But given different cultural norms, private-sphere activities are much easier to hide and more resistant to change.

Trafficking in women and children is another form of violence against women. While prohibited under the CEDAW convention, the practice has become more ubiquitous, facilitated by open borders, pressures to keep labor costs low, poverty that drives women and families to seek any kind of employment, and the high profitability of the sex trade. While the number of women and children forced into bonded sweatshop labor and domestic servitude will never be known, estimates for those trafficked for the purposes of the sex trade vary from between 600,000 to 1.75 million women and children annually. This problem is especially vexing, because unlike rape where consent is not given, women may choose to be trafficked for economic reasons. Yet, the international community speaking through several treaties (Convention on the Rights of the Child, Convention on Suppression of International Trafficking, Convention on the Abolition of Slavery, Slave Trade and Institutions and Practices Similar to Slavery) has made the practice illegal. While the standards have been set, monitoring and enforcement will be twenty-first-century tasks.

Different feminist groups have placed different priorities on the various types of human rights protection. Liberal feminists have found solace in granting women political and civil human rights, providing them the opportunity to secure privileges that were once exclusively male prerogatives. Socialist feminists point to the economic forces that have disadvantaged women and seek economic changes. In their view, as women become economically empowered, they will be able to alter patriarchal gender relations. More radical feminists highlight the distinctiveness of women and seek protection from all forms of gendered violence in both the public and private spheres.

While the legal stage has been set by the protection provided in various human rights treaties under the auspices of international organizations, the mainstay of enforcement will continue to be at the state level. It is states, prodded by the normative requirements of international treaties and lobbied by prominent individuals and human rights networks, that undertake domestic reform. And it is states that, unilaterally or multilaterally, undertake punitive action against offending states.

The Impact of Globalizing Issues

Globalizing issues have effects on four major areas of international relations theory and practice.

First, the interconnectedness of the plethora of subissues within health, environmental, and human rights issues affect international bargaining. When states choose to go to the bargaining table, a multiplicity of issues is often at stake. Many issues are fungible; states are willing to make trade-offs between issues to achieve the desired result. For example, in the aftermath of the 1973 oil embargo and in the face of supply shortages, the United States was willing to negotiate with Mexico on cleaning up the Colorado River. The

POLICY
DEBATE

Has the global war on terror made human rights issues obsolete?

YES:

◆ During a war, the right to security is paramount. A key right in President Franklin Roosevelt's famous "Four Freedoms" speech from 1941 is freedom from fear.

◆ Terrorists who indiscriminately attack innocent men, women, and children lose their right to be treated according to accepted political and civil rights standards.

◆ Laws of war and humanitarian law apply only to individuals acting in the name of the state. So nonstate terrorists enjoy no universal human rights protections.

◆ Terrorists have no respect for the human rights of their targets. So the targets have no responsibility to treat them any better.

NO:

◆ Not respecting the political and civil rights of terrorists dehumanizes everyone, placing both the terrorist and the target on equal footing.

◆ The rise of terrorism underlines the importance of economic and social rights; it is often the absence of economic rights that gives rise to terrorists.

◆ Not respecting the rights of terrorists will only create more angry individuals willing to use force.

◆ If the rights of suspected terrorists are abrogated, then the cycle of violence and hatred will likely continue into the future, while each side responds to the wrongs of the other.

◆ Respect of human rights is the foundation of a democracy, so if the ultimate goal is to create a democratic state, then respect for human rights must be a priority.

United States built a desalinization plant at the U.S.-Mexican border and helped Mexican residents reclaim land in the Mexicali Valley for agriculture. To win an ally in the supply of petroleum resources, the United States made this major concession and also accepted responsibility for past legal violations.

Other issues, however, are less fungible, particularly if key concerns of national security are at stake. The United States was unwilling to compromise by signing the Antipersonnel Landmines Treaty—a treaty designed to prohibit and eliminate the use of land mines—because of the security imperative to preserve the heavily mined border between North and South Korea. Supporters of the treaty framed the argument in human rights terms: innocent individuals, including vulnerable women and children, are being maimed by the use of such weapons; these weapons need to be eliminated. Yet in this case, the United States decided not to sign the treaty because of Korean security. While some states, eager for U.S. participation, were willing to make concessions, others, afraid that the treaty would be weakened by too many exceptions, were not. Bargaining is a much more complicated process in the age of globalizing issues.

Second, these globalizing issues themselves may be the source of conflict, just as the Marxists predicted in the nineteenth century. The need to protect the petroleum supply was the primary motivation for the West's involvement in the 1991 Gulf War. Jared Diamond's recent book, *Collapse*, documents how the struggle for scarce resources led to the collapse of empires in the past and to state failure in Rwanda and Burundi, resulting in the abrogation of human rights. The relationship between environmental and resource issues and conflict is a complex one.[21]

Issues of resource depletion and degradation, usually attenuated by population increase and pressure on resources, are apt to result in conflicts when some groups try to capture use of the scarce resource. For example, on the west bank of the Jordan River, where Israeli authorities control access to scarce water, conflict between the Israelis and the Palestinians is exacerbated. Israel permits its own settlers greater access to the resource and restricts access to the Palestinians. In the Gaza strip, where population is growing 4.6 percent annually, resources have been depleted, exacerbating the conflict with Israel.

Nonrenewable resources like oil lead to particularly violent conflicts, because these resources are vital; there are few viable substitutes. Changes in the distribution of these resources may lead to a shift in the balance of power, creating an instability that leads to war, just as realists fear. In contrast, issues such as ozone depletion or global warming are not particularly conducive to violent interstate conflict. In both cases, the commons and responsibility for its management are diffuse. Future generations will feel the effects.

Third, these globalizing issues pose direct challenges to state sovereignty. Thus, these new issues have set off a major debate about the nature of sovereignty. In Chapter 2, we traced the roots of sovereignty in the Westphalian revolution. The notion developed that states enjoy an internal autonomy and cannot be subjected to external authority. That norm—noninterference in the domestic affairs of other states—was embedded in the U.N. Charter. Yet the rise of nonstate actors, including multinational corporations, nongovernmental organizations, and supranational organizations like the European Union, and the forces of globalization, whether economic, cultural, or political, undermine the Westphalian notions of state sovereignty. The issues of health, the environment, and human rights were traditionally sovereign state concerns, where interference by outside actors was unacceptable. After World War II, those norms began to change and are still in the process of changing. This is one of the main reasons that discussion has turned to a power shift, an erosion of state authority and the potential demise of state power overall. Issues that once were the exclusive hallmark of state sovereignty are increasingly susceptible to scrutiny by global actors.

How then should sovereignty be reconceptualized? How has sovereignty been transformed? Mainstream theories in the realist and liberal traditions tend to talk of an erosion of sovereignty. Constructivists go further, probing how sovereignty is and has always been a contested concept. There have always been some issues where state control and authority are secure and others where authority is shared or even undermined. After all, sovereignty is a socially constructed institution that varies across time and place. Globalizing issues like health, the environment, and human rights permit us to examine long-standing but varying practices of sovereignty in depth. These issues give rise to new forms of authority and new forms of governance. They stimulate us to reorient our views of sovereignty.[22]

Fourth, globalizing issues pose critical problems for international relations scholars and for the theoretical frameworks introduced at the beginning of the text. Adherents of each of the frameworks have been forced to rethink key assumptions and values, as well as the discourse of their theoretical perspective, to accommodate globalizing issues.

For realists, the very core propositions of their theory—including the primacy of the state, the clear separation between domestic and international politics, and the emphasis on state security—are made problematic by globalizing issues. The globalizing issues of health and disease, the environment, human rights, drug and human trafficking, and international crime are problems that no one state can effectively address alone. These are issues in which the divide between the international and the domestic has broken down. These are issues that may threaten state security yet for which there may be no traditional military solution.

Responding to globalizing issues, realists have generally adopted a more nuanced argument consonant with realist precepts. While most realists admit that there may be other actors that have gained power

In Focus

EFFECTS OF GLOBALIZING ISSUES

◆ *On international bargaining:*
  More policy trade-offs
  Greater complexity
◆ *On international conflict:*
  May increase at international and substate level
◆ *On state sovereignty:*
  Traditional notion challenged
  Need for reconceptualization
◆ *On study of international relations:*
  Core assumptions of theories jeopardized
  Theories modified and broadened

relative to the state, they contend that state primacy is not in jeopardy. Competitive centers of power either at the local, transnational, or international level do not necessarily or automatically lead to the erosion or demise of state power. Most important, the fundamentals of state security are no less important in an age of globalization than they were in the past. What has changed is that security discourse has been broadened to encompass human security. For humans to be secure, not only must state security be assured but economic security, environmental security, human rights security, and health and well-being must be secured as well. One form of security does not replace the other; one augments the other. Thus, while globalizing issues have forced realists to add qualifications to the theory, they have thereby preserved it and enhanced its theoretical usefulness.

For liberals, the globalizing issues can be more easily integrated into their theoretical picture. After all, liberals at the outset asserted the importance of individuals and the possibility of both cooperative and conflictual interests. They introduced the notion of multiple issues that may be as important as security. They see power as a multidimensional concept. Later versions of liberal thinking, like neoliberal institutionalism, recognized the need for international institutions to facilitate state interactions, to ensure transparency, and to add the new issues to the international agenda. While not denying the importance of state security, they quickly embraced the notion of other forms of security, compatible with health, environmental, and human rights issues.

Radicals have never been comfortable with the primacy of the state and the international system that the dominant coalition of states created. A shift in power away from the state and that international system is a desired transition. With their pronounced emphasis on economics over security, radicals may be able to accommodate globalizing issues like health, the environment, and human rights. However, a prominent radical interpretation of both health and the environment is that economic deprivation and perceived relative economic deprivation are the root causes of disparities in health care and environmental degradation. Human rights violations, according to radical thought, are caused by elites and privileged groups trying to maintain their edge over the less fortunate.

Constructivists have presented a different approach for tapping into the globalizing issues. They have alerted us to the nuances of the changing discourse embedded in discussions of health, the environment, and human rights. They have illustrated how both material factors and ideas shape the debates over the issues. They have called attention to the importance of norms in influencing and changing individual and state behavior. Better than other theorists, constructivists have begun to explore the variable impacts of these issues on the traditional concepts of the state, national identity, and sovereignty. Yet while sometimes pathbreaking and often suggestive, constructivism itself remains under construction.

As all globalizing issues assume greater salience in the twenty-first century, all international relations theories will need modification and reformulation.

Do Globalizing Issues Lead to Global Governance?

Recognition of globalizing issues and their effects has led some scholars and pundits to conclude that governance processes need to be conceptualized differently than they have been in the past. The processes of interaction among the various actors in international politics are now more frequent and intense, ranging from conventional ad hoc cooperation and formal organizational collaboration to nongovernmental and network collaboration and even "virtual" communal interaction on the World Wide Web. These changes have led some to think of there being various pieces of global governance. **Global governance** implies that through various structures and processes, actors can coordinate interests and needs although there is no unifying political authority.

Yet for global governance to come together, for the international relations puzzle to be whole and complete, there must be a global civil society. Political scientist Ronnie Lipschutz describes the essential component of global civil society: "While global civil society must interact with states, the code of global civil society denies the primacy of states or their sovereign rights. This civil society is 'global' not only because of those connections that cross national boundaries and operate within the 'global, nonterritorial region,' but also as a result of a growing element of global consciousness in the way the members of global civil society act."[23] Some liberals would find this a desirable direction in which to be moving—a goal to be attained—while many fear that global governance might undermine democratic values: as the focus of governance moves further from individuals, democracy becomes more problematic.

Skeptics of global governance do not believe that anything approaching it, however defined, is possible or desirable. For realists, there can never be global governance in anarchy; outcomes are determined by relative power positions rather than law or other regulatory devices, however decentralized and diffuse those devices might be. For Kenneth Waltz, the quintessential neorealist, the anarchic structure of the international system is the core dynamic. For other realists, like Hans Morgenthau, there is space for both international law and international organization; his textbook includes chapters on both, but each is relatively insignificant in the face of power politics and the national interest. Few realists would talk in global governance terms. Radicals are also uncomfortable with global governance discourse. Rather than seeing global governance as a multiple-actor, multiple-process, decentralized framework, radicals fear domination by hegemons who would structure global governance processes to their own advantage. Skepticism about the possibility of global governance does not diminish the fact that there may be a need for such in the age of globalization.

In Sum: Changing You

In these ten chapters, we have explored the historical development of international relations from feudal times, to the development of the state system, and to notions of an international system and community and global governance. We have introduced different theories—namely liberalism, realism, and radicalism—that help us organize our perspectives about the role of the international system, the state, the individual, and intergovernmental and nongovernmental organizations in international relations. And we have introduced constructivist thinking on several issues. Using these perspectives, we have examined the major issues of the day. And we have confronted the emerging globalizing issues of the twenty-first century—health, the environment, and human rights—and analyzed how these issues affect interstate bargaining, conflict, sovereignty, and even how we study international politics.

A citizenry able to articulate these arguments is a citizenry better able to explain the whys and hows of events that affect our lives. A citizen who can understand these events is better able to make informed policy choices. In the globalizing era of the twenty-first century, as economic, political, social, and environmental forces both above the state and within the state assume greater saliency, the role of individuals becomes all the more demanding.

Notes

1. International Crisis Group, "HIV/AIDS as a Security Issue" (June 19, 2001), www.intl-crisis-group.org.
2. Peter M. Haas, "Introduction: Epistemic Communities and International Policy Coordination," *International Organization* 46:1 (Winter 1992), 3.
3. Karen T. Litfin, "Constructing Environmental Security and Ecological Interdependency," *Global Governance* 5.3 (July–September 1999), 367.
4. Thomas Malthus, "An Essay on the Principle of Population: Text, Sources, and Background Criticism" (1789), ed. Philip Appleman (New York: Norton, 1976).
5. Dennis Meadows et al., *The Limits to Growth* (New York: Signet, 1972).
6. Garrett Hardin, "The Tragedy of the Commons," *Science* 162 (December 13, 1968), 1243–48.
7. Randal C. Archibold, "Border Fight Focuses on Water, Not Immigration," *New York Times* (July 7, 2006), 1.

8. Rachel Carson, *Silent Spring* (Boston: Houghton Mifflin, 1962). See also Jacques Yves Cousteau with Frederick Dames, *The Silent World* (New York: Harper and Row, 1953); and Jacques Yves Cousteau with James Dugan, *The Living Sea* (New York: Harper and Row, 1963).

9. Thomas F. Homer-Dixon, "Environmental Scarcities and Violent Conflict: Evidence and Cases," *International Security* 19:1 (Summer 1994), 5–40.

10. See Karen T. Litfin, *Ozone Discourses: Science and Politics in Global Environmental Cooperation* (New York: Columbia University Press, 1994).

11. For excellent overviews, see Jack Donnelly, *International Human Rights* (3rd ed.; Boulder, Colo.; Westview, 2006); and David P. Forsythe, *Human Rights in International Relations* (2nd ed.; Cambridge, Eng.: Cambridge University Press, 2006).

12. Stephen D. Krasner, "Structural Causes and Regime Consequences: Regimes as Intervening Variables," *International Organization* 36:2 (Spring 1982), 186.

13. See Joanne R. Bauer and Daniel A. Bell, eds., *The East Asian Challenge for Human Rights* (Cambridge, Eng.: Cambridge University Press, 1999); and Amartya Sen, "Universal Truths: Human Rights and the Westernizing Illusion," *Harvard International Review* 20:3 (Summer 1998), 40–43.

14. Karen A. Mingst and Margaret P. Karns, *The United Nations in the 21ˢᵗ Century* (3rd ed.; Boulder, Colo.: Westview, 2007), Chap. 6.

15. David Cortright and George A. Lopez, *The Sanctions Decade: Assessing UN Strategies in the 1990s* (Boulder, Colo.: Lynne Rienner, 2000).

16. Henry Kissinger, *Diplomacy* (New York: Simon and Schuster, 1994).

17. See Margaret E. Keck and Kathryn Sikkink, *Activists Beyond Borders: Advocacy Networks in International Networks* (Ithaca, N.Y.: Cornell University Press, 1998); and Charles Tilly, *Social Movements, 1768–2004* (Boulder, Colo.: Paradigm, 2004).

18. V. Spike Peterson and Anne Sisson Runyan, *Global Gender Issues* (2d ed.; Boulder, Colo.: Westview, 1999).

19. Esther Boserup, *Women's Role in Economic Development* (London: George Allen and Unwin, 1970).

20. U.N. Conference on Human Rights, *Declaration* (Vienna, 1993), Art. 18.

21. Jared Diamond, *Collapse: How Societies Choose to Fail or Succeed* (New York: Penguin, 2005).

22. See Stephen D. Krasner, *Sovereignty: Organized Hypocrisy* (Princeton, N.J.: Princeton University Press, 1999); and Karen T. Litfin, ed., *The Greening of Sovereignty in World Politics* (Cambridge, Mass.: MIT Press, 1998).

23. Ronnie Lipschutz, "Reconstructing World Politics: The Emergence of Global Civil Society," *Millennium: Journal of International Studies* 21:3 (1992), 398–99.

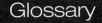

Glossary

anarchy the absence of governmental authority (6)

arms control restrictions on the research, manufacture, or deployment of weapons systems and certain types of troops (234)

asymmetric warfare war between parties of unequal strength, in which the weaker party tries to neutralize its opponent's strength by exploiting the opponent's weaknesses (223)

balance of payments the flow of money into and out of a country from trade, tourism, foreign aid, sale of services, profits, etc., for a period of time (261)

balance of power an international system in which states enjoy relatively equal power, states form alliances or make policies to counteract the acquisition of power by other states, and no one state is able to dominate the international system (30)

behavioralism an approach to the study of social science and international relations that posits that individuals and units like states act in regularized ways; leads to a belief that behaviors can be described, explained, and predicted (9)

belief system the organized and integrated perceptions of individuals in a society, including foreign-policy decisionmakers, often based on past history, that guide them to select certain policies over others (147)

bipolarity an international system in which there are two great powers or blocs of roughly equal strength or weight (52)

bureaucratic politics the model of foreign-policy decisionmaking that posits that national decisions are the outcomes of bargaining among bureaucratic groups having competing interests; decisions reflect the relative strength of the individual bureaucratic players or of the organizations they represent (125)

capitalism the economic system in which the ownership of the means of production is in private hands; the system operates according to market forces whereby capital and labor move freely; according to radicals, an exploitative relationship between the owners of production and the workers (38)

civil wars   armed conflicts within a state between factions that wish to control the government or exercise jurisdiction over territory; may have international repercussions with the flow of armaments and refugees, often leading to intervention by other states (219)

cognitively consistent   the tendency of individuals to accept information that is compatible with what has previously been accepted, often by ignoring inconsistent information; linked to the desire of individuals to be consistent in their attitudes (148)

Cold War   the era in international relations between the end of World War II and 1990, distinguished by ideological, economic, and political differences between the Soviet Union and the United States (37)

collective good   public goods that are available to all regardless of individual contribution—e.g., the air, the oceans, or Antarctica—but that no one owns or is individually responsible for; with collective goods, decisions by one group or state have effects on other groups or states (165)

collective security   the concept that aggression against a state should be defeated collectively because aggression against one state is aggression against all; basis of League of Nations and United Nations (61)

comparative advantage   the ability of a country to make and export a good relatively more efficiently than other countries; the basis for the liberal economic principle that countries benefit from free trade among nations (251)

compellence   the policy of threatening or intimidating an adversary in order to get it to either take or refrain from taking a particular action (117)

complex peacekeeping   multidimensional operations using military and civilian personnel, often including traditional peacekeeping and nation-building activities; more dangerous because not all parties have consented and because force is usually used (175)

constructivism   an alternative international relations theory that hypothesizes how ideas, norms, and institutions shape state identity and interests (72)

containment   a foreign policy designed to prevent the expansion of an adversary by blocking its opportunities to expand, by supporting weaker states through foreign aid programs, and by using coercive force against the adversary to harness its expansion; the major U.S. policy toward the Soviet Union during the Cold War era (38)

cultural relativism   the belief that human rights, ethics, and morality are determined by cultures and history and therefore are not universally the same (312)

demographic transition   the situation in which increasing levels of economic development lead to falling death rates, followed by falling birth rates (296)

dependency theorists   individuals whose ideas are derived from radicalism, and explain poverty and underdevelopment in developing countries based on their historical dependence on and domination by rich countries (71)

deterrence   the policy of maintaining a large military force and arsenal to discourage any potential aggressor from taking action; states commit themselves to punish an aggressor state (48)

diplomacy   the practice of states trying to influence the behavior of other states by bargaining, negotiating, taking specific noncoercive actions or refraining from such actions, or appealing to the foreign public for support of a position (112)

disarmament   the policy of eliminating a state's offensive weaponry; may occur for all classes of weapons or for specified weapons only; the logic of the policy is that fewer weapons leads to greater security (234)

diversionary war   the theory that leaders start conflicts to divert attention from domestic problems (212)

domino effect   a metaphor that posits that the loss of influence over one state to an adversary will lead to a subsequent loss of control over neighboring states, just as dominos fall one after another; used by the United States as a justification to support South Vietnam, fearing that if that country became communist, neighboring countries would also fall under communist influence (45)

elasticity   the responsiveness of demand and supply levels to price changes (277)

epistemic community   a transnational community of experts and technical specialists who share a set of beliefs and a way to approach problems (293)

ethnonational movements   the participation in organized political activity of self-conscious communities sharing an ethnic affiliation; some movements seek autonomy within an organized state; others desire separation and the formation of a new state; still others want to join with a different state (132)

European Union (EU)   a union of twenty-seven European states, formerly the European Economic Community; designed originally during the 1950s for economic integration, but since expanded into a closer political and economic union (182)

evoked set   the tendency to look for details in a contemporary situation that are similar to information previously obtained (148)

externalities   in economics, unintended side effects that can have positive or negative consequences (302)

first-generation human rights political or civil rights of citizens that prevent governmental authority from interfering with private individuals or civil society (negative rights) (310)

first-strike capability being able to launch a nuclear attack against an enemy that is designed to eliminate the possibility of its being able to launch a second strike (118)

game theory a technique developed by mathematicians and economists and used by political scientists to evaluate the choices made in decision situations, where one state's or individual's choice affects that of other actors; based on the assumption that each player knows its and the others' unique sets of options and the payoffs for each actor associated with these options; among the various types of games is the prisoner's dilemma (119)

general war war designed to conquer and occupy enemy territory, using all available weapons of warfare and targeting both military establishments and civilian facilities (218)

General Assembly one of the major organs of the United Nations; generally addresses issues other than those of peace and security; each member state has one vote; operates with six functional committees composed of all member states (172)

General Agreement on Tariffs and Trade (GATT) founded by treaty in 1947 as the Bretton Woods institution responsible for negotiating a liberal international trade regime that included the principles of nondiscrimination in trade and most-favored-nation status; re-formed as the World Trade Organization in 1995 (258)

global governance structures and processes that enable actors to coordinate interdependent needs and interests in the absence of a unifying political authority (325)

globalization the process of increasing integration of the world in terms of economics, politics, communications, social relations, and culture; increasingly undermines traditional state sovereignty (129)

Group of 77 a coalition of about 125 developing countries that press for reforms in economic relations between developing and developed countries; also referred to as the South (172)

groupthink the tendency for small groups to form a consensus and resist criticism of a core position, often disregarding contradictory information in the process; group may ostracize members holding a different position (150)

guerrilla warfare an approach used by irregular militaries, hiding in the civilian population, using hit and run tactics to wear down the enemy (223)

hegemon a dominant state that has a preponderance of power; often establishes and enforces the rules and norms in the international system (30)

humanitarian intervention   actions by states, international organizations, or the international community in general, to intervene, usually with coercive force, to alleviate human suffering without necessarily obtaining consent of the state (231)

human security   the notion that security includes not security of state and territory, but protection of individuals from turmoil, environmental degradation, and health disasters (172)

hypotheses   tentative statements about causal relationships put forward to explore and test its logical and usually its empirical consequences (57)

imperialism   the policy and practice of extending the domination of one state over another through territorial conquest or economic domination; in radicalism, the final stage of expansion of the capitalist system (69)

intergovernmental organizations (IGOs)   international agencies or bodies established by states and controlled by member states that deal with areas of common interests (163)

International Monetary Fund (IMF)   the Bretton Woods institution originally charged with helping states deal with temporary balance-of-payments problems; now plays a broader role in assisting debtor developing states by offering loans to those who institute specific policies, or structural adjustment programs (255)

international regimes   the rules, norms, and procedures that are developed by states and international organizations out of their common concerns and are used to organize common activities (167)

international relations   the study of the interactions among various actors (states, international organizations, nongovernmental organizations, and subnational entities like bureaucracies, local governments, and individuals) that participate in international politics (2)

international society   the states and substate actors in the international system and the institutions and norms that regulate their interaction; implies that these actors communicate, sharing common interests and a common identity; identified with British school of political theory (82)

irredentism   the demands of ethnonationalist groups to take political control of territory historically or ethnically related to them by separating from their parent state or taking territory from other states (133)

Islamic fundamentalism   believers within Islam who offer a critique of secular states and seek to change states and individual behaviors to conform to a strict reading of Islamic texts (131)

just war tradition   the idea that there are criteria that if met can make going to war ethical and that there are standards for how war should ethically be fought (229)

League of Nations   the international organization formed at the conclusion of World War I for the purpose of preventing another war; based on collective security (34)

legitimacy   the moral and legal right to rule, which is based on law, custom, heredity, or the consent of the governed (27)

levels of analysis   analytical framework based on the ideas that events in international relations can be explained by looking at individuals, states, or the international system and that causes at each level can be separated from causes at other levels (57)

liberalism   the theoretical perspective based on the assumption of the innate goodness of the individual and the value of political institutions in promoting social progress (59)

limited wars   wars fought for limited objectives with selected types of weapons or targets; the objective will be less than the total subjugation of the enemy (220)

Malthusian dilemma   the situation that population growth rates will increase faster than agricultural productivity, leading to food shortages; named after Thomas Malthus (296)

mirror images   the tendency of individuals and groups to see in one's opponent the opposite characteristics as those seen in one's self (149)

multinational corporations (MNCs)   private enterprises with production facilities, sales, or activities in several states (71)

multipolar   an international system in which there are several states or great powers of roughly equal strength or weight (52)

nation   a group of people sharing a common language, history, or culture (100)

national interest   the interest of the state, most basically the protection of territory and sovereignty; in realist thinking, the interest is a unitary one defined in terms of the pursuit of power; in liberal thinking, there are many national interests; in radical thinking, it is the interest of a ruling elite (63)

nationalism   devotion and allegiance to the nation and the shared characteristics of its peoples; used to motivate people to patriotic acts, sometimes leading a group to seek dominance over another group (27)

nation-building   the process of helping a state create administrative structures and capacity (175)

nation-state   the entity formed when people sharing the same historical, cultural, or linguistic roots form their own state with borders, a government, and international recognition; trend began with French and American Revolutions (101)

neoliberal institutionalism   a reinterpretation of liberalism that posits that even in an anarchic international system, states will cooperate because of their continuous interactions with each other and because it is in their self-interest to do so; institutions provide the framework for cooperative interactions (61)

neorealism   a reinterpretation of realism that posits that the structure of the international system is the most important level to study; states behave the way they do because of the structure of the international system; includes the belief that general laws can be found to explain events (66)

New International Economic Order (NIEO)   a list of demands by the Group of 77 to reform economic relations between the North and the South, that is, between the developed countries and the developing countries (93)

nongovernmental organizations (NGOs)   private associations of individuals or groups that engage in political, economic, or social activities usually across national borders (163)

normative   relating to ethical rules; in foreign policy and international affairs, standards suggesting what a policy should be (7)

North   the developed countries, mostly in the Northern Hemisphere, including the countries of North America, the European countries, and Japan (91)

North Atlantic Treaty Organization (NATO)   military and political alliance between Western European states and the United States established in 1948 for the purpose of defending Europe from aggression by the Soviet Union and its allies; post–Cold War expansion to Eastern Europe (42)

nuclear proliferation   the spread of nuclear weapons or nuclear weapons technology; Nuclear Nonproliferation Treaty obligates nuclear powers not to transfer their nuclear technology to third countries and to work toward nuclear disarmament and obligates nonnuclear signatories to refrain from acquiring or developing the technology (235)

organizational politics   the foreign-policy decisionmaking model that posits that national decisions are the products of subnational governmental organizations and units; the standard operating procedures and processes of the organizations largely determine the policy; major changes in policy are unlikely (125)

pluralist model   a model of foreign-policy decisionmaking that suggests that policy is formed as a result of the bargaining among the various domestic sources of foreign policy, including the public, private interest groups, and multinational corporations; these interests are generally channeled through democratic institutions like legislatures or persons holding elective positions (127)

power   the ability to influence others and also to control outcomes so as to produce results that would not have occurred naturally (107)

power potential   a measure of the power an entity like a state could have, derived from a consideration of both its tangible and its intangible resources; states may not always be able to transfer their power potential into actual power (107)

prisoner's dilemma   a theoretical game in which rational players (states or individuals) choose options that lead to outcomes (payoffs) such that all players are worse off than under a different set of choices (61)

public diplomacy   use of certain diplomatic methods to create a favorable image of the state or its people in the eyes of other states and their publics; methods include, for example, goodwill tours, cultural and student exchanges, and media presentations (114)

radicalism   a social theory, formulated by Karl Marx and modified by other theorists, that posits that class conflict between owners and workers will cause the eventual demise of capitalism; offers a critique of capitalism (68)

rational actors   in realist thinking, an individual or state that uses logical reasoning to select a policy; that is, it has a defined goal to achieve, considers a full range of alternative strategies, and selects the policy that best achieves the goal (64)

realism   a theory of international relations that emphasizes states' interest in accumulating power to ensure security in an anarchic world; based on the notion that individuals are power seeking and that states act in pursuit of their own national interest defined in terms of power (63)

responsibility to protect   emerging norm that the international community should help individuals suffering at the hands of their own state or others (231)

sanctions   economic, diplomatic, and even coercive military force for enforcing an international policy or another state's policy; sanctions can be positive (offering an incentive to a state) or negative (punishing a state) (114)

satisfice   in decisionmaking theory, the tendency of states and their leaders to settle for the minimally acceptable solution, not the best possible outcome, in order to reach a consensus and formulate a policy (126)

second-generation human rights   social and economic rights that states are obligated to provide their citizenry, including the rights to medical care, jobs, and housing (positive rights) (310)

second-strike capability   in the age of nuclear weapons, the ability of a state to respond and hurt an adversary after a first strike has been launched against that state by the adversary; ensures that both sides will suffer an unacceptable level of damage (118)

security dilemma   the situation in which one state improves its military capabilities, especially its defenses, and those improvements are seen by other states as threats; each state in an anarchic international system tries to increase its own level of protection leading to insecurity in others, often leading to an arms race (208)

Security Council   one of the major organs of the United Nations charged with the responsibility for peace and security issues; includes five permanent members with veto power and ten nonpermanent members chosen from the General Assembly (172)

socialism   an economic and social system that relies on intensive government intervention or public ownership of the means of production in order to distribute wealth among the population more equitably; in radical theory, the stage between capitalism and communism (38)

South   the developing countries of Africa, Latin America, and southern Asia (91)

sovereignty   the authority of the state, based on recognition by other states and by nonstate actors, to govern matters within its own borders that affect its people, economy, security, and form of government (23)

state   an organized political unit that has a geographic territory, a stable population, and a government to which the population owes allegiance and that is legally recognized by other states (99)

stratification   the uneven distribution of resources among different groups of individuals and states (91)

structural adjustment programs   IMF policies and recommendations aimed to guide states out of balance-of-payment difficulties and economic crises (256)

summits   talks and meetings among the highest-level government officials from different countries; designed to promote good relations and provide a forum to discuss issues and conclude formal negotiations (47)

superpowers   highest-power states as distinguished from other great powers; term coined during the Cold War to refer to the United States and the Soviet Union (37)

sustainable development   an approach to economic development that tries to reconcile current economic growth and environmental protection with the needs of future generations (255)

system   a group of units or parts united by some form of regular interaction, in which a change in one unit causes changes in the others; these interactions occur in regularized ways (81)

terrorism   the use of violence by groups or states usually against noncombatants to intimidate, cause fear, or punish their victims to achieve political goals; a form of asymmetric warfare (225)

theory   generalized statements about political, social, or economic activities that seek to describe and explain those activities; used in many cases as a basis of prediction (56)

third-generation human rights   collective rights of groups, including the rights of ethnic or indigenous minorities and designated special groups such as women and children, and the rights to democracy and development, among others (310)

track-two diplomacy   unofficial overtures by private individuals or groups to try and resolve an ongoing international crisis or civil war (151)

traditional peacekeeping   the use of multilateral third-party military forces to achieve several different objectives, generally to address and contain interstate conflict, including the enforcement of cease-fires and separation of forces; used during the Cold War to prevent conflict among the great powers from escalating (175)

transnational   across national or traditional state boundaries; can refer to actions of various nonstate actors, such as private individuals and nongovernmental organizations (48)

transnational movements   groups of people from different states who share religious, ideological, or policy beliefs and who work together to change the status quo (130)

Treaty of Westphalia   treaty ending the Thirty Years War in Europe in 1648; in international relations represents the beginning of state sovereignty within a territorial space (24)

unipolar   an international system in which there is only one great power, or hegemon (52)

unitary actor   the state as an actor that speaks with one voice and has a single national interest; realists assume states are unitary actors (64)

universal jurisdiction   a legal concept that permits states to claim legal authority beyond their national territory for the purpose of punishing a particularly heinous criminal that violates the laws of all states or protecting human rights (197)

universal rights   human rights believed to be basically the same at all times and in all cultures, a controversial notion (310)

Warsaw Pact   the military alliance formed by the states of the Soviet bloc in 1955 in response to the rearmament of West Germany and its inclusion in NATO; permitted the stationing of Soviet troops in Eastern Europe (42)

Washington Consensus   the liberal belief that only through specific liberal economic policies, especially privatization, can development result (255)

weapons of mass destruction   nuclear, chemical, and biological weapons, distinguished by their lethality and inability to discriminate targets (223)

World Trade Organization (WTO) intergovernmental organization designed to support the principles of liberal free trade; includes enforcement measures and dispute settlement mechanisms; established in 1995 to replace the General Agreement on Tariffs and Trade (259)

World Bank a global lending agency focused on financing projects in developing countries; formally known as the International Bank for Reconstruction and Development, established as one of the key Bretton Woods institutions to deal with reconstruction and development after World War II (253)

Index

Page numbers in *italics* refer to boxes, maps, figures, and tables.